Items should be returned on or before the last date shown below. Items not already requested by other borrowers may be renewed in person, in writing or by telephone. To renew, please quote the number on the barcode label. To renew online a PIN is required. This can be requested at your local library.
Renew online @ **www.dublincitypubliclibraries.ie**
Fines charged for overdue items will include postage incurred in recovery. Damage to or loss of items will be charged to the borrower.

Leabharlanna Poiblí Chathair Bhaile Átha Cliath
Dublin City Public Libraries

Baile Átha Cliath
Dublin City

Brainse Rátheanaigh
Raheny Branch
Tel: 8315521

Date Due	Date Due	Date Due

D1428894

ISOCRATES
III

LCL 373

ISOCRATES

VOLUME III

WITH AN ENGLISH TRANSLATION BY
LARUE VAN HOOK

HARVARD UNIVERSITY PRESS
CAMBRIDGE, MASSACHUSETTS
LONDON, ENGLAND

First published 1945

LOEB CLASSICAL LIBRARY® is a registered trademark
of the President and Fellows of Harvard College

ISBN 978-0-674-99411-9

*Printed on acid-free paper and bound by
The Maple-Vail Book Manufacturing Group*

CONTENTS

PREFACE

This third and concluding volume of the works of Isocrates contains a translation of all the discourses, and of the letters, which are not found in the previously published Volumes I and II of the Loeb Library Isocrates in the translation of Dr. George Norlin.

The text of this edition of Volume III is based on that of Friedrich Blass, *Isocratis Orationes*, Leipzig, Teubner, last impression, Vol. I, 1913 ; Vol. II, 1937.

Not only have the critical notes in the Introduction to the Teubner Text of Isocrates as published by Blass been consulted, but also the detailed Critical Apparatus of E. Drerup in his *Isocratis Opera Omnia*, Vol. I, Leipzig, 1906. Drerup's exhaustive Apparatus available in his edition, which contains all the discourses in this Vol. III of Isocrates except *Oration XIV* and the *Letters*, makes unnecessary in this volume the citation of numerous textual variants which would be of interest only to the specialist. Critical notes with the more important readings are likewise to be found in the Budé edition of Isocrates with translation into French, by G. Mathieu and E. Brémond, Paris (Vol. I, 1928 ; Vol. II, 1938). There is also an edition in the Dutch language of the *Trapeziticus* by J. C. Bongenaar, Utrecht, 1933.

The Greek text of Isocrates is fortunately so good that extensive emendation has not been necessary in

vii

PREFACE

the past.   In this volume important departures from
the text are noted in the footnotes.   Changes in the
accentuation and punctuation as found in the Teubner
text edited by Blass are numerous.

For a general account of Manuscripts, Editions,
Translations, etc., of Isocrates' works the reader is
referred to Norlin's General Introduction in Volume I
of the Loeb Library Isocrates, pages xlvi-li.   Biblio-
graphical references of value to the study of the
discourses in this volume will be found in the Intro-
ductions and footnotes to the translation.

LaRue Van Hook

New York, 1944

THE WORKS OF ISOCRATES

THE WORKS OF ISOCRATES

IX. EVAGORAS

INTRODUCTION

THE discourse entitled *Evagoras* is the third of the
" Cyprian " orations. The first of these, *To Nicocles*,[a]
is addressed to the son of Evagoras, king of Cyprus,
who succeeded his father on the throne, and gives
the young ruler advice on how a king should conduct
himself toward his subjects. The second, *Nicocles
or The Cyprians*,[b] discusses the duties of a king's
subjects. The third, *Evagoras*, is an *encomium*
(rhetorical eulogy) and was composed for a festival
held by Nicocles in memory of his father Evagoras,
king of the Cyprian kingdom of Salamis.

The main facts of the life of Evagoras, his accession
to the monarchy and his deeds as ruler, are narrated
in Isocrates' discourse although, in accordance with
the rhetorical rules of this form of composition, they
are embellished by the author.

Evagoras gained the throne not later than 411 B.C.,
and died in 374 B.C. Aristotle in the *Politics* (1311 b)
states that Evagoras was murdered, but Isocrates is
silent with respect to the manner of the death of
his hero.

The date of the composition is not known with
exactness. No doubt it was delivered not many years

---

[a] See Isocrates, *Or.* II and Introd. to that discourse
(Vol. I, pp. 38-39, L.C.L.).
[b] See Isocrates, *Or.* III (Vol. I, pp. 74-75, L.C.L.).

after the death of Evagoras. Blass [a] dates it about
370 B.C. ; Jebb [b] places it as late as 365 B.C. The
later date is preferred by Mathieu.[c] Isocrates himself, at the time of writing the discourse, was advanced
in years.[d]

The *Evagoras*, like the *Encomium of Helen* and the
Busiris, belongs to the *epideictic* or *display* group of
Isocratean compositions and in its style shows the
influence of the rhetorician Gorgias,[e] but it is unlike
these discourses on mythical personages in that it
is a sincere panegyric of the murdered king whom
Isocrates personally knew and admired. There is,
however, much exaggeration in the delineation of
the character of the hero. This embellishment was
always present in eulogies and was an inevitable
characteristic of the rhetorical *funeral oration* as it
was developed by the Sophists. In consequence,
Isocrates relates only the successes of Evagoras and
omits all mention of the reverses of the king.[f]

[a] *Die attische Beredsamkeit* ii. p. 285.
[b] *Attic Orators* ii. p. 104.
[c] *Isocrate* ii. p. 143.   [d] See § 73.
[e] See § 46, note *a*.
See *Busiris* 4, where such a procedure is justified.

ΙΣΟΚΡΑΤΟΥΣ

9. ΕΥΑΓΟΡΑΣ

[189] Ὁρῶν, ὦ Νικόκλεις, τιμῶντά σε τὸν τάφον τοῦ
πατρὸς οὐ μόνον τῷ πλήθει καὶ τῷ κάλλει τῶν
ἐπιφερομένων, ἀλλὰ καὶ χοροῖς καὶ μουσικῇ καὶ
γυμνικοῖς ἀγῶσιν, ἔτι δὲ πρὸς τούτοις ἵππων τε
καὶ τριήρων ἁμίλλαις, καὶ λείποντ' οὐδεμίαν τῶν
2 τοιούτων ὑπερβολήν, ἡγησάμην Εὐαγόραν, εἴ τίς
ἐστιν αἴσθησις τοῖς τετελευτηκόσι περὶ τῶν ἐνθάδε
γιγνομένων, εὐμενῶς μὲν ἀποδέχεσθαι καὶ ταῦτα,
καὶ χαίρειν ὁρῶντα τήν τε περὶ αὐτὸν ἐπιμέλειαν
καὶ τὴν σὴν μεγαλοπρέπειαν, πολὺ δ' ἂν ἔτι πλείω
χάριν ἔχειν ἢ τοῖς ἄλλοις ἅπασιν, εἴ τις δυνηθείη
περὶ τῶν ἐπιτηδευμάτων αὐτοῦ καὶ τῶν κινδύνων
3 ἀξίως διελθεῖν τῶν ἐκείνῳ πεπραγμένων· εὑρήσομεν γὰρ τοὺς φιλοτίμους καὶ μεγαλοψύχους
τῶν ἀνδρῶν οὐ μόνον ἀντὶ τῶν τοιούτων ἐπαινεῖ-
σθαι βουλομένους, ἀλλ' ἀντὶ τοῦ ζῆν ἀποθνήσκειν
εὐκλεῶς αἱρουμένους, καὶ μᾶλλον περὶ τῆς δόξης
ἢ τοῦ βίου σπουδάζοντας, καὶ πάντα ποιοῦντας,
ὅπως ἀθάνατον τὴν περὶ αὐτῶν μνήμην καταλεί-
4 ψουσιν. αἱ μὲν οὖν δαπάναι τῶν μὲν τοιούτων

4

THE ORATIONS OF ISOCRATES

IX. EVAGORAS

WHEN I saw you, Nicocles,[a] honouring the tomb of your father, not only with numerous and beautiful offerings, but also with dances, music, and athletic contests, and, furthermore, with races of horses and triremes, and leaving to others no possibility of surpassing you [b] in such celebrations, I judged that Evagoras (if the dead have any perception of that which takes place in this world),[c] while gladly accepting these offerings and rejoicing in the spectacle of your devotion and princely magnificence in honouring him, would feel far greater gratitude to anyone who could worthily recount his principles in life and his perilous deeds than to all other men; for we shall find that men of ambition and greatness of soul not only are desirous of praise for such things, but prefer a glorious death to life, zealously seeking glory rather than existence,[d] and doing all that lies in their power to leave behind a memory of themselves that shall never die. Expenditure of money

---

[a] For Nicocles see Introd. to this discourse.
[b] A favourite expression of Isocrates; cf. *Panegyr.* 5 and *De Bigis* 34.
[c] *Cf.* Isocrates, *Aegin.* 42 and *Plat.* 61; also Plato, *Apology* 40 c. [d] *Cf. To Philip* 135.

οὐδὲν ἐξεργάζονται, τοῦ δὲ πλούτου σημεῖόν εἰσιν·
οἱ δὲ περὶ τὴν μουσικὴν καὶ τὰς ἄλλας ἀγωνίας
ὄντες, οἱ μὲν τὰς δυνάμεις τὰς αὐτῶν, οἱ δὲ τὰς
τέχνας ἐπιδειξάμενοι, σφᾶς αὐτοὺς ἐντιμοτέρους
κατέστησαν· ὁ δὲ λόγος εἰ καλῶς διέλθοι τὰς
ἐκείνου πράξεις, ἀείμνηστον ἂν τὴν ἀρετὴν τὴν
Εὐαγόρου παρὰ πᾶσιν ἀνθρώποις ποιήσειεν.

5 Ἐχρῆν μὲν οὖν καὶ τοὺς ἄλλους ἐπαινεῖν τοὺς
ἐφ᾽ αὑτῶν ἄνδρας ἀγαθοὺς γεγενημένους, ἵν᾽ οἵ τε
δυνάμενοι τὰ τῶν ἄλλων ἔργα κοσμεῖν ἐν εἰδόσι
[190] ποιούμενοι τοὺς λόγους ταῖς ἀληθείαις ἐχρῶντο
περὶ αὐτῶν, οἵ τε νεώτεροι φιλοτιμοτέρως διέκειντο
πρὸς τὴν ἀρετήν, εἰδότες ὅτι τούτων εὐλογήσονται
μᾶλλον ὧν ἂν ἀμείνους σφᾶς αὐτοὺς παράσχωσιν.

6 νῦν δὲ τίς οὐκ ἂν ἀθυμήσειεν, ὅταν ὁρᾷ τοὺς μὲν
περὶ τὰ Τρωϊκὰ καὶ τοὺς ἐπέκεινα γενομένους ὑμ-
νουμένους καὶ τραγῳδουμένους, αὐτὸν δὲ προειδῇ,
μηδ᾽ ἂν ὑπερβάλλῃ τὰς ἐκείνων ἀρετάς, μηδέποτε
τοιούτων ἐπαίνων ἀξιωθησόμενον; τούτων δ᾽ αἴτιος ὁ φθόνος, ᾧ τοῦτο μόνον ἀγαθὸν πρόσεστιν,
ὅτι μέγιστον κακὸν τοῖς ἔχουσίν ἐστιν. οὕτω γάρ
τινες δυσκόλως πεφύκασιν, ὥσθ᾽ ἥδιον ἂν εὐλογου-
μένων ἀκούοιεν οὓς οὐκ ἴσασιν εἰ γεγόνασιν, ἢ
τούτων, ὑφ᾽ ὧν εὖ πεπονθότες αὐτοὶ τυγχάνουσιν.

7 οὐ μὴν δουλευτέον τοὺς νοῦν ἔχοντας τοῖς οὕτω
κακῶς φρονοῦσιν, ἀλλὰ τῶν μὲν τοιούτων ἀμελη-
τέον, τοὺς δ᾽ ἄλλους ἐθιστέον ἀκούειν περὶ ὧν καὶ
λέγειν δίκαιόν ἐστιν, ἄλλως τ᾽ ἐπειδὴ καὶ τὰς

---

* *e.g.*, Heracles, Theseus, and the Argonauts.

can effect nothing of this kind, but is an indication of wealth only; and those who devote themselves to music and letters and to the various contests, some by exhibiting their strength and others their artistic skill, win for themselves greater honour. But the spoken words which should adequately recount the deeds of Evagoras would make his virtues never to be forgotten among all mankind.

Now other writers should have praised those who in their own time had proved themselves good men, to the end that those who have the ability to glorify the deeds of their contemporaries, by speaking in the presence of those who knew the facts might have employed the truth concerning them, and also that the younger generation might with greater emulation have striven for virtue, knowing well that they would be praised more highly than those whom they have excelled in merit. But as it is, who would not be disheartened when he sees those who lived in the time of the Trojan War, and even earlier,[a] celebrated in song and tragedy, and yet foresees that even if he himself surpass their valorous achievements he will never be thought worthy of such praise? The cause of this is envy, which has this as its only good—it is the greatest evil to those who feel it. For some are so ungenerous by nature that they would listen more gladly to the praise of men of whose existence they are uncertain rather than of those who may have been their own benefactors. Men of intelligence, however, should not let themselves be enslaved by men whose minds are so perverted; on the contrary, they should ignore such as these and accustom their fellows to hear about those whom we are in duty bound to praise,

ἐπιδόσεις ἴσμεν γιγνομένας καὶ τῶν τεχνῶν καὶ
τῶν ἄλλων ἁπάντων οὐ διὰ τοὺς ἐμμένοντας τοῖς
καθεστῶσιν, ἀλλὰ διὰ τοὺς ἐπανορθοῦντας καὶ τολμῶντας ἀεί τι κινεῖν τῶν μὴ καλῶς ἐχόντων.

8 Οἶδα μὲν οὖν ὅτι χαλεπόν ἐστιν ὃ μέλλω ποιεῖν,
ἀνδρὸς ἀρετὴν διὰ λόγων ἐγκωμιάζειν. σημεῖον δὲ
μέγιστον· περὶ μὲν γὰρ ἄλλων πολλῶν καὶ παντοδαπῶν λέγειν τολμῶσιν οἱ περὶ τὴν φιλοσοφίαν
ὄντες, περὶ δὲ τῶν τοιούτων οὐδεὶς πώποτ' αὐτῶν
συγγράφειν ἐπεχείρησεν. καὶ πολλὴν αὐτοῖς ἔχω
συγγνώμην. τοῖς μὲν γὰρ ποιηταῖς πολλοὶ δέ-
9 δονται κόσμοι· καὶ γὰρ πλησιάζοντας τοὺς θεοὺς
τοῖς ἀνθρώποις οἷόν τ' αὐτοῖς ποιῆσαι καὶ διαλεγο-
μένους καὶ συναγωνιζομένους οἷς ἂν βουληθῶσι,
καὶ περὶ τούτων δηλῶσαι μὴ μόνον τοῖς τεταγ-
μένοις ὀνόμασιν, ἀλλὰ τὰ μὲν ξένοις, τὰ δὲ καινοῖς,
τὰ δὲ μεταφοραῖς, καὶ μηδὲν παραλιπεῖν, ἀλλὰ πᾶσι
10 τοῖς εἴδεσι διαποικῖλαι τὴν ποίησιν· τοῖς δὲ περὶ
τοὺς λόγους οὐδὲν ἔξεστι τῶν τοιούτων, ἀλλ' ἀπο-
τόμως καὶ τῶν ὀνομάτων τοῖς πολιτικοῖς μόνον καὶ
[191] τῶν ἐνθυμημάτων τοῖς περὶ αὐτὰς τὰς πράξεις
ἀναγκαῖόν ἐστι χρῆσθαι. πρὸς δὲ τούτοις οἱ μὲν
μετὰ μέτρων καὶ ῥυθμῶν ἅπαντα ποιοῦσιν, οἱ
δ' οὐδενὸς τούτων κοινωνοῦσιν· ἃ τοσαύτην ἔχει
χάριν, ὥστ' ἂν καὶ τῇ λέξει καὶ τοῖς ἐνθυμήμασιν
ἔχῃ κακῶς, ὅμως αὐταῖς ταῖς εὐρυθμίαις καὶ ταῖς

ᵃ Really oratory and rhetoric; for the meaning of

8

especially since we are aware that progress is made, not only in the arts, but in all other activities, not through the agency of those that are satisfied with things as they are, but through those who correct, and have the courage constantly to change, anything which is not as it should be.

I am fully aware that what I propose to do is difficult—to eulogize in prose the virtues of a man. The best proof is this : Those who devote themselves to philosophy [a] venture to speak on many subjects of every kind, but no one of them has ever attempted to compose a discourse on such a theme.[b] And I can make much allowance for them. For to the poets is granted the use of many embellishments of language, since they can represent the gods as associating with men, conversing with and aiding in battle whomsoever they please, and they can treat of these subjects not only in conventional expressions, but in words now exotic, now newly coined, and now in figures of speech, neglecting none, but using every kind with which to embroider their poesy.[c] Orators, on the contrary, are not permitted the use of such devices ; they must use with precision only words in current use and only such ideas as bear upon the actual facts. Besides, the poets compose all their works with metre and rhythm, while the orators do not share in any of these advantages ; and these lend such charm that even though the poets may be deficient in style and thoughts, yet by the very spell of their rhythm and harmony

" philosophy " in Isocrates see the General Introd., Vol. I, p. xxvi.
    [b] Prose *encomia* existed before this time, but they were mostly *exercises* on mythical subjects written by Sophists.
    [c] With this passage compare Arist. *Poetics* 1457 b.

11 συμμετρίαις ψυχαγωγοῦσι τοὺς ἀκούοντας. γνοίη
δ᾽ ἄν τις ἐκεῖθεν τὴν δύναμιν αὐτῶν· ἦν γάρ τις
τῶν ποιημάτων τῶν εὐδοκιμούντων τὰ μὲν ὀνόματα
καὶ τὰς διανοίας καταλίπῃ, τὸ δὲ μέτρον διαλύσῃ,
φανήσεται πολὺ καταδεέστερα τῆς δόξης ἧς νῦν
ἔχομεν περὶ αὐτῶν. ὅμως δὲ καίπερ τοσοῦτον
πλεονεκτούσης τῆς ποιήσεως, οὐκ ὀκνητέον, ἀλλ᾽
ἀποπειρατέον τῶν λόγων ἐστίν, εἰ καὶ τοῦτο δυνή-
σονται, τοὺς ἀγαθοὺς ἄνδρας εὐλογεῖν μηδὲν χεῖρον
τῶν ἐν ταῖς ᾠδαῖς καὶ τοῖς μέτροις ἐγκωμιαζόντων.

12 Πρῶτον μὲν οὖν περὶ τῆς φύσεως τῆς Εὐαγόρου,
καὶ τίνων ἦν ἀπόγονος, εἰ καὶ πολλοὶ προεπί-
στανται, δοκεῖ μοι πρέπειν κἀμὲ τῶν ἄλλων ἕνεκα
διελθεῖν περὶ αὐτῶν, ἵνα πάντες εἰδῶσιν ὅτι καλλίστων αὐτῷ καὶ μεγίστων παραδειγμάτων καταλειφθέντων οὐδὲν καταδεέστερον αὐτὸν ἐκείνων

13 παρέσχεν. ὁμολογεῖται μὲν γὰρ τοὺς ἀπὸ Διὸς
εὐγενεστάτους τῶν ἡμιθέων εἶναι, τούτων δ᾽ αὐτῶν
οὐκ ἔστιν ὅστις οὐκ ἂν Αἰακίδας προκρίνειεν· ἐν
μὲν γὰρ τοῖς ἄλλοις γένεσιν εὑρήσομεν τοὺς μὲν
ὑπερβάλλοντας, τοὺς δὲ καταδεεστέρους ὄντας,
οὗτοι δ᾽ ἅπαντες ὀνομαστότατοι τῶν καθ᾽ αὑτοὺς

14 γεγόνασιν. τοῦτο μὲν γὰρ Αἰακὸς ὁ Διὸς μὲν
ἔκγονος, τοῦ δὲ γένους τοῦ Τευκριδῶν πρόγονος,
τοσοῦτον διήνεγκεν ὥστε γενομένων αὐχμῶν ἐν
τοῖς Ἕλλησι καὶ πολλῶν ἀνθρώπων διαφθαρέντων,
ἐπειδὴ τὸ μέγεθος τῆς συμφορᾶς ὑπερέβαλεν, ἦλθον οἱ προεστῶτες τῶν πόλεων ἱκετεύοντες αὐτόν,
νομίζοντες διὰ τῆς συγγενείας καὶ τῆς εὐσεβείας
τῆς ἐκείνου τάχιστ᾽ ἂν εὑρέσθαι παρὰ τῶν θεῶν

---

[a] Cf. Plato, Rep. 601 b.   [b] Cf. Nicocles 42.

they bewitch their listeners.[a] The power of poetry may be understood from this consideration ; if one should retain the words and ideas of poems which are held in high esteem, but do away with the metre, they will appear far inferior to the opinion we now have of them. Nevertheless, although poetry has advantages so great, we must not shrink from the task, but must make the effort and see if it will be possible in prose to eulogize good men in no worse fashion than their encomiasts do who employ song and verse.

In the first place, with respect to the birth and ancestry of Evagoras,[b] even if many are already familiar with the facts, I believe it is fitting that I also should recount them for the sake of the others, that all may know that he proved himself not inferior to the noblest and greatest examples of excellence which were of his inheritance. For it is acknowledged that the noblest of the demigods are the sons of Zeus, and there is no one who would not award first place among these to the Aeacidae ; for while in the other families we shall find some of superior and some of inferior worth, yet all the Aeacidae have been most renowned of all their contemporaries. In the first place Aeacus,[c] son of Zeus and ancestor of the family of the Teucridae, was so distinguished that when a drought visited the Greeks and many persons had perished, and when the magnitude of the calamity had passed all bounds, the leaders of the cities came as suppliants to him ; for they thought that, by reason of his kinship with Zeus and his piety, they would most quickly obtain from

[c] Aeacus, son of Zeus and Aegina, was renowned for his piety.

15 τῶν παρόντων κακῶν ἀπαλλαγήν. σωθέντες δὲ
καὶ τυχόντες ὧν ἐδεήθησαν, ἱερὸν ἐν Αἰγίνῃ κατ-
εστήσαντο κοινὸν τῶν Ἑλλήνων, οὗπερ ἐκεῖνος
[192] ἐποιήσατο τὴν εὐχήν. καὶ κατ᾽ ἐκεῖνόν τε τὸν
χρόνον ἕως ἦν μετ᾽ ἀνθρώπων, μετὰ καλλίστης ὧν
δόξης διετέλεσεν· ἐπειδή τε μετήλλαξε τὸν βίον,
λέγεται παρὰ Πλούτωνι καὶ Κόρῃ μεγίστας τιμὰς
ἔχων παρεδρεύειν ἐκείνοις.

16   Τούτου δὲ παῖδες ἦσαν Τελαμὼν καὶ Πηλεύς, ὧν
ὁ μὲν ἕτερος μεθ᾽ Ἡρακλέους ἐπὶ Λαομέδοντα
στρατευσάμενος ἀριστείων ἠξιώθη, Πηλεὺς δ᾽ ἔν
τε τῇ μάχῃ τῇ πρὸς Κενταύρους ἀριστεύσας καὶ
κατὰ πολλοὺς ἄλλους κινδύνους εὐδοκιμήσας Θέτιδι
τῇ Νηρέως, θνητὸς ὢν ἀθανάτῃ, συνῴκησε, καὶ
μόνου τούτου φασὶ τῶν προγεγενημένων ὑπὸ θεῶν
17 ἐν τοῖς γάμοις ὑμέναιον ᾀσθῆναι. τούτοιν δ᾽ ἑκατέρου, Τελαμῶνος μὲν Αἴας καὶ Τεῦκρος ἐγενέσθην,
Πηλέως δ᾽ Ἀχιλλεύς, οἳ μέγιστον καὶ σαφέστατον
ἔλεγχον ἔδοσαν τῆς αὑτῶν ἀρετῆς· οὐ γὰρ ἐν ταῖς
αὑτῶν πόλεσι μόνον ἐπρώτευσαν, οὐδ᾽ ἐν τοῖς τόποις ἐν οἷς κατῴκουν, ἀλλὰ στρατείας τοῖς Ἕλλησιν ἐπὶ τοὺς βαρβάρους γενομένης, καὶ πολλῶν
18 μὲν ἑκατέρων ἀθροισθέντων, οὐδενὸς δὲ τῶν ὀνο-
μαστῶν ἀπολειφθέντος, ἐν τούτοις τοῖς κινδύνοις
Ἀχιλλεὺς μὲν ἁπάντων διήνεγκεν. Αἴας δὲ μετ᾽
ἐκεῖνον ἠρίστευσε, Τεῦκρος δὲ τῆς τε τούτων
συγγενείας ἄξιος καὶ τῶν ἄλλων οὐδενὸς χείρων
γενόμενος, ἐπειδὴ Τροίαν συνεξεῖλεν, ἀφικόμενος
εἰς Κύπρον Σαλαμῖνά τε κατῴκισεν, ὁμώνυμον

---

[a] This was the Aiakeion, described by Pausanias ii. 29.
[b] Persephonê.

the gods relief from the woes that afflicted them.
Having gained their desire, they were saved and
built in Aegina a temple [a] to be shared by all the
Greeks on the very spot where he had offered his
prayer. During his entire stay among men he ever
enjoyed the fairest repute, and after his departure
from life it is said that he sits by the side of Pluto
and Korê [b] in the enjoyment of the highest honours.[c]

The sons of Aeacus were Telamôn and Peleus ;
Telamôn won the meed of valour in an expedition
with Heracles against Laomedon,[d] and Peleus, having
distinguished himself in the battle with the Centaurs
and having won glory in many other hazardous enterprises, wedded Thetis, the daughter of Nereus, he
a mortal winning an immortal bride. And they say
that at his wedding alone, of all the human race who
have ever lived, the wedding-song was sung by gods.
To each of these two were born sons—to Telamôn
Ajax and Teucer, and to Peleus Achilles, and these
heroes gave proof of their valour in the clearest and
most convincing way ; for not alone in their own
cities were they pre-eminent, or in the places where
they made their homes, but when an expedition was
organized by the Greeks against the barbarians,[e]
and a great army was assembled on either side and
no warrior of repute was absent, Achilles above all
distinguished himself in these perils. And Ajax
was second to him in valour, and Teucer, who proved
himself worthy of their kinship and inferior to none
of the other heroes, after he had helped in the capture of Troy, went to Cyprus and founded Salamis,

[e] Aeacus, Minos, and Rhadamanthys were reputed to be
the judges in the world of the dead.
[d] Laomedon, with the help of Poseidon, built Troy.
[e] *i.e.*, the Trojans.

ποιήσας τῆς πρότερον αὐτῷ πατρίδος οὔσης, καὶ
τὸ γένος τὸ νῦν βασιλεῦον κατέλιπεν.

19 Τὰ μὲν οὖν ἐξ ἀρχῆς Εὐαγόρᾳ παρὰ τῶν προγόνων ὑπάρξαντα τηλικαῦτα τὸ μέγεθός ἐστιν. τοῦτον δὲ τὸν τρόπον τῆς πόλεως κατοικισθείσης κατὰ
μὲν ἀρχὰς οἱ γεγονότες ἀπὸ Τεύκρου τὴν βασιλείαν
εἶχον, χρόνῳ δ' ὕστερον ἀφικόμενος ἐκ Φοινίκης
ἀνὴρ φυγὰς καὶ πιστευθεὶς ὑπὸ τοῦ τότε βασιλεύοντος καὶ μεγάλας δυναστείας λαβὼν οὐ χάριν
20 ἔσχε τούτων, ἀλλὰ κακὸς μὲν γενόμενος περὶ τὸν
ὑποδεξάμενον, δεινὸς δὲ πρὸς τὸ πλεονεκτῆσαι, τὸν
μὲν εὐεργέτην ἐξέβαλεν, αὐτὸς δὲ τὴν βασιλείαν
κατέσχεν. ἀπιστῶν δὲ τοῖς πεπραγμένοις καὶ
βουλόμενος ἀσφαλῶς κατασκευάσασθαι τὰ περὶ
αὑτὸν τήν τε πόλιν ἐξεβαρβάρωσε καὶ τὴν νῆσον
[193] ὅλην βασιλεῖ τῷ μεγάλῳ κατεδούλωσεν.

21 Οὕτω δὲ τῶν πραγμάτων καθεστώτων καὶ τῶν
ἐκγόνων τῶν ἐκείνου τὴν ἀρχὴν ἐχόντων Εὐαγόρας
γίγνεται· περὶ οὗ τὰς μὲν φήμας καὶ τὰς μαντείας
καὶ τὰς ὄψεις τὰς ἐν τοῖς ὕπνοις γενομένας, ἐξ ὧν
μειζόνως ἂν φανείη γεγονὼς ἢ κατ' ἄνθρωπον,
αἱροῦμαι παραλιπεῖν, οὐκ ἀπιστῶν τοῖς λεγομένοις,
ἀλλ' ἵνα πᾶσι ποιήσω φανερὸν ὅτι τοσούτου δέω
πλασάμενος εἰπεῖν τι περὶ τῶν ἐκείνῳ πεπραγμένων, ὥστε καὶ τῶν ὑπαρχόντων ἀφίημι τὰ
τοιαῦτα περὶ ὧν ὀλίγοι τινὲς ἐπίστανται καὶ μὴ
πάντες οἱ πολῖται συνίσασιν. ἄρξομαι δ' ἐκ τῶν
ὁμολογουμένων λέγειν περὶ αὐτοῦ.

22 Παῖς μὲν γὰρ ὢν ἔσχε κάλλος καὶ ῥώμην καὶ
σωφροσύνην, ἅπερ τῶν ἀγαθῶν πρεπωδέστατα τοῖς

ᵃ The island Salamis near Athens.

giving to it the name of his former native land ^a; and he left behind him the family that now reigns.

So distinguished from the beginning was the heritage transmitted to Evagoras by his ancestors. After the city had been founded in this manner, the rule at first was held by Teucer's descendants; at a later time, however, there came from Phoenicia a fugitive, who, after he had gained the confidence of the king who then reigned, and had won great power, showed no proper gratitude for the favour shown him; on the contrary, he acted basely toward his host, and being skilled at grasping, he expelled his benefactor and himself seized the throne. But distrustful of the consequences of his measures and wishing to make his position secure, he reduced the city to barbarism, and brought the whole island into subservience to the Great King.[b]

Such was the state of affairs in Salamis, and the descendants of the usurper were in possession of the throne when Evagoras was born. I prefer to say nothing of the portents, the oracles, the visions appearing in dreams, from which the impression might be gained that he was of superhuman birth, not because I disbelieve the reports, but that I may make it clear to all that I am so far from resorting to invention in speaking of his deeds that even of those matters which are in fact true I dismiss such as are known only to the few and of which not all the citizens are cognizant. And I shall begin my account of him with the generally acknowledged facts.

When Evagoras was a boy he possessed beauty, bodily strength, and modesty, the very qualities that

---

^b The king of Persia, Artaxerxes.

15

τηλικούτοις ἐστίν. καὶ τούτων μάρτυρας ἄν τις
ποιήσαιτο, τῆς μὲν σωφροσύνης τοὺς συμπαιδευ-
θέντας τῶν πολιτῶν, τοῦ δὲ κάλλους ἅπαντας τοὺς
ἰδόντας, τῆς δὲ ῥώμης ἅπαντας τοὺς ἀγῶνας[1] ἐν
23 οἷς ἐκεῖνος τῶν ἡλικιωτῶν ἐκρατίστευσεν. ἀνδρὶ
δὲ γενομένῳ ταῦτά τε πάντα συνηυξήθη καὶ πρὸς
τούτοις ἀνδρία προσεγένετο καὶ σοφία καὶ δικαιοσύνη, καὶ ταῦτ᾽ οὐ μέσως οὐδ᾽ ὥσπερ ἑτέροις
τισίν, ἀλλ᾽ ἕκαστον αὐτῶν εἰς ὑπερβολήν· τοσοῦτον
γὰρ καὶ ταῖς τοῦ σώματος καὶ ταῖς τῆς ψυχῆς
24 ἀρεταῖς διήνεγκεν, ὥσθ᾽ ὁπότε μὲν αὐτὸν ὁρῷεν οἱ
τότε βασιλεύοντες, ἐκπλήττεσθαι καὶ φοβεῖσθαι
περὶ τῆς ἀρχῆς, ἡγουμένους οὐχ οἷόν τ᾽ εἶναι τὸν
τοιοῦτον τὴν φύσιν ἐν ἰδιώτου μέρει διαγαγεῖν,
ὁπότε δ᾽ εἰς τοὺς τρόπους ἀποβλέψειαν, οὕτω
σφόδρα πιστεύειν, ὥστ᾽ εἰ καί τις ἄλλος τολμῴη
περὶ αὐτοὺς ἐξαμαρτάνειν, νομίζειν Εὐαγόραν αὑ-
25 τοῖς ἔσεσθαι βοηθόν. καὶ τοσοῦτον τῆς δόξης
παραλλαττούσης οὐδετέρου τούτων ἐψεύσθησαν·
οὔτε γὰρ ἰδιώτης ὢν διετέλεσεν οὔτε περὶ ἐκείνους
ἐξήμαρτεν, ἀλλὰ τοσαύτην ὁ δαίμων ἔσχεν αὐτοῦ
πρόνοιαν, ὅπως καλῶς λήψεται τὴν βασιλείαν,
ὥσθ᾽ ὅσα μὲν ἀναγκαῖον ἦν παρασκευασθῆναι δι᾽
26 ἀσεβείας, ταῦτα μὲν ἕτερος ἔπραξεν, ἐξ ὧν δ᾽ οἷόν
τ᾽ ἦν ὁσίως καὶ δικαίως λαβεῖν τὴν ἀρχήν, Εὐαγόρᾳ
διεφύλαξεν. εἷς γὰρ τῶν δυναστευόντων ἐπιβουλεύσας τόν τε τύραννον ἀπέκτεινε καὶ συλλαβεῖν
Εὐαγόραν ἐπεχείρησεν, ἡγούμενος οὐ δυνήσεσθαι
κατασχεῖν τὴν ἀρχήν, εἰ μὴ κἀκεῖνον ἐκποδὼν

---

[1] ἅπαντας τοὺς ἀγῶνας ΓΔΕ. Blass added θεασαμένους
before τούς.

16

are most becoming to that age. Witnesses could be produced for these assertions : for his modesty—fellow-citizens who were educated with him ; for his beauty—all who beheld him ; for his strength—all the contests [a] in which he vanquished his age-mates. When he attained to manhood not only did all these qualities grow up with him, but to them were also added manly courage, wisdom, and justice, and that too in no ordinary measure, as is the case with some others, but each of these characteristics in extraordinary degree. So surpassing was his excellence of both body and mind, that when the kings of that time looked upon him they were terrified and feared for their throne, thinking that a man of such nature could not possibly pass his life in the status of a private citizen, but whenever they observed his character, they felt such confidence in him that they believed that even if anyone else should dare to injure them, Evagoras would be their champion. And although opinions of him were so at variance, they were mistaken in neither respect ; for he neither remained in private life, nor did them injury ; on the contrary, the Deity took such thought for him that he should honourably assume the throne, that all the preparations which necessarily involved impiety were made by another, while he preserved for Evagoras those means whereby it was possible for him to gain the rule in accordance with piety and justice. For one of the princes,[b] starting a conspiracy, slew the tyrant and attempted to arrest Evagoras, believing that he would not be able to retain the rule himself unless he should get him out

---

[a] *i.e.*, the official records of winners in the contests sanctioned by the state.   [b] Abdemon ; *cf.* Diodorus xiv. 98.

[194]

27 ποιήσαιτο. διαφυγὼν δὲ τὸν κίνδυνον καὶ σωθεὶς
εἰς Σόλους τῆς Κιλικίας οὐ τὴν αὐτὴν γνώμην ἔσχε
τοῖς ταῖς τοιαύταις συμφοραῖς περιπίπτουσιν. οἱ
μὲν γὰρ ἄλλοι, κἂν ἐκ τυραννίδος ἐκπέσωσι, διὰ
τὰς παρούσας τύχας ταπεινοτέρας τὰς ψυχὰς ἔχου-
σιν· ἐκεῖνος δ' εἰς τοσοῦτον μεγαλοφροσύνης ἦλθεν,
ὥστε τὸν ἄλλον χρόνον ἰδιώτης ὤν, ἐπειδὴ φεύγειν
28 ἠναγκάσθη, τυραννεῖν ᾠήθη δεῖν. καὶ τοὺς μὲν
πλάνους τοὺς φυγαδικοὺς καὶ τὸ δι' ἑτέρων ζητεῖν
τὴν κάθοδον καὶ θεραπεύειν αὐτοῦ χείρους ὑπερεῖδεν, λαβὼν δὲ ταύτην ἀφορμήν, ἥνπερ χρὴ τοὺς
εὐσεβεῖν βουλομένους, ἀμύνεσθαι καὶ μὴ προτέ-
ρους ὑπάρχειν, καὶ προελόμενος ἢ κατορθώσας
τυραννεῖν ἢ διαμαρτὼν ἀποθανεῖν, παρακαλέσας
ἀνθρώπους, ὡς οἱ τοὺς πλείστους λέγοντες, περὶ
πεντήκοντα, μετὰ τούτων παρεσκευάζετο ποιεῖσθαι
29 τὴν κάθοδον. ὅθεν καὶ μάλιστ' ἄν τις καὶ τὴν φύσιν τὴν ἐκείνου καὶ τὴν δόξαν ἣν εἶχε παρὰ τοῖς
ἄλλοις θεωρήσειεν· μέλλοντος γὰρ πλεῖν μετὰ
τοσούτων ἐπὶ τηλικαύτην πρᾶξιν[1] τὸ μέγεθος καὶ
πάντων τῶν δεινῶν πλησίον ὄντων οὔτ' ἐκεῖνος ἠθύ-
μησεν οὔτε τῶν παρακληθέντων οὐδεὶς ἀποστῆναι
τῶν κινδύνων ἠξίωσεν, ἀλλ' οἱ μὲν ὥσπερ θεῷ συν-
ακολουθοῦντες ἅπαντες ἐνέμειναν τοῖς ὡμολογη-
μένοις, ὁ δ' ὥσπερ ἢ στρατόπεδον ἔχων κρεῖττον
τῶν ἀντιπάλων ἢ προειδὼς τὸ συμβησόμενον οὕτω
30 διέκειτο τὴν γνώμην. δῆλον δ' ἐκ τῶν ἔργων· ἀπο-
βὰς γὰρ εἰς τὴν νῆσον οὐχ ἡγήσατο δεῖν χωρίον
ἐχυρὸν καταλαβὼν καὶ τὸ σῶμ' ἐν ἀσφαλείᾳ κατα-

---

[1] πρᾶξιν ΔΘΛ vulg. : πόλιν Γ.

18

of the way. But Evagoras escaped this peril, and having saved himself by fleeing to Soli in Cilicia did not show the same spirit as those who are the victims of like misfortune. For other exiles from royal power are humbled in spirit because of their misfortunes, whereas Evagoras attained to such greatness of soul that, although until that time he had lived as a private citizen, when he was driven into exile he determined to gain the throne. The wandering life of an exile, the dependence upon the help of others in seeking his restoration and the paying of court to his inferiors—all these he scorned; but this he took as his guiding principle, which those who would be god-fearing men must take—to act only in self-defence and never to be the aggressor; and he chose either by success to regain the throne or, failing in that, to die. And so, calling to his side men numbering, according to the highest estimates, about fifty, with these he prepared to effect his return from exile. And from this venture especially the character of Evagoras and his reputation among his associates may be seen; for although he was on the point of sailing with so few companions for the accomplishment of so great a design, and although all the attendant dangers were near at hand, neither did he himself lose heart, nor did any of his companions see fit to shrink from these dangers; nay, as if a god were their leader, they one and all held fast to their promises, and Evagoras, just as if either he had an army superior to that of his adversaries or foresaw the outcome, held to his opinion. This is evident from his acts; for, when he had landed on the island, he did not think it necessary to seize a strong position, make sure of his own safety, and then to wait and see

στήσας περιιδεῖν εἴ τινες αὐτῷ τῶν πολιτῶν βοη-
θήσουσιν· ἀλλ' εὐθύς, ὥσπερ εἶχε, ταύτης τῆς
νυκτὸς διελὼν τοῦ τείχους πυλίδα καὶ ταύτῃ τοὺς
μεθ' αὑτοῦ διαγαγὼν προσέβαλλε πρὸς τὸ βασί-
31 λειον. καὶ τοὺς μὲν θορύβους τοὺς ἐν τοῖς τοιούτοις καιροῖς γιγνομένους καὶ τοὺς φόβους τοὺς τῶν
ἄλλων καὶ τὰς παρακελεύσεις τὰς ἐκείνου τί δεῖ
λέγοντα διατρίβειν; γενομένων δ' αὐτῷ τῶν μὲν
περὶ τὸν τύραννον ἀνταγωνιστῶν, τῶν δ' ἄλλων
[195] πολιτῶν θεατῶν, δεδιότες γὰρ τοῦ μὲν τὴν ἀρχήν,
32 τοῦ δὲ τὴν ἀρετήν, ἡσυχίαν εἶχον, οὐ πρότερον
ἐπαύσατο μαχόμενος καὶ μόνος πρὸς πολλοὺς καὶ
μετ' ὀλίγων πρὸς ἅπαντας τοὺς ἐχθρούς,[1] πρὶν ἑλεῖν
τὸ βασίλειον, καὶ τούς τ' ἐχθροὺς ἐτιμωρήσατο καὶ
τοῖς φίλοις ἐβοήθησεν, ἔτι δὲ τῷ γένει τὰς τιμὰς
τὰς πατρίους ἐκομίσατο, καὶ τύραννον αὑτὸν τῆς
πόλεως κατέστησεν.

33 Ἡγοῦμαι μὲν οὖν, εἰ καὶ μηδενὸς ἄλλου μνησ-
θείην, ἀλλ' ἐνταῦθα καταλίποιμι τὸν λόγον, ῥᾴδιον
ἐκ τούτων εἶναι γνῶναι τήν τ' ἀρετὴν τὴν Εὐαγόρου
καὶ τὸ μέγεθος τῶν πεπραγμένων· οὐ μὴν ἀλλ' ἔτι
γε σαφέστερον περὶ ἀμφοτέρων τούτων ἐκ τῶν
34 ἐχομένων οἶμαι δηλώσειν. τοσούτων γὰρ τυράννων ἐν ἅπαντι τῷ χρόνῳ γεγενημένων οὐδεὶς
φανήσεται τὴν τιμὴν ταύτην κάλλιον ἐκείνου κτησάμενος. εἰ μὲν οὖν πρὸς ἕκαστον αὐτῶν τὰς
πράξεις τὰς Εὐαγόρου παραβάλλοιμεν, οὔτ' ἂν ὁ
λόγος ἴσως τοῖς καιροῖς ἁρμόσειεν οὔτ' ἂν ὁ χρόνος
τοῖς λεγομένοις ἀρκέσειεν· ἢν δὲ προελόμενοι τοὺς
εὐδοκιμωτάτους ἐπὶ τούτων σκοπῶμεν, οὐδὲν μὲν

---

[1] τοὺς ἐχθρούς ΘΛ vulg. is bracketed by Blass.

if some of the citizens would rally to his aid; but immediately, just as he was, on that very night he broke through a little gate in the wall, and leading his followers through this opening, attacked the palace. The confusion attendant upon such occasions, the fears of his followers, the exhortations of their leader—why need I take the time to describe? [a] When the supporters of the tyrant opposed him and the citizens generally were observers (for they held their peace because they feared either the authority of the one party or the valour of the other), he did not cease from fighting, whether alone against many or with few opposing all the foe, until, having captured the palace, he had taken vengeance upon the enemy and had succoured his friends; furthermore, he restored its ancestral honours to his family [b] and established himself as ruler of the city.

I think that even if I should mention nothing more, but should discontinue my discourse at this point, from what I have said the valour of Evagoras and the greatness of his deeds would be readily manifest: nevertheless, I consider that both will be yet more clearly revealed from what remains to be said. For of all the many sovereigns since time began, none will be found to have won this honour more gloriously than Evagoras. If we were to compare the deeds of Evagoras with those of each one, such an account would perhaps be inappropriate to the occasion, and the time would not suffice for the telling. But if we select the most illustrious of these rulers and examine their exploits in the light of his, our investigation

---

[a] *Cf. Panegyr.* 97 for a similar passage in reference to the sea-fight at Salamis. In *To Philip* 93-94 Isocrates justifies such "autoplagiarism."   [b] *Cf. Nicocles* 28.

χεῖρον ἐξετῶμεν, πολὺ δὲ συντομώτερον διαλεχ-
θησόμεθα περὶ αὐτῶν.

35 Τῶν μὲν οὖν τὰς πατρικὰς βασιλείας παρα-
λαβόντων τίς οὐκ ἂν τοὺς Εὐαγόρου κινδύνους
προκρίνειεν; οὐδεὶς γάρ ἐστιν οὕτω ῥάθυμος,
ὅστις ἂν δέξαιτο παρὰ τῶν προγόνων τὴν ἀρχὴν
ταύτην παραλαβεῖν μᾶλλον ἢ κτησάμενος ὥσπερ
36 ἐκεῖνος τοῖς παισὶ τοῖς αὑτοῦ καταλιπεῖν. καὶ μὴν
τῶν γε παλαιῶν καθόδων αὗται μάλιστ᾽ εὐδοκι-
μοῦσιν ἃς παρὰ τῶν ποιητῶν ἀκούομεν· οὗτοι γὰρ
οὐ μόνον τῶν γεγενημένων τὰς καλλίστας ἡμῖν
ἀπαγγέλλουσιν, ἀλλὰ καὶ παρ᾽ αὑτῶν καινὰς συν-
τιθέασιν. ἀλλ᾽ ὅμως οὐδεὶς αὐτῶν μεμυθολόγηκεν,
ὅστις οὕτω δεινοὺς καὶ φοβεροὺς ποιησάμενος τοὺς
κινδύνους εἰς τὴν αὑτοῦ κατῆλθεν· ἀλλ᾽ οἱ μὲν
πλεῖστοι πεποίηνται διὰ τύχην λαβόντες τὰς βασιλείας, οἱ δὲ μετὰ δόλου καὶ τέχνης περιγενόμενοι
37 τῶν ἐχθρῶν. ἀλλὰ μὴν τῶν γ᾽ ἐπὶ τάδε γεγενημένων, ἴσως δὲ καὶ τῶν ἁπάντων, Κῦρον τὸν
Μήδων μὲν ἀφελόμενον τὴν ἀρχήν, Πέρσαις δὲ
196] κτησάμενον, καὶ πλεῖστοι καὶ μάλιστα θαυμάζουσιν. ἀλλ᾽ ὁ μὲν τῷ Περσῶν στρατοπέδῳ τὸ
Μήδων ἐνίκησεν, ὃ πολλοὶ καὶ τῶν Ἑλλήνων καὶ
τῶν βαρβάρων ῥᾳδίως ἂν ποιήσειαν· ὁ δὲ διὰ τῆς
ψυχῆς τῆς αὑτοῦ καὶ τοῦ σώματος τὰ πλεῖστα
38 φαίνεται τῶν προειρημένων διαπραξάμενος. ἔπειτ᾽
ἐκ μὲν τῆς Κύρου στρατηγίας οὔπω δῆλον ὅτι καὶ
τοὺς Εὐαγόρου κινδύνους ἂν ὑπέμεινεν, ἐκ δὲ τῶν
τούτῳ πεπραγμένων ἅπασι φανερόν, ὅτι ῥᾳδίως ἂν
κἀκείνοις τοῖς ἔργοις ἐπεχείρησεν. πρὸς δὲ τούτοις

will lose nothing thereby and our discussion will be much more brief.

Who, then, would not choose the perilous deeds of Evagoras before the fortunes of those who inherited their kingdoms from their fathers ? For surely there is no one so mean of spirit that he would prefer to receive that power from his ancestors than first to acquire it, as he did, and then to bequeath it to his children. Furthermore, of the returns to their thrones by princes of ancient times the most renowned are those of which the poets tell us ; indeed they not only chronicle for us those which have been most glorious, but also compose new ones of their own invention. Nevertheless, no poet has told the story of any legendary prince who has faced hazards so formidable and yet regained his throne ; on the contrary, most of their heroes have been represented as having regained their kingdoms by chance, others as having employed deceit and artifice to overcome their foes. Nay, of those who lived later, perhaps indeed of all, the one hero who was most admired by the greatest number was Cyrus, who deprived the Medes of their kingdom and gained it for the Persians. But while Cyrus with a Persian army conquered the Medes, a deed which many a Greek or a barbarian could easily do, Evagoras manifestly accomplished the greater part of the deeds which have been mentioned through strength of his own mind and body. Again, while it is not at all certain from the expedition of Cyrus that he would have endured the dangers of Evagoras, yet it is obvious to all from the deeds of Evagoras that the latter would have readily attempted the exploits of Cyrus. In addition, while piety and justice characterized

τῷ μὲν ὁσίως καὶ δικαίως ἅπαντα πέπρακται, τῷ
δ᾽ οὐκ εὐσεβῶς ἔνια συμβέβηκεν· ὁ μὲν γὰρ τοὺς
ἐχθροὺς ἀπώλεσε, Κῦρος δὲ τὸν πατέρα τὸν τῆς
μητρὸς ἀπέκτεινεν. ὥστ᾽ εἴ τινες βούλοιντο μὴ τὸ
μέγεθος τῶν συμβάντων ἀλλὰ τὴν ἀρετὴν τὴν
ἑκατέρου κρίνειν, δικαίως ἂν Εὐαγόραν καὶ τούτου
39 μᾶλλον ἐπαινέσειαν. εἰ δὲ δεῖ συντόμως καὶ μηδὲν
ὑποστειλάμενον μηδὲ δείσαντα τὸν φθόνον, ἀλλὰ
παρρησίᾳ χρησάμενον εἰπεῖν, οὐδεὶς οὔτε θνητὸς
οὔθ᾽ ἡμίθεος οὔτ᾽ ἀθάνατος εὑρεθήσεται κάλλιον
οὐδὲ λαμπρότερον οὐδ᾽ εὐσεβέστερον λαβὼν ἐκείνου
τὴν βασιλείαν. καὶ τούτοις ἐκείνως ἄν τις μάλιστα
πιστεύσειεν, εἰ σφόδρα τοῖς λεγομένοις ἀπιστήσας
ἐξετάζειν ἐπιχειρήσειεν, ὅπως ἕκαστος ἐτυράννευ-
σεν. φανήσομαι γὰρ οὐκ ἐκ παντὸς τρόπου μεγάλα
λέγειν προθυμούμενος, ἀλλὰ διὰ τὴν τοῦ πράγματος
ἀλήθειαν οὕτω περὶ αὐτοῦ θρασέως εἰρηκώς.

40 Εἰ μὲν οὖν ἐπὶ μικροῖς διήνεγκε, τοιούτων ἂν καὶ
τῶν λόγων αὐτῷ προσῆκεν ἀξιοῦσθαι· νῦν δ᾽ ἅ-
παντες ἂν ὁμολογήσειαν τυραννίδα καὶ τῶν θείων
ἀγαθῶν καὶ τῶν ἀνθρωπίνων μέγιστον καὶ σεμνό-
τατον καὶ περιμαχητότατον εἶναι. τὸν δὴ τὸ κάλλιστον τῶν ὄντων κάλλιστα κτησάμενον τίς ἂν ἢ
ποιητὴς ἢ λόγων εὑρετὴς ἀξίως τῶν πεπραγμένων
ἐπαινέσειεν;

41 Οὐ τοίνυν ἐν τούτοις ὑπερβαλόμενος ἐν τοῖς
ἄλλοις εὑρεθήσεται καταδεέστερος γενόμενος, ἀλλὰ

---

[a] Astyages, father of Mandanê, who married Cambyses,
father of Cyrus. That Cyrus slew Astyages is not stated by
any other writer.

every act of Evagoras, some of the successes of
Cyrus were gained impiously; for the former destroyed his enemies, but Cyrus slew his mother's
father.[a] Consequently if any should wish to judge,
not of the greatness of their successes, but of the
essential merit of each, they would justly award
greater praise to Evagoras than even to Cyrus. And
if there is need to speak concisely, without reser-
vation or fear of arousing ill-feeling, but with the
utmost frankness, I would say that no one, whether
mortal, demigod, or immortal, will be found to have
obtained his throne more nobly, more splendidly, or
more piously. Anyone would in the highest degree
be confirmed in this belief if, distrusting completely
what I have said, he were to set about examining
how each gained royal power. For it will be manifest
that it is through no desire whatever of grandilo-
quence, but because of the truth of the matter, that
I have spoken thus boldly about Evagoras.

Now if he had distinguished himself in unimportant
ways only, he would fittingly be thought worthy also
of praise of like nature; but as it is, all would admit
that of all blessings whether human or divine supreme
power is the greatest, the most august, and the object
of greatest strife. That man, therefore, who has
most gloriously acquired the most glorious of possessions, what poet or what artificer of words [b] could
praise in a manner worthy of his deeds?

Nor again, though he was a man of surpassing
merit in these respects, will Evagoras be found deficient in all others, but, in the first place, although

---

[b] λόγων εὑρετής is found also in *To Philip* 144. It means
"prose-writer," and refers especially to composers of " set
discourses " or " show-pieces."

πρῶτον μὲν εὐφυέστατος ὢν τὴν γνώμην καὶ
πλεῖστα κατορθοῦν δυνάμενος ὅμως οὐκ ᾠήθη δεῖν
ὀλιγωρεῖν οὐδ' αὐτοσχεδιάζειν περὶ τῶν πραγ-
[197] μάτων, ἀλλ' ἐν τῷ ζητεῖν καὶ φροντίζειν καὶ
βουλεύεσθαι τὸν πλεῖστον τοῦ χρόνου διέτριβεν,
ἡγούμενος μέν, εἰ καλῶς τὴν αὑτοῦ φρόνησιν
παρασκευάσειεν, καλῶς¹ αὑτῷ καὶ τὴν βασιλείαν
ἕξειν, θαυμάζων δ' ὅσοι τῶν μὲν ἄλλων ἕνεκα τῆς
ψυχῆς ποιοῦνται τὴν ἐπιμέλειαν, αὐτῆς δὲ ταύτης
42 μηδὲν τυγχάνουσι φροντίζοντες. ἔπειτα καὶ περὶ
τῶν πραγμάτων τὴν αὐτὴν διάνοιαν εἶχεν· ὁρῶν
γὰρ τοὺς ἄριστα τῶν ὄντων ἐπιμελουμένους ἐλά-
χιστα λυπουμένους, καὶ τὰς ἀληθινὰς τῶν ῥαθυμιῶν
οὐκ ἐν ταῖς ἀργίαις ἀλλ' ἐν ταῖς εὐπραγίαις καὶ
καρτερίαις ἐνούσας, οὐδὲν ἀνεξέταστον παρέλειπεν,
ἀλλ' οὕτως ἀκριβῶς καὶ τὰς πράξεις ᾔδει καὶ τῶν
πολιτῶν ἕκαστον ἐγίγνωσκεν ὥστε μήτε τοὺς ἐπιβουλεύοντας αὐτῷ φθάνειν μήτε τοὺς ἐπιεικεῖς
ὄντας λανθάνειν, ἀλλὰ πάντας τυγχάνειν τῶν
προσηκόντων· οὐ γὰρ ἐξ ὧν ἑτέρων ἤκουεν οὔτ'
ἐκόλαζεν οὔτ' ἐτίμα τοὺς πολίτας, ἀλλ' ἐξ ὧν
αὐτὸς συνῄδει τὰς κρίσεις ἐποιεῖτο περὶ αὐτῶν.

43   Ἐν τοιαύταις δ' ἐπιμελείαις αὑτὸν καταστήσας
οὐδὲ περὶ τῶν κατὰ τὴν ἡμέραν ἑκάστην προσπι-
πτόντων οὐδὲ περὶ ἓν πεπλανημένως εἶχεν, ἀλλ'
οὕτω θεοφιλῶς καὶ φιλανθρώπως διῴκει τὴν πόλιν
ὥστε τοὺς εἰσαφικνουμένους μὴ μᾶλλον Εὐαγόραν
τῆς ἀρχῆς ζηλοῦν ἢ τοὺς ἄλλους τῆς ὑπ' ἐκείνου
βασιλείας· ἅπαντα γὰρ τὸν χρόνον διετέλεσεν οὐδένα μὲν ἀδικῶν, τοὺς δὲ χρηστοὺς τιμῶν, καὶ
σφόδρα μὲν ἁπάντων ἄρχων, νομίμως δὲ τοὺς

---

¹ καλῶς Γ : ὁμοίως Blass.

gifted by nature with the highest intelligence and capable of successful action in very many fields, yet he judged that he should not slight any matter or act on the spur of the moment in public affairs; nay, he spent most of his time in inquiring, in deliberation, and in taking counsel, for he believed that if he should prepare his mind well, all would be well with his kingdom also [a]; and he marvelled at those who, while they cultivate the mind for all other ends, take no thought of the mind itself. Again, in public affairs he held to the same opinion; for, seeing that those persons who look best after realities are least worried, and that the true freedom from anxiety is to be found, not in inactivity, but in success and patient endurance, he left nothing unexamined; on the contrary, so thoroughly was he cognizant of public affairs and so thorough was his knowledge of each of the citizens, that neither those who conspired against him took him unawares, nor did the good citizens remain unknown to him, but all got their deserts: for he neither punished nor honoured them on the basis of what he heard from others, but from his own knowledge he judged them.

When he had engaged himself in the care of such matters he made not a single mistake in dealing with the unexpected incidents which daily befell, but he governed the city so reverently and humanely that visitors to the island [b] did not so much envy Evagoras his office as they did the citizens their government under him; for throughout his whole life he never acted unjustly toward anyone but ever honoured the good; and while he ruled all his subjects with strictness, yet he punished wrongdoers in accordance with

---

[a] *Cf. To Nicocles* 10.　　　　[b] *Cf.* § 51.

44 ἐξαμαρτόντας κολάζων· οὐδὲν μὲν συμβούλων δεόμενος, ὅμως δὲ τοῖς φίλοις συμβουλευόμενος· πολλὰ
μὲν τῶν χρωμένων ἡττώμενος, ἅπαντα δὲ τῶν
ἐχθρῶν περιγιγνόμενος· σεμνὸς ὢν οὐ ταῖς τοῦ
προσώπου συναγωγαῖς ἀλλὰ ταῖς τοῦ βίου κατα-
σκευαῖς· οὐδὲ πρὸς ἓν ἀτάκτως οὐδ' ἀνωμάλως
διακείμενος, ἀλλ' ὁμοίως τὰς ἐν τοῖς ἔργοις ὁμολο-
45 γίας ὥσπερ τὰς ἐν τοῖς λόγοις διαφυλάττων· μέγα
φρονῶν οὐκ ἐπὶ τοῖς διὰ τύχην ἀλλ' ἐπὶ τοῖς δι'
αὑτὸν γιγνομένοις· τοὺς μὲν φίλους ταῖς εὐεργεσίαις
[198] ὑφ' αὑτῷ ποιούμενος, τοὺς δ' ἄλλους τῇ μεγαλο-
ψυχίᾳ καταδουλούμενος· φοβερὸς ὢν οὐ τῷ πολλοῖς
χαλεπαίνειν, ἀλλὰ τῷ πολὺ τὴν τῶν ἄλλων φύσιν
ὑπερβάλλειν· ἡγούμενος τῶν ἡδονῶν, ἀλλ' οὐκ ἀγό-
μενος ὑπ' αὐτῶν· ὀλίγοις πόνοις πολλὰς ῥᾳστώνας
κτώμενος, ἀλλ' οὐ διὰ μικρὰς ῥᾳθυμίας μεγάλους
46 πόνους ὑπολειπόμενος· ὅλως οὐδὲν παραλείπων
ὧν προσεῖναι δεῖ τοῖς βασιλεῦσιν, ἀλλ' ἐξ ἑκά-
στης τῆς πολιτείας ἐξειλεγμένος τὸ βέλτιστον,
καὶ δημοτικὸς μὲν ὢν τῇ τοῦ πλήθους θεραπείᾳ,
πολιτικὸς δὲ τῇ τῆς πόλεως ὅλης διοικήσει, στρατ-
ηγικὸς δὲ τῇ πρὸς τοὺς κινδύνους εὐβουλίᾳ, τυραννικὸς[1] δὲ τῷ πᾶσι τούτοις διαφέρειν. καὶ ταῦθ'
ὅτι προσῆν Εὐαγόρᾳ, καὶ πλείω τούτων, ἐξ αὐτῶν
τῶν ἔργων ῥᾴδιον καταμαθεῖν.

47 Παραλαβὼν γὰρ τὴν πόλιν ἐκβαρβαρωμένην καὶ
διὰ τὴν Φοινίκων ἀρχὴν οὔτε τοὺς Ἕλληνας προσ-
δεχομένην οὔτε τέχνας ἐπισταμένην οὔτ' ἐμπορίῳ
χρωμένην οὔτε λιμένα κεκτημένην ταῦτά τε πάντα

---

[1] τυραννικὸς ΘΛ : μεγαλόφρων ΓΔ.

the laws; and while he was in no need of advisers, yet he sought the counsel of his friends. He yielded often to his intimates, but in everything dominated his enemies; he inspired respect, not by the frownings of his brow, but by the principles of his life—in no thing was he disposed to carelessness or caprice, but observed his agreements in deed as well as word; he was proud, not of successes that were due to Fortune, but of those that came about through his own efforts; his friends he made subject to himself by his benefactions, the rest by his magnanimity he enslaved; he inspired fear, not by venting his wrath upon many, but because in character he far surpassed all others; of his pleasures he was the master and not their servant; by little labour he gained much leisure, but would not, to gain a little respite, leave great labours undone; in general, he fell in no respect short of the qualities which belong to kings, but choosing from each kind of government the best characteristic, he was democratic in his service to the people, statesmanlike in the administration of the city as a whole, an able general in his good counsel in the face of dangers, and princely in his superiority in all these qualities. That these attributes were inherent in Evagoras, and even more than these, it is easy to learn from his deeds themselves.[a]

After he had taken over the government of the city, which had been reduced to a state of barbarism and, because it was ruled by Phoenicians, was neither hospitable to the Greeks nor acquainted with the arts, nor possessed of a trading-port or harbour,

---

[a] In §§ 43-46 the strong influence of Gorgias is obvious in the long series of artificial antitheses and in the varied assonance.

διώρθωσε καὶ πρὸς τούτοις καὶ χώραν πολλὴν
προσεκτήσατο καὶ τείχη προσπεριεβάλετο καὶ
τριήρεις ἐναυπηγήσατο καὶ ταῖς ἄλλαις κατασκευαῖς οὕτως ηὔξησε τὴν πόλιν ὥστε μηδεμιᾶς τῶν
Ἑλληνίδων ἀπολελεῖφθαι, καὶ δύναμιν τοσαύτην
ἐνεποίησεν ὥστε πολλοὺς φοβεῖσθαι τῶν πρότερον
48 καταφρονούντων αὐτῆς.   καίτοι τηλικαύτας ἐπιδόσεις τὰς πόλεις λαμβάνειν οὐχ οἷόν τ᾽ ἐστίν, ἢν
μή τις αὐτὰς διοικῇ τοιούτοις ἤθεσιν οἵοις Εὐαγόρας μὲν εἶχεν ἐγὼ δ᾽ ὀλίγῳ πρότερον ἐπειράθην
διελθεῖν.   ὥστ᾽ οὐ δέδοικα μὴ φανῶ μείζω λέγων
τῶν ἐκείνῳ προσόντων, ἀλλὰ μὴ πολὺ λίαν ἀπο-
49 λειφθῶ τῶν πεπραγμένων αὐτῷ. τίς γὰρ ἂν ἐφ-
ίκοιτο τοιαύτης φύσεως, ὃς οὐ μόνον τὴν αὐτοῦ
πόλιν πλείονος ἀξίαν ἐποίησεν ἀλλὰ καὶ τὸν τόπον
ὅλον τὸν περιέχοντα τὴν νῆσον ἐπὶ πραότητα καὶ
μετριότητα προήγαγεν; πρὶν μέν γε λαβεῖν Εὐαγόραν τὴν ἀρχὴν οὕτως ἀπροσοίστως καὶ χαλεπῶς
εἶχον, ὥστε καὶ τῶν ἀρχόντων τούτους ἐνόμιζον
[199] εἶναι βελτίστους οἵτινες ὠμότατα πρὸς τοὺς Ἕλ-
50 ληνας διακείμενοι τυγχάνοιεν· νῦν δὲ τοσοῦτον
μεταπεπτώκασιν ὥσθ᾽ ἁμιλλᾶσθαι μὲν οἵτινες
αὐτῶν δόξουσι φιλέλληνες εἶναι μάλιστα, παιδο-
ποιεῖσθαι δὲ τοὺς πλείστους αὐτῶν γυναῖκας λαμ-
βάνοντας παρ᾽ ἡμῶν, χαίρειν δὲ καὶ τοῖς κτήμασι
καὶ τοῖς ἐπιτηδεύμασι τοῖς Ἑλληνικοῖς μᾶλλον ἢ
τοῖς παρὰ σφίσιν αὐτοῖς, πλείους δὲ καὶ τῶν περὶ
τὴν μουσικὴν καὶ τῶν περὶ τὴν ἄλλην παίδευσιν ἐν
τούτοις τοῖς τόποις διατρίβειν ἢ παρ᾽ οἷς πρότερον
εἰωθότες ἦσαν.   καὶ τούτων ἁπάντων οὐδεὶς ὅστις
οὐκ ἂν Εὐαγόραν αἴτιον εἶναι προσομολογήσειεν.

Evagoras remedied all these defects and, besides, acquired much additional territory, surrounded it all with new walls and built triremes, and with other construction so increased the city that it was inferior to none of the cities of Greece. And he caused it to become so powerful that many who formerly despised it, now feared it.[a] And yet it is not possible that cities should take on such increase unless there are those who govern them by such principles as Evagoras had and as I endeavoured to describe a little before. In consequence I am not afraid of appearing to exaggerate in speaking of the qualities of the man, but rather lest I greatly fall short of doing justice to his deeds. For who could do justice to a man of such natural gifts, a man who not only increased the importance of his own city, but advanced the whole region surrounding the island to a régime of mildness and moderation ? Before Evagoras gained the throne the inhabitants were so hostile to strangers and fierce that they considered the best rulers to be those who treated the Greeks in the most cruel fashion. At present, however, they have undergone so great a change that they strive with one another to see who shall be regarded as most friendly to the Greeks, and the majority of them take their wives from us and from them beget children, and they have greater pleasure in owning Greek possessions and observing Greek institutions than in their own, and more of those who occupy themselves with the liberal arts and with education in general now dwell in these regions than in the communities in which they formerly used to live. And for all these changes, no one could deny that Evagoras is responsible.

[a] See *Panegyr.* 141 for the fleet and army of Evagoras.

51 Μέγιστον δὲ τεκμήριον καὶ τοῦ τρόπου καὶ τῆς ὁσιότητος τῆς ἐκείνου· τῶν γὰρ Ἑλλήνων πολλοὶ καὶ καλοὶ κἀγαθοὶ τὰς αὑτῶν πατρίδας ἀπολιπόντες ἦλθον εἰς Κύπρον οἰκήσοντες, ἡγούμενοι κουφοτέραν καὶ νομιμωτέραν εἶναι τὴν Εὐαγόρου βασιλείαν τῶν οἴκοι πολιτειῶν· ὧν τοὺς μὲν ἄλλους 52 ὀνομαστὶ διελθεῖν πολὺ ἂν ἔργον εἴη· Κόνωνα δὲ τὸν διὰ πλείστας ἀρετὰς πρωτεύσαντα τῶν Ἑλλήνων τίς οὐκ οἶδεν ὅτι δυστυχησάσης τῆς πόλεως[1] ἐξ ἁπάντων ἐκλεξάμενος ὡς Εὐαγόραν ἦλθε, νομίσας καὶ τῷ σώματι βεβαιοτάτην εἶναι τὴν παρ' ἐκείνῳ καταφυγὴν καὶ τῇ πόλει τάχιστ' ἂν αὐτὸν γενέσθαι βοηθόν. καὶ πολλὰ πρότερον ἤδη κατωρθωκὼς οὐδὲ περὶ ἑνὸς πώποτε πράγματος ἔδοξεν 53 ἄμεινον ἢ περὶ τούτου βουλεύσασθαι· συνέβη γὰρ αὐτῷ διὰ τὴν ἄφιξιν τὴν εἰς Κύπρον καὶ ποιῆσαι καὶ παθεῖν πλεῖστ' ἀγαθά. πρῶτον μὲν γὰρ οὐκ ἔφθασαν ἀλλήλοις πλησιάσαντες καὶ περὶ πλείονος ἐποιήσαντο σφᾶς αὐτοὺς ἢ τοὺς πρότερον οἰκείους ὄντας. ἔπειτα περί τε τῶν ἄλλων ὁμονοοῦντες ἅπαντα τὸν χρόνον διετέλεσαν καὶ περὶ τῆς ἡμε-54 τέρας πόλεως τὴν αὐτὴν γνώμην εἶχον. ὁρῶντες γὰρ αὐτὴν ὑπὸ Λακεδαιμονίοις οὖσαν καὶ μεγάλῃ μεταβολῇ κεχρημένην λυπηρῶς καὶ βαρέως ἔφερον, ἀμφότεροι προσήκοντα ποιοῦντες· τῷ μὲν γὰρ ἦν

---

[1] δυστυχησάσης τῆς πόλεως Γ²ΘΛ : δυστυχήσας, omitting τῆς πόλεως, Γ¹, Arist. *Rhet.* 1399 a 5, Blass.

---

* *e.g.*, Andocides, the Athenian orator, who had an estate

The most convincing proof of the character and uprightness of Evagoras is this—that many of the most reputable Greeks left their own fatherlands and came to Cyprus to dwell, because they considered Evagoras's rule less burdensome and more equitable than that of their own governments at home.[a] To mention all the others by name would be too great a task : but who does not know about Conon, first among the Greeks for his very many glorious deeds, that when his own city had met with ill-fortune,[b] he chose out of all the world Evagoras and came to him, believing that for himself Evagoras would provide the most secure asylum and for his country the most speedy assistance. And indeed Conon, although he had been successful in many previous ventures, in no one of them, it is believed, had he planned more wisely than in this ; for the result of his visit to Cyprus was that he both conferred and received most benefits. In the first place, no sooner had Evagoras and Conon met one another than they esteemed each other more highly than those who before had been their intimate friends. Again, they not only were in complete harmony all their lives regarding all other matters, but also in matters relating to our own city they held to the same opinion. For when they beheld Athens under the domination of the Lacedaemonians and the victim of a great reversal of fortune, they were filled with grief and indignation, both acting fittingly ; for Conon was a native

in Cyprus (*cf.* Andoc. *On the Mysteries* 4), and other Greeks who were forced into exile.

[b] The Athenian fleet under Conon was defeated by the Spartans at Aegospotami in 405 B.C. After this " ill-fortune " Conon, with eight triremes, took refuge with Evagoras, where he remained until 397 B.C.

φύσει πατρίς, τὸν δὲ διὰ πολλὰς καὶ μεγάλας
εὐεργεσίας νόμῳ πολίτην ἐπεποίηντο. σκοπου-
μένοις δ' αὐτοῖς ὅπως τῶν συμφορῶν αὐτὴ
200] ἀπαλλάξουσι, ταχὺν τὸν καιρὸν Λακεδαιμόνιο
παρεσκεύασαν· ἄρχοντες γὰρ τῶν Ἑλλήνων καὶ
κατὰ γῆν καὶ κατὰ θάλατταν εἰς τοῦτ' ἀπληστίας
ἦλθον, ὥστε καὶ τὴν Ἀσίαν κακῶς ποιεῖν ἐπεχεί-
55 ρησαν. λαβόντες δ' ἐκεῖνοι τοῦτον τὸν καιρὸν
καὶ τῶν στρατηγῶν τῶν βασιλέως ἀπορούντων ὅ τι
χρήσωνται τοῖς πράγμασιν, ἐδίδασκον αὐτοὺς μὴ
κατὰ γῆν ἀλλὰ κατὰ θάλατταν ποιεῖσθαι τὸν πόλεμον τὸν πρὸς Λακεδαιμονίους, νομίζοντες, εἰ
μὲν πεζὸν στρατόπεδον καταστήσαιντο καὶ τούτῳ
περιγένοιντο, τὰ περὶ τὴν ἤπειρον μόνον καλῶς
ἕξειν, εἰ δὲ κατὰ θάλατταν κρατήσειαν, ἅπασαν
56 τὴν Ἑλλάδα τῆς νίκης ταύτης μεθέξειν. ὅπερ
συνέβη· πεισθέντων γὰρ ταῦτα τῶν στρατηγῶν καὶ
ναυτικοῦ συλλεγέντος Λακεδαιμόνιοι μὲν κατεναυ-
μαχήθησαν καὶ τῆς ἀρχῆς ἀπεστερήθησαν, οἱ δ'
Ἕλληνες ἠλευθερώθησαν, ἡ δὲ πόλις ἡμῶν τῆς τε
παλαιᾶς δόξης μέρος τι πάλιν ἀνέλαβε καὶ τῶ
συμμάχων ἡγεμὼν κατέστη. καὶ ταῦτ' ἐπράχθη
Κόνωνος μὲν στρατηγοῦντος, Εὐαγόρου δὲ τοῦτό
τε παρασχόντος καὶ τῆς δυνάμεως τὴν πλείστην
57 παρασκευάσαντος. ὑπὲρ ὧν ἡμεῖς μὲν αὐτοὺς
ἐτιμήσαμεν ταῖς μεγίσταις τιμαῖς καὶ τὰς εἰκόνας
αὐτῶν ἐστήσαμεν οὗπερ τὸ τοῦ Διὸς ἄγαλμα τοῦ
σωτῆρος, πλησίον ἐκείνου τε καὶ σφῶν αὐτῶν,
ἀμφοτέρων ὑπόμνημα καὶ τοῦ μεγέθους τῆς εὐεργεσίας καὶ τῆς φιλίας τῆς πρὸς ἀλλήλους.

---

[a] This is attested by Demosthenes, *Philip's Letter* 10.
[b] Agesilaus, king of Sparta, was leader.

son of Athens, and Evagoras, because of his many generous benefactions, had legally been given citizenship by the Athenians.[a] And while they were deliberating how they might free Athens from her misfortunes, the Lacedaemonians themselves soon furnished the opportunity; for, as rulers of the Greeks on land and sea, they became so insatiate that they attempted to ravage Asia[b] also. Conon and Evagoras seized this opportunity, and, as the generals of the Persian king were at a loss to know how to handle the situation, these two advised them to wage war against the Lacedaemonians, not upon land but upon the sea, their opinion being that if the Persians should organize an army on land and with this should gain a victory, the mainland alone would profit, whereas, if they should be victors on the sea, all Hellas would have a share in the victory. And that in fact is what happened: the generals followed this advice, a fleet was assembled, the Lacedaemonians were defeated in a naval battle[c] and lost their supremacy, while the Greeks regained their freedom and our city recovered in some measure its old-time glory and became leader of the allies. And although all this was accomplished with Conon as commander, yet Evagoras both made the outcome possible and furnished the greater part of the armament. In gratitude we honoured them with the highest honours and set up their statues[d] where stands the image of Zeus the Saviour, near to it and to one another, a memorial both of the magnitude of their benefactions and of their mutual friendship.

[c] Off Cnidus, 394 B.C.
[d] In front of the Zeus Stoa in the Agora; *cf.* Pausanias i. 3. 2.

Βασιλεὺς δ' οὐ τὴν αὐτὴν γνώμην ἔσχε περὶ
αὐτῶν, ἀλλ' ὅσῳ μείζω καὶ πλείονος ἄξια κατειρ-
γάσαντο, τοσούτῳ μᾶλλον ἔδεισεν αὐτούς. περὶ
μὲν οὖν Κόνωνος ἄλλος ἡμῖν ἔσται λόγος· ὅτι δὲ
πρὸς Εὐαγόραν οὕτως ἔσχεν, οὐδ' αὐτὸς λαθεῖν
58 ἐζήτησεν. φαίνεται γὰρ μᾶλλον μὲν σπουδάσας
περὶ τὸν ἐν Κύπρῳ πόλεμον ἢ περὶ τοὺς ἄλλους
ἅπαντας, μείζω δὲ καὶ χαλεπώτερον ἐκεῖνον ἀντ-
αγωνιστὴν νομίσας ἢ Κῦρον τὸν περὶ τῆς βασιλείας ἀμφισβητήσαντα. μέγιστον δὲ τεκμήριον·
τοῦ μὲν γὰρ ἀκούων τὰς παρασκευὰς τοσοῦτον
κατεφρόνησεν ὥστε διὰ τὸ μὴ φροντίζειν μικροῦ
δεῖν ἔλαθεν αὐτὸν ἐπὶ τὸ βασίλειον ἐπιστάς· πρὸς
δὲ τοῦτον οὕτως ἐκ πολλοῦ περιδεῶς ἔσχεν, ὥστε
μεταξὺ πάσχων εὖ πολεμεῖν πρὸς αὐτὸν ἐπεχείρησε,
[201] δίκαια μὲν οὐ ποιῶν, οὐ μὴν παντάπασιν ἀλόγως
59 βουλευσάμενος. ἠπίστατο μὲν γὰρ πολλοὺς καὶ
τῶν Ἑλλήνων καὶ τῶν βαρβάρων ἐκ ταπεινῶν καὶ
φαύλων πραγμάτων μεγάλας δυναστείας κατεργασα-
μένους, ᾐσθάνετο δὲ τὴν Εὐαγόρου μεγαλοψυχίαν
καὶ τὰς ἐπιδόσεις αὐτῷ καὶ τῆς δόξης καὶ τῶν
πραγμάτων οὐ κατὰ μικρὸν γιγνομένας, ἀλλὰ καὶ
τὴν φύσιν ἀνυπέρβλητον ἔχοντα καὶ τὴν τύχην
60 αὐτῷ συναγωνιζομένην· ὥστ' οὐχ ὑπὲρ τῶν γεγενημένων ὀργιζόμενος ἀλλὰ περὶ τῶν μελλόντων
φοβούμενος, οὐδὲ περὶ Κύπρου μόνον δεδιώς, ἀλλὰ

---

[a] Isocrates gives a brief discussion of Conon's affairs in
To Philip 62-64.

[b] Cf. Xenophon, *Anab.* i. for the famous expedition of
Cyrus the Younger against his brother Artaxerxes II. See
Panegyr. 145.

The king of Persia, however, did not have the same opinion of them ; on the contrary, the greater and more illustrious their deeds the more he feared them. Concerning Conon I will give an account elsewhere [a] ; but that toward Evagoras he entertained this feeling not even the king himself sought to conceal. For he was manifestly more concerned about the war in Cyprus than about any other, and regarded Evagoras as a more powerful and formidable antagonist than Cyrus, who had disputed the throne with him.[b] The most convincing proof of this statement is this : when the king heard of the preparations Cyrus was making he viewed him with such contempt that because of his indifference Cyrus almost stood at the doors of his palace before he was aware of him.[c] With regard to Evagoras, however, the king had stood in terror of him for so long a time that even while he was receiving benefits from him he had undertaken to make war upon him—a wrongful act, indeed, but his purpose was not altogether unreasonable. For the king well knew that many men, both Greeks and barbarians, starting from low and insignificant beginnings, had overthrown great dynasties, and he was aware too of the lofty ambition of Evagoras and that the growth of both his prestige and of his political activities was not taking place by slow degrees ; also that Evagoras had unsurpassed natural ability and that Fortune was fighting with him as an ally. Therefore it was not in anger for the events of the past, but with forebodings for the future, nor yet fearing for Cyprus alone, but for

[c] The battle of Cunaxa (401 B.C.) in which Cyrus was slain. The distance from Babylon, according to Xenophon, was 360 stades (c. 45 miles).

πολὺ περὶ μειζόνων ἐποιήσατο τὸν πόλεμον πρὸς
αὐτόν. οὕτω δ' οὖν ὥρμησεν ὥστ' εἰς τὴν στρατείαν ταύτην πλέον ἢ τάλαντα πεντακισχίλια καὶ
μύρια κατηνάλωσεν.

61 Ἀλλ' ὅμως Εὐαγόρας πάσαις ἀπολελειμμένος
ταῖς δυνάμεσιν, ἀντιτάξας τὴν αὑτοῦ γνώμην πρὸς
τὰς οὕτως ὑπερμεγέθεις παρασκευάς, ἐπέδειξεν
αὑτὸν ἐν τούτοις πολὺ θαυμαστότερον ἢ τοῖς ἄλλοις τοῖς προειρημένοις. ὅτε μὲν γὰρ αὐτὸν εἴων
62 εἰρήνην ἄγειν, τὴν αὑτοῦ πόλιν μόνην εἶχεν· ἐπειδὴ
δ' ἠναγκάσθη πολεμεῖν, τοιοῦτος ἦν καὶ τοιοῦτον
εἶχε Πνυταγόραν τὸν υἱὸν τὸν αὑτοῦ συναγωνι-
στὴν ὥστε μικροῦ μὲν ἐδέησε Κύπρον ἅπασαν
κατασχεῖν, Φοινίκην δ' ἐπόρθησε, Τύρον δὲ κατὰ
κράτος εἷλε, Κιλικίαν δὲ βασιλέως ἀπέστησε,
τοσούτους δὲ τῶν πολεμίων ἀπώλεσεν ὥστε πολλοὺς Περσῶν πενθοῦντας τὰς αὑτῶν συμφορὰς
63 μεμνῆσθαι τῆς ἀρετῆς τῆς ἐκείνου· τελευτῶν δ'
οὕτως ἐνέπλησεν αὐτοὺς τοῦ πολεμεῖν, ὥστ' εἰθισμένων τὸν ἄλλον χρόνον τῶν βασιλέων μὴ διαλλάτ-
τεσθαι τοῖς ἀποστᾶσι πρὶν κύριοι γένοιντο τῶν
σωμάτων, ἄσμενοι τὴν εἰρήνην ἐποιήσαντο, λύ-
σαντες μὲν τὸν νόμον τοῦτον, οὐδὲν δὲ κινήσαντες
64 τῆς Εὐαγόρου τυραννίδος. καὶ Λακεδαιμονίων μὲν
τῶν καὶ δόξαν καὶ δύναμιν μεγίστην ἐχόντων κατ'
ἐκεῖνον τὸν χρόνον ἐντὸς τριῶν ἐτῶν ἀφείλετο τὴν
ἀρχήν, Εὐαγόρᾳ δὲ πολεμήσας ἔτη δέκα τῶν αὐτῶν
κύριον αὐτὸν κατέλιπεν, ὧνπερ ἦν καὶ πρὶν εἰς
τὸν πόλεμον εἰσελθεῖν. ὃ δὲ πάντων δεινότατον·

---

[a] A talent of gold was worth about $1200 or £300.
[b] Cf. Isocrates, Panegyr. 161.
[c] A Homeric reminiscence.

reasons far weightier, that he undertook the war against Evagoras. In any case he threw himself into it with such ardour that he expended on this expedition more than fifteen thousand talents.[a]

But nevertheless, although Evagoras was inferior in all the resources of war, after he had marshalled in opposition to these extraordinarily immense preparations of the king his own determination, he proved himself in these circumstances to be far more worthy of admiration than in all those I have mentioned before. For when his enemies permitted him to be at peace, all he possessed was his own city ; but when he was forced to go to war, he proved so valiant, and had so valiant an ally in his son Pnytagoras, that he almost subdued the whole of Cyprus, ravaged Phoenicia, took Tyre by storm, caused Cilicia to revolt from the king, and slew so many of his enemies that many of the Persians, when they mourn over their sorrows, recall the valour of Evagoras.[b] And finally he so glutted them with war [c] that the Persian kings, who at other times were not accustomed to make peace with their rebellious subjects until they had become masters of their persons, gladly made peace,[d] abandoning this custom and leaving entirely undisturbed the authority of Evagoras. And although the king within three years [e] destroyed the dominion of the Lacedaemonians,[f] who were then at the height of their glory and power, yet after he had waged war against Evagoras for ten years,[g] he left him lord of all that he had possessed before he entered upon the war. But the most amazing

[a] For the actual facts see Diodorus xv. 9.

[e] 397-394 B.C.

[f] An exaggeration ; it was the Spartan sea-power only that was destroyed.   [g] 390-380 (?) B.C.

[202] τὴν γὰρ πόλιν, ἣν Εὐαγόρας ἑτέρου τυραννοῦντος μετὰ πεντήκοντ' ἀνδρῶν εἷλε, ταύτην βασιλεὺς ὁ μέγας τοσαύτην δύναμιν ἔχων οὐχ οἷός τ' ἐγένετο χειρώσασθαι.

65 Καίτοι πῶς ἄν τις τὴν ἀνδρίαν ἢ τὴν φρόνησιν ἢ σύμπασαν τὴν ἀρετὴν τὴν Εὐαγόρου φανερώτερον ἐπιδείξειεν ἢ διὰ τοιούτων ἔργων καὶ κινδύνων; οὐ γὰρ μόνον φανεῖται τοὺς ἄλλους πολέμους, ἀλλὰ καὶ τὸν τῶν ἡρώων ὑπερβαλόμενος, τὸν ὑπὸ πάντων ἀνθρώπων ὑμνούμενον. οἱ μὲν γὰρ μεθ' ἁπάσης τῆς Ἑλλάδος Τροίαν μόνην εἷλον, ὁ δὲ μίαν πόλιν ἔχων πρὸς ἅπασαν τὴν Ἀσίαν ἐπολέμησεν· ὥστ' εἰ τοσοῦτοι τὸ πλῆθος ἐγκωμιάζειν αὐτὸν ἠβουλήθησαν ὅσοι περ ἐκείνους, πολὺ ἂν μείζω καὶ τὴν

66 δόξαν αὐτῶν ἔλαβεν. τίνα γὰρ εὑρήσομεν τῶν τότε γενομένων, εἰ τοὺς μύθους ἀφέντες τὴν ἀλήθειαν σκοποῖμεν, τοιαῦτα διαπεπραγμένον, ἢ τίνα τοσ-ούτων μεταβολῶν ἐν τοῖς πράγμασιν αἴτιον γε-γενημένον; ὃς αὐτὸν μὲν ἐξ ἰδιώτου τύραννον κατέστησε, τὸ δὲ γένος ἅπαν ἀπεληλαμένον τῆς πολιτείας εἰς τὰς προσηκούσας τιμὰς πάλιν ἐπαν-ήγαγε, τοὺς δὲ πολίτας ἐκ βαρβάρων μὲν Ἕλληνας

67 ἐποίησεν, ἐξ ἀνάνδρων δὲ πολεμικούς, ἐξ ἀδόξων δ' ὀνομαστούς, τὸν δὲ τόπον ἄμικτον ὅλον παρα-λαβὼν καὶ παντάπασιν ἐξηγριωμένον ἡμερώτερον καὶ πραότερον κατέστησεν, ἔτι δὲ πρὸς τούτοις εἰς ἔχθραν μὲν βασιλεῖ καταστὰς οὕτως αὐτὸν ἠμύνατο καλῶς ὥστ' ἀείμνηστον γεγενῆσθαι τὸν πόλεμον τὸν περὶ Κύπρον, ὅτε δ' ἦν αὐτῷ σύμμαχος, τοσ-ούτω χρησιμώτερον αὐτὸν παρέσχε τῶν ἄλλων

68 ὥσθ' ὁμολογουμένως μεγίστην αὐτῷ συμβαλέσθαι

<hr />

^a Cf. Panegyr. 83.

thing of all is this : the city which, held by another prince, Evagoras had captured with fifty men, the Great King, with all his vast power, was unable to subdue at all.

In truth, how could one reveal the courage, the wisdom, or the virtues generally of Evagoras more clearly than by pointing to such deeds and perilous enterprises ? For he will be shown to have surpassed in his exploits, not only those of other wars, but even those of the war of the heroes which is celebrated in the songs of all men. For they, in company with all Hellas, captured Troy only,[a] but Evagoras, although he possessed but one city, waged war against all Asia. Consequently, if the number of those who wished to praise him had equalled those who lauded the heroes at Troy, he would have gained far greater renown than they. For whom shall we find of the men of that age—if we disregard the fabulous tales and look at the truth—who has accomplished such feats or has brought about changes so great in political affairs ? Evagoras, from private estate, made himself a sovereign ; his entire family, which had been driven from political power, he restored again to their appropriate honours ; the citizens of barbarian birth he transformed into Hellenes, cravens into warriors, and obscure individuals into men of note ; and having taken over a country wholly inhospitable and utterly reduced to savagery, he made it more civilized and gentler ; furthermore, when he became hostile to the king, he defended himself so gloriously that the Cyprian War has become memorable for ever ; and when he was the ally of the king, he made himself so much more serviceable than the others that, in the opinion of all, the forces he contributed to the naval

δύναμιν εἰς τὴν ναυμαχίαν τὴν περὶ Κνίδον, ἧς
γενομένης βασιλεὺς μὲν ἁπάσης τῆς Ἀσίας κύριος
κατέστη, Λακεδαιμόνιοι δ᾽ ἀντὶ τοῦ τὴν ἤπειρον
πορθεῖν περὶ τῆς αὑτῶν κινδυνεύειν ἠναγκάσθησαν,
οἱ δ᾽ Ἕλληνες ἀντὶ δουλείας αὐτονομίας ἔτυχον,
Ἀθηναῖοι δὲ τοσοῦτον ἐπέδοσαν ὥστε τοὺς πρότερον αὐτῶν ἄρχοντας ἐλθεῖν αὐτοῖς τὴν ἀρχὴν
69 δώσοντας. ὥστ᾽ εἴ τις ἔροιτό με, τί νομίζω
[203] μέγιστον εἶναι τῶν Εὐαγόρᾳ πεπραγμένων, πότερον
τὰς ἐπιμελείας καὶ τὰς παρασκευὰς τὰς πρὸς
Λακεδαιμονίους ἐξ ὧν τὰ προειρημένα γέγονεν, ἢ
τὸν τελευταῖον πόλεμον, ἢ τὴν κατάληψιν τῆς
βασιλείας, ἢ τὴν ὅλην τῶν πραγμάτων διοίκησιν,
εἰς πολλὴν ἀπορίαν ἂν κατασταίην· ἀεὶ γάρ μοι
δοκεῖ μέγιστον εἶναι καὶ θαυμαστότατον καθ᾽ ὅ τι
ἂν αὐτῶν ἐπιστήσω τὴν διάνοιαν.

70 Ὥστ᾽ εἴ τινες τῶν προγεγενημένων δι᾽ ἀρετὴν
ἀθάνατοι γεγόνασιν, οἶμαι κἀκεῖνον ἠξιῶσθαι ταύτης τῆς δωρεᾶς, σημείοις χρώμενος ὅτι καὶ τὸν
ἐνθάδε χρόνον εὐτυχέστερον καὶ θεοφιλέστερον
ἐκείνων διαβεβίωκεν. τῶν μὲν γὰρ ἡμιθέων τοὺς
πλείστους καὶ τοὺς ὀνομαστοτάτους εὑρήσομεν ταῖς
μεγίσταις συμφοραῖς περιπεσόντας, Εὐαγόρας δ᾽
οὐ μόνον θαυμαστότατος ἀλλὰ καὶ μακαριστότατος
71 ἐξ ἀρχῆς ὢν διετέλεσεν. τί γὰρ ἀπέλιπεν εὐδαιμονίας, ὃς τοιούτων μὲν προγόνων ἔτυχεν οἵων
οὐδεὶς ἄλλος, πλὴν εἴ τις ἀπὸ τῶν αὐτῶν ἐκείνῳ
γέγονεν, τοσοῦτον δὲ καὶ τῷ σώματι καὶ τῇ γνώμῃ
τῶν ἄλλων διήνεγκεν ὥστε μὴ μόνον Σαλαμῖνος

battle at Cnidus were the largest, and as the result of this battle, while the king became master of all Asia, the Lacedaemonians instead of ravaging the continent were compelled to fight for their own land, and the Greeks, in place of servitude, gained independence, and the Athenians increased in power so greatly that those who formerly were their rulers [a] came to offer them the hegemony. Consequently, if anyone should ask me what I regard as the greatest of the achievements of Evagoras, whether the careful military preparations directed against the Lacedaemonians which resulted in the aforesaid successes, or the last war, or the recovery of his throne, or his general administration of affairs, I should be at a great loss what to say in reply; for each achievement to which I happen to direct my attention seems to me the greatest and most admirable.

Therefore, I believe that, if any men of the past have by their merit become immortal, Evagoras also has earned this preferment; and my evidence for that belief is this—that the life he lived on earth has been more blessed by fortune and more favoured by the gods than theirs. For of the demigods the greater number and the most renowned were, we shall find, afflicted by the most grievous misfortunes, but Evagoras continued from the beginning to be not only the most admired, but also the most envied for his blessings. For in what respect did he lack utter felicity? Such ancestors Fortune gave to him as to no other man, unless it has been one sprung from the same stock, and so greatly in body and mind did he excel others that he was worthy to hold sway over

---

[a] A reference to the Lacedaemonians before the battle of Cnidus; see *Areop.* 65.

ἀλλὰ καὶ τῆς Ἀσίας ἁπάσης ἄξιος εἶναι τυραννεῖν,
κάλλιστα δὲ κτησάμενος τὴν βασιλείαν ἐν ταύτῃ
τὸν βίον διετέλεσε, θνητὸς δὲ γενόμενος ἀθάνατον
τὴν περὶ αὐτοῦ μνήμην κατέλιπε, τοσοῦτον δ' ἐβίω
χρόνον ὥστε μήτε τοῦ γήρως ἄμοιρος γενέσθαι
μήτε τῶν νόσων μετασχεῖν τῶν διὰ ταύτην τὴν
72 ἡλικίαν γιγνομένων. πρὸς δὲ τούτοις, ὃ δοκεῖ
σπανιώτατον εἶναι καὶ χαλεπώτατον, εὐπαιδίας τυχεῖν ἅμα καὶ πολυπαιδίας, οὐδὲ τούτου διήμαρτεν,
ἀλλὰ καὶ τοῦτ' αὐτῷ συνέπεσεν. καὶ τὸ μέγιστον,
ὅτι τῶν ἐξ αὐτοῦ γεγονότων οὐδένα[1] κατέλιπεν
ἰδιωτικοῖς ὀνόμασι προσαγορευόμενον, ἀλλὰ τὸν
μὲν βασιλέα καλούμενον, τοὺς δ' ἄνακτας, τὰς δ'
ἀνάσσας. ὥστ' εἴ τινες τῶν ποιητῶν περί τινος
τῶν προγεγενημένων ὑπερβολαῖς κέχρηνται, λέγοντες ὡς ἦν θεὸς ἐν ἀνθρώποις ἢ δαίμων θνητός,
ἅπαντα τὰ τοιαῦτα περὶ τὴν ἐκείνου φύσιν ῥηθῆναι
μάλιστ' ἂν ἁρμόσειεν.

73 Τῶν μὲν οὖν εἰς Εὐαγόραν πολλὰ μὲν οἶμαι
[204] παραλιπεῖν· ὑστερίζω γὰρ τῆς ἀκμῆς τῆς ἐμαυτοῦ,
μεθ' ἧς ἀκριβέστερον καὶ φιλοπονώτερον ἐξειρ-
γασάμην ἂν τὸν ἔπαινον τοῦτον· οὐ μὴν ἀλλὰ καὶ
νῦν, ὅσον κατὰ τὴν ἐμὴν δύναμιν, οὐκ ἀνεγκω-
μίαστός ἐστιν. ἐγὼ δ', ὦ Νικόκλεις, ἡγοῦμαι
καλὰ μὲν εἶναι μνημεῖα καὶ τὰς τῶν σωμάτων
εἰκόνας, πολὺ μέντοι πλείονος ἀξίας τὰς τῶν πράξ-

---

[1] οὐδένα mss. : οὐδὲν Γ[1] and Blass.

[a] Evagoras seized the power not later than 411 B.C., when
the Athenian orator Andocides, in exile, found him reigning

not only Salamis but the whole of Asia also ; and having acquired most gloriously his kingdom he continued in its possession all his life ; and though a mortal by birth, he left behind a memory of himself that is immortal, and he lived just so long that he was neither unacquainted with old age, nor afflicted with the infirmities attendant upon that time of life.[a] In addition to these blessings, that which seems to be the rarest and most difficult thing to win—to be blessed with many children who are at the same time good—not even this was denied him, but this also fell to his lot.   And the greatest blessing was this : of his offspring he left not one who was addressed merely by a private title ; on the contrary, one was called king,[b] others princes, and others princesses.   In view of these facts, if any of the poets have used extravagant expressions in characterizing any man of the past, asserting that he was a god among men, or a mortal divinity, all praise of that kind would be especially in harmony with the noble qualities of Evagoras.

No doubt I have omitted much that might be said of Evagoras ; for I am past my prime of life,[c] in which I should have worked out this eulogy with greater finish and diligence.   Nevertheless, even at my age, to the best of my ability he has not been left without his encomium.   For my part, Nicocles, I think that while effigies of the body are fine memorials, yet likenesses of deeds and of the character are of far greater

He died in 374–373 B.C. Isocrates, in his depiction of the happy lot of the king, naturally must ignore the fact that Evagoras seems to have been assassinated !

  [b] A reference to Nicocles.

  [c] Isocrates was perhaps seventy years of age when he wrote the *Evagoras.*

εων καὶ τῆς διανοίας, ἃς ἐν τοῖς λόγοις ἄν τις
74 μόνον τοῖς τεχνικῶς ἔχουσι θεωρήσειεν. προκρίνω
δὲ ταύτας πρῶτον μὲν εἰδὼς τοὺς καλοὺς κἀγαθοὺς
τῶν ἀνδρῶν οὐχ οὕτως ἐπὶ τῷ κάλλει τοῦ σώματος
σεμνυνομένους ὡς ἐπὶ τοῖς ἔργοις καὶ τῇ γνώμῃ
φιλοτιμουμένους· ἔπειθ' ὅτι τοὺς μὲν τύπους ἀναγκαῖον παρὰ τούτοις εἶναι μόνοις, παρ' οἷς ἂν στα-
θῶσι, τοὺς δὲ λόγους ἐξενεχθῆναί θ' οἷόν τ' ἐστὶν
εἰς τὴν Ἑλλάδα καί, διαδοθέντας ἐν ταῖς τῶν εὖ
φρονούντων διατριβαῖς, ἀγαπᾶσθαι παρ' οἷς κρεῖττόν ἐστιν ἢ παρὰ τοῖς ἄλλοις ἅπασιν εὐδοκιμεῖν·
75 πρὸς δὲ τούτοις ὅτι τοῖς μὲν πεπλασμένοις καὶ τοῖς
γεγραμμένοις οὐδεὶς ἂν τὴν τοῦ σώματος φύσιν
ὁμοιώσειε, τοὺς δὲ τρόπους τοὺς ἀλλήλων καὶ τὰς
διανοίας τὰς ἐν τοῖς λεγομένοις ἐνούσας ῥᾴδιόν ἐστι
μιμεῖσθαι τοῖς μὴ ῥαθυμεῖν αἱρουμένοις, ἀλλὰ χρη-
76 στοῖς εἶναι βουλομένοις. ὧν ἕνεκα καὶ μᾶλλον
ἐπεχείρησα γράφειν τὸν λόγον τοῦτον, ἡγούμενος
καὶ σοὶ καὶ τοῖς σοῖς παισὶ καὶ τοῖς ἄλλοις τοῖς
ἀπ' Εὐαγόρου γεγονόσι πολὺ καλλίστην ἂν γενέσθαι
ταύτην παράκλησιν, εἴ τις ἀθροίσας τὰς ἀρετὰς
τὰς ἐκείνου καὶ τῷ λόγῳ κοσμήσας παραδοίη θεω-
77 ρεῖν ὑμῖν καὶ συνδιατρίβειν αὐταῖς. τοὺς μὲν γὰρ
ἄλλους προτρέπομεν ἐπὶ τὴν φιλοσοφίαν ἑτέρους
ἐπαινοῦντες, ἵνα ζηλοῦντες τοὺς εὐλογουμένους τῶν
αὐτῶν ἐκείνοις ἐπιτηδευμάτων ἐπιθυμῶσιν, ἐγὼ δὲ
σὲ καὶ τοὺς σοὺς οὐκ ἀλλοτρίοις παραδείγμασι
χρώμενος ἀλλ' οἰκείοις παρακαλῶ, καὶ συμβουλεύω
46

value,[a] and these are to be observed only in discourses composed according to the rules of art. These I prefer to statues because I know, in the first place, that honourable men pride themselves not so much on bodily beauty as they desire to be honoured for their deeds and their wisdom ; in the second place, because I know that images must of necessity remain solely among those in whose cities they were set up, whereas portrayals in words may be published throughout Hellas, and having been spread abroad in the gatherings of enlightened men, are welcomed among those whose approval is more to be desired than that of all others ; and finally, while no one can make the bodily nature resemble moulded statues and portraits in painting, yet for those who do not choose to be slothful, but desire to be good men, it is easy to imitate the character of their fellow-men and their thoughts and purposes—those, I mean, that are embodied in the spoken word. For these reasons especially I have undertaken to write this discourse because I believed that for you, for your children, and for all the other descendants of Evagoras, it would be by far the best incentive, if someone should assemble his achievements, give them verbal adornment, and submit them to you for your contemplation and study. For we exhort young men to the study of philosophy [b] by praising others in order that they, emulating those who are eulogized, may desire to adopt the same pursuits, but I appeal to you and yours, using as examples not aliens, but members of your own family, and I counsel you to devote your attention to this,

[a] Cf. To Nicocles 36.
[b] Cf. Vol. I, Introd. pp. xxvi and xxvii for the " philosophy " of Isocrates.

προσέχειν τὸν νοῦν, ὅπως καὶ λέγειν καὶ πράττειν
μηδενὸς ἧττον δυνήσει τῶν Ἑλλήνων.

78 Καὶ μὴ νόμιζέ με καταγιγνώσκειν, ὡς νῦν ἀμε-
λεῖς, ὅτι πολλάκις σοι διακελεύομαι περὶ τῶν αὐτῶν. οὐ γὰρ οὔτ' ἐμὲ λέληθας οὔτε τοὺς ἄλλους
[207] ὅτι καὶ πρῶτος καὶ μόνος τῶν ἐν τυραννίδι καὶ
πλούτῳ καὶ τρυφαῖς ὄντων φιλοσοφεῖν καὶ πονεῖν
ἐπικεχείρηκας, οὐδ' ὅτι πολλοὺς τῶν βασιλέων
ποιήσεις ζηλώσαντας τὴν σὴν παίδευσιν τούτων
τῶν διατριβῶν ἐπιθυμεῖν, ἀφεμένους ἐφ' οἷς νῦν
79 λίαν χαίρουσιν. ἀλλ' ὅμως ἐγὼ ταῦτ' εἰδὼς οὐδὲν
ἧττον καὶ ποιῶ καὶ ποιήσω ταὐτὸν ὅπερ ἐν τοῖς
γυμνικοῖς ἀγῶσιν οἱ θεαταί· καὶ γὰρ ἐκεῖνοι παρα-
κελεύονται τῶν δρομέων οὐ τοῖς ἀπολελειμμένοις
ἀλλὰ τοῖς περὶ τῆς νίκης ἁμιλλωμένοις.

80 Ἐμὸν μὲν οὖν ἔργον καὶ τῶν ἄλλων φίλων
τοιαῦτα καὶ λέγειν καὶ γράφειν ἐξ ὧν μέλλομέν σε
παροξύνειν ὀρέγεσθαι τούτων, ὧνπερ καὶ νῦν τυγχάνεις ἐπιθυμῶν· σοὶ δὲ προσήκει μηδὲν ἐλλείπειν
ἀλλ' ὥσπερ ἐν τῷ παρόντι καὶ τὸν λοιπὸν χρόνον
ἐπιμελεῖσθαι καὶ τὴν ψυχὴν ἀσκεῖν, ὅπως ἄξιος
ἔσει καὶ τοῦ πατρὸς καὶ τῶν ἄλλων προγόνων.
ὡς ἅπασι μὲν προσήκει περὶ πολλοῦ ποιεῖσθαι τὴν
φρόνησιν, μάλιστα δ' ὑμῖν τοῖς πλείστων καὶ με-
81 γίστων κυρίοις οὖσιν. χρὴ δ' οὐκ ἀγαπᾶν, εἰ τῶν
παρόντων τυγχάνεις ὢν ἤδη κρείττων, ἀλλ' ἀγανακ-
τεῖν, εἰ τοιοῦτος μὲν ὢν αὐτὸς τὴν φύσιν, γεγονὼς
δὲ τὸ μὲν παλαιὸν ἀπὸ Διός, τὸ δ' ὑπογυιότατον ἐξ
ἀνδρὸς τοιούτου τὴν ἀρετήν, μὴ πολὺ διοίσεις καὶ

ᵃ See Isocrates, Vol. I, p. 39, L.C.L., Introd. to the discourse To Nicocles.

that you may not be surpassed in either word or deed by any of the Hellenes.

And do not imagine that I am reproaching you for indifference at present, because I often admonish you on the same subject.[a] For it has not escaped the notice of either me or anyone else that you, Nicocles, are the first and the only one of those who possess royal power, wealth, and luxury who has undertaken to pursue the study of philosophy, nor that you will cause many kings, emulating your culture, to desire these studies and to abandon the pursuits in which they now take too great pleasure. Although I am aware of these things, none the less I am acting, and shall continue to act, in the same fashion as spectators at the athletic games; for they do not shout encouragement to the runners who have been distanced in the race, but to those who still strive for the victory.

It is my task, therefore, and that of your other friends, to speak and to write in such fashion as may be likely to incite you to strive eagerly after those things which even now you do in fact desire; and you it behooves not to be negligent, but as at present so in the future to pay heed to yourself and to discipline your mind that you may be worthy of your father and of all your ancestors. For though it is the duty of all to place a high value upon wisdom, yet you kings especially should do so, who have power over very many and weighty affairs. You must not be content if you chance to be already superior to your contemporaries, but you should be chagrined if, endowed as you are by nature, distantly descended from Zeus and in our own time from a man of such distinguished excellence, you shall not far surpass,

τῶν ἄλλων καὶ τῶν ἐν ταῖς αὐταῖς σοι τιμαῖς ὄντων. ἔστι δ' ἐπὶ σοὶ μὴ διαμαρτεῖν τούτων· ἂν
γὰρ ἐμμένῃς τῇ φιλοσοφίᾳ καὶ τοσοῦτον ἐπιδιδῷς
ὅσον περ νῦν, ταχέως γενήσει τοιοῦτος οἷόν σε
προσήκει.

not only all others, but also those who possess the
same high station as yourself. It is in your power
not to fail in this ; for if you persevere in the study of
philosophy and make as great progress as heretofore,
you will soon become the man it is fitting you
should be.

X. HELEN

INTRODUCTION

THE *Encomium on Helen* is an epideictic, or display, composition on a theme which subsequently became extremely popular in the schools of rhetoric. Although Helen of Sparta was a woman of divine beauty and a Homeric heroine of compelling charm, yet she was condemned and execrated by the poets as the cause of countless woes to the Greeks. Thus Aeschylus characterizes her in *Agamemnon* 689 as ἐλένας, ἐλάνδρος, ἐλέπτολις.[a]

A vindication of this glorious but shameless woman, whose misconduct in abandoning her husband Menelaüs to elope with Paris to Troy had caused the Trojan War, was a difficult undertaking and was a challenge to the powers of the most accomplished rhetorician. Gorgias of Sicily had attempted the task in his extant *Encomium on Helen*, a brilliant *tour de force*, but he confesses, at the end of his composition, that his composition was, after all, a παίγνιον, or " sportive essay."

In § 14 of his *Helen*, Isocrates praises an individual who has chosen Helen as his theme, but rebukes him for having composed, not a real encomium of his heroine, but a plea in defence of her conduct. This is undoubtedly a reference to the discourse of the Sicilian rhetorician Gorgias, who had been the teacher of Isocrates, since the criticism exactly applies to

---

[a] " Ship's hell, Man's hell, City's hell " (Browning's translation).

the extant discourse *Helen* attributed to Gorgias. Jebb, *Attic Orators* ii. p. 98, makes the strange assertion that this work does not "bear any distinctive marks of the style of Gorgias." On the contrary, in my opinion, it fairly bristles with them. For a discussion of this matter and an English translation by Van Hook of this extraordinary discourse by Gorgias see *The Classical Weekly*, Feb. 15, 1913. The translation of certain sections of the *Helen* of Gorgias, in which an effort has been made to reproduce in English the effect of the original Greek, is here reprinted, as it may be of interest to the reader :

The Encomium on Helen by Gorgias

Embellishment to a city is the valour of its citizens ; to a person, comeliness ; to a soul, wisdom ; to a deed, virtue ; to discourse, truth. But the opposite to these is lack of embellishment. Now a man, woman, discourse, work, city, deed, if deserving of praise, must be honoured with praise, but if undeserving must be censured. For it is alike aberration and stultification to censure the commendable and commend the censurable.

It is the duty of the same individual both to proclaim justice wholly, and to declaim against injustice holily, to confute the detractors of Helen, a woman concerning whom there has been uniform and universal praise of poets and the celebration of her name has been the commemoration of her fame. But I desire by rational calculation to free the lady's reputation, by disclosing her detractors as prevaricators, and, by revealing the truth, to put an end to error.

That in nature and nurture the lady was the fairest flower of men and women is not unknown, not even to the few, for her maternity was of Leda, her paternity immortal by generation, but mortal by reputation, Tyndareüs and Zeus, of whom the one was reputed in the being, the other was asserted in the affirming ; the former, the greatest of humanity, the latter, the lordliest of divinity. Of such origin, she was endowed with godlike beauty, expressed not suppressed, which inspired in many men many mad moods of love, and

she, one lovely person, assembled many personalities of proud ambition, of whom some possessed opulent riches, others the fair fame of ancient ancestry ; others the vigour of native strength, others the power of acquired wisdom ; and all came because of amorous contention and ambitious pretention.

Who he was, however, who won Helen and attained his heart's desire, and why, and how, I will not say, since to give information to the informed conduces to confirmation, but conveys no delectation. Passing over in my present discourse the time now past, I will proceed to the beginning of my intended discussion and will predicate the causes by reason of which it was natural that Helen went to Troy. For either by the disposition of fortune and the ratification of the gods and the determination of necessity she did what she did, or by violence confounded, or by persuasion dumbfounded, or to Love surrendered. If, however, it was against her will, the culpable should not be exculpated. For it is impossible to forestall divine disposals by human proposals. It is a law of nature that the stronger is not subordinated to the weaker, but the weaker is subjugated and dominated by the stronger ; the stronger is the leader, while the weaker is the entreater. Divinity surpasses humanity in might, in sight, and in all else. Therefore, if on fortune and the deity we must visit condemnation, the infamy of Helen should find no confirmation.

But if by violence she was defeated and unlawfully she was treated and to her injustice was meted, clearly her violator as a terrifier was importunate, while she, translated and violated, was unfortunate. Therefore, the barbarian who verbally, legally, actually attempted the barbarous attempt, should meet with verbal accusation, legal reprobation, and actual condemnation. For Helen, who was violated, and from her fatherland separated, and from her friends segregated, should justly meet with commiseration rather than with defamation. For he was the victor and she was the victim. It is just, therefore, to sympathize with the latter and anathematize the former.

But if it was through persuasion's reception and the soul's deception, it is not difficult to defend the situation and forfend the accusation, thus. Persuasion is a powerful potentate, who with frailest, feeblest frame works wonders. For it can

put an end to fear and make vexation vanish ; it can inspire exultation and increase compassion. I will show how this is so. For I must indicate this to my hearers for them to predicate. All poetry I ordain and proclaim to be composition in metre, the listeners of which are affected by passionate trepidation and compassionate perturbation and likewise tearful lamentation, since through discourse the soul suffers, as if its own, the felicity and infelicity of property and person of others.

Come, let us turn to another consideration. Inspired incantations are provocative of charm and revocative of harm. For the power of song in association with the belief of the soul captures and enraptures and translates the soul with witchery. For there have been discovered arts twain of witchery and sorcery, which are consternation to the heart and perturbation to art.

Now, it has been shown that, if Helen was won over by persuasion, she is deserving of commiseration, and not condemnation. The fourth accusation I shall now proceed to answer with a fourth refutation. For if love was the doer of all these deeds, with no difficulty will she be acquitted of the crime attributed to her. The nature of that which we see is not that which we wish it to be, but as it chances to be. For through the vision the soul is also in various ways smitten.

If, then, the eye of Helen, charmed by Alexander's beauty, gave to her soul excitement and amorous incitement, what wonder ? How could one who was weaker, repel and expel him who, being divine, had power divine ? If it was physical diversion and psychical perversion, we should not execrate it as reprehensible, but deprecate it as indefensible. For it came to whom it came by fortuitous insinuations, not by judicious resolutions ; by erotic compulsions, not by despotic machinations.

How, then, is it fair to blame Helen who, whether by love captivated, or by word persuaded, or by violence dominated, or by divine necessity subjugated, did what she did, and is completely absolved from blame ?

By this discourse I have freed a woman from evil reputation ; I have kept the promise which I made in the beginning ; I have essayed to dispose of the injustice of defamation and the folly of allegation ; I have prayed to compose a lucubration for Helen's adulation and my own delectation.

Isocrates asserts that he will show this writer how this theme ought to have been treated and that he intends to avoid topics previously discussed by others and in this treatise Isocrates makes good his promise to compose a real encomium. The topics, however, which he elaborates can hardly be called original with him.

The *Helen* purports to be a serious work and is composed with care. But it is a " show-piece," a rhetorical exercise, and follows the conventional pattern for an encomium of this nature. To students of rhetoric the *Helen* is of interest, but for the modern reader it, like its companion-piece, *Busiris*, must be put among the least important of the compositions of Isocrates.

The praise of Theseus, to which a lengthy discussion (*Helen* 18-38) is devoted is, as Norlin says (Isocrates, Vol. II, p. 418, L.C.L.), an effective element of variety, but because of its disproportionate length it is open to adverse criticism in an encomium of Helen. It is true that in any discourse written for Athenians the praise of their national hero would be pleasing and effective, and for Isocrates the theme was an inviting one. But the orator himself had his qualms. In *Helen* 29 he apologetically states : " I perceive that I am being carried beyond the proper limits of my theme, and I fear that some may think that I am more concerned with Theseus than with the subject which I originally chose." And in *Panathenaicus* 126 he regretfully says : " I would give much not to have spoken about the virtue and the achievements of Theseus on a former occasion, for it would have been more appropriate to discuss this topic in my discourse about our city."

HELEN

The date of the *Helen* of Isocrates is generally put about 370 B.C.[a]

[a] For a discussion of the discourse and of its date see Jebb, *Attic Orators* ii. pp. 96-103; Blass, *Die attische Beredsamkeit* ii. pp. 242 ff. Mathieu et Brémond, *Isocrate* i. p. 160, would give an earlier date to the composition.

10. ΕΛΕΝΗ

[208] Εἰσί τινες οἳ μέγα φρονοῦσιν, ἢν ὑπόθεσιν ἄτοπον καὶ παράδοξον ποιησάμενοι περὶ ταύτης ἀνεκτῶς εἰπεῖν δυνηθῶσι· καὶ καταγεγηράκασιν οἱ μὲν οὐ φάσκοντες οἷόν τ' εἶναι ψευδῆ λέγειν οὐδ' ἀντιλέγειν οὐδὲ δύο λόγω περὶ τῶν αὐτῶν πραγμάτων ἀντειπεῖν, οἱ δὲ διεξιόντες ὡς ἀνδρία καὶ σοφία καὶ δικαιοσύνη ταὐτόν ἐστι, καὶ φύσει μὲν οὐδὲν αὐτῶν ἔχομεν, μία δ' ἐπιστήμη καθ' ἁπάντων ἐστίν· ἄλλοι δὲ περὶ τὰς ἔριδας διατρίβουσι τὰς οὐδὲν μὲν ὠφελούσας, πράγματα δὲ παρέχειν τοῖς πλησιάζουσι δυναμένας.

2 Ἐγὼ δ' εἰ μὲν ἑώρων νεωστὶ τὴν περιεργίαν ταύτην ἐν τοῖς λόγοις ἐγγεγενημένην καὶ τούτους ἐπὶ τῇ καινότητι τῶν εὑρημένων φιλοτιμουμένους, οὐκ ἂν ὁμοίως ἐθαύμαζον αὐτῶν· νῦν δὲ τίς ἐστιν οὕτως ὀψιμαθής, ὅστις οὐκ οἶδε Πρωταγόραν καὶ τοὺς κατ' ἐκεῖνον τὸν χρόνον γενομένους σοφιστάς, ὅτι καὶ τοιαῦτα καὶ πολὺ τούτων πραγματωδέστερα

3 συγγράμματα κατέλιπον ἡμῖν; πῶς γὰρ ἄν τις ὑπερβάλοιτο Γοργίαν τὸν τολμήσαντα λέγειν ὡς

---

[a] So Antisthenes and the Cynics ; cf. Plato, Soph. 240 c.

60

X. HELEN

THERE are some who are much pleased with themselves if, after setting up an absurd and self-contradictory subject, they succeed in discussing it in tolerable fashion ; and men have grown old, some asserting that it is impossible to say, or to gainsay, what is false,ᵃ or to speak on both sides of the same questions, others maintaining that courage and wisdom and justice are identical,ᵇ and that we possess none of these as natural qualities, but that there is only one sort of knowledge concerned with them all ; and still others waste their time in captious disputations that are not only entirely useless, but are sure to make trouble for their disciples.

For my part, if I observed that this futile affectation had arisen only recently in rhetoric and that these men were priding themselves upon the novelty of their inventions, I should not be surprised at them to such degree ; but as it is, who is so backward in learning as not to know that Protagoras and the sophists of his time have left to us compositions of similar character and even far more overwrought than these ? For how could one surpass Gorgias,ᶜ who dared to assert that nothing exists of the things that

---

ᵇ A reference to the views of Plato and the Academy.

ᶜ Cf. Antid. 268. Gorgias of Leontini in Sicily, pupil of Teisias, came to Athens on an embassy in 427 B.C.

ISOCRATES

οὐδὲν τῶν ὄντων ἔστιν, ἢ Ζήνωνα τὸν ταὐτὰ δυνατὰ
καὶ πάλιν ἀδύνατα πειρώμενον ἀποφαίνειν, ἢ Μέ-
λισσον ὃς ἀπείρων τὸ πλῆθος πεφυκότων τῶν πραγμάτων ὡς ἑνὸς ὄντος τοῦ παντὸς ἐπεχείρησεν
4 ἀποδείξεις εὑρίσκειν; ἀλλ' ὅμως οὕτω φανερῶς
ἐκείνων ἐπιδειξάντων ὅτι ῥάδιόν ἐστι, περὶ ὧν ἄν
τις πρόθηται, ψευδῆ μηχανήσασθαι λόγον, ἔτι περὶ
[209] τὸν τόπον τοῦτον διατρίβουσιν· οὓς ἐχρῆν ἀφεμένους ταύτης τῆς τερθρείας, τῆς ἐν μὲν τοῖς λόγοις
ἐξελέγχειν προσποιουμένης, ἐν δὲ τοῖς ἔργοις πολὺν
ἤδη χρόνον ἐξεληλεγμένης, τὴν ἀλήθειαν διώκειν,
5 καὶ περὶ τὰς πράξεις ἐν αἷς πολιτευόμεθα, τοὺς
συνόντας παιδεύειν, καὶ περὶ τὴν ἐμπειρίαν τὴν
τούτων γυμνάζειν, ἐνθυμουμένους ὅτι πολὺ κρεῖττόν
ἐστι περὶ τῶν χρησίμων ἐπιεικῶς δοξάζειν ἢ περὶ
τῶν ἀχρήστων ἀκριβῶς ἐπίστασθαι, καὶ μικρὸν
προέχειν ἐν τοῖς μεγάλοις μᾶλλον ἢ πολὺ διαφέρειν
ἐν τοῖς μικροῖς καὶ τοῖς μηδὲν πρὸς τὸν βίον
ὠφελοῦσιν.
6 Ἀλλὰ γὰρ οὐδενὸς αὐτοῖς ἄλλου μέλει πλὴν τοῦ
χρηματίζεσθαι παρὰ τῶν νεωτέρων. ἔστι δ' ἡ περὶ
τὰς ἔριδας φιλοσοφία δυναμένη τοῦτο ποιεῖν· οἱ γὰρ
μήτε τῶν ἰδίων πω μήτε τῶν κοινῶν φροντίζοντες
τούτοις μάλιστα χαίρουσι τῶν λόγων οἳ μηδὲ πρὸς
7 ἓν χρήσιμοι τυγχάνουσιν ὄντες. τοῖς μὲν οὖν τηλικούτοις πολλὴ συγγνώμη ταύτην ἔχειν τὴν διά-
νοιαν· ἐπὶ γὰρ ἁπάντων τῶν πραγμάτων πρὸς τὰς
περιττότητας καὶ τὰς θαυματοποιίας οὕτω διακείμενοι διατελοῦσι· τοῖς δὲ παιδεύειν προσποιου-
μένοις ἄξιον ἐπιτιμᾶν, ὅτι κατηγοροῦσι μὲν τῶν

---

[a] This is Zeno of Elea, in Italy, and not the founder of the

are, or Zeno,[a] who ventured to prove the same
things as possible and again as impossible, or Melissus
who, although things in nature are infinite in number,
made it his task to find proofs that the whole is one !
Nevertheless, although these men so clearly have
shown that it is easy to contrive false statements on
any subject that may be proposed, they still waste
time on this commonplace. They ought to give up
the use of this claptrap, which pretends to prove
things by verbal quibbles, which in fact have long
since been refuted, and to pursue the truth, to instruct
their pupils in the practical affairs of our government
and train to expertness therein, bearing in mind that
likely conjecture about useful things is far preferable
to exact knowledge of the useless, and that to be a
little superior in important things is of greater worth
than to be pre-eminent in petty things that are
without value for living.

But the truth is that these men care for naught
save enriching themselves at the expense of the
youth. It is their " philosophy " applied to eristic
disputations [b] that effectively produces this result ;
for these rhetoricians, who care nothing at all for
either private or public affairs, take most pleasure in
those discourses which are of no practical service in
any particular. These young men, to be sure, may well
be pardoned for holding such views ; for in all matters
they are and always have been inclined toward what
is extraordinary and astounding. But those who
profess to give them training are deserving of censure

Stoic School of philosophy. Zeno and Melissus were disciples
of Parmenides.

[b] *eristics*—" wordy wrangling "; " mere disputation for
its own sake "; *cf.* General Introd., Vol. I, p. xxi and
Against the Sophists 1.

ἐπὶ τοῖς ἰδίοις συμβολαίοις ἐξαπατώντων καὶ μὴ
δικαίως τοῖς λόγοις χρωμένων, αὐτοὶ δ᾽ ἐκείνων
δεινότερα ποιοῦσιν· οἱ μὲν γὰρ ἄλλους τινὰς ἐζημί-
ωσαν, οὗτοι δὲ τοὺς συνόντας μάλιστα βλάπτου-
8 σιν. τοσοῦτον δ᾽ ἐπιδεδωκέναι πεποιήκασι τὸ
ψευδολογεῖν ὥστ᾽ ἤδη τινές, ὁρῶντες τούτους ἐκ
τῶν τοιούτων ὠφελουμένους, τολμῶσι γράφειν ὡς
ἔστιν ὁ τῶν πτωχευόντων καὶ φευγόντων βίος
ζηλωτότερος ἢ τῶν ἄλλων ἀνθρώπων, καὶ ποιοῦνται
τεκμήριον, ὡς εἰ περὶ πονηρῶν πραγμάτων ἔχουσί
τι λέγειν, περί γε τῶν καλῶν κἀγαθῶν ῥᾳδίως
9 εὐπορήσουσιν. ἐμοὶ δὲ δοκεῖ πάντων εἶναι κατα-
γελαστότατον τὸ διὰ τούτων τῶν λόγων ζητεῖν
πείθειν ὡς περὶ τῶν πολιτικῶν ἐπιστήμην ἔχουσιν,
ἐξὸν ἐν αὐτοῖς οἷς ἐπαγγέλλονται τὴν ἐπίδειξιν
ποιεῖσθαι· τοὺς γὰρ ἀμφισβητοῦντας τοῦ φρονεῖν
καὶ φάσκοντας εἶναι σοφιστὰς οὐκ ἐν τοῖς ἠμελη-
[210] μένοις ὑπὸ τῶν ἄλλων, ἀλλ᾽ ἐν οἷς ἅπαντές εἰσιν
ἀνταγωνισταί, προσήκει διαφέρειν καὶ κρείττους
10 εἶναι τῶν ἰδιωτῶν. νῦν δὲ παραπλήσιον ποιοῦσιν.
ὥσπερ ἂν εἴ τις προσποιοῖτο κράτιστος εἶναι τῶν
ἀθλητῶν ἐνταῦθα καταβαίνων, οὗ μηδεὶς ἂν ἄλλος
ἀξιώσειεν. τίς γὰρ ἂν τῶν εὖ φρονούντων συμφορὰς ἐπαινεῖν ἐπιχειρήσειεν; ἀλλὰ δῆλον, ὅτι δι᾽
11 ἀσθένειαν ἐνταῦθα καταφεύγουσιν. ἔστι γὰρ τῶν
μὲν τοιούτων συγγραμμάτων μία τις ὁδός, ἣν οὔθ᾽
εὑρεῖν οὔτε μαθεῖν οὔτε μιμήσασθαι δύσκολόν ἐστιν·
οἱ δὲ κοινοὶ καὶ πιστοὶ καὶ τούτοις ὅμοιοι τῶν
λόγων διὰ πολλῶν ἰδεῶν καὶ καιρῶν δυσκαταμαθή

because, while they condemn those who deceive in cases involving private contracts in business and those who are dishonest in what they say, yet they themselves are guilty of more reprehensible conduct; for the former wrong sundry other persons, but the latter inflict most injury upon their own pupils. And they have caused mendacity to increase to such a degree that now certain men, seeing these persons prospering from such practices, have the effrontery to write that the life of beggars and exiles is more enviable than that of the rest of mankind, and they use this as a proof that, if they can speak ably on ignoble subjects, it follows that in dealing with subjects of real worth they would easily find abundance of arguments. The most ridiculous thing of all, in my opinion, is this, that by these arguments they seek to convince us that they possess knowledge of the science of government, when they might be demonstrating it by actual work in their professed subject; for it is fitting that those who lay claim to learning and profess to be wise men should excel laymen and be better than they, not in fields neglected by everybody else, but where all are rivals. But as it is, their conduct resembles that of an athlete who, although pretending to be the best of all athletes, enters a contest in which no one would condescend to meet him. For what sensible man would undertake to praise misfortunes ? No, it is obvious that they take refuge in such topics because of weakness. Such compositions follow one set road and this road is neither difficult to find, nor to learn, nor to imitate. On the other hand, discourses that are of general import, those that are trustworthy, and all of similar nature, are devised and expressed through the medium

τῶν εὑρίσκονταί τε καὶ λέγονται, καὶ τοσούτῳ
χαλεπωτέραν ἔχουσι τὴν σύνθεσιν, ὅσῳ περ τὸ
σεμνύνεσθαι τοῦ σκώπτειν καὶ τὸ σπουδάζειν τοῦ
παίζειν ἐπιπονώτερόν ἐστιν. σημεῖον δὲ μέγιστον·
12 τῶν μὲν γὰρ τοὺς βομβυλιοὺς καὶ τοὺς ἅλας καὶ
τὰ τοιαῦτα βουληθέντων ἐπαινεῖν οὐδεὶς πώποτε
λόγων ἠπόρησεν, οἱ δὲ περὶ τῶν ὁμολογουμένων
ἀγαθῶν ἢ καλῶν ἢ τῶν διαφερόντων ἐπ' ἀρετῇ
λέγειν ἐπιχειρήσαντες πολὺ καταδεέστερον τῶν ὑπ-
13 αρχόντων ἅπαντες εἰρήκασιν. οὐ γὰρ τῆς αὐτῆς γνώμης ἐστὶν ἀξίως εἰπεῖν περὶ ἑκατέρων αὐτῶν, ἀλλὰ
τὰ μὲν μικρὰ ῥᾴδιον τοῖς λόγοις ὑπερβαλέσθαι,
τῶν δὲ χαλεπὸν τοῦ μεγέθους ἐφικέσθαι· καὶ περὶ
μὲν τῶν δόξαν ἐχόντων σπάνιον εὑρεῖν, ἃ μηδεὶς
πρότερον εἴρηκε, περὶ δὲ τῶν φαύλων καὶ ταπεινῶν
ὅ τι ἂν τις τύχῃ φθεγξάμενος ἅπαν ἴδιόν ἐστιν.
14 Διὸ καὶ τὸν γράψαντα περὶ τῆς Ἑλένης ἐπαινῶ
μάλιστα τῶν εὖ λέγειν τι βουληθέντων, ὅτι περὶ
τοιαύτης ἐμνήσθη γυναικός, ἣ καὶ τῷ γένει καὶ τῷ
κάλλει καὶ τῇ δόξῃ πολὺ διήνεγκεν. οὐ μὴν ἀλλὰ
καὶ τοῦτον μικρόν τι παρέλαθεν· φησὶ μὲν γὰρ
ἐγκώμιον γεγραφέναι περὶ αὐτῆς, τυγχάνει δ' ἀπολογίαν εἰρηκὼς ὑπὲρ τῶν ἐκείνῃ πεπραγμένων.
15 ἔστι δ' οὐκ ἐκ τῶν αὐτῶν ἰδεῶν οὐδὲ περὶ τῶν
αὐτῶν ἔργων[1] ὁ λόγος, ἀλλὰ πᾶν τοὐναντίον· ἀπο-

---

[1] ἔργων mss. is bracketed by Blass who prefers, without
good reason, ἀνθρώπων. Drerup retains ἔργων. Capps
suggests ἔργων ἑκάτερος ὁ λόγος, which is tempting.

[a] Cf. Plato, Symp. 177 B, where there is reference to an
Encomium of Salt by an unknown writer. See Panath. 135.
Cf. Lucian's comic encomium, Praise of the Fly (see L.C.L.
Lucian, Vol. I, pp. 81 ff.). [b] Cf. Panath. 36.

of a variety of forms and occasions of discourse whose opportune use is hard to learn, and their composition is more difficult as it is more arduous to practise dignity than buffoonery and seriousness than levity. The strongest proof is this : no one who has chosen to praise bumble-bees and salt [a] and kindred topics has ever been at a loss for words, yet those who have essayed to speak on subjects recognized as good or noble, or of superior moral worth have all fallen far short of the possibilities which these subjects offer. For it does not belong to the same mentality to do justice to both kinds of subjects ; on the contrary, while it is easy by eloquence to overdo the trivial themes, it is difficult to reach the heights of greatness of the others [b] ; and while on famous subjects one rarely finds thoughts which no one has previously uttered, yet on trifling and insignificant topics whatever the speaker may chance to say is entirely original.

This is the reason why, of those who have wished to discuss a subject with eloquence, I praise especially him who chose to write of Helen,[c] because he has recalled to memory so remarkable a woman, one who in birth, and in beauty, and in renown far surpassed all others. Nevertheless, even he committed a slight inadvertence—for although he asserts that he has written an encomium of Helen, it turns out that he has actually spoken a defence of her conduct ! But the composition in defence does not draw upon the same topics as the encomium, nor indeed does it deal with actions of the same kind, but quite the

[c] This statement certainly seems to refer to Gorgias, *Helen* (see particularly the end of that composition which is translated by Van Hook, *Greek Life and Thought*, pp. 162 ff. See also the Introduction to this discourse).

λογεῖσθαι μὲν γὰρ προσήκει περὶ τῶν ἀδικεῖν αἰτίαν
[211] ἐχόντων, ἐπαινεῖν δὲ τοὺς ἐπ' ἀγαθῷ τινὶ διαφέροντας.

Ἵνα δὲ μὴ δοκῶ τὸ ῥᾷστον ποιεῖν, ἐπιτιμᾶν τοῖς
ἄλλοις μηδὲν ἐπιδεικνὺς τῶν ἐμαυτοῦ, πειράσομαι
περὶ τῆς αὐτῆς ταύτης εἰπεῖν, παραλιπὼν ἅπαντα
τὰ τοῖς ἄλλοις εἰρημένα.

16   Τὴν μὲν οὖν ἀρχὴν τοῦ λόγου ποιήσομαι τὴν
ἀρχὴν τοῦ γένους αὐτῆς. πλείστων γὰρ ἡμιθέων
ὑπὸ Διὸς γεννηθέντων μόνης ταύτης γυναικὸς πατὴρ
ἠξίωσε κληθῆναι. σπουδάσας δὲ μάλιστα περί τε
τὸν ἐξ Ἀλκμήνης καὶ τοὺς ἐκ Λήδας, τοσούτῳ
μᾶλλον Ἑλένην Ἡρακλέους προὐτίμησεν ὥστε τῷ
μὲν ἰσχὺν ἔδωκεν, ἣ βίᾳ τῶν ἄλλων κρατεῖν δύναται,
τῇ δὲ κάλλος ἀπένειμεν, ὃ καὶ τῆς ῥώμης αὐτῆς
17 ἄρχειν πέφυκεν. εἰδὼς δὲ τὰς ἐπιφανείας καὶ τὰς
λαμπρότητας οὐκ ἐκ τῆς ἡσυχίας, ἀλλ' ἐκ τῶν
πολέμων καὶ τῶν ἀγώνων γιγνομένας, βουλόμενος
αὐτῶν μὴ μόνον τὰ σώματ' εἰς θεοὺς ἀναγαγεῖν
ἀλλὰ καὶ τὰς δόξας ἀειμνήστους καταλιπεῖν, τοῦ
μὲν ἐπίπονον καὶ φιλοκίνδυνον τὸν βίον κατέστησε,
τῆς δὲ περίβλεπτον καὶ περιμάχητον τὴν φύσιν
ἐποίησεν.

18   Καὶ πρῶτον μὲν Θησεύς, ὁ λεγόμενος μὲν Αἰ-
γέως, γενόμενος δ' ἐκ Ποσειδῶνος, ἰδὼν αὐτὴν

---

[a] The same sentiment is found in *Busiris* 9.
[b] Heracles.   [c] Castor and Pollux.
[d] Quoted and discussed by Demetrius, *On Style* 23.
[e] For Isocrates' view of Theseus see *Panath.* 126 ff., with his
references to this discussion of the hero.   For Theseus see Euri-

contrary ; for a plea in defence is appropriate only
when the defendant is charged with a crime, whereas
we praise those who excel in some good quality.

But that I may not seem to be taking the easiest
course, criticizing others without exhibiting any
specimen of my own,[a] I will try to speak of this
same woman, disregarding all that any others have
said about her.

I will take as the beginning of my discourse the beginning of her family. For although Zeus begat very
many of the demigods, of this woman alone he con-
descended to be called father. While he was devoted
most of all to the son of Alcmena [b] and to the sons
of Leda,[c] yet his preference for Helen, as compared
with Heracles, was so great that, although he conferred upon his son strength of body, which is
able to overpower all others by force, yet to her he
gave the gift of beauty, which by its nature brings
even strength itself into subjection to it. And knowing that all distinction and renown accrue, not from
a life of ease, but from wars and perilous combats,
and since he wished, not only to exalt their persons
to the gods, but also to bequeath to them glory that
would be immortal, he gave his son a life of labours
and love of perils, and to Helen he granted the
gift of nature which drew the admiration of all be-
holders and which in all men inspired contention.[d]

In the first place Theseus,[e] reputedly the son of
Aegeus, but in reality the progeny of Poseidon, seeing

pides, *Hippolytus* 887 ff. and Plutarch's *Theseus*. Theseus,
reputed son of Aegeus and of Aethra, daughter of Pittheus,
king of Troezen in Argolis, was honoured as the founder of
the political institutions of Athens. *Cf.* p. 79 and note.

οὔπω μὲν ἀκμάζουσαν, ἤδη δὲ τῶν ἄλλων δια-
φέρουσαν, τοσοῦτον ἡττήθη τοῦ κάλλους ὁ κρατεῖν
τῶν ἄλλων εἰθισμένος, ὥσθ' ὑπαρχούσης αὐτῷ καὶ
πατρίδος μεγίστης καὶ βασιλείας ἀσφαλεστάτης
ἡγησάμενος οὐκ ἄξιον εἶναι ζῆν ἐπὶ τοῖς παροῦσιν
19 ἀγαθοῖς ἄνευ τῆς πρὸς ἐκείνην οἰκειότητος, ἐπειδὴ
παρὰ τῶν κυρίων οὐχ οἷός τ' ἦν αὐτὴν λαβεῖν, ἀλλ'
ἐπέμενον τήν τε τῆς παιδὸς ἡλικίαν καὶ τὸν χρησ-
μὸν τὸν παρὰ τῆς Πυθίας, ὑπεριδὼν τὴν ἀρχὴν
τὴν Τυνδάρεω καὶ καταφρονήσας τῆς ῥώμης τῆς
Κάστορος καὶ Πολυδεύκους καὶ πάντων τῶν ἐν
Λακεδαίμονι δεινῶν ὀλιγωρήσας, βίᾳ λαβὼν αὐτὴν
20 εἰς Ἄφιδναν τῆς Ἀττικῆς κατέθετο, καὶ τοσαύτην
χάριν ἔσχε Πειρίθῳ τῷ μετασχόντι τῆς ἁρπαγῆς,
ὥστε βουληθέντος αὐτοῦ μνηστεῦσαι Κόρην τὴν
Διὸς καὶ Δήμητρος, καὶ παρακαλοῦντος ἐπὶ τὴν εἰς
[212] Ἅιδου κατάβασιν, ἐπειδὴ συμβουλεύων οὐχ οἷός τ'
ἦν ἀποτρέπειν, προδήλου τῆς συμφορᾶς οὔσης ὅμως
αὐτῷ συνηκολούθησε, νομίζων ὀφείλειν τοῦτον τὸν
ἔρανον, μηδενὸς ἀποστῆναι τῶν ὑπὸ Πειρίθου προσ-
ταχθέντων ἀνθ' ὧν ἐκεῖνος αὐτῷ συνεκινδύνευσεν.
21 Εἰ μὲν οὖν ὁ ταῦτα πράξας εἷς ἦν τῶν τυχόντων
ἀλλὰ μὴ τῶν πολὺ διενεγκόντων, οὐκ ἄν πω δῆλος
ἦν ὁ λόγος, πότερον Ἑλένης ἔπαινος ἢ κατηγορία
Θησέως ἐστίν· νῦν δὲ τῶν μὲν ἄλλων τῶν εὐδοκιμησάντων εὑρήσομεν τὸν μὲν ἀνδρίας, τὸν δὲ
σοφίας, τὸν δ' ἄλλου τινὸς τῶν τοιούτων μερῶν

Helen not as yet in the full bloom of her beauty, but already surpassing other maidens, was so captivated by her loveliness that he, accustomed as he was to subdue others, and although the possessor of a fatherland most great and a kingdom most secure, thought life was not worth living amid the blessings he already had unless he could enjoy intimacy with her. And when he was unable to obtain her from her guardians —for they were awaiting her maturity and the fulfilment of the oracle which the Pythian priestess had given—scorning the royal power of Tyndareüs,[a] disdaining the might of Castor and Pollux,[b] and belittling all the hazards in Lacedaemon, he seized her by force and established her at Aphidna in Attica. So grateful was Theseus to Peirithoüs, his partner in the abduction, that when Peirithoüs wished to woo Persephonê, the daughter of Zeus and Demeter, and summoned him to the descent into Hades to obtain her, when Theseus found that he could not by his warnings dissuade his friend, although the danger was manifest he nevertheless accompanied him, for he was of opinion that he owed this debt[c] of gratitude—to decline no task enjoined by Peirithoüs in return for his help in his own perilous enterprise.

If the achiever of these exploits had been an ordinary person and not one of the very distinguished, it would not yet be clear whether this discourse is an encomium of Helen or an accusation of Theseus ; but as it is, while in the case of other men who have won renown we shall find that one is deficient in courage, another in wisdom, and another in some kindred

---

[a] Father of Helen. [b] Brothers of Helen.
[c] For the figure of speech in ἔρανος see *Busiris* 1 and Plato, *Symp.* 177 c.

ἀπεστερημένον, τοῦτον δὲ μόνον οὐδ' ἑνὸς ἐνδεᾶ
γενόμενον, ἀλλὰ παντελῆ τὴν ἀρετὴν κτησάμενον.
22 δοκεῖ δέ μοι πρέπειν περὶ αὐτοῦ καὶ διὰ μακροτέρων εἰπεῖν· ἡγοῦμαι γὰρ ταύτην μεγίστην εἶναι πίστιν τοῖς βουλομένοις Ἑλένην ἐπαινεῖν, ἢν
ἐπιδείξωμεν τοὺς ἀγαπήσαντας καὶ θαυμάσαντας
ἐκείνην αὐτοὺς τῶν ἄλλων θαυμαστοτέρους ὄντας.
ὅσα μὲν γὰρ ἐφ' ἡμῶν γέγονεν, εἰκότως ἂν ταῖς
δόξαις ταῖς ἡμετέραις αὐτῶν διακρίνοιμεν, περὶ
δὲ τῶν οὕτω παλαιῶν προσήκει τοῖς κατ' ἐκεῖνον τὸν χρόνον εὖ φρονήσασιν ὁμονοοῦντας ἡμᾶς
φαίνεσθαι.

23 Κάλλιστον μὲν οὖν ἔχω περὶ Θησέως τοῦτ' εἰπεῖν,
ὅτι κατὰ τὸν αὐτὸν χρόνον Ἡρακλεῖ γενόμενος
ἐνάμιλλον τὴν αὐτοῦ δόξαν πρὸς τὴν ἐκείνου κατέστησεν. οὐ γὰρ μόνον τοῖς ὅπλοις ἐκοσμήσαντο
παραπλησίοις, ἀλλὰ καὶ τοῖς ἐπιτηδεύμασιν ἐχρή-
σαντο τοῖς αὐτοῖς, πρέποντα τῇ συγγενείᾳ ποιοῦν-
τες. ἐξ ἀδελφῶν γὰρ γεγονότες, ὁ μὲν ἐκ Διός,
ὁ δ' ἐκ Ποσειδῶνος, ἀδελφὰς καὶ τὰς ἐπιθυμίας
ἔσχον. μόνοι γὰρ οὗτοι τῶν προγεγενημένων ὑπὲρ
τοῦ βίου τοῦ τῶν ἀνθρώπων ἀθληταὶ κατέστησαν.
24 συνέβη δὲ τὸν μὲν ὀνομαστοτέρους καὶ μείζους, τὸν
δ' ὠφελιμωτέρους καὶ τοῖς Ἕλλησιν οἰκειοτέρους
ποιήσασθαι τοὺς κινδύνους. τῷ μὲν γὰρ Εὐρυ-
σθεὺς προσέταττε τάς τε βοῦς τὰς ἐκ τῆς Ἐρυθείας
ἀγαγεῖν καὶ τὰ μῆλα τὰ τῶν Ἑσπερίδων ἐνεγκεῖν
καὶ τὸν Κέρβερον ἀναγαγεῖν καὶ τοιούτους ἄλλους
πόνους, ἐξ ὧν ἤμελλεν οὐ τοὺς ἄλλους ὠφελήσειν

virtue, yet this hero alone was lacking in naught, but had attained consummate virtue. And it seems to me appropriate to speak of Theseus at still greater length; for I think this will be the strongest assurance for those who wish to praise Helen, if we can show that those who loved and admired her were themselves more deserving of admiration than other men. For contemporary events we should with good reason judge in accordance with our own opinions, but concerning events in times so remote it is fitting that we show our opinion to be in accord with the opinion of those men of wisdom who were at that time living.

The fairest praise that I can award to Theseus is this—that he, a contemporary of Heracles, won a fame which rivalled his. For they not only equipped themselves with similar armour, but followed the same pursuits, performing deeds that were worthy of their common origin. For being in birth the sons of brothers, the one of Zeus, the other of Poseidon, they cherished also kindred ambitions; for they alone of all who have lived before our time made themselves champions of human life. It came to pass that Heracles undertook perilous labours more celebrated and more severe, Theseus those more useful, and to the Greeks of more vital importance. For example, Heracles was ordered by Eurystheus [a] to bring the cattle from Erytheia [b] and to obtain the apples of the Hesperides and to fetch Cerberus up from Hades and to perform other labours of that kind, labours which would bring no benefit to mankind, but only danger

---

[a] Eurystheus, king of Mycenae, imposed the twelve labours upon Heracles; see *Panegyr.* 56 and note.

[b] An island near the coast of Spain.

25 ἀλλ' αὐτὸς κινδυνεύσειν· ὁ δ' αὐτὸς αὑτοῦ κύριος
[213] ὢν τούτους προῃρεῖτο τῶν ἀγώνων ἐξ ὧν ἤμελλεν
ἢ τῶν Ἑλλήνων ἢ τῆς αὑτοῦ πατρίδος εὐεργέτης
γενήσεσθαι. καὶ τόν τε ταῦρον τὸν ἀνεθέντα μὲν
ὑπὸ Ποσειδῶνος, τὴν δὲ χώραν λυμαινόμενον, ὃν
πάντες οὐκ ἐτόλμων ὑπομένειν, μόνος χειρωσά-
μενος μεγάλου φόβου καὶ πολλῆς ἀπορίας τοὺς
26 οἰκοῦντας τὴν πόλιν ἀπήλλαξεν· καὶ μετὰ ταῦτα
Λαπίθαις σύμμαχος γενόμενος, στρατευσάμενος ἐπὶ
Κενταύρους τοὺς διφυεῖς, οἳ καὶ τάχει καὶ ῥώμῃ
καὶ τόλμῃ διενεγκόντες τὰς μὲν ἐπόρθουν, ταῖς δ'
ἤμελλον, ταῖς δ' ἠπείλουν τῶν πόλεων, τούτους
μάχῃ νικήσας εὐθὺς μὲν αὐτῶν τὴν ὕβριν ἔπαυσεν,
οὐ πολλῷ δ' ὕστερον τὸ γένος ἐξ ἀνθρώπων ἠφάνι-
27 σεν. περὶ δὲ τοὺς αὐτοὺς χρόνους τὸ τέρας τὸ
τραφὲν μὲν ἐν Κρήτῃ, γενόμενον δ' ἐκ Πασιφάης
τῆς Ἡλίου θυγατρός, ᾧ κατὰ μαντείαν δασμὸν τῆς
πόλεως δὶς ἑπτὰ παῖδας ἀποστελλούσης, ἰδὼν αὐτοὺς ἀγομένους καὶ πανδημεὶ προπεμπομένους ἐπὶ
θάνατον ἄνομον καὶ προῦπτον καὶ πενθουμένους
ἔτι ζῶντας, οὕτως ἠγανάκτησεν ὥσθ' ἡγήσατο
κρεῖττον εἶναι τεθνάναι μᾶλλον ἢ ζῆν ἄρχων τῆς
πόλεως τῆς οὕτως οἰκτρὸν τοῖς ἐχθροῖς φόρον ὑπο-
28 τελεῖν ἠναγκασμένης. σύμπλους δὲ γενόμενος, καὶ
κρατήσας φύσεως ἐξ ἀνδρὸς μὲν καὶ ταύρου μεμιγ-
μένης, τὴν δ' ἰσχὺν ἐχούσης οἵαν προσήκει τὴν
ἐκ τοιούτων σωμάτων συγκειμένην, τοὺς μὲν παῖδας διασώσας τοῖς γονεῦσιν ἀπέδωκε, τὴν δὲ
74

to himself; Theseus, however, being his own master, gave preference to those struggles which would make him a benefactor of either the Greeks at large or of his native land. Thus, the bull let loose by Poseidon which was ravaging the land of Attica, a beast which all men lacked the courage to confront, Theseus singlehanded subdued, and set free the inhabitants of the city from great fear and anxiety. And after this, allying himself with the Lapiths, he took the field against the Centaurs, those creatures of double nature, endowed with surpassing swiftness, strength, and daring, who were sacking, or about to sack, or were threatening, one city after another. These he conquered in battle and straightway put an end to their insolence, and not long thereafter he caused their race to disappear from the sight of men. At about the same time appeared the monster [a] reared in Crete, the offspring of Pasiphaë, daughter of Helius, to whom our city was sending, in accordance with an oracle's command, tribute of twice seven children. When Theseus saw these being led away, and the entire populace escorting them, to a death savage and foreseen, and being mourned as dead while yet living, he was so incensed that he thought it better to die than to live as ruler of a city that was compelled to pay to the enemy a tribute so lamentable. Having embarked with them for Crete, he subdued this monster, half-man and half-bull, which possessed strength commensurate with its composite origin, and having rescued the children, he restored them to their parents, and thus freed the city

[a] The Minotaur, "the bull of Minos," to whom seven boys and seven girls were annually sent as tribute by the Athenians; cf. Plato, *Phaedo* 58 A.

πόλιν οὕτως ἀνόμου καὶ δεινοῦ καὶ δυσαπαλλάκτου
προστάγματος ἠλευθέρωσεν.

29 Ἀπορῶ δ' ὅ τι χρήσωμαι τοῖς ἐπιλοίποις· ἐπι-
στὰς γὰρ ἐπὶ τὰ Θησέως ἔργα καὶ λέγειν ἀρξάμενος
περὶ αὐτῶν ὀκνῶ μὲν μεταξὺ παύσασθαι καὶ παραλιπεῖν τήν τε Σκίρωνος καὶ Κερκύονος καὶ τῶν
ἄλλων τῶν τοιούτων παρανομίαν, πρὸς οὓς ἀντ-
αγωνιστὴς γενόμενος ἐκεῖνος πολλῶν καὶ μεγάλων
συμφορῶν τοὺς Ἕλληνας ἀπήλλαξεν, αἰσθάνομαι
δ' ἐμαυτὸν ἔξω φερόμενον τῶν καιρῶν καὶ δέδοικα
30 μή τισι δόξω περὶ τούτου μᾶλλον σπουδάζειν ἢ
[214] περὶ ἧς τὴν ἀρχὴν ὑπεθέμην. ἐξ ἀμφοτέρων οὖν
τούτων αἱροῦμαι τὰ μὲν πλεῖστα παραλιπεῖν διὰ
τοὺς δυσκόλως ἀκροωμένους, περὶ δὲ τῶν ἄλλων
ὡς ἂν δύνωμαι συντομώτατα διελθεῖν, ἵνα τὰ μὲν
ἐκείνοις, τὰ δ' ἐμαυτῷ χαρίσωμαι, καὶ μὴ παντάπασιν ἡττηθῶ τῶν εἰθισμένων φθονεῖν καὶ τοῖς
λεγομένοις ἅπασιν ἐπιτιμᾶν.

31 Τὴν μὲν οὖν ἀνδρίαν ἐν τούτοις ἐπεδείξατο τοῖς
ἔργοις ἐν οἷς αὐτὸς καθ' αὑτὸν ἐκινδύνευσε, τὴν δ'
ἐπιστήμην ἣν εἶχε πρὸς τὸν πόλεμον, ἐν ταῖς μάχαις
αἷς μεθ' ὅλης τῆς πόλεως ἠγωνίσατο, τὴν δ' εὐσέβειαν τὴν πρὸς τοὺς θεοὺς ἔν τε ταῖς Ἀδράστου
καὶ ταῖς τῶν παίδων τῶν Ἡρακλέους ἱκετείαις, τοὺς
μὲν γὰρ μάχῃ νικήσας Πελοποννησίους διέσωσε,
τῷ δὲ τοὺς ὑπὸ τῇ Καδμείᾳ τελευτήσαντας βίᾳ
Θηβαίων θάψαι παρέδωκε, τὴν δ' ἄλλην ἀρετὴν καὶ

---

[a] A mythical robber who haunted the rocks between
Attica and Megara.

[b] See the Introduction to this discourse.

[c] Cf. Euripides, Heraclidae for the story and also Isocrates,
Panegyr. 56.

from an obligation so savage, so terrible, and so ineluctable.

But I am at a loss how to deal with what remains to be said ; for, now that I have taken up the deeds of Theseus and begun to speak of them, I hesitate to stop midway and leave unmentioned the lawlessness of Sciron *a* and of Cercyon and of other robbers like them whom he fought and vanquished and thereby delivered the Greeks from many great calamities. But, on the other hand, I perceive that I am being carried beyond the proper limits of my theme and I fear that some may think that I am more concerned with Theseus than with the subject which I originally chose.*b* In this dilemma I prefer to omit the greater part of what might be said, out of regard for impatient hearers, and to give as concise an account as I can of the rest, that I may gratify both them and myself and not make a complete surrender to those whose habit it is out of jealousy to find fault with everything that is said.

His courage Theseus displayed in these perilous exploits which he hazarded alone ; his knowledge of war in the battles he fought in company with the whole city ; his piety toward the gods in con-nexion with the supplications of Adrastus and the children of Heracles when, by defeating the Pelopon-nesians in battle, he saved the lives of the children,*c* and to Adrastus he restored for burial, despite the Thebans, the bodies of those who had died beneath the walls of the Cadmea *d* ; and finally, he revealed

---

a Cf. Euripides, *Suppliants*. The story of Adrastus is told in detail in *Panath*. 168 ff. Adrastus, king of Argos, led the expedition of the " Seven against Thebes " (*cf.* Aeschylus, *Septem*), which met with defeat.

τὴν σωφροσύνην ἔν τε τοῖς προειρημένοις καὶ
μάλιστ᾽ ἐν οἷς τὴν πόλιν διῴκησεν.

32 Ὁρῶν γὰρ τοὺς βίᾳ τῶν πολιτῶν ἄρχειν ζητοῦν-
τας ἑτέροις δουλεύοντας καὶ τοὺς ἐπικίνδυνον τὸν
βίον τοῖς ἄλλοις καθιστάντας αὐτοὺς περιδεῶς
ζῶντας, καὶ πολεμεῖν ἀναγκαζομένους μετὰ μὲν
τῶν πολιτῶν πρὸς τοὺς ἐπιστρατευομένους, μετὰ
33 δ᾽ ἄλλων τινῶν πρὸς τοὺς συμπολιτευομένους, ἔτι
δὲ συλῶντας μὲν τὰ τῶν θεῶν, ἀποκτείνοντας δὲ
τοὺς βελτίστους τῶν πολιτῶν, ἀπιστοῦντας δὲ τοῖς
οἰκειοτάτοις, οὐδὲν δὲ ῥαθυμότερον ζῶντας τῶν ἐπὶ
θανάτῳ συνειλημμένων, ἀλλὰ τὰ μὲν ἔξω ζηλουμένους, αὐτοὺς δὲ παρ᾽ αὑτοῖς μᾶλλον τῶν ἄλλων
34 λυπουμένους· τί γάρ ἐστιν ἄλγιον ἢ ζῆν ἀεὶ δεδι-
ότα μή τις αὐτὸν τῶν παρεστώτων ἀποκτείνῃ, καὶ
μηδὲν ἧττον φοβούμενον τοὺς φυλάττοντας ἢ τοὺς
ἐπιβουλεύοντας; τούτων ἁπάντων καταφρονήσας
καὶ νομίσας οὐκ ἄρχοντας ἀλλὰ νοσήματα τῶν
πόλεων εἶναι τοὺς τοιούτους, ἐπέδειξεν ὅτι ῥᾴδιόν
ἐστιν ἅμα τυραννεῖν καὶ μηδὲν χεῖρον διακεῖσθαι
35 τῶν ἐξ ἴσου πολιτευομένων. καὶ πρῶτον μὲν τὴν
πόλιν σποράδην καὶ κατὰ κώμας οἰκοῦσαν εἰς ταὐτὸν συναγαγὼν τηλικαύτην ἐποίησεν ὥστ᾽ ἔτι καὶ
[215] νῦν ἀπ᾽ ἐκείνου τοῦ χρόνου μεγίστην τῶν Ἑλληνίδων εἶναι· μετὰ δὲ ταῦτα κοινὴν τὴν πατρίδα
καταστήσας καὶ τὰς ψυχὰς τῶν συμπολιτευομένων

his other virtues and his prudence, not only in the deeds already recited, but especially in the manner in which he governed our city.

For he saw that those who seek to rule their fellow-citizens by force are themselves the slaves of others, and that those who keep the lives of their fellow-citizens in peril themselves live in extreme fear, and are forced to make war, on the one hand, with the help of citizens against invaders from abroad, and, on the other hand, with the help of auxiliaries against their fellow citizens ; further, he saw them despoiling the temples of the gods, putting to death the best of their fellow-citizens, distrusting those nearest to them, living lives no more free from care than do men who in prison await their death; he saw that, although they are envied for their external blessings, yet in their own hearts they are more miserable than all other men—for what, pray, is more grievous than to live in constant fear lest some bystander kill you, dreading no less your own guards than those who plot against you ? Theseus, then, despising all these and considering such men to be not rulers, but pests, of their states, demonstrated that it is easy to exercise the supreme power and at the same time to enjoy as good relations as those who live as citizens on terms of perfect equality. In the first place, the scattered settlements and villages of which the state was composed he united, and made Athens into a city-state [a] so great that from then even to the present day it is the greatest state of Hellas : and after this, when he had established a common fatherland and had set free

---

[a] A reference to the συνοικισμός attributed to Theseus, *i.e.*, the uniting of the scattered villages in Attica into a *polis* or city-state. *Cf.* Thucydides ii. 15.

ἐλευθερώσας ἐξ ἴσου τὴν ἅμιλλαν αὐτοῖς περὶ τῆς
ἀρετῆς ἐποίησε, πιστεύων μὲν ὁμοίως αὐτῶν προ-
έξειν ἀσκούντων ὥσπερ ἀμελούντων, εἰδὼς δὲ τὰς
τιμὰς ἡδίους οὔσας τὰς παρὰ τῶν μέγα φρονούντων
36 ἢ τὰς παρὰ τῶν δουλευόντων. τοσούτου δ' ἐδέησεν
ἀκόντων τι ποιεῖν τῶν πολιτῶν ὥσθ' ὁ μὲν τὸν
δῆμον καθίστη κύριον τῆς πολιτείας, οἱ δὲ μόνον
αὐτὸν ἄρχειν ἠξίουν, ἡγούμενοι πιστοτέραν καὶ
κοινοτέραν εἶναι τὴν ἐκείνου μοναρχίαν τῆς αὐτῶν
δημοκρατίας. οὐ γὰρ ὥσπερ ἕτεροι τοὺς μὲν
πόνους ἄλλοις προσέταττε, τῶν δ' ἡδονῶν αὐτὸς
μόνος ἀπέλαυεν, ἀλλὰ τοὺς μὲν κινδύνους ἰδίους
ἐποιεῖτο, τὰς δ' ὠφελείας ἅπασιν εἰς τὸ κοινὸν
37 ἀπεδίδου. καὶ γάρ τοι διετέλεσε τὸν βίον οὐκ
ἐπιβουλευόμενος ἀλλ' ἀγαπώμενος, οὐδ' ἐπακτῷ
δυνάμει τὴν ἀρχὴν διαφυλάττων, ἀλλὰ τῇ τῶν
πολιτῶν εὐνοίᾳ δορυφορούμενος, τῇ μὲν ἐξουσίᾳ
τυραννῶν, ταῖς δ' εὐεργεσίαις δημαγωγῶν· οὕτω
γὰρ νομίμως καὶ καλῶς διῴκει τὴν πόλιν ὥστ'
ἔτι καὶ νῦν ἴχνος τῆς ἐκείνου πραότητος ἐν τοῖς
ἤθεσιν ἡμῶν καταλελεῖφθαι.

38   Τὴν δὴ γεννηθεῖσαν μὲν ὑπὸ Διός, κρατήσασαν
δὲ τοιαύτης ἀρετῆς καὶ σωφροσύνης, πῶς οὐκ
ἐπαινεῖν χρὴ καὶ τιμᾶν καὶ νομίζειν πολὺ τῶν
πώποτε γενομένων διενεγκεῖν; οὐ γὰρ δὴ μάρτυρά
γε πιστότερον οὐδὲ κριτὴν ἱκανώτερον ἕξομεν ἐπαγ-
αγέσθαι περὶ τῶν Ἑλένῃ προσόντων ἀγαθῶν τῆς
Θησέως διανοίας. ἵνα δὲ μὴ δοκῶ δι' ἀπορίαν περὶ

ᵃ With this passage (§§ 34-35) *Panegyr.* 38-39, with note,
should be compared.   ᵇ *Cf.* To *Nicocles* 21.

the minds of his fellow-citizens, he instituted for them on equal terms that rivalry of theirs for distinction based on merit, confident that he would stand out as their superior in any case, whether they practised that privilege or neglected it, and he also knew that honours bestowed by high-minded men are sweeter than those that are awarded by slaves.[a] And he was so far from doing anything contrary to the will of the citizens that he made the people masters of the government, and they on their part thought it best that he should rule alone, believing that his sole rule was more to be trusted and more equitable than their own democracy. For he did not, as the other rulers did habitually, impose the labours upon the citizens and himself alone enjoy the pleasures ; but the dangers he made his own, and the benefits he bestowed upon the people in common. In consequence, Theseus passed his life beloved of his people and not the object of their plots, not preserving his sovereignty by means of alien military force, but protected, as by a bodyguard, by the goodwill of the citizens,[b] by virtue of his authority ruling as a king, but by his benefactions as a popular leader ; for so equitably and so well did he administer the city that even to this day traces of his clemency may be seen remaining in our institutions.

As for Helen, daughter of Zeus, who established her power over such excellence and sobriety, should she not be praised and honoured, and regarded as far superior to all the women who have ever lived ? For surely we shall never have a more trustworthy witness or more competent judge of Helen's good attributes than the opinion of Theseus. But lest I seem through poverty of ideas to be dwelling unduly upon the same

τὸν αὐτὸν τόπον διατρίβειν, μηδ' ἀνδρὸς ἑνὸς δόξῃ
καταχρώμενος ἐπαινεῖν αὐτήν, βούλομαι καὶ περὶ
τῶν ἐχομένων διελθεῖν.

39 Μετὰ γὰρ τὴν Θησέως εἰς Ἅιδου κατάβασιν
ἐπανελθούσης αὖθις εἰς Λακεδαίμονα καὶ πρὸς τὸ
μνηστεύεσθαι λαβούσης ἡλικίαν ἅπαντες οἱ τότε
βασιλεύοντες καὶ δυναστεύοντες τὴν αὐτὴν γνώμην
[216] ἔσχον περὶ αὐτῆς· ἐξὸν γὰρ αὐτοῖς λαμβάνειν ἐν
ταῖς αὑτῶν πόλεσι γυναῖκας τὰς πρωτευούσας,
ὑπεριδόντες τοὺς οἴκοι γάμους ἦλθον ἐκείνην μνηστεύ-
40 σοντες. οὔπω δὲ κεκριμένου τοῦ μέλλοντος αὐτῇ
συνοικήσειν ἀλλ' ἔτι κοινῆς τῆς τύχης οὔσης
οὕτω πρόδηλος ἦν ἅπασιν ἐσομένη περιμάχητος
ὥστε συνελθόντες πίστεις ἔδοσαν ἀλλήλοις ἦ μὴν
βοηθήσειν, εἴ τις ἀποστεροίη τὸν ἀξιωθέντα λαβεῖν
αὐτήν, νομίζων ἕκαστος τὴν ἐπικουρίαν ταύτην
41 αὑτῷ παρασκευάζειν. τῆς μὲν οὖν ἰδίας ἐλπίδος
πλὴν ἑνὸς ἀνδρὸς ἅπαντες ἐψεύσθησαν, τῆς δὲ
κοινῆς δόξης ἧς ἔσχον περὶ ἐκείνης οὐδεὶς αὐτῶν
διήμαρτεν. οὐ πολλοῦ γὰρ χρόνου διελθόντος, γενομένης ἐν θεοῖς περὶ κάλλους ἔριδος ἧς Ἀλέξανδρος
ὁ Πριάμου κατέστη κριτής, καὶ διδούσης Ἥρας
μὲν ἁπάσης αὐτῷ τῆς Ἀσίας βασιλεύειν, Ἀθηνᾶς
42 δὲ κρατεῖν ἐν τοῖς πολέμοις, Ἀφροδίτης δὲ τὸν
γάμον τὸν Ἑλένης, τῶν μὲν σωμάτων οὐ δυνηθεὶς
λαβεῖν διάγνωσιν ἀλλ' ἡττηθεὶς τῆς τῶν θεῶν
ὄψεως, τῶν δὲ δωρεῶν ἀναγκασθεὶς γενέσθαι κριτής, εἵλετο τὴν οἰκειότητα τὴν Ἑλένης ἀντὶ τῶν
ἄλλων ἁπάντων, οὐ πρὸς τὰς ἡδονὰς ἀποβλέψας,—
καίτοι καὶ τοῦτο τοῖς εὖ φρονοῦσι πολλῶν αἱρετώ-
43 τερόν ἐστιν, ἀλλ' ὅμως οὐκ ἐπὶ τοῦθ' ὥρμησεν, ἀλλ'

ᵃ *i.e.*, Paris.

theme and by misusing the glory of one man to be praising Helen, I wish now to review the subsequent events also.

After the descent of Theseus to Hades, when Helen returned to Lacedaemon, and was now of marriageable age, all the kings and potentates of that time formed of her the same opinion ; for although it was possible for them in their own cities to wed women of the first rank, they disdained wedlock at home and went to Sparta to woo Helen. And before it had yet been decided who was to be her husband and all her suitors still had an equal chance, it was so evident to all that Helen would be the object of armed contention that they met together and exchanged solemn pledges of assistance if anyone should attempt to take her away from him who had been adjudged worthy of winning her ; for each thought he was providing this alliance for himself. In this their private hope all, it is true, save one man, were disappointed, yet in the general opinion which all had formed concerning her no one was mistaken. For not much later when strife arose among the goddesses for the prize of beauty, and Alexander,[a] son of Priam, was appointed judge and when Hera offered him sovereignty over all Asia, Athena victory in war, and Aphrodite Helen as his wife, finding himself unable to make a distinction regarding the charms of their persons, but overwhelmed by the sight of the goddesses, Alexander, compelled to make a choice of their proffered gifts, chose living with Helen before all else. In so doing he did not look to its pleasures —although even this is thought by the wise to be preferable to many things, but nevertheless it was not this he strove for—but because he was eager to

ἐπεθύμησε Διὸς γενέσθαι κηδεστής, νομίζων πολὺ
μείζω καὶ καλλίω ταύτην εἶναι τὴν τιμὴν ἢ τὴν
τῆς Ἀσίας βασιλείαν, καὶ μεγάλας μὲν ἀρχὰς καὶ
δυναστείας καὶ φαύλοις ἀνθρώποις ποτὲ παραγίγνε-
σθαι, τοιαύτης δὲ γυναικὸς οὐδένα τῶν ἐπιγιγνο-
μένων ἀξιωθήσεσθαι, πρὸς δὲ τούτοις οὐδὲν ἂν
κτῆμα κάλλιον καταλιπεῖν τοῖς παισὶν ἢ παρασκευ-
άσας αὐτοῖς ὅπως μὴ μόνον πρὸς πατρὸς ἀλλὰ καὶ
44 πρὸς μητρὸς ἀπὸ Διὸς ἔσονται γεγονότες. ἠπίστατο
γὰρ τὰς μὲν ἄλλας εὐτυχίας ταχέως μεταπιπτού-
σας, τὴν δ' εὐγένειαν ἀεὶ τοῖς αὐτοῖς παραμένουσαν,
ὥστε ταύτην μὲν τὴν αἵρεσιν ὑπὲρ ἅπαντος τοῦ
γένους ἔσεσθαι, τὰς δ' ἑτέρας δωρεὰς ὑπὲρ τοῦ
χρόνου μόνον τοῦ καθ' αὑτόν.

45 Τῶν μὲν οὖν εὖ φρονούντων οὐδεὶς ἂν τοῖς λογισ-
[217] μοῖς τούτοις ἐπιτιμήσειεν, τῶν δὲ μηδὲν πρὸ τοῦ
πράγματος ἐνθυμουμένων ἀλλὰ τὸ συμβαῖνον μόνον
σκοπουμένων ἤδη τινὲς ἐλοιδόρησαν αὐτόν· ὧν τὴν
ἄνοιαν ἐξ ὧν ἐβλασφήμησαν περὶ ἐκείνου ῥάδιον
46 ἅπασι καταμαθεῖν. πῶς γὰρ οὐ καταγέλαστον
πεπόνθασιν, εἰ τὴν αὑτῶν φύσιν ἱκανωτέραν εἶναι
νομίζουσι τῆς ὑπὸ τῶν θεῶν προκριθείσης; οὐ
γὰρ δή που περὶ ὧν εἰς τοσαύτην ἔριν κατέστησαν
τὸν τυχόντα διαγνῶναι κύριον ἐποίησαν, ἀλλὰ δῆλον ὅτι τοσαύτην ἔσχον σπουδὴν ἐκλέξασθαι κριτὴν
τὸν βέλτιστον, ὅσηνπερ περὶ αὐτοῦ τοῦ πράγματος
47 ἐπιμέλειαν ἐποιήσαντο. χρὴ δὲ σκοπεῖν ὁποῖός τις
ἦν καὶ δοκιμάζειν αὐτὸν οὐκ ἐκ τῆς ὀργῆς τῆς τῶν
ἀποτυχουσῶν, ἀλλ' ἐξ ὧν ἅπασαι βουλευσάμεναι
προείλοντο τὴν ἐκείνου διάνοιαν. κακῶς μὲν γὰρ

---

* *i.e.*, Alexander's.

become a son of Zeus by marriage, considering this a much greater and more glorious honour than sovereignty over Asia, and thinking that while great dominions and sovereignties fall at times even to quite ordinary men, no man would ever in all time to come be considered worthy of such a woman ; and furthermore, that he could leave no more glorious heritage to his children than by seeing to it that they should be descendants of Zeus, not only on their father's side, but also on their mother's. For he knew that while other blessings bestowed by Fortune soon change hands, nobility of birth abides forever with the same possessors ; therefore he foresaw that this choice would be to the advantage of all his race, whereas the other gifts would be enjoyed for the duration of his own life only.

No sensible person surely could find fault with this reasoning, but some, who have not taken into consideration the antecedent events but look at the sequel alone, have before now reviled Alexander ; but the folly of these accusers is easily discerned by all from the calumnies they have uttered. Are they not in a ridiculous state of mind if they think their own judgement is more competent than that which the gods chose as best ? [a] For surely they did not select any ordinary arbiter to decide a dispute about an issue that had got them into so fierce a quarrel, but obviously they were as anxious to select the most competent judge as they were concerned about the matter itself. There is need, moreover, to consider his real worth and to judge him, not by the resentment of those who were defeated for the prize, but by the reasons which caused the goddesses unanimously to choose his judgement. For nothing

παθεῖν ὑπὸ τῶν κρειττόνων οὐδὲν κωλύει καὶ τοὺς
μηδὲν ἐξημαρτηκότας· τοιαύτης δὲ τιμῆς τυχεῖν
ὥστε θνητὸν ὄντα θεῶν γενέσθαι κριτήν, οὐχ οἷόν
τε μὴ οὐ τὸν πολὺ τῇ γνώμῃ διαφέροντα.

48 Θαυμάζω δ᾽ εἴ τις οἴεται κακῶς βεβουλεῦσθαι
τὸν μετὰ ταύτης ζῆν ἑλόμενον, ἧς ἕνεκα πολλοὶ
τῶν ἡμιθέων ἀποθνῄσκειν ἠθέλησαν. πῶς δ᾽ οὐκ
ἂν ἦν ἀνόητος, εἰ τοὺς θεοὺς εἰδὼς περὶ κάλλους
φιλονικοῦντας αὐτὸς κάλλους κατεφρόνησε, καὶ μὴ
ταύτην ἐνόμισε μεγίστην εἶναι τῶν δωρεῶν, περὶ
ἧς κἀκείνας ἑώρα μάλιστα σπουδαζούσας;

49 Τίς δ᾽ ἂν τὸν γάμον τὸν Ἑλένης ὑπερεῖδεν, ἧς
ἁρπασθείσης οἱ μὲν Ἕλληνες οὕτως ἠγανάκτησαν
ὥσπερ ὅλης τῆς Ἑλλάδος πεπορθημένης, οἱ δὲ
βάρβαροι τοσοῦτον ἐφρόνησαν, ὅσον περ ἂν εἰ
πάντων ἡμῶν ἐκράτησαν. δῆλον δ᾽ ὡς ἑκάτεροι
διετέθησαν· πολλῶν γὰρ αὐτοῖς πρότερον ἐγκλημάτων γενομένων περὶ μὲν τῶν ἄλλων ἡσυχίαν
ἦγον, ὑπὲρ δὲ ταύτης τηλικοῦτον συνεστήσαντο
πόλεμον οὐ μόνον τῷ μεγέθει τῆς ὀργῆς ἀλλὰ καὶ
τῷ μήκει τοῦ χρόνου καὶ τῷ πλήθει τῶν παρα-
50 σκευῶν ὅσος οὐδεὶς πώποτε γέγονεν. ἐξὸν δὲ τοῖς
μὲν ἀποδοῦσιν Ἑλένην ἀπηλλάχθαι τῶν παρόντων
[218] κακῶν, τοῖς δ᾽ ἀμελήσασιν ἐκείνης ἀδεῶς οἰκεῖν
τὸν ἐπίλοιπον χρόνον, οὐδέτεροι ταῦτ᾽ ἠθέλησαν·
ἀλλ᾽ οἱ μὲν περιεώρων καὶ πόλεις ἀναστάτους
γιγνομένας καὶ τὴν χώραν πορθουμένην, ὥστε
μὴ προέσθαι τοῖς Ἕλλησιν αὐτήν, οἱ δ᾽ ᾑροῦντο
μένοντες ἐπὶ τῆς ἀλλοτρίας καταγηράσκειν καὶ

prevents even innocent persons from being ill-treated by the stronger, but only a mortal man of greatly superior intelligence could have received such honour as to become a judge of immortals.

I am astonished that anyone should think that Alexander was ill-advised in choosing to live with Helen, for whom many demigods were willing to die. Would he not have been a fool if, knowing that the deities themselves were contending for the prize of beauty, he had himself scorned beauty, and had failed to regard as the greatest of gifts that for the possession of which he saw even those goddesses most earnestly striving ?

What man would have rejected marriage with Helen, at whose abduction the Greeks were as incensed as if all Greece had been laid waste, while the barbarians were as filled with pride as if they had conquered us all ? It is clear how each party felt about the matter ; for although there had been many causes of contention between them before, none of these disturbed their peace, whereas for her they waged so great a war, not only the greatest of all wars in the violence of its passions, but also in the duration of the struggle and in the extent of the preparations the greatest of all time. And although the Trojans might have rid themselves of the misfortunes which encompassed them by sur-rendering Helen, and the Greeks might have lived in peace for all time by being indifferent to her fate, neither so wished ; on the contrary, the Trojans allowed their cities to be laid waste and their land to be ravaged, so as to avoid yielding Helen to the Greeks, and the Greeks chose rather, remaining in a foreign land to grow old there and never to see their

μηδέποτε τοὺς αὑτῶν ἰδεῖν μᾶλλον ἢ 'κείνην κατα-
51 λιπόντες εἰς τὰς αὑτῶν πατρίδας ἀπελθεῖν. καὶ
ταῦτ' ἐποίουν οὐχ ὑπὲρ 'Αλεξάνδρου καὶ Μενελάου
φιλονικοῦντες, ἀλλ' οἱ μὲν ὑπὲρ τῆς 'Ασίας, οἱ
δ' ὑπὲρ τῆς Εὐρώπης, νομίζοντες, ἐν ὁποτέρᾳ τὸ
σῶμα τοὐκείνης κατοικήσειε, ταύτην εὐδαιμονε-
στέραν τὴν χώραν ἔσεσθαι.

52 Τοσοῦτος δ' ἔρως ἐνέπεσε τῶν πόνων καὶ τῆς
στρατείας ἐκείνης οὐ μόνον τοῖς Ἕλλησι καὶ τοῖς
βαρβάροις ἀλλὰ καὶ τοῖς θεοῖς, ὥστ' οὐδὲ τοὺς ἐξ
αὑτῶν γεγονότας ἀπέτρεψαν τῶν ἀγώνων τῶν περὶ
Τροίαν, ἀλλὰ Ζεὺς μὲν προειδὼς τὴν Σαρπηδόνος
εἱμαρμένην, 'Ηὼς δὲ τὴν Μέμνονος, Ποσειδῶν δὲ
τὴν Κύκνου, Θέτις δὲ τὴν 'Αχιλλέως, ὅμως αὐτοὺς
53 συνεξώρμησαν καὶ συνεξέπεμψαν, ἡγούμενοι κάλλιον αὐτοῖς εἶναι τεθνάναι μαχομένοις περὶ τῆς
Διὸς θυγατρὸς μᾶλλον ἢ ζῆν ἀπολειφθεῖσι τῶν περὶ
ἐκείνης κινδύνων. καὶ τί δεῖ θαυμάζειν, ἃ περὶ
τῶν παίδων διενοήθησαν; αὐτοὶ γὰρ πολὺ μείζω
καὶ δεινοτέραν ἐποιήσαντο παράταξιν τῆς πρὸς
Γίγαντας αὐτοῖς γενομένης· πρὸς μὲν γὰρ ἐκείνους
μετ' ἀλλήλων ἐμαχέσαντο, περὶ δὲ ταύτης πρὸς
σφᾶς αὐτοὺς ἐπολέμησαν.

54 Εὐλόγως δὲ κἀκεῖνοι ταῦτ' ἔγνωσαν, κἀγὼ τηλικαύταις ὑπερβολαῖς ἔχω χρήσασθαι περὶ αὐτῆς·
κάλλους γὰρ πλεῖστον μέρος μετέσχεν, ὃ σεμνό-
τατον καὶ τιμιώτατον καὶ θειότατον τῶν ὄντων
ἐστίν. ῥᾴδιον δὲ γνῶναι τὴν δύναμιν αὐτοῦ· τῶν

• Cf. Panath. 81.
⁑ Sarpedon, son of Zeus and Laodameia, prominent in the

own again, than, leaving her behind, to return to their
fatherland. And they were not acting in this way
as eager champions of Alexander or of Menelaus ;
nay, the Trojans were upholding the cause of Asia,
the Greeks of Europe, in the belief that the land in
which Helen in person resided would be the more
favoured of Fortune.

So great a passion for the hardships of that expedition and for participation in it took possession not
only of the Greeks and the barbarians, but also of
the gods, that they did not dissuade even their own
children from joining in the struggles around Troy [a] ;
nay, Zeus, though foreseeing the fate of Sarpedon,[b]
and Eos that of Memnon, and Poseidon that of
Cycnus, and Thetis that of Achilles, nevertheless
they all urged them on and sent them forth, thinking
it more honourable for them to die fighting for the
daughter of Zeus than to live without having taken
part in the perils undergone on her account. And
why should we be astonished that the gods felt thus
concerning their children ? For they themselves
engaged in a far greater and more terrible struggle
than when they fought the Giants ; for against those
enemies they had fought a battle in concert, but for
Helen they fought a war against one another.

With good reason in truth they came to this decision, and I, for my part, am justified in employing
extravagant language in speaking of Helen ; for
beauty she possessed in the highest degree, and
beauty is of all things the most venerated, the most
precious, and the most divine. And it is easy to
determine its power ; for while many things which

Iliad, was killed by Patroclus ; Memnon and Cycnus were
slain by Achilles.

μὲν γὰρ ἀνδρίας ἢ σοφίας ἢ δικαιοσύνης μὴ μετεχόντων πολλὰ φανήσεται τιμώμενα μᾶλλον ἢ τούτων ἕκαστον, τῶν δὲ κάλλους ἀπεστερημένων οὐδὲν
εὑρήσομεν ἀγαπώμενον ἀλλὰ πάντα καταφρονού-
μενα, πλὴν ὅσα ταύτης τῆς ἰδέας κεκοινώνηκε, καὶ
τὴν ἀρετὴν διὰ τοῦτο μάλιστ' εὐδοκιμοῦσαν, ὅτι
55
[217 bis] κάλλιστον τῶν ἐπιτηδευμάτων ἐστίν. γνοίη δ' ἂν
τις κἀκεῖθεν ὅσον διαφέρει τῶν ὄντων, ἐξ ὧν αὐτοὶ
διατιθέμεθα πρὸς ἕκαστον αὐτῶν. τῶν μὲν γὰρ
ἄλλων ὧν ἂν ἐν χρείᾳ γενώμεθα, τυχεῖν μόνον
βουλόμεθα, περαιτέρω δὲ περὶ αὐτῶν οὐδὲν τῇ
ψυχῇ προσπεπόνθαμεν· τῶν δὲ καλῶν ἔρως ἡμῖν
ἐγγίγνεται, τοσούτῳ μείζω τοῦ βούλεσθαι ῥώμην
56 ἔχων, ὅσῳ περ καὶ τὸ πρᾶγμα κρεῖττόν ἐστιν. καὶ
τοῖς μὲν κατὰ σύνεσιν ἢ κατ' ἄλλο τι προέχουσι
φθονοῦμεν, ἢν μὴ τῷ ποιεῖν ἡμᾶς εὖ καθ' ἑκάστην
τὴν ἡμέραν προσαγάγωνται καὶ στέργειν σφᾶς αὐτοὺς ἀναγκάσωσι· τοῖς δὲ καλοῖς εὐθὺς ἰδόντες
εὖνοι γιγνόμεθα, καὶ μόνους αὐτοὺς ὥσπερ τοὺς
57 θεοὺς οὐκ ἀπαγορεύομεν θεραπεύοντες, ἀλλ' ἥδιον
δουλεύομεν τοῖς τοιούτοις ἢ τῶν ἄλλων ἄρχομεν,
πλείω χάριν ἔχοντες τοῖς πολλὰ προστάττουσιν ἢ
τοῖς μηδὲν ἐπαγγέλλουσιν. καὶ τοὺς μὲν ὑπ' ἄλλῃ
τινὶ δυνάμει γιγνομένους λοιδοροῦμεν καὶ κόλακας
ἀποκαλοῦμεν, τοὺς δὲ τῷ κάλλει λατρεύοντας
58 φιλοκάλους καὶ φιλοπόνους εἶναι νομίζομεν. τοσ-
αύτῃ δ' εὐσεβείᾳ καὶ προνοίᾳ χρώμεθα περὶ τὴν
ἰδέαν τὴν τοιαύτην ὥστε καὶ τῶν ἐχόντων τὸ κάλλος τοὺς μὲν μισθαρνήσαντας καὶ κακῶς βουλευσα-
μένους περὶ τῆς αὑτῶν ἡλικίας μᾶλλον ἀτιμάζομεν
ἢ τοὺς εἰς τὰ τῶν ἄλλων σώματ' ἐξαμαρτοντας·

do not have any attributes of courage, wisdom, or justice will be seen to be more highly valued than any one of these attributes, yet of those things which lack beauty we shall find not one that is beloved ; on the contrary, all are despised, except in so far as they possess in some degree this outward form, beauty, and it is for this reason that virtue is most highly esteemed, because it is the most beautiful of ways of living.   And we may learn how superior beauty is to all other things by observing how we ourselves are affected by each of them severally.   For in regard to the other things which we need, we only wish to possess them and our heart's desire is set on nothing further than this ; for beautiful things, however, we have an inborn passion whose strength of desire corresponds to the superiority of the thing sought. And while we are jealous of those who excel us in intelligence or in anything else, unless they win us over by daily benefactions and compel us to be fond of them, yet at first sight we become well-disposed toward those who possess beauty, and to these alone as to the gods we do not fail in our homage ; on the contrary, we submit more willingly to be the slaves of such than to rule all others, and we are more grateful to them when they impose many tasks upon us than to those who demand nothing at all.   We revile those who fall under the power of anything other than beauty and call them flatterers, but those who are subservient to beauty we regard as lovers of beauty and lovers of service. So strong are our feelings of reverence and solicitude for such a quality, that we hold in greater dishonour those of its possessors who have trafficked in it and ill-used their own youth than those who do violence

ὅσοι δ' ἂν τὴν αὑτῶν ὥραν διαφυλάξωσιν ἄβατον
τοῖς πονηροῖς ὥσπερ ἱερὸν ποιήσαντες, τούτους εἰς
τὸν ἐπίλοιπον χρόνον ὁμοίως τιμῶμεν ὥσπερ τοὺς
ὅλην τὴν πόλιν ἀγαθόν τι ποιήσαντας.

59 Καὶ τί δεῖ τὰς ἀνθρωπίνας δόξας λέγοντα διατρίβειν; ἀλλὰ Ζεὺς ὁ κρατῶν πάντων ἐν μὲν τοῖς
ἄλλοις τὴν αὑτοῦ δύναμιν ἐνδείκνυται, πρὸς δὲ
τὸ κάλλος ταπεινὸς γιγνόμενος ἀξιοῖ πλησιάζειν.
Ἀμφιτρύωνι μὲν γὰρ εἰκασθεὶς ὡς Ἀλκμήνην ἦλθε,
χρυσὸς δὲ ῥυεὶς Δανάῃ συνεγένετο, κύκνος δὲ γενόμενος εἰς τοὺς Νεμέσεως κόλπους κατέφυγε, τούτῳ
δὲ πάλιν ὁμοιωθεὶς Λήδαν ἐνύμφευσεν· ἀεὶ δὲ μετὰ
τέχνης ἀλλ' οὐ μετὰ βίας θηρώμενος φαίνεται τὴν
60 φύσιν τὴν τοιαύτην. τοσούτῳ δὲ μᾶλλον προτετίμη-
[218 bis] ται τὸ κάλλος παρ' ἐκείνοις ἢ παρ' ἡμῖν ὥστε καὶ
ταῖς γυναιξὶ ταῖς αὑτῶν ὑπὸ τούτου κρατουμέναις
συγγνώμην ἔχουσι, καὶ πολλὰς ἄν τις ἐπιδείξειε
τῶν ἀθανάτων, αἳ θνητοῦ κάλλους ἡττήθησαν, ὧν
οὐδεμία λαθεῖν τὸ γεγενημένον ὡς αἰσχύνην ἔχον
ἐζήτησεν, ἀλλ' ὡς καλῶν ὄντων τῶν πεπραγμένων
ὑμνεῖσθαι μᾶλλον ἢ σιωπᾶσθαι περὶ αὐτῶν ἠβουλήθησαν. μέγιστον δὲ τῶν εἰρημένων τεκμήριον[1].
πλείους γὰρ ἂν εὕροιμεν διὰ τὸ κάλλος ἀθανάτους
γεγενημένους ἢ διὰ τὰς ἄλλας ἀρετὰς ἁπάσας.

61 Ὧν Ἑλένη τοσούτῳ πλέον ἔσχεν, ὅσῳ περ καὶ
τὴν ὄψιν αὐτῶν διήνεγκεν. οὐ γὰρ μόνον ἀθανασίας
ἔτυχεν, ἀλλὰ καὶ τὴν δύναμιν ἰσόθεον λαβοῦσα
πρῶτον μὲν τοὺς ἀδελφοὺς ἤδη κατεχομένους ὑπὸ
τῆς πεπρωμένης εἰς θεοὺς ἀνήγαγε, βουλομένη δὲ
πιστὴν ποιῆσαι τὴν μεταβολὴν οὕτως αὐτοῖς τὰς
τιμὰς ἐναργεῖς ἔδωκεν ὥσθ' ὁρωμένους ὑπὸ τῶν

---

[1] τεκμήριον omitted by Blass following Γ[1].

to the persons of others ; whereas those who guard their youthful beauty as a holy shrine, inaccessible to the base, are honoured by us for all time equally with those who have benefited the city as a whole.

But why need I waste time in citing the opinions of men ? Nay, Zeus, lord of all, reveals his power in all else, but deigns to approach beauty in humble guise. For in the likeness of Amphitryon he came to Alcmena, and as a shower of gold he united with Danaë, and in the guise of a swan he took refuge in the bosom of Nemesis, and again in this form he espoused Leda ; ever with artifice manifestly, and not with violence, does he pursue beauty in women. And so much greater honour is paid to beauty among the gods than among us that they pardon their own wives when they are vanquished by it ; and one could cite many instances of goddesses who succumbed to mortal beauty, and no one of these sought to keep the fact concealed as if it involved disgrace ; on the contrary, they desired their adventures to be celebrated in song as glorious deeds rather than to be hushed in silence. The greatest proof of my statements is this : we shall find that more mortals have been made immortal because of their beauty than for all other excellences.

All these personages Helen surpassed in proportion as she excelled them in the beauty of her person. For not only did she attain immortality but, having won power equalling that of a god, she first raised to divine station her brothers,[a] who were already in the grip of Fate, and wishing to make their transformation believed by men, she gave to them honours [b] so

---

[a] Castor and Pollux ; cf. § 19.
[b] A reference to " St. Elmo's fire " ; cf. Pliny ii. 37.

ἐν τῇ θαλάττῃ κινδυνευόντων σῴζειν, οἵτινες ἂν
62 αὐτοὺς εὐσεβῶς κατακαλέσωνται. μετὰ δὲ ταῦτα
τοσαύτην Μενελάῳ χάριν ἀπέδωκεν ὑπὲρ τῶν πόνων καὶ τῶν κινδύνων οὓς δι' ἐκείνην ὑπέμεινεν,
ὥστε τοῦ γένους ἅπαντος τοῦ Πελοπιδῶν δια-
φθαρέντος καὶ κακοῖς ἀνηκέστοις περιπεσόντος οὐ
μόνον αὐτὸν τῶν συμφορῶν τούτων ἀπήλλαξεν
ἀλλὰ καὶ θεὸν ἀντὶ θνητοῦ ποιήσασα σύνοικον αὐτῇ
καὶ πάρεδρον εἰς ἅπαντα τὸν αἰῶνα κατεστήσατο.
63 καὶ τούτοις ἔχω τὴν πόλιν τὴν Σπαρτιατῶν τὴν μάλιστα τὰ παλαιὰ διασῴζουσαν ἔργῳ παρασχέσθαι
μαρτυροῦσαν· ἔτι γὰρ καὶ νῦν ἐν Θεράπναις τῆς
Λακωνικῆς θυσίας αὐτοῖς ἁγίας καὶ πατρίας ἀπο-
τελοῦσιν οὐχ ὡς ἥρωσιν ἀλλ' ὡς θεοῖς ἀμφοτέροις
οὖσιν.
64   Ἐνεδείξατο δὲ καὶ Στησιχόρῳ τῷ ποιητῇ τὴν
αὑτῆς δύναμιν· ὅτε μὲν γὰρ ἀρχόμενος τῆς ᾠδῆς
ἐβλασφήμησέ τι περὶ αὐτῆς, ἀνέστη τῶν ὀφθαλμῶν
ἐστερημένος, ἐπειδὴ δὲ γνοὺς τὴν αἰτίαν τῆς συμφορᾶς τὴν καλουμένην παλινῳδίαν ἐποίησε, πάλιν
65 αὐτὸν εἰς τὴν αὐτὴν φύσιν κατέστησεν. λέγουσι δέ
τινες καὶ τῶν Ὁμηριδῶν ὡς ἐπιστᾶσα τῆς νυκτὸς
Ὁμήρῳ προσέταξε ποιεῖν περὶ τῶν στρατευσα-
μένων ἐπὶ Τροίαν, βουλομένη τὸν ἐκείνων θάνατον ζηλωτότερον ἢ τὸν βίον τὸν τῶν ἄλλων
καταστῆσαι· καὶ μέρος μέν τι καὶ διὰ τὴν Ὁμήρου
τέχνην, μάλιστα δὲ διὰ ταύτην οὕτως ἐπαφρόδιτον
καὶ παρὰ πᾶσιν ὀνομαστὴν αὐτοῦ γενέσθαι τὴν
ποίησιν.
66   Ὡς οὖν καὶ δίκην λαβεῖν καὶ χάριν ἀποδοῦναι

---

[a] Just outside Sparta were the tombs of Menelaus and

manifest that they have power to save when they are seen by sailors in peril on the sea, if they but piously invoke them.   After this she so amply recompensed Menelaus for the toils and perils which he had undergone because of her, that when all the race of the Pelopidae had perished and were the victims of irremediable disasters, not only did she free him from these misfortunes but, having made him god instead of mortal, she established him as partner of her house and sharer of her throne forever.   And I can produce the city of the Spartans, which preserves with especial care its ancient traditions, as witness for the fact ; for even to the present day at Therapnê *a* in Laconia the people offer holy and traditional sacrifices to them both, not as to heroes, but as to gods.

And she displayed her own power to the poet Stesichorus *b* also ; for when, at the beginning of his ode, he spoke in disparagement of her, he arose deprived of his sight ; but when he recognized the cause of his misfortune and composed the *Recantation,c* as it is called, she restored to him his normal sight. And some of the Homeridae also relate that Helen appeared to Homer by night and commanded him to compose a poem on those who went on the expedition to Troy, since she wished to make their death more to be envied than the life of the rest of mankind ; and they say that while it is partly because of Homer's art, yet it is chiefly through her that his poem has such charm and has become so famous among all men.

Since, then, Helen has power to punish as well as to

Helen (see Pausanias iii. 19. 9) and their sanctuary (Herodotus vi. 61).

b The famous lyric poet of Himera, in Sicily.

c The well-known *palinode* ; for this legend and the fragment of the poem see Plato, *Phaedrus* 243 A.

δυναμένην, τοὺς μὲν τοῖς χρήμασι προέχοντας
ἀναθήμασι καὶ θυσίαις καὶ ταῖς ἄλλαις προσόδοις
ἱλάσκεσθαι καὶ τιμᾶν αὐτὴν χρή, τοὺς δὲ φιλο-
σόφους πειρᾶσθαί τι λέγειν περὶ αὐτῆς ἄξιον τῶν
ὑπαρχόντων ἐκείνῃ· τοῖς γὰρ πεπαιδευμένοις πρέπει
τοιαύτας ποιεῖσθαι τὰς ἀπαρχάς.

67   Πολὺ δὲ πλείω τὰ παραλελειμμένα τῶν εἰρημένων ἐστίν. χωρὶς γὰρ τεχνῶν καὶ φιλοσοφιῶν
καὶ τῶν ἄλλων ὠφελειῶν, ἃς ἔχοι τις ἂν εἰς ἐκείνην
καὶ τὸν πόλεμον τὸν Τρωϊκὸν ἀνενεγκεῖν, δικαίως
ἂν καὶ τοῦ μὴ δουλεύειν ἡμᾶς τοῖς βαρβάροις
Ἑλένην αἰτίαν εἶναι νομίζοιμεν. εὑρήσομεν γὰρ
τοὺς Ἕλληνας δι' αὐτὴν ὁμονοήσαντας καὶ κοινὴν
στρατείαν ἐπὶ τοὺς βαρβάρους ποιησαμένους, καὶ
τότε πρῶτον τὴν Εὐρώπην τῆς Ἀσίας τρόπαιον
68   στήσασαν· ἐξ ὧν τοσαύτης μεταβολῆς ἐτύχομεν
ὥστε τὸν μὲν ἐπέκεινα χρόνον οἱ δυστυχοῦντες
ἐν τοῖς βαρβάροις τῶν Ἑλληνίδων πόλεων ἄρχειν
ἠξίουν, καὶ Δαναὸς μὲν ἐξ Αἰγύπτου φυγὼν Ἄργος
κατέσχε, Κάδμος δὲ Σιδώνιος Θηβῶν ἐβασίλευσε,
Κᾶρες δὲ τὰς νήσους κατῴκουν, Πελοποννήσου δὲ
συμπάσης ὁ Ταντάλου Πέλοψ ἐκράτησεν, μετὰ δ'
ἐκεῖνον τὸν πόλεμον τοσαύτην ἐπίδοσιν τὸ γένος
ἡμῶν ἔλαβεν ὥστε καὶ πόλεις μεγάλας καὶ χώραν
69   πολλὴν ἀφελέσθαι τῶν βαρβάρων. ἢν οὖν τινες
βούλωνται ταῦτα διεργάζεσθαι καὶ μηκύνειν, οὐκ
ἀπορήσουσιν ἀφορμῆς, ὅθεν Ἑλένην ἔξω τῶν
εἰρημένων ἕξουσιν ἐπαινεῖν, ἀλλὰ πολλοῖς καὶ
καινοῖς λόγοις ἐντεύξονται περὶ αὐτῆς.

96

reward, it is the duty of those who have great wealth
to propitiate and to honour her with thank-offerings,
sacrifices, and processions, and philosophers should
endeavour to speak of her in a manner worthy of her
merits ; for such are the first-fruits it is fitting that
men of cultivation should offer.

Far more has been passed over than has been said.
Apart from the arts and philosophic studies and all
the other benefits which one might attribute to her
and to the Trojan War, we should be justified in
considering that it is owing to Helen that we are not
the slaves of the barbarians.   For we shall find that it
was because of her that the Greeks became united in
harmonious accord and organized a common expedition against the barbarians, and that it was then for
the first time that Europe set up a trophy of victory
over Asia ; and in consequence, we experienced a
change so great that, although in former times any
barbarians who were in misfortune presumed to be
rulers over the Greek cities (for example, Danaus, an
exile from Egypt, occupied Argos, Cadmus of Sidon
became king of Thebes, the Carians colonized the
islands,[a] and Pelops, son of Tantalus, became master
of all the Peloponnese), yet after that war our race
expanded so greatly that it took from the barbarians
great cities and much territory.   If, therefore, any
orators wish to dilate upon these matters and dwell
upon them, they will not be at a loss for material
apart from what I have said, wherewith to praise
Helen ; on the contrary, they will discover many new
arguments that relate to her.

> [a] *Cf.* Thucydides i. 4 and *Panath.* 43.

XI. BUSIRIS

INTRODUCTION

The *Busiris*, like the *Encomium on Helen*, is an epideictic essay of the " display " type, written as an eulogy of a famous personage ; in this case, the subject of extravagant praise is Busiris, mythical king of Egypt.

The immediate inspiration for the *Encomium on Helen* was a brilliant paradoxical discourse, or *jeu d'esprit*, by a rhetorician who was, in all probability, the Sicilian Gorgias.[a] In his *Helen* Isocrates criticizes this rhetorician and shows how the subject should have been treated. In the *Busiris*, likewise, the situation is similar. Polycrates,[b] who had entered upon the career of a professional rhetorician because of financial need, had composed a defence

---

[a] *Cf.* Introduction to *Helen*.
[b] According to the Greek introduction (*hypothesis*) to this composition Polycrates was an Athenian who practised the profession of Sophist at Cyprus. At the time when the *Busiris* was written Polycrates was a beginner in the field of rhetoric. Before 380 B.C. Polycrates had achieved fame at Athens and is mentioned by later writers on rhetoric in company with such noted persons as Antiphon, Thrasymachus, Anaximenes and Isaeus. He is severely criticized, however, by the critics Dionysius of Halicarnassus and Demetrius. Dionysius attacks him as " empty in practical oratory, frigid and vulgar in epideictic (display rhetoric), and lacking in grace " (*Isaeus* ch. 20), and Demetrius deplores his lack of earnestness (*On Style* 120).

of Busiris. Isocrates, who had never met the writer, having read this composition, addresses Polycrates and, in his customary rather patronizing manner, tells him that his work is seriously faulty in that he has written an accusation rather than a defence, and then proceeds to show him by actual example how the subject should have been handled.

The *Busiris* is not a work of particular merit. Isocrates himself, in the Introduction to his *Panathenaicus*, disparages subjects of this nature as trivial and unworthy, and in *Busiris* § 9 he admits that the topic is not a serious one and does not demand a dignified style. This discourse is a rhetorical exercise, artificial in its nature, composed near the beginning of Isocrates' professional career in Athens, probably between the years 390–385 B.C.[a]

---

[a] See Jebb, *Attic Orators* ii. p. 91, " perhaps in 391 or 390 B.C." Blass, *Die attische Beredsamkeit* ii. p. 248 gives 391 B.C. *Cf.* Mathieu et Brémond, *Isocrate* i. p. 184.

11. ΒΟΥΣΙΡΙΣ

[221] Τὴν μὲν ἐπιείκειαν τὴν σήν, ὦ Πολύκρατες, καὶ
τὴν τοῦ βίου μεταβολὴν παρ' ἄλλων πυνθανόμενος
οἶδα· τῶν δὲ λόγων τινὰς ὧν γέγραφας, αὐτὸς
ἀνεγνωκὼς ἥδιστα μὲν ἄν σοι περὶ ὅλης ἐπαρρησι-
ασάμην τῆς παιδεύσεως περὶ ἣν ἠνάγκασαι δια-
τρίβειν· ἡγοῦμαι γὰρ τοῖς ἀναξίως μὲν δυστυχοῦ-
σιν, ἐκ δὲ φιλοσοφίας χρηματίζεσθαι ζητοῦσιν,
ἅπαντας τοὺς πλείω πεπραγματευμένους καὶ μᾶλλον ἀπηκριβωμένους προσήκειν ἐθελοντὰς τοῦτον
2 εἰσφέρειν τὸν ἔρανον· ἐπειδὴ δ' οὔπω περιτετυχή-
καμεν ἀλλήλοις, περὶ μὲν τῶν ἄλλων, ἤν ποτ' εἰς
ταὐτὸν ἔλθωμεν, τόθ' ἡμῖν ἐξέσται διὰ πλειόνων
ποιήσασθαι τὴν συνουσίαν, ἃ δ' ἐν τῷ παρόντι
δυναίμην ἂν εὐεργετῆσαί σε, ταῦτα δ'[1] ᾠήθην
χρῆναι σοὶ μὲν ἐπιστεῖλαι, πρὸς δὲ τοὺς ἄλλους ὡς
3 οἷόν τε μάλιστ' ἀποκρύψασθαι. γιγνώσκω μὲν οὖν
ὅτι τοῖς πλείστοις τῶν νουθετουμένων ἔμφυτόν
[222] ἐστι μὴ πρὸς τὰς ὠφελείας ἀποβλέπειν, ἀλλὰ τοσούτῳ χαλεπώτερον ἀκούειν τῶν λεγομένων, ὅσῳ

---

[1] ταῦτά γ' Warmington.

[a] That is, from the teaching of the subject.

XI. BUSIRIS

I HAVE learned of your fairmindedness, Polycrates, and of the reversal in your life, through information from others ; and having myself read certain of the discourses which you have written, I should have been greatly pleased to discuss frankly with you and fully the education with which you have been obliged to occupy yourself. For I believe that when men through no fault of their own are unfortunate and so seek in philosophy a source of gain,[a] it is the duty of all who have had a wider experience in that occupation, and have become more thoroughly versed in it, to make this contribution [b] voluntarily for their benefit. But since we have not yet met one another, we shall be able, if we ever do come together, to discuss the other topics at greater length ; concerning those suggestions, however, by which at the present time I might be of service to you, I have thought I should advise you by letter, though concealing my views, to the best of my ability, from everyone else. I am well aware, however, that it is instinctive with most persons when admonished, not to look to the benefits they receive but, on the contrary, to listen to what is said with the greater displeasure in proportion to the rigour with which

[b] For the figure of speech in ἔρανος see *Helen* 20 and Plato, *Symp.* 177 c.

περ ἂν αὐτῶν τις ἀκριβέστερον ἐξετάζῃ τὰς ἁμαρ-
τίας· ὅμως δ' οὐκ ὀκνητέον ὑπομένειν τὴν ἀπ-
έχθειαν ταύτην τοῖς εὐνοϊκῶς πρός τινας ἔχουσιν,
ἀλλὰ πειρατέον μεθιστάναι τὴν δόξαν τῶν οὕτω
πρὸς τοὺς συμβουλεύοντας διακειμένων.

4 Αἰσθόμενος οὖν οὐχ ἥκιστά σε μεγαλαυχούμενον
ἐπί τε τῇ Βουσίριδος ἀπολογίᾳ καὶ τῇ Σωκράτους
κατηγορίᾳ, πειράσομαί σοι ποιῆσαι καταφανὲς ὅτι
πολὺ τοῦ δέοντος ἐν ἀμφοτέροις τοῖς λόγοις δι-
ήμαρτες. ἁπάντων γὰρ εἰδότων ὅτι δεῖ τοὺς μὲν
εὐλογεῖν τινὰς βουλομένους πλείω τῶν ὑπαρχόντων
ἀγαθῶν αὐτοῖς προσόντ' ἀποφαίνειν, τοὺς δὲ κατ-
5 ηγοροῦντας τἀναντία τούτων ποιεῖν, τοσούτου δεῖς
οὕτω κεχρῆσθαι τοῖς λόγοις, ὥσθ' ὑπὲρ μὲν Βουσίριδος ἀπολογήσασθαι φάσκων, οὐχ ὅπως τῆς
ὑπαρχούσης αὐτὸν διαβολῆς ἀπήλλαξας, ἀλλὰ καὶ
τηλικαύτην αὐτῷ τὸ μέγεθος παρανομίαν προσῆψας
ἧς οὐκ ἔσθ' ὅπως ἄν τις δεινοτέραν ἐξευρεῖν δυνη-
θείη· τῶν γὰρ ἄλλων τῶν ἐπιχειρησάντων ἐκεῖνον
λοιδορεῖν τοσοῦτον μόνον περὶ αὐτοῦ βλασφη-
μούντων, ὡς ἔθυε τῶν ξένων τοὺς ἀφικνουμένους,
σὺ καὶ κατεσθίειν αὐτὸν τοὺς ἀνθρώπους ᾐτιάσω·
Σωκράτους δὲ κατηγορεῖν ἐπιχειρήσας, ὥσπερ ἐγ-
κωμιάσαι βουλόμενος, Ἀλκιβιάδην ἔδωκας αὐτῷ
μαθητήν, ὃν ὑπ' ἐκείνου μὲν οὐδεὶς ᾔσθετο παιδευό-
μενον, ὅτι δὲ πολὺ διήνεγκε τῶν ἄλλων ἅπαντες
6 ἂν ὁμολογήσειαν. τοιγαροῦν εἰ γένοιτ' ἐξουσία τοῖς

---

^a For the legend of Busiris see Apollodorus ii. 5. 7 and
Herodotus ii. 45. Busiris, in obedience to an oracle, sacrificed strangers on the altar of Zeus. Herodotus doubts the
truth of the legend that the Egyptians sacrificed men.

their critic passes their faults in review. Nevertheless, those who are well disposed toward any persons must not shrink from incurring such resentment, but must try to effect a change in the opinion of those who feel this way toward those who offer them counsel.

Having observed, therefore, that you take especial pride in your *Defence of Busiris* and in your *Accusation of Socrates*, I shall try to make it clear to you that in both these discourses you have fallen far short of what the subject demands. For although everyone knows that those who wish to praise a person must attribute to him a larger number of good qualities than he really possesses, and accusers must do the contrary, you have so far fallen short of following these principles of rhetoric that, though you profess to defend Busiris, you have not only failed to absolve him of the calumny with which he is attacked, but have even imputed to him a lawlessness of such enormity that it is impossible for one to invent wickedness more atrocious. For the other writers whose aim was to malign him went only so far in their abuse as to charge him with sacrificing the strangers[a] who came to his country; you, however, accused him of actually devouring his victims. And when your purpose was to accuse Socrates, as if you wished to praise him, you gave Alcibiades to him as a pupil who, as far as anybody observed, never was taught by Socrates,[b] but that Alcibiades far excelled all his contemporaries all would agree. Hence, if the dead should acquire the power of

---

[b] Alcibiades, if not a disciple of Socrates, was intimately associated with the philosopher; *cf.* Plato, *Symp.* For praise of Alcibiades see Isocrates, *De Bigis.*

τετελευτηκόσι βουλεύσασθαι περὶ τῶν εἰρημένων,
ὁ μὲν ἄν σοι τοσαύτην ἔχοι χάριν ὑπὲρ τῆς κατηγορίας, ὅσην οὐδενὶ τῶν ἐπαινεῖν αὐτὸν εἰθισμένων, ὁ δ' εἰ καὶ περὶ τοὺς ἄλλους πραότατος ἦν,
ἀλλ' οὖν ἐπί γε τοῖς ὑπὸ σοῦ λεγομένοις οὕτως
ἂν ἀγανακτήσειεν ὥστε μηδεμιᾶς ἀποσχέσθαι τιμωρίας. καίτοι πῶς οὐκ αἰσχύνεσθαι μᾶλλον ἢ
σεμνύνεσθαι προσήκει τὸν παρὰ τοῖς λοιδορουμέ-
νοις ὑφ' αὑτοῦ μᾶλλον ἀγαπώμενον ἢ παρὰ τοῖς
ἐγκωμιαζομένοις;

7 Οὕτω δ' ἠμέλησας εἰ μηδὲν ὁμολογούμενον ἐρεῖς,
ὥστε φῂς μὲν αὐτὸν τὴν Αἰόλου καὶ τὴν Ὀρφέως
ζηλῶσαι δόξαν, ἀποφαίνεις δ' οὐδὲν τῶν αὐτῶν
ἐκείνοις ἐπιτηδεύσαντα. πότερα γὰρ τοῖς περὶ
[223] Αἰόλου λεγομένοις αὐτὸν παρατάξωμεν; ἀλλ' ἐκεῖνος μὲν τῶν ξένων τοὺς ἐπὶ τὴν χώραν ἐκπίπτον-
τας εἰς τὰς αὑτῶν πατρίδας ἀπέστελλεν, ὁ δ' εἰ
χρὴ τοῖς ὑπὸ σοῦ λεγομένοις πιστεύειν, θύσας
8 κατήσθιεν. ἢ τοῖς Ὀρφέως ἔργοις ὁμοιώσωμεν;
ἀλλ' ὁ μὲν ἐξ Ἅιδου τοὺς τεθνεῶτας ἀνῆγεν, ὁ δὲ
πρὸ μοίρας τοὺς ζῶντας ἀπώλλυεν. ὥσθ' ἡδέως
ἂν εἰδείην τί ποτ' ἂν ἐποίησεν, εἰ καταφρονῶν
αὐτῶν ἐτύγχανεν, ὃς θαυμάζων τὴν ἀρετὴν τὴν
ἐκείνων ἅπαντα φαίνεται τἀναντία διαπραττόμενος.
ὃ δὲ πάντων ἀτοπώτατον, ὅτι περὶ τὰς γενεαλογίας
ἐσπουδακὼς ἐτόλμησας εἰπεῖν, ὡς τούτους ἐζήλω-
σεν ὧν οὐδ' οἱ πατέρες πω κατ' ἐκεῖνον τὸν χρόνον
γεγονότες ἦσαν.

9 Ἵνα δὲ μὴ δοκῶ τὸ προχειρότατον ποιεῖν, ἐπι-

---

[a] Cf. *Odys.* x. 17-27, where Aeolus furnishes escort for
Odysseus.

judging what has been said of them, Socrates would be as grateful to you for your accusation as to any who have been wont to eulogize him; while Busiris, even if he had been most tender-hearted toward his guests, would be so enraged by your account of him that he would abstain from no vengeance whatever! And yet ought not that man to feel shame, rather than pride, who is more loved by those whom he has reviled than by those whom he has praised?

And you have been so careless about committing inconsistencies that you say Busiris emulated the fame of Aeolus and Orpheus, yet you do not show that any of his pursuits was identical with theirs. What, can we compare his deeds with the reported exploits of Aeolus? But Aeolus restored to their native lands strangers who were cast on his shores,[a] whereas Busiris, if we are to give credence to your account, sacrificed and ate them! Or, are we to liken his deeds to those of Orpheus? But Orpheus led the dead back from Hades,[b] whereas Busiris brought death to the living before their day of destiny. Consequently, I should be glad to know what, in truth, Busiris would have done if he had happened to despise Aeolus and Orpheus, seeing that, while admiring their virtues, all his own deeds are manifestly the opposite of theirs. But the greatest absurdity is this—though you have made a specialty of genealogies, you have dared to say that Busiris emulated those whose fathers even at that time had not yet been born![c]

But that I may not seem to be doing the easiest

---

[b] A reference to the myth of Orpheus and Eurydicê.
[c] Cf. § 37 for the same argument.

λαμβάνεσθαι τῶν εἰρημένων μηδὲν ἐπιδεικνὺς τῶν
ἐμαυτοῦ,[1] πειράσομαί σοι διὰ βραχέων δηλῶσαι
περὶ τὴν αὐτὴν ὑπόθεσιν, καίπερ οὐ σπουδαίαν
οὖσαν οὐδὲ σεμνοὺς λόγους ἔχουσαν, ἐξ ὧν ἔδει
καὶ τὸν ἔπαινον καὶ τὴν ἀπολογίαν ποιήσασθαι.

10 Περὶ μὲν οὖν τῆς Βουσίριδος εὐγενείας τίς οὐκ
ἂν δυνηθείη ῥᾳδίως εἰπεῖν; ὃς πατρὸς μὲν ἦν
Ποσειδῶνος, μητρὸς δὲ Λιβύης τῆς Ἐπάφου τοῦ
Διός, ἥν φασι πρώτην γυναῖκα βασιλεύσασαν ὁμώνυμον αὐτῇ τὴν χώραν καταστῆσαι. τυχὼν δὲ
τοιούτων προγόνων οὐκ ἐπὶ τούτοις μόνοις μέγ᾽
ἐφρόνησεν, ἀλλ᾽ ᾠήθη δεῖν καὶ τῆς ἀρετῆς τῆς
αὑτοῦ μνημεῖον εἰς ἅπαντα τὸν χρόνον καταλιπεῖν.

11 Τὴν μὲν οὖν μητρῴαν ἀρχὴν ὑπερεῖδεν ἐλάττω
νομίσας ἢ κατὰ τὴν αὑτοῦ φύσιν εἶναι, πλείστους
δὲ καταστρεψάμενος καὶ μεγίστην δύναμιν κτησάμενος ἐν Αἰγύπτῳ κατεστήσατο τὴν βασιλείαν, οὐκ
ἐκ τῶν παρουσῶν μόνον ἀλλ᾽ ἐξ ἁπασῶν προκρίνας

12 τὴν ἐκεῖ πολὺ διαφέρειν οἴκησιν. ἑώρα γὰρ τοὺς
μὲν ἄλλους τόπους οὐκ εὐκαίρως οὐδ᾽ εὐαρμόστως
πρὸς τὴν τοῦ σύμπαντος φύσιν ἔχοντας, ἀλλὰ τοὺς
μὲν ὑπ᾽ ὄμβρων κατακλυζομένους, τοὺς δ᾽ ὑπὸ
καυμάτων διαφθειρομένους, ταύτην δὲ τὴν χώραν
ἐν καλλίστῳ μὲν τοῦ κόσμου κειμένην, πλεῖστα
[224] δὲ καὶ παντοδαπώτατα φέρειν δυναμένην, ἀθανάτῳ
13 δὲ τείχει τῷ Νείλῳ τετειχισμένην, ὃς οὐ μόνον

---

[1] μηδὲν ἐπιδεικνὺς τῶν ἐμαυτοῦ is without justification
bracketed by Blass following Γ[1]. It occurs in *Helen* 15,
but is equally pertinent here.

[a] The same sentiment occurs in *Helen* 15.
[b] Cf. Aeschylus, *Prometheus* 850, where Epaphus is said
to be the son of Zeus and Io.

thing in assailing what others have said without exhibiting any specimen of my own,[a] I will try briefly to expound the same subject—even though it is not serious and does not call for a dignified style—and show out of what elements you ought to have composed the eulogy and the speech in defence.

Of the noble lineage of Busiris who would not find it easy to speak? His father was Poseidon, his mother Libya the daughter of Epaphus[b] the son of Zeus, and she, they say, was the first woman to rule as queen and to give her own name to her country. Although fortune had given him such ancestors, these alone did not satisfy his pride, but he thought he must also leave behind an everlasting monument to his own valour.

He was not content with his mother's kingdom, considering it too small for one of his endowment; and when he had conquered many peoples and had acquired supreme power he established his royal seat in Egypt, because he judged that country to be far superior as his place of residence, not only to the lands which then were his, but even to all other countries in the world. For he saw that all other regions are neither seasonably nor conveniently situated in relation to the nature of the universe, but some are deluged by rains and others scorched by heat; Egypt,[c] however, having the most admirable situation of the universe,[d] was able to produce the most abundant and most varied products, and was defended by the immortal ramparts of the Nile, a river which by its nature provides not only protec-

---

[c] Egypt here means the Delta of the Nile; *cf.* Herodotus ii. 14. Praise of Egypt is found in Plato, *Tim.* 22 D.

[d] *i.e.,* as regards climate and fertility.

φυλακὴν ἀλλὰ καὶ τροφὴν ἱκανὴν αὐτῇ παρέχειν
πέφυκεν, ἀνάλωτος μὲν ὢν καὶ δύσμαχος τοῖς ἐπι-
βουλεύουσιν, εὐαγωγὸς δὲ καὶ πρὸς πολλὰ χρήσιμος τοῖς ἐντὸς αὐτοῦ κατοικοῦσιν. πρὸς γὰρ τοῖς
προειρημένοις καὶ τὴν δύναμιν αὐτῶν πρὸς τὴν τῆς
γῆς ἐργασίαν ἰσόθεον πεποίηκεν· τῶν γὰρ ὄμβρων
καὶ τῶν αὐχμῶν τοῖς μὲν ἄλλοις ὁ Ζεὺς ταμίας
ἐστίν, ἐκείνων δ' ἕκαστος ἀμφοτέρων τούτων αὐτὸς
14 αὑτῷ κύριος καθέστηκεν. εἰς τοσαύτην δ' ὑπερβολὴν εὐδαιμονίας ἥκουσιν, ὥστε τῇ μὲν ἀρετῇ καὶ
τῇ φύσει τῆς χώρας καὶ τῷ πλήθει τῶν πεδίων
ἤπειρον καρποῦνται, τῇ δὲ τῶν περιόντων διαθέσει
καὶ τῇ τῶν ἐλλειπόντων κομιδῇ διὰ τὴν τοῦ ποτα-
μοῦ δύναμιν νῆσον οἰκοῦσιν· κύκλῳ γὰρ αὐτὴν
περιέχων καὶ πᾶσαν διαρρέων πολλὴν αὐτοῖς εὐπορίαν ἀμφοτέρων τούτων πεποίηκεν.

15 Ἤρξατο μὲν οὖν ἐντεῦθεν, ὅθεν περ χρὴ τοὺς
εὖ φρονοῦντας, ἅμα τόν τε τόπον ὡς κάλλιστον
καταλαβεῖν καὶ τροφὴν ἱκανὴν τοῖς περὶ αὐτὸν
ἐξευρεῖν. μετὰ δὲ ταῦτα διελόμενος χωρὶς ἑκάστους τοὺς μὲν ἐπὶ τὰς ἱερωσύνας κατέστησε, τοὺς
δ' ἐπὶ τὰς τέχνας ἔτρεψε, τοὺς δὲ τὰ περὶ τὸν
πόλεμον μελετᾶν ἠνάγκασεν, ἡγούμενος τὰ μὲν
ἀναγκαῖα καὶ τὰς περιουσίας ἔκ τε τῆς χώρας καὶ
τῶν τεχνῶν δεῖν ὑπάρχειν, τούτων δ' εἶναι φυλακὴν
ἀσφαλεστάτην τήν τε περὶ τὸν πόλεμον ἐπιμέλειαν
16 καὶ τὴν πρὸς τοὺς θεοὺς εὐσέβειαν. ἅπαντας δὲ
τοὺς ἀριθμοὺς περιλαβὼν ἐξ ὧν ἄριστ' ἄν τις
τὰ κοινὰ διοικήσειεν, ἀεὶ τοῖς αὐτοῖς τὰς αὐτὰς

---

[a] Cf. *Iliad* iv. 84.
[b] A reference to the Delta, enclosed and watered by the branches of the Nile.

tion to the land, but also its means of subsistence in abundance, being impregnable and difficult for foes to conquer, yet convenient for commerce and in many respects serviceable to dwellers within its bounds. For in addition to the advantages I have mentioned, the Nile has bestowed upon the Egyptians a godlike power in respect to the cultivation of the land; for while Zeus is the dispenser *a* of rains and droughts to the rest of mankind, of both of these each Egyptian has made himself master on his own account. And to so perfect a state of happiness have the Egyptians come that with respect to the excellence and fertility of their land and the extent of their plains they reap the fruits of a continent, and as regards the disposition of their superfluous products and the importation of what they lack, the river's possibilities are such that they inhabit an island *b*; for the Nile, encircling the land and flowing through its whole extent, has given them abundant means for both.

So Busiris thus began, as wise men should, by occupying the fairest country and also by finding sustenance sufficient for his subjects. Afterwards, he divided them into classes *c* : some he appointed to priestly services, others he turned to the arts and crafts, and others he forced to practise the arts of war. He judged that, while necessities and superfluous products must be provided by the land and the arts, the safest means of protecting these was practice in warfare and reverence for the gods. Including in all classes the right numbers for the best administration of the commonwealth, he gave orders that the same

c Isocrates here praises the caste system. *Cf.* Plato in the *Republic.*

πράξεις μεταχειρίζεσθαι προσέταξεν, εἰδὼς τοὺς
μὲν μεταβαλλομένους τὰς ἐργασίας οὐδὲ πρὸς ἓν
τῶν ἔργων ἀκριβῶς ἔχοντας, τοὺς δ' ἐπὶ ταῖς αὐταῖς
πράξεσι συνεχῶς διαμένοντας εἰς ὑπερβολὴν ἕκα-
17 στον ἀποτελοῦντας. τοιγαροῦν καὶ πρὸς τὰς τέχνας
εὑρήσομεν αὐτοὺς πλέον διαφέροντας τῶν περὶ τὰς
αὐτὰς ἐπιστήμας ἢ τοὺς ἄλλους δημιουργοὺς τῶν
ἰδιωτῶν, καὶ πρὸς τὴν σύνταξιν δι' ἧς τήν τε
βασιλείαν καὶ τὴν ἄλλην πολιτείαν διαφυλάττουσιν,
οὕτω καλῶς ἔχοντας ὥστε καὶ τῶν φιλοσόφων
τοὺς ὑπὲρ τῶν τοιούτων λέγειν ἐπιχειροῦντας καὶ
[225] μάλιστ' εὐδοκιμοῦντας τὴν ἐν Αἰγύπτῳ προαιρεῖσθαι πολιτείαν, καὶ Λακεδαιμονίους μέρος τι τῶν
ἐκεῖθεν μιμουμένους ἄριστα διοικεῖν τὴν αὐτῶν
18 πόλιν. καὶ γὰρ τὸ μηδένα τῶν μαχίμων ἄνευ τῆς
τῶν ἀρχόντων γνώμης ἀποδημεῖν καὶ τὰ συσσίτια
καὶ τὴν τῶν σωμάτων ἄσκησιν, ἔτι δὲ τὸ μηδενὸς
τῶν ἀναγκαίων ἀποροῦντας τῶν κοινῶν προσταγ-
μάτων ἀμελεῖν, μηδ' ἐπὶ ταῖς ἄλλαις τέχναις
διατρίβειν, ἀλλὰ τοῖς ὅπλοις καὶ ταῖς στρατείαις
προσέχειν τὸν νοῦν, ἐκεῖθεν ἅπαντα ταῦτ' εἰλήφα-
19 σιν. τοσούτῳ δὲ χεῖρον κέχρηνται τούτοις τοῖς
ἐπιτηδεύμασιν, ὅσον οὗτοι μὲν ἅπαντες στρατιῶται
καταστάντες βίᾳ τὰ τῶν ἄλλων λαμβάνειν ἀξιοῦσιν,
ἐκεῖνοι δ' οὕτως οἰκοῦσιν ὥσπερ χρὴ τοὺς μήτε
τῶν ἰδίων ἀμελοῦντας μήτε τοῖς ἀλλοτρίοις ἐπιβουλεύοντας. γνοίη δ' ἄν τις ἐνθένδε τὸ διάφορον

---

[a] It is natural to think that there is a reference here to
Plato and his *Republic*, but it is not certain.
[b] *Cf.* Herodotus ii. 80 and vi. 60.

112

individuals should always engage in the same pursuits, because he knew that those who continually change their occupations never achieve proficiency in even a single one of their tasks, whereas those who apply themselves constantly to the same activities perform each thing they do surpassingly well. Hence we shall find that in the arts the Egyptians surpass those who work at the same skilled occupations elsewhere more than artisans in general excel the laymen ; also with respect to the system which enables them to preserve royalty and their political institutions in general, they have been so successful that philosophers [a] who undertake to discuss such topics and have won the greatest reputation prefer above all others the Egyptian form of government, and that the Lacedaemonians, on the other hand, govern their own city in admirable fashion because they imitate certain of the Egyptian customs. For instance, the provision that no citizen fit for military service could leave the country without official authorization, the meals taken in common, and the training of their bodies ; furthermore, the fact that lacking none of the necessities of life, they do not neglect the edicts of the State, and that none engage in any other crafts, but that all devote themselves to arms and warfare, all these practices they have taken from Egypt.[b] But the Lacedaemonians have made so much worse use of these institutions that all of them, being professional soldiers, claim the right to seize by force the property of everybody else, whereas the Egyptians live as people should who neither neglect their own possessions, nor plot how they may acquire the property of others. The difference in the aims of the two polities may be seen from

20 ἑκατέρας τῆς πολιτείας. εἰ μὲν γὰρ ἅπαντες μιμη-
σαίμεθα τὴν Λακεδαιμονίων ἀργίαν καὶ πλεονεξίαν, εὐθὺς ἂν ἀπολοίμεθα καὶ διὰ τὴν ἔνδειαν
τῶν καθ' ἡμέραν καὶ διὰ τὸν πόλεμον τὸν πρὸς ἡμᾶς
αὐτούς· εἰ δὲ τοῖς Αἰγυπτίων νόμοις χρῆσθαι
βουληθεῖμεν, καὶ τοῖς μὲν ἐργάζεσθαι, τοῖς δὲ τὰ
τούτων σῴζειν δόξειεν, ἕκαστοι τὴν αὑτῶν ἔχοντες
εὐδαιμόνως ἂν τὸν βίον διατελοῖμεν.

21 Καὶ μὲν δὴ καὶ τῆς περὶ τὴν φρόνησιν ἐπιμελείας
εἰκότως ἄν τις ἐκεῖνον αἴτιον νομίσειεν. τοῖς γὰρ
ἱερεῦσι παρεσκεύασεν εὐπορίαν μὲν ταῖς ἐκ τῶν
ἱερῶν προσόδοις, σωφροσύνην δὲ ταῖς ἁγνείαις ταῖς
ὑπὸ τῶν νόμων προστεταγμέναις, σχολὴν δὲ ταῖς
22 τῶν κινδύνων καὶ τῶν ἄλλων ἔργων ἀτελείαις· μεθ'
ὧν ἐκεῖνοι βιοτεύοντες τοῖς μὲν σώμασιν ἰατρικὴν
ἐξεῦρον ἐπικουρίαν, οὐ διακεκινδυνευμένοις φαρ-
μάκοις χρωμένην ἀλλὰ τοιούτοις, ἃ τὴν μὲν ἀσφάλειαν ὁμοίαν ἔχει τῇ τροφῇ τῇ καθ' ἡμέραν, τὰς δ'
ὠφελείας τηλικαύτας ὥστ' ἐκείνους ὁμολογουμένως
ὑγιεινοτάτους εἶναι καὶ μακροβιωτάτους, ταῖς δὲ
ψυχαῖς φιλοσοφίας ἄσκησιν κατέδειξαν, ἣ καὶ
νομοθετῆσαι καὶ τὴν φύσιν τῶν ὄντων ζητῆσαι
23 δύναται. καὶ τοὺς μὲν πρεσβυτέρους ἐπὶ τὰ μέγιστα
[226] τῶν πραγμάτων ἔταξεν, τοὺς δὲ νεωτέρους ἀμελή-
σαντας τῶν ἡδονῶν ἐπ' ἀστρολογίᾳ καὶ λογισμοῖς
καὶ γεωμετρίᾳ διατρίβειν ἔπεισεν, ὧν τὰς δυνάμεις
οἱ μὲν ὡς πρός ἔνια χρησίμους ἐπαινοῦσιν, οἱ δ'
ὡς πλεῖστα πρὸς ἀρετὴν συμβαλλομένας ἀποφαίνειν
ἐπιχειροῦσιν.

---

[a] *Cf.* Herodotus ii. 84 and iii. 129.
[b] For the views of Isocrates in regard to the sciences see
Panath. 26-27.

the following : if we should all imitate the sloth and greed of the Lacedaemonians, we should straightway perish through both the lack of the necessities of daily life and civil war ; but if we should wish to adopt the laws of the Egyptians which prescribe that some must work and that the rest must protect the property of the workers, we should all possess our own goods and pass our days in happiness.

Furthermore, the cultivation of practical wisdom may also reasonably be attributed to Busiris. For example, he saw to it that from the revenues of the sacrifices the priests should acquire affluence, but self-control through the purifications prescribed by the laws, and leisure by exemption from the hazards of fighting and from all work. And the priests, because they enjoyed such conditions of life, discovered for the body the aid which the medical art affords,[a] not that which uses dangerous drugs, but drugs of such a nature that they are as harmless as daily food, yet in their effects are so beneficial that all men agree the Egyptians are the healthiest and most long of life among men ; and then for the soul they introduced philosophy's training, a pursuit which has the power, not only to establish laws but also to investigate the nature of the universe. The older men Busiris appointed to have charge of the most important matters, but the younger he persuaded to forgo all pleasures and devote themselves to the study of the stars, to arithmetic, and to geometry ; the value of these sciences [b] some praise for their utility in certain ways, while others attempt to demonstrate that they are conducive in the highest measure to the attainment of virtue.

115

24 Μάλιστα δ' ἄξιον ἐπαινεῖν καὶ θαυμάζειν τὴν εὐσέβειαν αὐτῶν καὶ τὴν περὶ τοὺς θεοὺς θεραπείαν. ὅσοι μὲν γὰρ σφᾶς αὐτοὺς οὕτω κατεσχημάτισαν ὥστ' ἢ κατὰ σοφίαν ἢ κατ' ἄλλην τιν' ἀρετὴν ὑπολαμβάνεσθαι μειζόνως ἢ κατὰ τὴν ἀξίαν, οὗτοι μὲν βλάπτουσι τοὺς ἐξαπατηθέντας· ὅσοι δὲ τῶν θείων πραγμάτων οὕτω προέστησαν ὥστε καὶ τὰς ἐπιμελείας καὶ τὰς τιμωρίας εἶναι δοκεῖν ἀκριβεστέρας τῶν συμβαινόντων, οἱ δὲ τοιοῦτοι πλεῖστα τὸν βίον τὸν τῶν ἀνθρώπων ὠφελοῦσιν.

25 καὶ γὰρ τὴν ἀρχὴν οἱ τὸν φόβον ἡμῖν ἐνεργασάμενοι τοῦτον αἴτιοι γεγόνασι τοῦ μὴ παντάπασι θηριωδῶς διακεῖσθαι πρὸς ἀλλήλους. ἐκεῖνοι τοίνυν οὕτως ἁγίως περὶ ταῦτα καὶ σεμνῶς ἔχουσιν ὥστε καὶ τοὺς ὅρκους πιστοτέρους εἶναι τοὺς ἐν τοῖς ἐκείνων ἱεροῖς ἢ τοὺς παρὰ τοῖς ἄλλοις καθεστῶτας, καὶ τῶν ἁμαρτημάτων ἕκαστον οἴεσθαι παραχρῆμα δώσειν δίκην, ἀλλ' οὐ διαλήσειν τὸν παρόντα χρόνον, οὐδ'

26 εἰς τοὺς παῖδας ἀναβληθήσεσθαι τὰς τιμωρίας. καὶ ταῦτ' εἰκότως δοξάζουσιν· πολλὰς γὰρ αὐτοῖς καὶ παντοδαπὰς ἀσκήσεις τῆς ὁσιότητος ἐκεῖνος κατέστησεν, ὅστις καὶ τῶν ζῴων τῶν παρ' ἡμῖν καταφρονουμένων ἔστιν ἃ σέβεσθαι καὶ τιμᾶν ἐνομοθέτησεν, οὐκ ἀγνοῶν τὴν δύναμιν αὐτῶν, ἀλλ' ἅμα μὲν ἐθίζειν οἰόμενος δεῖν τὸν ὄχλον ἐμμένειν ἅπασι τοῖς ὑπὸ τῶν ἀρχόντων παραγγελλο-

27 μένοις, ἅμα δὲ βουλόμενος πεῖραν λαμβάνειν ἐν τοῖς φανεροῖς, ἥντινα περὶ τῶν ἀφανῶν διάνοιαν ἔχουσιν. ἐνόμιζε γὰρ τοὺς μὲν τούτων ὀλιγωροῦν-

---

a In *Nicocles* 6 Isocrates affirms that the power of speech and of reason has enabled us to escape the life of wild beasts. See also *Panegyr.* 48 ff.

The piety of the Egyptians and their worship of the gods are especially deserving of praise and admiration. For all persons who have so bedizened themselves as to create the impression that they possess greater wisdom, or some other excellence, than they can rightly claim, certainly do harm to their dupes ; but those persons who have so championed the cause of religion that divine rewards and punishments are made to appear more certain than they prove to be, such men, I say, benefit in the greatest measure the lives of men. For actually those who in the beginning inspired in us our fear of the gods, brought it about that we in our relations to one another are not altogether like wild beasts.[a] So great, moreover, is the piety and the solemnity with which the Egyptians deal with these matters that not only are the oaths taken in their sanctuaries more binding than is the case elsewhere, but each person believes that he will pay the penalty for his misdeeds immediately and that he will neither escape detection for the present nor will the punishment be deferred to his children's time. And they have good reason for this belief ; for Busiris established for them numerous and varied practices of piety and ordered them by law even to worship and to revere certain animals which among us are regarded with contempt, not because he misapprehended their power, but because he thought that the crowd ought to be habituated to obedience to all the commands of those in authority, and at the same time he wished to test in visible matters how they felt in regard to the invisible. For he judged that those who belittled these instructions would perhaps look with contempt upon the more

117

τας τυχὸν καὶ τῶν μειζόνων καταφρονήσειν, τοὺς
δ' ἐπὶ πάντων ὁμοίως ἐμμένοντας τῇ τάξει βεβαίως
ἔσεσθαι τὴν αὑτῶν εὐσέβειαν ἐπιδεδειγμένους.

28 Ἔχοι δ' ἄν τις μὴ σπεύδειν ὡρμημένος πολλὰ
καὶ θαυμαστὰ περὶ τῆς ὁσιότητος αὐτῶν διελθεῖν,
ἣν οὔτε μόνος οὔτε πρῶτος ἐγὼ τυγχάνω καθεω-
[227] ρακώς, ἀλλὰ πολλοὶ καὶ τῶν ὄντων καὶ τῶν προγεγενημένων, ὧν καὶ Πυθαγόρας ὁ Σάμιός ἐστιν·
ὃς ἀφικόμενος εἰς Αἴγυπτον καὶ μαθητὴς ἐκείνων
γενόμενος τήν τ' ἄλλην φιλοσοφίαν πρῶτος εἰς τοὺς
Ἕλληνας ἐκόμισε, καὶ τὰ περὶ τὰς θυσίας καὶ τὰς
ἁγιστείας τὰς ἐν τοῖς ἱεροῖς ἐπιφανέστερον τῶν
ἄλλων ἐσπούδασεν, ἡγούμενος, εἰ καὶ μηδὲν αὐτῷ
διὰ ταῦτα πλέον γίγνοιτο παρὰ τῶν θεῶν, ἀλλ' οὖν
παρά γε τοῖς ἀνθρώποις ἐκ τούτων μάλιστ' εὐδοκι-
29 μήσειν. ὅπερ αὐτῷ καὶ συνέβη· τοσοῦτον γὰρ
εὐδοξίᾳ τοὺς ἄλλους ὑπερέβαλεν, ὥστε καὶ τοὺς
νεωτέρους ἅπαντας ἐπιθυμεῖν αὐτοῦ μαθητὰς εἶναι,
καὶ τοὺς πρεσβυτέρους ἥδιον ὁρᾶν τοὺς παῖδας τοὺς
αὑτῶν ἐκείνῳ συγγιγνομένους ἢ τῶν οἰκείων ἐπιμελουμένους. καὶ τούτοις οὐχ οἷόν τ' ἀπιστεῖν· ἔτι
γὰρ καὶ νῦν τοὺς προσποιουμένους ἐκείνου μαθητὰς
εἶναι μᾶλλον σιγῶντας θαυμάζουσιν ἢ τοὺς ἐπὶ τῷ
λέγειν μεγίστην δόξαν ἔχοντας.

30 Ἴσως ἂν οὖν τοῖς εἰρημένοις ἀπαντήσειας, ὅτι
τὴν μὲν χώραν καὶ τοὺς νόμους καὶ τὴν εὐσέβειαν,
ἔτι δὲ τὴν φιλοσοφίαν ἐπαινῶ τὴν Αἰγυπτίων, ὡς
δὲ τούτων αἴτιος ἦν, ὃν ὑπεθέμην, οὐδεμίαν ἔχω
λέγειν ἀπόδειξιν. ἐγὼ δ' εἰ μὲν ἄλλος τίς μοι
τὸν τρόπον τοῦτον ἐπέπληττεν, ἡγούμην ἂν αὐτὸν
πεπαιδευμένως ἐπιτιμᾶν· σοὶ δ' οὐ προσήκει ταύτην

118

important commands also, but that those who gave strict obedience equally in everything would have given proof of their steadfast piety.

If one were not determined to make haste, one might cite many admirable instances of the piety of the Egyptians, that piety which I am neither the first nor the only one to have observed; on the contrary, many contemporaries and predecessors have remarked it, of whom Pythagoras of Samos is one.[a] On a visit to Egypt he became a student of the religion of the people, and was first to bring to the Greeks all philosophy, and more conspicuously than others he seriously interested himself in sacrifices and in ceremonial purity, since he believed that even if he should gain thereby no greater reward from the gods, among men, at any rate, his reputation would be greatly enhanced. And this indeed happened to him. For so greatly did he surpass all others in reputation that all the younger men desired to be his pupils, and their elders were more pleased to see their sons staying in his company than attending to their private affairs. And these reports we cannot disbelieve; for even now persons who profess to be followers of his teaching are more admired when silent than are those who have the greatest renown for eloquence.

Perhaps, however, you would reply against all I have said, that I am praising the land, the laws, and the piety of the Egyptians, and also their philosophy, but that Busiris was their author, as I have assumed, I am able to offer no proof whatever. If any other person criticized me in that fashion, I should believe that his censure was that of a scholar;

[a] The celebrated philosopher; *cf.* Herodotus iv. 95.

31 ποιεῖσθαι τὴν ἐπίληψιν.¹ βουληθεὶς γὰρ Βούσιριν
εὐλογεῖν προείλου λέγειν, ὡς τόν τε Νεῖλον περὶ
τὴν χώραν περιέρρηξε καὶ τῶν ξένων τοὺς ἀφικνουμένους θύων κατήσθιεν· ὡς δὲ ταῦτ' ἐποίησεν
οὐδεμίαν πίστιν εἴρηκας. καίτοι πῶς οὐ καταγέ-
λαστόν ἐστι ταῦτα παρὰ τῶν ἄλλων ἀπαιτεῖν, οἷς
αὐτὸς μηδὲ κατὰ μικρὸν τυγχάνεις κεχρημένος;
32 ἀλλὰ τοσούτῳ πλέον ἡμῶν ἀπέχεις τοῦ πιστὰ
λέγειν, ὅσον ἐγὼ μὲν οὐδενὸς αὐτὸν αἰτιῶμαι τῶν
ἀδυνάτων ἀλλὰ νόμων καὶ πολιτείας, αἵπερ εἰσὶ
πράξεις τῶν ἀνδρῶν τῶν καλῶν κἀγαθῶν· σὺ
δὲ τοιούτων δημιουργὸν ἀποφαίνεις, ὧν οὐδέτερον
οὐδεὶς ἂν ἀνθρώπων ποιήσειεν, ἀλλὰ τὸ μὲν τῆς
τῶν θηρίων ὠμότητος, τὸ δὲ τῆς τῶν θεῶν δυνά-
33 μεως ἔργον ἐστίν. ἔπειτ' εἰ καὶ τυγχάνομεν ἀμφό-
[228] τεροι ψευδῆ λέγοντες, ἀλλ' οὖν ἐγὼ μὲν κέχρημαι
τούτοις τοῖς λόγοις, οἷσπερ χρὴ τοὺς ἐπαινοῦντας,
σὺ δ' οἷς προσήκει τοὺς λοιδοροῦντας· ὥστ' οὐ
μόνον τῆς ἀληθείας αὐτῶν ἀλλὰ καὶ τῆς ἰδέας ὅλης
δι' ἧς εὐλογεῖν δεῖ, φαίνει διημαρτηκώς.
34 Χωρὶς δὲ τούτων εἰ δεῖ τῶν σῶν ἀπαλλαγέντα
τὸν ἐμὸν λόγον ἐξετάζειν, οὐδεὶς ἂν αὐτῷ δικαίως
ἐπιπλήξειεν. εἰ μὲν γὰρ ἄλλος τις ἦν φανερὸς ὁ
ταῦτα πράξας, ἀγώ φημι γεγενῆσθαι δι' ἐκεῖνον,
ὁμολογῶ λίαν εἶναι τολμηρός, εἰ περὶ ὧν ἅπαντες
35 ἐπίστανται, περὶ τούτων μεταπείθειν ἐπιχειρῶ. νῦν
δ' ἐν κοινῷ τῶν πραγμάτων ὄντων καὶ δοξάσαι

¹ ἐπίληψιν Corais : ὑπόληψιν mss.

---

* Cf. Herodotus ii. 16, where the same verb (περιρρήγνυμι)

120

but you are not the one to reprove me. For, when you wished to praise Busiris, you chose to say that he forced the Nile to break into branches and surround the land,[a] and that he sacrificed and ate strangers who came to his country ; but you gave no proof that he did these things. And yet is it not ridiculous to demand that others follow a procedure which you yourself have not used in the slightest degree ? Nay, your account is far less credible than mine, since I attribute to him no impossible deed, but only laws and political organization, which are the accomplishments of honourable men, whereas you represent him as the author of two astounding acts which no human being would commit, one requiring the cruelty of wild beasts, the other the power of the gods. Further, even if both of us, perchance, are wrong, I, at any rate, have used only such arguments as authors of eulogies must use ; you, on the contrary, have employed ·those which are appropriate to revilers. Consequently, it is obvious that you have gone astray, not only from the truth, but also from the entire pattern which must be employed in eulogy.

Apart from these considerations, if your discourse should be put aside and mine carefully examined, no one would justly find fault with it. For if it were manifest that another had done the deeds which I assert were done by him, I acknowledge that I am exceedingly audacious in trying to change men's views about matters of which all the world has knowledge. But as it is, since the question is open to the judgement of all and one must resort to

is used in connexion with the branches of the Nile in the Delta.

δέον περὶ αὐτῶν, τίν᾽ ἄν τις τῶν ἐκεῖ καθεστώτων
ἐκ τῶν εἰκότων σκοπούμενος αἰτιώτερον εἶναι νομίσειεν ἢ τὸν ἐκ Ποσειδῶνος μὲν γεγονότα, πρὸς δὲ
μητρὸς ἀπὸ Διὸς ὄντα, μεγίστην δὲ δύναμιν τῶν
καθ᾽ αὑτὸν κτησάμενον καὶ παρὰ τοῖς ἄλλοις
ὀνομαστότατον γεγενημένον; οὐ γὰρ δή που τοὺς
ἁπάντων τούτων ἀπολελειμμένους προσήκει μᾶλλον
ἢ ᾽κεῖνον τηλικούτων ἀγαθῶν εὑρετὰς γενέσθαι.

36 Καὶ μὲν δὴ καὶ τοῖς χρόνοις ῥᾳδίως ἄν τις τοὺς
λόγους τοὺς τῶν λοιδορούντων ἐκεῖνον ψευδεῖς
ὄντας ἐπιδείξειεν. οἱ γὰρ αὐτοὶ τῆς τε Βουσίριδος
ξενοφονίας κατηγοροῦσι καί φασιν αὐτὸν ὑφ᾽ Ἡρα-
37 κλέους ἀποθανεῖν· ὁμολογεῖται δὲ παρὰ πάντων
τῶν λογοποιῶν Περσέως τοῦ Διὸς καὶ Δανάης
Ἡρακλέα μὲν εἶναι τέτταρσι γενεαῖς νεώτερον,
Βούσιριν δὲ πλέον ἢ διακοσίοις ἔτεσι πρεσβύτερον.
καίτοι τὸν βουλόμενον ἀπολύσασθαι τὴν ὑπὲρ ἐκείνου διαβολὴν πῶς οὐκ ἄτοπόν ἐστι ταύτην τὴν
πίστιν παραλιπεῖν, τὴν οὕτως ἐναργῆ καὶ τηλικαύτην δύναμιν ἔχουσαν;

38 Ἀλλὰ γὰρ οὐδέν σοι τῆς ἀληθείας ἐμέλησεν,
ἀλλὰ ταῖς τῶν ποιητῶν βλασφημίαις ἐπηκολούθη-
σας, οἳ δεινότερα μὲν πεποιηκότας καὶ πεπονθότας
ἀποφαίνουσι τοὺς ἐκ τῶν ἀθανάτων γεγονότας ἢ
τοὺς ἐκ τῶν ἀνθρώπων τῶν ἀνοσιωτάτων, τοιούτους δὲ λόγους περὶ αὐτῶν τῶν θεῶν εἰρήκασιν,
οἵους οὐδεὶς ἂν περὶ τῶν ἐχθρῶν εἰπεῖν τολμήσειεν·
οὐ γὰρ μόνον κλοπὰς καὶ μοιχείας καὶ παρ᾽ ἀνθρώ-
[229] ποις θητείας αὐτοῖς ὠνείδισαν, ἀλλὰ καὶ παίδων
βρώσεις καὶ πατέρων ἐκτομὰς καὶ μητέρων δε-

conjecture, who, reasoning from what is probable, would be considered to have a better claim to the authorship of the institutions of Egypt rather than a son of Poseidon, a descendant of Zeus on his mother's side, the most powerful personage of his time and the most renowned among all other peoples? For surely it is not fitting that any who were in all these respects inferior should, in preference to Busiris, have the credit of being the authors of those great benefactions.

Furthermore, it could be easily proved on chronological grounds also that the statements of the detractors of Busiris are false. For the same writers who accuse Busiris of slaying strangers also assert that he died at the hands of Heracles; but all chroniclers agree that Heracles was later by four generations than Perseus, son of Zeus and Danaë, and that Busiris lived more than two hundred years earlier than Perseus. And yet what can be more absurd than that one who was desirous of clearing Busiris of the calumny has failed to mention that evidence, so manifest and so conclusive?

But the fact is that you had no regard for the truth; on the contrary, you followed the calumnies of the poets, who declare that the offspring of the immortals have perpetrated as well as suffered things more atrocious than any perpetrated or suffered by the offspring of the most impious of mortals; aye, the poets have related about the gods themselves tales more outrageous than anyone would dare tell concerning their enemies. For not only have they imputed to them thefts and adulteries, and vassalage among men, but they have fabricated tales of the eating of children, the castrations of fathers, the

123

σμοὺς καὶ πολλὰς ἄλλας ἀνομίας κατ' αὐτῶν
39 ἐλογοποίησαν. ὑπὲρ ὧν τὴν μὲν ἀξίαν δίκην οὐκ
ἔδοσαν, οὐ μὴν ἀτιμώρητοί γε διέφυγον, ἀλλ' οἱ
μὲν αὐτῶν ἀλῆται καὶ τῶν καθ' ἡμέραν ἐνδεεῖς
κατέστησαν, οἱ δ' ἐτυφλώθησαν, ἄλλος δὲ φεύγων
τὴν πατρίδα καὶ τοῖς οἰκειοτάτοις πολεμῶν ἅπαντα
τὸν χρόνον διετέλεσεν, Ὀρφεὺς δ' ὁ μάλιστα τούτων τῶν λόγων ἁψάμενος, διασπασθεὶς τὸν βίον
40 ἐτελεύτησεν· ὥστ' ἢν σωφρονῶμεν, οὐ μιμησόμεθα
τοὺς λόγους τοὺς ἐκείνων, οὐδὲ περὶ μὲν τῆς πρὸς
ἀλλήλους κακηγορίας νομοθετήσομεν, τῆς δ' εἰς
τοὺς θεοὺς παρρησίας ὀλιγωρήσομεν, ἀλλὰ φυλαξό-
μεθα καὶ νομιοῦμεν ὁμοίως ἀσεβεῖν τούς τε λέγοντας τὰ τοιαῦτα καὶ τοὺς πιστεύοντας αὐτοῖς.

41 Ἐγὼ μὲν οὖν οὐχ ὅπως τοὺς θεούς, ἀλλ' οὐδὲ
τοὺς ἐξ ἐκείνων γεγονότας οὐδεμιᾶς ἡγοῦμαι κα-
κίας μετασχεῖν, ἀλλ' αὐτούς τε πάσας ἔχοντας τὰς
ἀρετὰς φῦναι καὶ τοῖς ἄλλοις τῶν καλλίστων ἐπιτηδευμάτων ἡγεμόνας καὶ διδασκάλους γεγενῆσθαι.
καὶ γὰρ ἄλογον, εἰ τῆς μὲν ἡμετέρας εὐπαιδίας εἰς
τοὺς θεοὺς τὴν αἰτίαν ἀναφέρομεν, τῆς δὲ σφετέρας
42 αὐτῶν μηδὲν αὐτοὺς φροντίζειν νομίζοιμεν. ἀλλ'
εἰ μὲν ἡμῶν τις τῆς τῶν ἀνθρώπων φύσεως κατα-
σταίη κύριος, οὐδ' ἂν τοὺς οἰκέτας ἐάσειεν εἶναι
πονηρούς· ἐκείνων δὲ καταγιγνώσκομεν ὡς καὶ
τοὺς ἐξ αὐτῶν γεγονότας περιεῖδον οὕτως ἀσεβεῖς
καὶ παρανόμους ὄντας. καὶ σὺ μὲν οἴει καὶ τοὺς

ᵃ e.g., Hermes steals Apollo's oxen (*Homeric Hymn to
Hermes*); the illicit love of Ares and Aphrodite (*Odyssey*
viii.); Apollo, servant of Admetus (Euripides, *Alcestis*);
Cronus devours his children and mutilates his father
Uranus; and Hephaestus fetters Hera.

fetterings of mothers, and many other crimes.[a] For
these blasphemies the poets, it is true, did not pay
the penalty they deserved, but assuredly they did
not escape punishment altogether : some became
vagabonds begging for their daily bread ; others
became blind ; another spent all his life in exile from
his fatherland and in warring with his kinsmen ; and
Orpheus, who made a point of rehearsing these tales,
died by being torn asunder.[b] Therefore if we are
wise we shall not imitate their tales, nor while passing
laws for the punishment of libels against each other,
shall we disregard loose-tongued vilification of the
gods ; on the contrary, we shall be on our guard and
consider equally guilty of impiety those who recite
and those who believe such lies.[c]

Now I, for my part, think that not only the gods
but also their offspring have no share in any wickedness but themselves are by nature endowed with all
the virtues and have become for all mankind guides
and teachers of the most honourable conduct. For
it is absurd that we should attribute to the gods the
responsibility for the happy fortunes of our children,
and yet believe them to be indifferent to those of
their own. Nay, if any one of us should obtain the
power of regulating human nature, he would not
allow even his slaves to be vicious ; yet we condemn
the gods by believing that they permitted their own
offspring to be so impious and lawless. And you,

[b] For example, Homer was represented as a blind wan-
derer ; Stesichorus was smitten with blindness for abuse of
Helen in his verses ; and Orpheus was torn to pieces by
the women of Thrace. Perhaps Archilochus is the poet in
exile.

[c] The poet Xenophanes, and later Plato, had strongly
protested against the attribution of immoralities to the gods.

μηδὲν προσήκοντας, ἤν σοι πλησιάσωσι, βελτίους
ποιήσειν, τοὺς δὲ θεοὺς οὐδεμίαν ἡγεῖ τῆς τῶν
43 παίδων ἀρετῆς ἔχειν ἐπιμέλειαν. καίτοι κατὰ τὸν
σὸν λόγον δυοῖν τοῖν αἰσχίστοιν οὐ διαμαρτάνουσιν·
εἰ μὲν γὰρ μηδὲν δέονται χρηστοὺς αὐτοὺς εἶναι,
χείρους εἰσὶ τῶν ἀνθρώπων τὴν διάνοιαν, εἰ δὲ βούλονται μέν, ἀποροῦσι δ' ὅπως ποιήσωσιν, ἐλάττω
τῶν σοφιστῶν τὴν δύναμιν ἔχουσιν.

44 Πολλῶν δ' ἐνόντων εἰπεῖν ἐξ ὧν ἄν τις καὶ τὸν
ἔπαινον καὶ τὴν ἀπολογίαν μηκύνειεν, οὐχ ἡγοῦμαι
δεῖν μακρολογεῖν· οὐ γὰρ ἐπίδειξιν τοῖς ἄλλοις ποι-
[230] ούμενος, ἀλλ' ὑποδεῖξαί σοι βουλόμενος ὡς χρὴ
τούτων ἑκάτερον ποιεῖν, διείλεγμαι περὶ αὐτῶν,
ἐπεὶ τόν γε λόγον ὃν σὺ γέγραφας, οὐκ ἀπολογίαν
ὑπὲρ Βουσίριδος, ἀλλ' ὁμολογίαν τῶν ἐπικαλου-
45 μένων δικαίως ἄν τις εἶναι νομίσειεν. οὐ γὰρ
ἀπολύεις αὐτὸν τῶν αἰτιῶν, ἀλλ' ἀποφαίνεις ὡς
καὶ τῶν ἄλλων τινὲς ταὐτὰ πεποιήκασι, ῥᾳθυμο-
τάτην τοῖς ἁμαρτάνουσιν εὑρίσκων καταφυγήν. εἰ
γὰρ τῶν μὲν ἀδικημάτων μὴ ῥᾴδιον εὑρεῖν ὃ μήπω
τυγχάνει γεγενημένον, τοὺς δ' ἐφ' ἑκάστοις αὐτῶν
ἁλισκομένους μηδὲν ἡγοίμεθα δεινὸν ποιεῖν, ὅταν
ἕτεροι ταὐτὰ φαίνωνται διαπεπραγμένοι, πῶς οὐκ
ἂν καὶ τὰς ἀπολογίας ἅπασι ῥᾳδίας ποιήσαιμεν,
καὶ τοῖς βουλομένοις εἶναι πονηροῖς πολλὴν ἐξου-
46 σίαν παρασκευάσαιμεν; μάλιστα δ' ἂν κατίδοις
τὴν εὐήθειαν τῶν εἰρημένων ἐπὶ σαυτοῦ θεωρήσας.
ἐνθυμήθητι γάρ· εἰ μεγάλων καὶ δεινῶν αἰτιῶν περὶ

Polycrates, assume that you will make men better
even if they are not related to you, provided that
they become your pupils, yet believe that the gods
have no care for the virtue of their own children !
And yet, according to your own reasoning, the gods
are not free from the two most disgraceful faults : for
if they do not want their children to be virtuous, they
are inferior in character to human beings ; but if, on
the other hand, they desire it but are at a loss how to
effect it, they are more impotent than the sophists !

Although the subject admits of many arguments
for the amplification of my theme of eulogy and
defence, I believe it unnecessary to speak at greater
length ; for my aim in this discourse is not to make
a display to impress others, but to show for your
benefit how each of these topics should be treated,
since the composition which you wrote may justly
be considered by anyone to be, not a defence of
Busiris, but an admission of all the crimes charged
against him. For you do not exonerate him from
the charges, but only declare that some others have
done the same things, inventing thus a very easy
refuge for all criminals. Why, if it is not easy to
find a crime which has not yet been committed, and
if we should consider that those who have been found
guilty of one or another of these crimes have done
nothing so very wrong, whenever others are found
to have perpetrated the same offences, should we not
be providing ready-made pleas in exculpation of all
criminals and be granting complete licence for those
who are bent on villainy ? You would best perceive
the inanity of your defence of Busiris if you should
imagine yourself in his position. Just suppose this
case : if you had been accused of grave and terrible

σὲ γεγονυιῶν τοῦτόν τις τὸν τρόπον σοι συνείποι,
πῶς ἂν διατεθείης; ἐγὼ μὲν γὰρ οἶδ' ὅτι μᾶλλον
ἂν αὐτὸν μισήσειας ἢ τοὺς κατηγοροῦντας. καίτοι
πῶς οὐκ αἰσχρὸν τοιαύτας ὑπὲρ τῶν ἄλλων ποιεῖσθαι τὰς ἀπολογίας, ἐφ' αἷς ὑπὲρ σαυτοῦ λεγομέναις
μάλιστ' ἂν ὀργισθείης;

47 Σκέψαι δὲ κἀκεῖνο καὶ δίελθε πρὸς αὐτόν. εἴ τις
τῶν σοι συνόντων ἐπαρθείη ποιεῖν ἃ σὺ τυγχάνεις
εὐλογῶν, πῶς οὐκ ἂν ἀθλιώτατος εἴη καὶ τῶν νῦν
ὄντων καὶ τῶν πώποτε γεγενημένων; ἆρ' οὖν
χρὴ τοιούτους λόγους γράφειν οἷς τοῦτο προσέσται
μέγιστον ἀγαθόν, ἢν μηδένα πεῖσαι τῶν ἀκουσάν-
των δυνηθῶσιν;

48 Ἀλλὰ γὰρ ἴσως ἂν εἴποις ὡς οὐδὲ σὲ τοῦτο
παρέλαθεν, ἀλλ' ἐβουλήθης τοῖς φιλοσόφοις παρά-
δειγμα καταλιπεῖν ὡς χρὴ περὶ τῶν αἰσχρῶν
αἰτιῶν καὶ δυσχερῶν πραγμάτων ποιεῖσθαι τὰς
ἀπολογίας. ἀλλ' εἰ καὶ πρότερον ἠγνόεις, οἶμαί
σοι νῦν γεγενῆσθαι φανερὸν ὅτι πολὺ θᾶττον ἄν τις
σωθείη μηδὲν φθεγξάμενος ἢ τοῦτον τὸν τρόπον
49 ἀπολογησάμενος. καὶ μὲν δὴ καὶ τοῦτο δῆλον, ὅτι
τῆς φιλοσοφίας ἐπικήρως διακειμένης καὶ φθονου-
μένης διὰ τοὺς τοιούτους τῶν λόγων ἔτι μᾶλλον
αὐτὴν μισήσουσιν.

[231] Ἢν οὖν ἐμοὶ πείθῃ, μάλιστα μὲν οὐ ποιήσει τοῦ
λοιποῦ πονηρὰς ὑποθέσεις, εἰ δὲ μή, τοιαῦτα ζητή-
σεις λέγειν ἐξ ὧν μήτ' αὐτὸς χείρων εἶναι δόξεις
μήτε τοὺς μιμουμένους λυμανεῖ μήτε τὴν περὶ τοὺς

ᵃ By " philosophy " Isocrates means τὴν περὶ τοὺς λόγους

crimes and an advocate should defend you in this fashion, what would be your state of mind ? I know very well that you would detest him more heartily than your accusers. And yet is it not disgraceful to compose for others a plea in defence of such kind that it would arouse your extreme anger if spoken on your own behalf ?

Again, consider this, and meditate upon it. If one of your pupils should be induced to do those things which you praise, would he not be the most wretched of men who are now alive and, in truth, of all who ever have lived ? Is it right, therefore, to compose discourses such that they will do the most good if they succeed in convincing no one among those who hear them ?

But perhaps you will say that you too were not unaware of all this but that you wished to bequeath to men of learning an example of how pleas in defence of shameful charges and difficult causes ought to be made. But I think it has now been made clear to you, even if you were previously in ignorance, that an accused person would sooner gain acquittal by not uttering a word than by pleading his cause in this way. And, furthermore, this too is evident, that philosophy,[a] which is already in mortal jeopardy and is hated, will be detested even more because of such discourses.

If, then, you will listen to me, you will preferably not deal in future with such base subjects, but if that cannot be, you will seek to speak of such things as will neither injure your own reputation, nor corrupt your imitators, nor bring the teaching of rhetoric

παίδευσιν of § 49, *fin.*—the training in, and cultivation of, the art of discourse.

50 λόγους παίδευσιν διαβαλεῖς. καὶ μὴ θαυμάσῃς, εἰ νεώτερος ὢν καὶ μηδέν σοι προσήκων οὕτω προχείρως ἐπιχειρῶ σε νουθετεῖν· ἡγοῦμαι γὰρ οὐ τῶν πρεσβυτάτων οὐδὲ τῶν οἰκειοτάτων, ἀλλὰ τῶν πλεῖστ᾽ εἰδότων καὶ βουλομένων ὠφελεῖν ἔργον εἶναι περὶ τῶν τοιούτων συμβουλεύειν.

into disrepute. And do not be astonished if I, who am younger than you and unrelated to you, essay so lightly to admonish you ; for, in my opinion, giving good counsel on such subjects is not the function of older men or of the most intimate friends, but of those who know most and desire most to render service.

XIV. PLATAICUS

INTRODUCTION

This speech is supposed to be spoken by a citizen of Plataea before the Ecclesia, or Assembly, of Athens. It is an eloquent plea to the Athenians for help against the Thebans, who in 373 B.C. had destroyed Plataea for the second time, and an appeal for aid in the restoration of the devastated town.

Plataea, a small city and district in southern Boeotia, had long been on very friendly terms with Athens. At Marathon the Plataeans, alone of all Greeks (*cf.* § 57), had fought against the Persians by the side of the Athenians.[a] In 427 B.C., after a long and desperate siege, Plataea was captured by the Thebans, the city destroyed, the citizens slain, and their territory given to the Thebans.[b] The survivors took refuge in Athens and were actually given the rights of citizenship by the Athenians.

In 386 B.C. Plataea was rebuilt by Sparta and the exiled Plataeans in considerable numbers returned. Inevitably they were regarded as allies by Sparta. In 377 or 376 B.C. Plataea was compelled to join the Boeotian Confederacy headed by the Thebans, who were destined to hold the hegemony of Greece for ten years. But the hatred of the Plataeans for the Thebans was so great that Diodorus (xv. 46) says

---

[a] See Isocrates, *Panath.* 93 and Herodotus vi. 108-111.
[b] Thucydides ii. 2.

that the Plataeans offered their city to Athens. In the year 373 B.C. (the date is probable, but not certain) the Thebans surprised the Plataeans, destroyed their town, and annexed their territory. Again, as in 427 B.C., the surviving Plataeans sought refuge at Athens.

The situation of the Plataeans was considered by the Athenian Assembly, but no help was offered and the restoration of their city at that time was not attempted. Years later, in 338 B.C., Philip of Macedon, enemy of Thebes, restored Plataea.

The date of the discourse falls between the capture of Plataea (373 B.C.) and the battle of Leuctra (371 B.C.). Mathieu [a] argues for the beginning of the year 371 B.C. and regards the *Plataicus* as a fictitious discourse, a work of democratic propaganda in favour of Athenian hegemony. Jebb [b] believes that it is a genuine work, written for a real occasion and for actual use.[c]

[a] *Isocrate* ii. p. 71 ; *cf.* Blass, *Die attische Beredsamkeit* ii. p. 265.
[b] *Attic Orators* ii. p. 176.
[c] So also does Grote.

14. ΠΛΑΤΑΙΚΟΣ

[296] Εἰδότες ὑμᾶς, ὦ ἄνδρες Ἀθηναῖοι, καὶ τοῖς
ἀδικουμένοις προθύμως βοηθεῖν εἰθισμένους καὶ
[297] τοῖς εὐεργέταις μεγίστην χάριν ἀποδιδόντας, ἥκομεν ἱκετεύσοντες μὴ περιδεῖν ἡμᾶς εἰρήνης οὔσης
ἀναστάτους ὑπὸ Θηβαίων γεγενημένους. πολλῶν
δ᾽ ἤδη πρὸς ὑμᾶς καταφυγόντων καὶ διαπραξα-
μένων ἅπανθ᾽ ὅσων ἐδεήθησαν, ἡγούμεθα μάλισθ᾽
ὑμῖν προσήκειν περὶ τῆς ἡμετέρας πόλεως ποιήσα-
2 σθαι πρόνοιαν· οὔτε γὰρ ἂν ἀδικώτερον οὐδένας
ἡμῶν εὕροιτε τηλικαύταις συμφοραῖς περιπεπτω-
κότας, οὔτ᾽ ἐκ πλείονος χρόνου πρὸς τὴν ὑμετέραν
πόλιν οἰκειότερον διακειμένους. ἔτι δὲ τοιούτων
δεησόμενοι πάρεσμεν ἐν οἷς κίνδυνος μὲν οὐδεὶς
ἔνεστιν, ἅπαντες δ᾽ ἄνθρωποι νομιοῦσιν ὑμᾶς πει-
θομένους ὁσιωτάτους καὶ δικαιοτάτους εἶναι τῶν
Ἑλλήνων.

3 Εἰ μὲν οὖν μὴ Θηβαίους ἑωρῶμεν ἐκ παντὸς
τρόπου παρεσκευασμένους πείθειν ὑμᾶς,[1] ὡς οὐδὲν
εἰς ἡμᾶς ἐξημαρτήκασι, διὰ βραχέων ἂν ἐποιησάμεθα τοὺς λόγους· ἐπειδὴ δ᾽ εἰς τοῦθ᾽ ἥκομεν ἀτυ-

---

[1] ὑμᾶς after πείθειν deleted, without good reason, by Blass.

XIV. PLATAICUS

SINCE we Plataeans know, Athenians, that it is your custom not only zealously to come to the rescue of victims of injustice, but also to requite your benefactors with the utmost gratitude, we have come as suppliants to beg you not to remain indifferent to our having been driven from our homes in time of peace by the Thebans. And since many peoples in the past have fled to you for protection and have obtained all they craved, we think it beseems you more than others to show solicitude for our city ; for victims of a greater injustice than ourselves, or any who have been plunged into calamities so great, you could not find anywhere, nor any people who for a longer time have maintained toward your city a more loyal friendship.[a] Furthermore, we have come here to ask you for assistance of such a kind that your granting it will involve you in no danger whatever and yet will cause all the world to regard you as the most scrupulous and most just of all the Greeks.

If we did not observe that the Thebans have schemed to win you over, by fair means or foul, to their contention that they have done us no wrong, we could have finished our plea in a few words. But since we have reached such a state of misfortune that

---

[a] *Cf.* Herodotus vi. 108. Athens and Plataea were allied as early as 510 B.C.

χίας ὥστε μὴ μόνον ἡμῖν εἶναι τὸν ἀγῶνα πρὸς
τούτους, ἀλλὰ καὶ τῶν ῥητόρων πρὸς τοὺς δυνα-
τωτάτους, οὓς ἀπὸ τῶν ἡμετέρων αὐτοῖς οὗτοι
παρεσκευάσαντο συνηγόρους, ἀναγκαῖον διὰ μακροτέρων δηλῶσαι περὶ αὐτῶν.

4 Χαλεπὸν μὲν οὖν μηδὲν καταδεέστερον εἰπεῖν ὧν
πεπόνθαμεν· ποῖος γὰρ ἂν λόγος ἐξισωθείη ταῖς
ἡμετέραις δυσπραξίαις, ἢ τίς ἂν ῥήτωρ ἱκανὸς
γένοιτο κατηγορῆσαι τῶν Θηβαίοις ἡμαρτημένων;
ὅμως δὲ πειρατέον οὕτως ὅπως ἂν δυνώμεθα
5 φανερὰν καταστῆσαι τὴν τούτων παρανομίαν. πολὺ
δὲ μάλιστ' ἀγανακτοῦμεν ὅτι τοσούτου δέομεν
τῶν ἴσων ἀξιοῦσθαι τοῖς ἄλλοις Ἕλλησιν, ὥστ'
εἰρήνης οὔσης καὶ συνθηκῶν γεγενημένων οὐχ
ὅπως τῆς κοινῆς ἐλευθερίας μετέχομεν, ἀλλ' οὐδὲ
δουλείας μετρίας τυχεῖν ἠξιώθημεν.

6 Δεόμεθ' οὖν ὑμῶν, ὦ ἄνδρες Ἀθηναῖοι, μετ'
εὐνοίας ἀκροάσασθαι τῶν λεγομένων, ἐνθυμηθέντας
ὅτι πάντων ἂν ἡμῖν ἀλογώτατον εἴη συμβεβηκός,
εἰ τοῖς μὲν ἅπαντα τὸν χρόνον δυσμενῶς πρὸς
τὴν πόλιν ὑμῶν διακειμένοις αἴτιοι γεγένησθε τῆς
ἐλευθερίας, ἡμεῖς δὲ μηδ' ἱκετεύοντες ὑμᾶς τῶν
αὐτῶν τοῖς ἐχθίστοις τύχοιμεν.

7 Περὶ μὲν οὖν τῶν γεγενημένων οὐκ οἶδ' ὅ τι δεῖ
[298] μακρολογεῖν· τίς γὰρ οὐκ οἶδεν ὅτι καὶ τὴν χώραν
ἡμῶν κατανενέμηνται καὶ τὴν πόλιν κατεσκάφασιν;
ἃ δὲ λέγοντες ἐλπίζουσιν ἐξαπατήσειν ὑμᾶς, περὶ
τούτων πειρασόμεθα διδάσκειν.

---

[a] Athenian venal advocates are meant.
[b] This seems to be a reference to the peace of 374 B.C.

we must struggle, not only against them, but also against the ablest of your orators, men whom they have hired with our resources to be their advocates,[a] we must explain our cause at greater length.

It is difficult indeed not to speak inadequately on the subject of our wrongs. For what eloquence could match our misfortunes, or what orator could adequately denounce the wrongs the Thebans have done? Nevertheless, we must try to the best of our ability to make their transgressions known. And the chief cause of our indignation is that we are so far from being judged worthy of equality with the rest of the Greeks that, although we are at peace [b] and although treaties exist, we not only have no share in the liberty which all the rest enjoy, but that we are not considered worthy of even a moderate condition of servitude.

We therefore beg of you, citizens of Athens, that you listen to our plea in a friendly spirit, reflecting that for us the most preposterous outcome of all would be, if those who have always been hostile to your city shall have regained their freedom through your efforts, but we, even when we supplicate you, should fail to obtain the same treatment as is accorded to your greatest enemies.

As for the events which have occurred in the past, I see no reason why I should speak of them at length. For who does not know that the Thebans have portioned out our land for pasturage and have razed our city to the ground? But it is with respect to their argument, by which they hope to deceive you, that we shall try to inform you.

made between Athens and Sparta (see Jebb, *Attic Orators* ii. p. 177).

8 Ἐνίοτε μὲν γὰρ ἐπιχειροῦσι λέγειν, ὡς διὰ τοῦτο
πρὸς ἡμᾶς οὕτω προσηνέχθησαν, ὅτι συντελεῖν
αὐτοῖς οὐκ ἠθέλομεν. ὑμεῖς δ' ἐνθυμεῖσθε πρῶτον
μὲν εἰ δίκαιόν ἐστιν ὑπὲρ τηλικούτων ἐγκλημάτων
οὕτως ἀνόμους καὶ δεινὰς ποιεῖσθαι τὰς τιμωρίας,
ἔπειτ' εἰ προσήκειν ὑμῖν δοκεῖ μὴ πεισθεῖσαν τὴν
Πλαταιέων πόλιν, ἀλλὰ βιασθεῖσαν Θηβαίοις συντελεῖν. ἐγὼ μὲν γὰρ οὐδένας ἡγοῦμαι τολμηροτέρους
εἶναι τούτων, οἵτινες τὰς μὲν ἰδίας ἡμῶν ἑκάστων
πόλεις ἀφανίζουσι, τῆς δὲ σφετέρας αὐτῶν πολιτείας οὐδὲν δεομένους κοινωνεῖν ἀναγκάζουσιν.
9 πρὸς δὲ τούτοις οὐδ' ὁμολογούμενα φαίνονται δια-
πραττόμενοι πρός τε τοὺς ἄλλους καὶ πρὸς ἡμᾶς.
ἐχρῆν γὰρ αὐτούς, ἐπειδὴ πείθειν ἡμῶν τὴν πόλιν
οὐχ οἷοί τ' ἦσαν, ὥσπερ τοὺς Θεσπιέας καὶ τοὺς
Ταναγραίους, συντελεῖν μόνον εἰς τὰς Θήβας ἀναγ-
κάζειν· οὐδὲν γὰρ ἂν τῶν ἀνηκέστων κακῶν ἦμεν
πεπονθότες. νῦν δὲ φανεροὶ γεγόνασιν οὐ τοῦτο
διαπράξασθαι βουληθέντες, ἀλλὰ τῆς χώρας ἡμῶν
10 ἐπιθυμήσαντες. θαυμάζω δὲ πρὸς τί τῶν γεγενημένων ἀναφέροντες καὶ πῶς ποτε τὸ δίκαιον
κρίνοντες ταῦτα φήσουσι προστάττειν ἡμῖν. εἰ μὲν
γὰρ τὰ πάτρια σκοποῦσιν, οὐ τῶν ἄλλων αὐτοῖς
ἀρκτέον, ἀλλὰ πολὺ μᾶλλον Ὀρχομενίοις φόρον
οἰστέον· οὕτω γὰρ εἶχε τὸ παλαιόν· εἰ δὲ τὰς
συνθήκας ἀξιοῦσιν εἶναι κυρίας, ὅπερ ἐστὶ δίκαιον,
πῶς οὐχ ὁμολογήσουσιν ἀδικεῖν καὶ παραβαίνειν

---

[a] That is, to join the Boeotian Confederation, of which
Thebes held the hegemony, and thus to be tributary (συντελεῖν) to the Thebans.
[b] Orchomenus, stronghold of the Minyans in prehistoric

At times, you know, they attempt to maintain that they have subjected us to this treatment because we were unwilling to be members of their federation.[a] But I ask you to consider, first, if on such grounds it is just to inflict penalties so contrary to justice and so cruel ; next, if it seems to you consistent with the dignity of the city of the Plataeans, without their consent but under compulsion, to accept such dependence under the Thebans. For my part, I consider that there exists no people more overbearing than those who blot out the cities of each of us and compel us, when we have no use for it, to participate in their form of polity. Besides this, they are clearly inconsistent in their dealings with others and with us. For when they were unable to gain our consent, they should have gone no farther than to compel us to submit to the hegemony of Thebes as they compelled Thespiae and Tanagra ; for in that case we should not have suffered irremediable misfortunes. But as it is, they have made it clear that it was not their intention to give us that status ; on the contrary, it was our territory they coveted. I wonder to what precedent in the past they will appeal, and what conceivable interpretation of justice they will give, when they admit that they dictate to us in such matters. For if it is to our ancestral customs they look, they ought not to be ruling over our other cities, but far rather to be paying tribute to the Orchomenians[b] ; for such was the case in ancient times. And if they hold that the treaties are valid, which indeed in justice they should be, how can they avoid admitting that they are guilty of wrong and are violating them ?

times, joined the Boeotian Confederacy after the battle of Leuctra, 371 B.C.

αὐτάς· ὁμοίως γὰρ τάς τε μικρὰς τῶν πόλεων καὶ
τὰς μεγάλας αὐτονόμους εἶναι κελεύουσιν.

11 Οἶμαι δὲ περὶ μὲν τούτων οὐ τολμήσειν αὐτοὺς
ἀναισχυντεῖν, ἐπ' ἐκεῖνον δὲ τρέψεσθαι τὸν λόγον,
ὡς μετὰ Λακεδαιμονίων ἐπολεμοῦμεν, καὶ πάσῃ τῇ
συμμαχίᾳ διαφθείραντες ἡμᾶς τὰ συμφέροντα πε-
12 ποιήκασιν. ἐγὼ δ' ἡγοῦμαι μὲν χρῆναι μηδεμίαν
[299] μήτ' αἰτίαν μήτε κατηγορίαν μεῖζον δύνασθαι τῶν
ὅρκων καὶ τῶν συνθηκῶν· οὐ μὴν ἀλλ' εἰ δεῖ τινὰς
κακῶς παθεῖν διὰ τὴν Λακεδαιμονίων συμμαχίαν,
οὐκ ἂν Πλαταιεῖς ἐξ ἁπάντων τῶν Ἑλλήνων
προὐκρίθησαν δικαίως· οὐ γὰρ ἑκόντες, ἀλλ' ἀναγ-
13 κασθέντες αὐτοῖς ἐδουλεύομεν. τίς γὰρ ἂν πιστεύσειεν εἰς τοῦθ' ἡμᾶς ἀνοίας ἐλθεῖν ὥστε περὶ
πλείονος ποιήσασθαι τοὺς ἐξανδραποδισαμένους
ἡμῶν τὴν πατρίδα μᾶλλον ἢ τοὺς τῆς πόλεως τῆς
αὐτῶν μεταδόντας; ἀλλὰ γάρ, οἶμαι, χαλεπὸν ἦν
νεωτερίζειν αὐτοὺς μὲν μικρὰν πόλιν οἰκοῦντας,
ἐκείνων δ' οὕτω μεγάλην δύναμιν κεκτημένων, ἔτι
δὲ πρὸς τούτοις ἁρμοστοῦ καθεστῶτος καὶ φρου-
ρᾶς ἐνούσης καὶ τηλικούτου στρατεύματος ὄντος
4 Θεσπιᾶσιν, ὑφ' ὧν οὐ μόνον ἂν θᾶττον ἢ Θηβαίων
διεφθάρημεν, ἀλλὰ καὶ δικαιότερον· τούτους μὲν
γὰρ εἰρήνης οὔσης οὐ προσῆκε μνησικακεῖν περὶ
τῶν τότε γεγενημένων, ἐκεῖνοι δ' ἐν τῷ πολέμῳ
προδοθέντες εἰκότως ἂν παρ' ἡμῶν τὴν μεγίστην

---

[a] Evidently a reference to the Second Athenian Confederacy, organized in 377 B.C. and directed against Sparta. *Cf.*
p. 147.

[b] That is, the Athenians; see Introduction.

[c] *Cf.* Xenophon, *Hell.* v. 4. 13-22. Cleombrotus, king of

For these treaties direct that our cities, the small as well as the large, shall all alike be autonomous.

But I imagine that on the subject of the treaties they will not venture to show their impudence, but will resort to the argument that we were taking the side of the Lacedaemonians in the war and that by destroying us they have benefited the entire confederacy.[a] In my opinion, however, no complaint and no accusation should have greater validity than the oaths and the treaties. Nevertheless, if any people are to suffer because of their alliance with the Lacedaemonians, it was not the Plataeans who, of all the Greeks, if justice were done, would have been selected ; for it was not of our own free will, but under compulsion, that we were subservient to the Lacedaemonians. Why, who could believe that we had reached such a degree of folly as to have valued more highly a people who reduced our fatherland to slavery than the people who had given us a share in their own city ?[b] No indeed, but it was difficult for us to attempt a revolt when we had so small a city ourselves and the Lacedaemonians possessed power so great, and when besides a Spartan governor occupied it with a garrison, and also a large army was stationed at Thespiae,[c] of such strength that we should have been destroyed by it not only more quickly than by the Thebans, but also with greater right. For it was not fitting that the Thebans in time of peace should harbour a grudge against us for what happened at that time, whereas the Lacedaemonians, if they had been betrayed by us during the war, with good reason would have punished us

Sparta, in the beginning of 378 B.C., occupied Plataea and Thespiae. Sphodrias was the governor or *harmost*.

15 δίκην ἐλάμβανον. ἡγοῦμαι δ' ὑμᾶς οὐκ ἀγνοεῖν ὅτι πολλοὶ καὶ τῶν ἄλλων Ἑλλήνων τοῖς μὲν σώμασι μετ' ἐκείνων ἀκολουθεῖν ἠναγκάζοντο, ταῖς δ' εὐνοίαις μεθ' ὑμῶν ἦσαν. οὓς τίνα χρὴ προσδοκᾶν γνώμην ἕξειν, ἢν ἀκούσωσιν ὅτι Θηβαῖοι τὸν δῆμον τὸν Ἀθηναίων πεπείκασιν ὡς οὐδενός ἐστι φειστέον τῶν ὑπὸ Λακεδαιμονίοις γενομένων;

16 ὁ γὰρ τούτων λόγος οὐδὲν ἄλλ' ἢ τοῦτο φανήσεται δυνάμενος· οὐ γὰρ ἰδίαν κατηγορίαν ποιούμενοι κατὰ τῆς πόλεως τῆς ἡμετέρας ἀπολωλέκασιν αὐτήν, ἀλλ' ἣν ὁμοίως καὶ κατ' ἐκείνων ἕξουσιν εἰπεῖν. ὑπὲρ ὧν βουλεύεσθαι χρὴ καὶ σκοπεῖν, ὅπως μὴ τοὺς πρότερον μισοῦντας τὴν ἀρχὴν τὴν Λακεδαιμονίων ἡ τούτων ὕβρις διαλλάξει καὶ ποιήσει τὴν ἐκείνων συμμαχίαν αὐτῶν νομίζειν εἶναι σωτηρίαν.

17 Ἐνθυμεῖσθε δ' ὅτι τὸν πόλεμον ἀνείλεσθε τὸν ὑπογυιότατον οὐχ ὑπὲρ τῆς ὑμετέρας οὐδ' ὑπὲρ τῆς τῶν συμμάχων ἐλευθερίας, ἅπασι γὰρ ὑπῆρχεν ὑμῖν, ἀλλ' ὑπὲρ τῶν παρὰ τοὺς ὅρκους καὶ τὰς συνθήκας τῆς αὐτονομίας ἀποστερουμένων. ὃ δὴ καὶ πάντων σχετλιώτατον, εἰ τὰς πόλεις ἃς οὐκ [300] ᾤεσθε δεῖν Λακεδαιμονίοις δουλεύειν, ταύτας περιόψεσθε νῦν ὑπὸ Θηβαίων ἀπολλυμένας· οἳ τοσούτου δέουσι μιμεῖσθαι τὴν πραότητα τὴν ὑμετέραν,

18 ὥσθ' ὃ δοκεῖ πάντων δεινότατον εἶναι, δοριαλώτους γενέσθαι, τοῦτο κρεῖττον ἦν ἡμῖν παθεῖν ὑπὸ ταύτης τῆς πόλεως ἢ τούτων τυχεῖν ὁμόρους ὄντας. οἱ μὲν γὰρ ὑφ' ὑμῶν κατὰ κράτος ἁλόντες εὐθὺς

_____
ᵃ 378–374 B.C.

144

most severely. And I think that you are not unaware that many other Greeks, although with their bodies they were compelled to follow the Lacedaemonians, yet in sympathy they were on your side. What conclusion must we suppose that these others will reach, if they hear that the Thebans have persuaded the Athenian people that none ought to be spared who have been subject to the Lacedaemonians ? For it will be clearly evident that the Thebans' argument has no other meaning ; since it is no accusation against our city in particular that has led them to destroy it but, on the contrary, they will be able to bring that same charge also against those others. These are matters which demand your deliberation and concern, lest the overbearing ways of the Thebans shall reconcile those who formerly hated the rule of the Lacedaemonians and cause them to believe that the alliance with them is their own salvation.

Remember also that you undertook your most recent war,[a] not to secure the freedom of either yourselves or your allies (for you all enjoyed that already), but in behalf of those who were being deprived of their autonomy in violation of the oaths and covenants. But surely it would be the most outrageous thing in the world, if you are going to permit these cities, which you thought ought not to be in servitude to the Lacedaemonians, now to be destroyed by the Thebans—men who are so far from emulating your clemency that it would have been better for us to suffer at the hands of this city that fate which is regarded as the most dreadful of all misfortunes, to be taken prisoners of war, than to have got them as neighbours ; for those whose cities were taken by you by storm were straightway

μὲν ἁρμοστοῦ καὶ δουλείας ἀπηλλάγησαν, νῦν δὲ
τοῦ συνεδρίου καὶ τῆς ἐλευθερίας μετέχουσιν· οἱ
δὲ τούτων πλησίον οἰκοῦντες οἱ μὲν οὐδὲν ἧττον
τῶν ἀργυρωνήτων δουλεύουσι, τοὺς δ' οὐ πρότερον
παύσονται πρὶν ἂν οὕτως ὥσπερ ἡμᾶς διαθῶσιν.
19 καὶ Λακεδαιμονίων μὲν κατηγοροῦσιν, ὅτι τὴν
Καδμείαν κατέλαβον καὶ φρουρὰς εἰς τὰς πόλεις
καθίστασαν, αὐτοὶ δ' οὐ φύλακας εἰσπέμποντες,
ἀλλὰ τῶν μὲν τὰ τείχη κατασκάπτοντες, τοὺς δ'
ἄρδην ἀπολλύοντες οὐδὲν οἴονται δεινὸν ποιεῖν, ἀλλ'
εἰς τοῦτ' ἀναισχυντίας ἐληλύθασιν, ὥστε τῆς μὲν
αὐτῶν σωτηρίας τοὺς συμμάχους ἅπαντας ἀξιοῦσιν
ἐπιμελεῖσθαι, τῆς δὲ τῶν ἄλλων δουλείας αὐτοὺς
20 κυρίους καθιστᾶσιν. καίτοι τίς οὐκ ἂν μισήσειε
τὴν τούτων πλεονεξίαν, οἳ τῶν μὲν ἀσθενεστέρων
ἄρχειν ζητοῦσι, τοῖς δὲ κρείττοσιν ἴσον ἔχειν
οἴονται δεῖν, καὶ τῇ μὲν ὑμετέρᾳ πόλει τῆς γῆς
τῆς ὑπ' Ὠρωπίων δεδομένης φθονοῦσιν, αὐτοὶ δὲ
βίᾳ τὴν ἀλλοτρίαν χώραν κατανέμονται;
21 Καὶ πρὸς τοῖς ἄλλοις κακοῖς λέγουσιν ὡς ὑπὲρ
τοῦ κοινοῦ τῶν συμμάχων ταῦτ' ἔπραξαν. καίτοι
χρῆν αὐτούς, ὄντος ἐνθάδε συνεδρίου καὶ τῆς ὑμετέρας πόλεως ἄμεινον βουλεύεσθαι δυναμένης ἢ τῆς
Θηβαίων, οὐχ ὑπὲρ τῶν πεπραγμένων ἥκειν ἀπο-
λογησομένους, ἀλλὰ πρὶν ποιῆσαί τι τούτων ἐλθεῖν
22 ὡς ὑμᾶς βουλευσομένους. νῦν δὲ τὰς μὲν οὐσίας

---

[a] Oropus, a town on the frontier between Attica and
Boeotia, was long a bone of contention. In 412 B.C. it was
treacherously taken by Thebes (Thucydides viii. 60); at
some time after 402 B.C. it was under Athenian protection;
in 366 B.C. Oropus was again seized by Thebes, but in
338 B.C. Philip gave the town to Athens.

freed of a Spartan governor and of slavery, and now they have share in a Council and in freedom, whereas, of those who live anywhere near the Thebans, some are no less slaves than those who have been bought with money, and as for the rest, the Thebans will not stop until they have brought them to the condition in which we now are. They accuse the Lacedaemonians because they occupied the Cadmea and established garrisons in their cities, yet they themselves, not sending garrisons, but razing the walls of some and entirely destroying others, think they have committed no atrocity; nay, they have come to such a pitch of shamelessness that while they demand that all their allies should be guardians of the safety of Thebes, yet they arrogate to themselves the right to impose slavery upon everybody else. And yet what man would not detest the greedy spirit of these Thebans, who seek to rule the weaker, but think they must be on terms of equality with the stronger and who begrudge your city the territory ceded by the Oropians,[a] yet themselves forcibly seize and portion out territory not their own?

And not content with their other base misrepresentations, they now say that they pursued this course for the common good of the allies. And yet what they ought to have done, inasmuch as there is an Hellenic Council[b] here and your city is more competent than Thebes to advise prudent measures, is, not to be here now to defend the acts they have already committed, but to have come to you for consultation before they took any such action. But as it

[b] Athens' Second Confederacy, organized in 377 B.C. For this Council cf. § 18 above.

τὰς ἡμετέρας ἰδίᾳ διηρπάκασι, τῆς δὲ διαβολῆς
ἅπασι τοῖς συμμάχοις ἥκουσι μεταδώσοντες. ἢν
ὑμεῖς, ἢν σωφρονῆτε, φυλάξεσθε· πολὺ γὰρ κάλλιον τούτους ἀναγκάσαι μιμήσασθαι τὴν ὁσιότητα
τὴν ὑμετέραν ἢ τῆς τούτων παρανομίας αὐτοὺς
πεισθῆναι μετασχεῖν, οἳ μηδὲν τῶν αὐτῶν τοῖς
23 ἄλλοις γιγνώσκουσιν. οἶμαι γὰρ ἅπασι φανερὸν
[301] εἶναι διότι προσήκει τοὺς εὖ φρονοῦντας ἐν μὲν τῷ
πολέμῳ σκοπεῖν ὅπως ἐκ παντὸς τρόπου πλέον
ἕξουσι τῶν ἐχθρῶν, ἐπειδὰν δ' εἰρήνη γένηται, μηδὲν περὶ πλείονος ποιεῖσθαι τῶν ὅρκων καὶ τῶν
24 συνθηκῶν. οὗτοι δὲ τότε μὲν ἐν ἁπάσαις ταῖς πρεσ-
βείαις ὑπὲρ τῆς ἐλευθερίας καὶ τῆς αὐτονομίας
ἐποιοῦντο τοὺς λόγους· ἐπειδὴ δὲ νομίζουσιν αὐτοῖς
ἄδειαν γεγενῆσθαι, πάντων τῶν ἄλλων ἀμελήσαντες
ὑπὲρ τῶν ἰδίων κερδῶν καὶ τῆς αὐτῶν βίας λέγειν
25 τολμῶσι, καὶ φασὶ τὸ Θηβαίους ἔχειν τὴν ἡμετέραν, τοῦτο συμφέρον εἶναι τοῖς συμμάχοις, κακῶς
εἰδότες ὡς οὐδ' αὐτοῖς τοῖς παρὰ τὸ δίκαιον πλεο-
νεκτοῦσιν οὐδὲ πώποτε συνήνεγκεν, ἀλλὰ πολλοὶ
δὴ τῆς ἀλλοτρίας ἀδίκως ἐπιθυμήσαντες περὶ
τῆς αὐτῶν δικαίως εἰς τοὺς μεγίστους κινδύνους
κατέστησαν.

26 Ἀλλὰ μὴν οὐδ' ἐκεῖνό γ' ἕξουσι λέγειν, ὡς αὐτοὶ
μέν, μεθ' ὧν ἂν γένωνται, πιστοὶ διατελοῦσιν
ὄντες, ἡμᾶς δ' ἄξιον φοβεῖσθαι, μὴ κομισάμενοι
τὴν χώραν πρὸς Λακεδαιμονίους ἀποστῶμεν· εὑρήσετε γὰρ ἡμᾶς μὲν δὶς ἐκπεπολιορκημένους ὑπὲρ
τῆς φιλίας τῆς ὑμετέρας, τούτους δὲ πολλάκις εἰς

ᵃ By the Thebans in 427 (Thucydides iii. 52) and again
in 373 B.C.

is, having now pillaged our possessions, acting alone, they have come here to give a share of their disrepute to all their allies. And that disrepute, if you are wise, you will shun, since it is far more honourable to compel them to emulate your scrupulousness than that you allow yourselves to be persuaded to share in the lawlessness of these people, whose principles are wholly alien to those of the rest of mankind. For I presume that it is clear to all that it is incumbent upon the wise, in time of war to strive in every way to get the better of the enemy, but when peace is made, to regard nothing as of greater importance than their oaths and their covenants. The Thebans, however, in the former circumstances, in all their embassies would plead the cause of " freedom " and " independence "; but now that they believe they have secured licence for themselves, disregarding everything else, they have the effrontery to speak in defence of their private gain and of their own acts of violence, and they assert that it is to the advantage of their allies that the Thebans should have our country—fools that they are, not to know that no advantage ever accrues to those who unjustly seek greedy gain; on the contrary, many a people that have unjustly coveted the territory of others have with justice brought into the greatest jeopardy their own.

But one thing the Thebans will not be able to say —that they remain loyal to their associates, though there is reason to fear that we, having recovered our country, will desert to the Lacedaemonians ; for you will find, Athenians, that we have twice been besieged *a* and forced to surrender because of our friendship for you, while the Thebans often have

27 ταύτην τὴν πόλιν ἐξημαρτηκότας. καὶ τὰς μὲν
παλαιὰς προδοσίας πολὺ ἂν ἔργον εἴη λέγειν· γενο-
μένου δὲ τοῦ Κορινθιακοῦ πολέμου διὰ τὴν ὕβριν
τὴν τούτων, καὶ Λακεδαιμονίων μὲν ἐπ' αὐτοὺς
στρατευσάντων, δι' ὑμᾶς δὲ σωθέντες οὐχ ὅπως
τούτων χάριν ἀπέδοσαν, ἀλλ' ἐπειδὴ διελέλυσθε[1]
τὸν πόλεμον, ἀπολιπόντες ὑμᾶς εἰς τὴν Λακεδαι-
28 μονίων συμμαχίαν εἰσῆλθον. καὶ Χῖοι μὲν καὶ
Μυτιληναῖοι καὶ Βυζάντιοι συμπαρέμειναν, οὗτοι
δὲ τηλικαύτην πόλιν οἰκοῦντες οὐδὲ κοινοὺς σφᾶς
αὐτοὺς παρασχεῖν ἐτόλμησαν, ἀλλ' εἰς τοῦτ' ἀν-
ανδρίας καὶ πονηρίας ἦλθον, ὥστ' ὤμοσαν ἦ μὴν
ἀκολουθήσειν μετ' ἐκείνων ἐφ' ὑμᾶς τοὺς διασώ-
σαντας τὴν πόλιν αὐτῶν· ὑπὲρ ὧν δόντες τοῖς θεοῖς
δίκην καὶ τῆς Καδμείας καταληφθείσης ἠναγκάσθησαν ἐνθάδε καταφυγεῖν. ὅθεν καὶ μάλιστ'
29 ἐπεδείξαντο τὴν αὐτῶν ἀπιστίαν· σωθέντες γὰρ
πάλιν διὰ τῆς ὑμετέρας δυνάμεως καὶ κατελθόντες
[302] εἰς τὴν αὐτῶν οὐδένα χρόνον ἐνέμειναν, ἀλλ' εὐθὺς
εἰς Λακεδαίμονα πρέσβεις ἀπέστελλον, ἕτοιμοι δουλεύειν ὄντες καὶ μηδὲν κινεῖν τῶν πρότερον πρὸς
αὐτοὺς ὡμολογημένων. καὶ τί δεῖ μακρολογεῖν;
εἰ γὰρ μὴ προσέταττον ἐκεῖνοι τούς τε φεύγοντας
καταδέχεσθαι καὶ τοὺς αὐτόχειρας ἐξείργειν, οὐδὲν
ἂν ἐκώλυεν αὐτοὺς μετὰ τῶν ἠδικηκότων ἐφ' ὑμᾶς
τοὺς εὐεργέτας στρατεύεσθαι.

30 Καὶ τοιοῦτοι μὲν νεωστὶ περὶ τὴν πόλιν τήνδε
γεγενημένοι, τὸ δὲ παλαιὸν ἁπάσης τῆς Ἑλλάδος
προδόται καταστάντες, αὐτοὶ μὲν ὑπὲρ οὕτως ἑκου-

---

[1] διελέλυσθε Γ: διελύσασθε Ε: διελύεσθε Priscian, read by
Blass.

wronged this city. It would be a laborious task to
recount their treacheries in the past, but when the
Corinthian war broke out because of their overbearing conduct and the Lacedaemonians had marched
against them, although the Thebans had been saved
by you, they were so far from showing their gratitude
for this service that, when you had put an end to
the war, they abandoned you and entered into the
alliance with the Lacedaemonians. The people of
Chios, of Mytilenê, and of Byzantium remained loyal,
but the Thebans, although they dwelt in a city of
such importance, did not have the fortitude even to
remain neutral, but were guilty of such cowardice
and baseness as to give their solemn oath to join the
Lacedaemonians in attacking you, the saviours of
their city. For this they were punished by the gods,
and, after the Cadmea was captured, they were
forced to take refuge here in Athens. By this they
furnished the crowning proof of their perfidy ; for
when they had again been saved by your power and
were restored to their city, they did not remain
faithful for a single instant, but immediately sent
ambassadors to Lacedaemon, showing themselves
ready to be slaves and to alter in no respect their
former agreements with Sparta. Why need I speak
at greater length ? For if the Lacedaemonians had
not ordered them to take back their exiles and exclude the murderers, nothing would have hindered
them from taking the field as allies of those who had
injured them, against you their benefactors.

And these Thebans, who have recently behaved
in such fashion toward your city and in times past
have been guilty of betraying Greece as a whole,[a]

_____
[a] In the Persian Wars.

σίων καὶ μεγάλων ἀδικημάτων συγγνώμης τυχεῖν
ἠξιώθησαν, ἡμῖν δ' ὑπὲρ ὧν ἠναγκάσθημεν, οὐδεμίαν ἔχειν οἴονται δεῖν, ἀλλὰ τολμῶσιν ὄντες
Θηβαῖοι λακωνισμὸν ἑτέροις ὀνειδίζειν, οὓς πάντες
ἴσμεν πλεῖστον χρόνον Λακεδαιμονίοις δεδουλευ-
κότας καὶ προθυμότερον ὑπὲρ τῆς ἐκείνων ἀρχῆς
31 ἢ τῆς αὑτῶν σωτηρίας πεπολεμηκότας. ποίας γὰρ
εἰσβολῆς ἀπελείφθησαν τῶν εἰς ταύτην τὴν χώραν
γεγενημένων; ἢ τίνων οὐκ ἐχθίους ὑμῖν καὶ δυσ-
μενέστεροι διετέλεσαν ὄντες; οὐκ ἐν τῷ Δεκελεικῷ
πολέμῳ πλειόνων αἴτιοι κακῶν ἐγένοντο τῶν ἄλλων τῶν συνεισβαλόντων; οὐ δυστυχησάντων ὑμῶν
μόνοι τῶν συμμάχων ἔθεντο τὴν ψῆφον, ὡς χρὴ
τήν τε πόλιν ἐξανδραποδίσασθαι καὶ τὴν χώραν
ἀνεῖναι μηλόβοτον ὥσπερ τὸ Κρισαῖον πεδίον;
32 ὥστ' εἰ Λακεδαιμόνιοι τὴν αὐτὴν γνώμην ἔσχον
Θηβαίοις, οὐδὲν ἂν ἐκώλυε τοὺς ἅπασι τοῖς Ἕλλησιν αἰτίους τῆς σωτηρίας γενομένους αὐτοὺς
ὑπὸ τῶν Ἑλλήνων ἐξανδραποδισθῆναι καὶ ταῖς
μεγίσταις συμφοραῖς περιπεσεῖν. καίτοι τίνα τηλικαύτην εὐεργεσίαν ἔχοιεν ἂν εἰπεῖν, ἥτις ἱκανὴ
γενήσεται διαλῦσαι τὴν ἔχθραν τὴν ἐκ τούτων
δικαίως ἂν ὑπάρχουσαν πρὸς αὐτούς;
33 Τούτοις μὲν οὖν οὐδεὶς λόγος ὑπολείπεται τηλικαῦτα τὸ μέγεθος ἐξημαρτηκόσι, τοῖς δὲ συναγο-

---

ᵃ The Decelean War is the name given to the latter part
(413–404 B.C.) of the Peloponnesian War when a Spartan
force occupied the Attic post, Decelea, in 413 B.C.

ᵇ A reference to the Athenian naval defeat at Aegospotami, in 405 B.C.

ᶜ This is an exaggeration ; not only the Thebans, but
the Corinthians and other Peloponnesians, voted for the

have seen fit to demand for themselves forgiveness
for their evil deeds willingly committed and so mon-
strous, yet to us, for acts done under compulsion,
they think no mercy ought to be shown, but they,
true Thebans as they are, have the effrontery to
reproach others for siding with the Lacedaemonians,
when they, as we all know, have for the longest
time been in servitude to them and have fought
more zealously for Spartan domination than for their
own security ! In what invasion into your country
of all that have ever been made have they failed to
take part ? Who, more consistently than they, have
been your enemies and ill-wishers ? In the Decelean
War [a] were they not authors of more mischief than
the other invaders ? When misfortune befell you,[b]
did not they alone of the allies [c] vote that your city
should be reduced to slavery and its territory be
abandoned to pasturage as was the plain of Crisa,[d]
so that if the Lacedaemonians had been of the same
opinion as the Thebans, there would have been
nothing to prevent the authors of the salvation of
all the Greeks [e] from being themselves enslaved by
the Greeks and from plunging into the most grievous
misfortunes ? And yet what benefaction of their own
could they adduce great enough to wipe out the
hatred caused by these wrongs which you would
justly feel toward them ?

Accordingly, to these Thebans no plea is left, such
is the magnitude of their crimes, and to those who

destruction of Athens, but Sparta refused; *cf.* Xenophon,
Hell. ii. 2. 19-20.
   [d] After the first Sacred War, at the end of the sixth century B.C., the plain of Crisa, between Delphi and the Corinthian Gulf, was declared holy ground and was dedicated
to Apollo.   [e] In the Persian Wars.

ρεύειν βουλομένοις ἐκεῖνος μόνος, ὡς νῦν μὲν ἡ
Βοιωτία προπολεμεῖ τῆς ὑμετέρας χώρας, ἢν δὲ
διαλύσησθε τὴν πρὸς τούτους φιλίαν, ἀσύμφορα
τοῖς συμμάχοις διαπράξεσθε· μεγάλην γὰρ ἔσεσθαι
τὴν ῥοπήν, εἰ μετὰ Λακεδαιμονίων ἢ τούτων
34 γενήσεται πόλις. ἐγὼ δ' οὔτε τοῖς συμμάχοις
[303] ἡγοῦμαι λυσιτελεῖν τοὺς ἀσθενεστέρους τοῖς κρείτ-
τοσι δουλεύειν, καὶ γὰρ τὸν παρελθόντα χρόνον
ὑπὲρ τούτων ἐπολεμήσαμεν, οὔτε Θηβαίους εἰς
τοῦτο μανίας ἥξειν ὥστ' ἀποστάντας τῆς συμμαχίας Λακεδαιμονίοις ἐνδώσειν τὴν πόλιν, οὐχ ὡς
πιστεύων τοῖς τούτων ἤθεσιν, ἀλλ' οἶδ' ὅτι γιγνώσκουσιν ὡς δυοῖν θάτερον ἀναγκαῖόν ἐστιν αὐτοῖς,
ἢ μένοντας ἀποθνήσκειν καὶ πάσχειν οἶά περ
ἐποίησαν, ἢ φεύγοντας ἀπορεῖν καὶ τῶν ἐλπίδων
ἁπασῶν ἐστερῆσθαι.

35 Πότερα γὰρ τὰ πρὸς τοὺς πολίτας αὐτοῖς ἔχει
καλῶς, ὧν τοὺς μὲν ἀποκτείναντες, τοὺς δ' ἐκ τῆς
πόλεως ἐκβαλόντες διηρπάκασι τὰς οὐσίας, ἢ τὰ
πρὸς τοὺς ἄλλους Βοιωτούς, ὧν οὐκ ἄρχειν μόνον
ἀδίκως ἐπιχειροῦσιν, ἀλλὰ τῶν μὲν τὰ τείχη κατ-
εσκάφασι, τῶν δὲ καὶ τὴν χώραν ἀπεστερήκασιν;
36 ἀλλὰ μὴν οὐδ' ἐπὶ τὴν ὑμετέραν πόλιν οἶόν τ' αὐτοῖς ἐπανελθεῖν ἐστίν, ἢν οὕτω συνεχῶς φανήσονται
προδιδόντες. ὥστ' οὐκ ἔστιν ὅπως βουλήσονται
πρὸς ὑμᾶς ὑπὲρ τῆς ἀλλοτρίας διενεχθέντες τὴν
αὑτῶν πόλιν οὕτως εἰκῇ καὶ προδήλως ἀποβαλεῖν,
ἀλλὰ πολὺ κοσμιώτερον διακείσονται πρὸς ἁπάσας
τὰς πράξεις, καὶ τοσούτῳ πλείω ποιήσονται θερα-

ᵃ That is, Plataea.

wish to speak on their behalf only this—that Boeotia is now fighting in defence of your country, and that, if you put an end to your friendship with them, you will be acting to the detriment of your allies; for it will be a matter of great consequence if the city of Thebes takes the side of the Lacedaemonians. My opinion is, however, that it is neither profitable to the allies that the weaker should be in servitude to the stronger (in past times, in fact, we went to war to protect the weak), nor that the Thebans will be so mad as to desert the alliance and hand over their city to the Lacedaemonians; this is not because I have confidence in the character of the Thebans, but because I know that they are well aware that one of two fates necessarily awaits them—either resisting, to die and to suffer such cruelties as they have inflicted, or else, going into exile, to be in want and deprived of all their hopes.

Well then, are their relations with their fellow-citizens agreeable, some of whom they have put to death and others they have banished and robbed of their property? Or are they on friendly terms with the other Boeotians, whom they not only attempt to rule without warrant of justice, but have also in some instances razed their walls and have dispossessed others of their territory? But assuredly they cannot again take refuge in your city either, Athenians, the city which they will be discovered to have so consistently betrayed. It is inconceivable, therefore, that they will care to get into a quarrel with you over an alien city *a* and on that account so rashly and so inevitably to lose their own; on the contrary, in all their dealings with you they will behave in much more seemly fashion, and the more they fear for

πείαν ὑμῶν, ὅσῳ περ ἂν μᾶλλον περὶ σφῶν αὐτῶν
37 δεδίωσιν. ἐπεδείξαντο δ' ὑμῖν ὡς χρὴ τῇ φύσει
χρῆσθαι τῇ τούτων ἐξ ὧν ἔπραξαν περὶ Ὠρωπόν·
ὅτε μὲν γὰρ ἐξουσίαν ἤλπισαν αὐτοῖς ἔσεσθαι
ποιεῖν, ὅ τι ἂν βουληθῶσιν, οὐχ ὡς συμμάχοις
ὑμῖν προσηνέχθησαν, ἀλλ' ἅπερ ἂν εἰς τοὺς πολε-
μιωτάτους ἐξαμαρτεῖν ἐτόλμησαν· ἐπειδὴ δ' ἐκ-
σπόνδους αὐτοὺς ἀντὶ τούτων ἐψηφίσασθε ποιῆσαι,
παυσάμενοι τῶν φρονημάτων ἦλθον ὡς ὑμᾶς τα-
πεινότερον διατεθέντες ἢ νῦν ἡμεῖς τυγχάνομεν
38 ἔχοντες. ὥστ' ἤν τινες ὑμᾶς ἐκφοβῶσι τῶν ῥητόρων ὡς κίνδυνός ἐστι, μὴ μεταβάλωνται καὶ
γένωνται μετὰ τῶν πολεμίων, οὐ χρὴ πιστεύειν·
τοιαῦται γὰρ αὐτοὺς ἀνάγκαι κατειλήφασιν, ὥστε
πολὺ ἂν θᾶττον τὴν ὑμετέραν ἀρχὴν ἢ τὴν Λακεδαιμονίων συμμαχίαν ὑπομείναιεν.
39 Εἰ δ' οὖν καὶ τἀναντία μέλλοιεν ἅπαντα πράξειν,
[304] οὐδ' οὕτως ἡγοῦμαι προσήκειν ὑμῖν τῆς Θηβαίων
πόλεως πλείω ποιήσασθαι λόγον ἢ τῶν ὅρκων καὶ
τῶν συνθηκῶν, ἐνθυμουμένους πρῶτον μὲν ὡς οὐ
τοὺς κινδύνους, ἀλλὰ τὰς ἀδοξίας καὶ τὰς αἰσχύνας
φοβεῖσθαι πάτριον ὑμῖν ἐστιν, ἔπειθ' ὅτι συμβαίνει
κρατεῖν ἐν τοῖς πολέμοις οὐ τοὺς βίᾳ τὰς πόλεις
καταστρεφομένους, ἀλλὰ τοὺς ὁσιώτερον καὶ πραό-
40 τερον τὴν Ἑλλάδα διοικοῦντας. καὶ ταῦτ' ἐπὶ
πλειόνων μὲν ἄν τις παραδειγμάτων ἔχοι διελθεῖν·
τὰ δ' οὖν ἐφ' ἡμῶν γενόμενα τίς οὐκ οἶδεν, ὅτι καὶ
Λακεδαιμόνιοι τὴν δύναμιν τὴν ὑμετέραν ἀνυπό-
στατον δοκοῦσαν εἶναι κατέλυσαν, μικρὰς μὲν ἀφορ-

Cf. § 20.
▸ 374 B.C., between Athens and Sparta.

themselves the more they will cultivate your friendship. Indeed they have proved to you how people of such character should be treated by their conduct in the matter of Oropus [a] ; for when they hoped that they would have licence to do as they pleased they did not treat you as allies, but as ruthlessly wronged you as they would have dared to act against their deadliest enemies. But as soon as you in requital voted to exclude them from the peace,[b] they left off their arrogance and came to you in more humble mood than we Plataeans are in now. If, then, some of their orators seek to frighten you, arguing that there is danger of the Thebans' changing sides and going over to the enemy, you must not credit what they say ; for they are constrained by compulsions so peremptory that they would much sooner submit to your government than tolerate the alliance with the Lacedaemonians.

But even if they were likely to act altogether otherwise, not even then, in my opinion, does it become you to have greater regard for the city of the Thebans than for your oaths and treaties, when you remember, first, that it is your ancient tradition to fear, not dangers, but acts of infamy and dishonour ; next, that it usually happens that victory in war is not for those who destroy cities by violence, but for those who govern Greece in a more scrupulous and clement manner.[c] And this could be proved by numerous instances ; but as for those which have occurred in our own time at any rate, who does not know that the Lacedaemonians shattered your power,[d] which was thought to be irresistible—

[c] Cf., however, Panath. 185.
[d] At Aegospotami, 405 B.C.

μὰς εἰς τὸν πόλεμον τὸν κατὰ θάλατταν τὸ πρῶτον
ἔχοντες, διὰ δὲ τὴν δόξαν ταύτην προσαγόμενοι
τοὺς Ἕλληνας, καὶ πάλιν ὑμεῖς τὴν ἀρχὴν ἀφεί-
λεσθε τὴν ἐκείνων, ἐξ ἀτειχίστου μὲν τῆς πόλεως
ὁρμηθέντες καὶ κακῶς πραττούσης, τὸ δὲ δίκαιον
41 ἔχοντες σύμμαχον; καὶ τούτων ὡς οὐ βασιλεὺς
αἴτιος ἦν ὁ τελευταῖος χρόνος σαφῶς ἐπέδειξεν·
ἔξω γὰρ αὐτοῦ τῶν πραγμάτων γεγενημένου, καὶ
τῶν μὲν ὑμετέρων ἀνελπίστως ἐχόντων, Λακεδαιμονίοις δὲ σχεδὸν ἁπασῶν τῶν πόλεων δου-
λευουσῶν, ὅμως αὐτῶν τοσοῦτον περιεγένεσθε
πολεμοῦντες ὥστ' ἐκείνους ἀγαπητῶς ἰδεῖν τὴν
εἰρήνην γενομένην.

42 Μηδεὶς οὖν ὑμῶν ὀρρωδείτω μετὰ τοῦ δικαίου
ποιούμενος τοὺς κινδύνους, μηδ' οἰέσθω συμμάχων
ἀπορήσειν, ἂν τοῖς ἀδικουμένοις ἐθέλητε βοηθεῖν
ἀλλὰ μὴ Θηβαίοις μόνοις· οἷς νῦν τἀναντία ψηφισά-
μενοι πολλοὺς ἐπιθυμεῖν ποιήσετε τῆς ὑμετέρας
φιλίας. ἢν γὰρ ἐνδείξησθ' ὡς ὁμοίως ἅπασιν ὑπὲρ
43 τῶν συνθηκῶν παρεσκευάσθε πολεμεῖν, τίνες εἰς
τοῦτ' ἀνοίας ἥξουσιν ὥστε βούλεσθαι μετὰ τῶν
καταδουλουμένων εἶναι μᾶλλον ἢ μεθ' ὑμῶν τῶν
ὑπὲρ τῆς αὐτῶν ἐλευθερίας ἀγωνιζομένων; εἰ δὲ
μή, τί λέγοντες, ἢν πάλιν γένηται πόλεμος, ἀξιώ-
σετε προσάγεσθαι τοὺς Ἕλληνας, εἰ τὴν αὐτονομίαν
προτείνοντες ἐκδώσετε πορθεῖν Θηβαίοις ἥντιν' ἂν
44 βούλωνται τῶν πόλεων; πῶς δ' οὐ τἀναντία φανή-
[305] σεσθε πράττοντες ὑμῖν αὐτοῖς, εἰ Θηβαίους μὲν μὴ
διακωλύσετε παραβαίνοντας τοὺς ὅρκους καὶ τὰς
συνθήκας, πρὸς δὲ Λακεδαιμονίους ὑπὲρ τῶν αὐ-

---

[a] A reference to the beginning of the Corinthian War.

although at first they possessed slight resources for the war waged at sea, but they won the Greeks over to their side because of that general belief— and that you in turn took the leadership away from them, although you depended on a city without walls and in evil plight,ᵃ but possessed Justice as your ally ? And that the Persian king was not responsible for this outcome recent years have clearly shown; for when he stood aloof from the conflict, and your situation was desperate, and when almost all the cities were in servitude to the Lacedaemonians, nevertheless you were so superior to them in the war that they were glad to see the conclusion of peace.

Let no one of you, then, be afraid, if Justice is with him, to take such dangers upon himself, nor think that allies will be lacking, if you are willing to aid all who are victims of wrong, and not the Thebans alone ; if you now cast your vote against them, you will cause many to desire your friendship. For if you show yourselves ready to war upon all alike in defence of the treaties, who will be so insane as to prefer to join those who try to enslave than to be in company with you who are fighting for their freedom ? But if you are not so minded, what reason will you give, if war breaks out again, to justify your demand that the Greeks should join you, if you hold out to them independence and then grant to the Thebans to destroy any city they desire ? How can you avoid the charge of acting with inconsistency if, while you do not prevent the Thebans from violating their oaths and treaties, yet you pretend that you

395 B.C. Athens had been compelled by Sparta to destroy her Long Walls and fortifications after her defeat in 404 B.C.

159

τῶν τούτων προσποιήσεσθε πολεμεῖν; καὶ τῶν μὲν
κτημάτων τῶν ὑμετέρων αὐτῶν ἀπέστητε, βουλόμενοι τὴν συμμαχίαν ὡς μεγίστην ποιῆσαι, τούτους
δὲ τὴν ἀλλοτρίαν ἔχειν ἐάσετε καὶ τοιαῦτα ποιεῖν
ἐξ ὧν ἅπαντες χείρους εἶναι νομιοῦσιν ὑμᾶς;

45 Ὁ δὲ πάντων δεινότατον, εἰ τοῖς μὲν συνεχῶς
μετὰ Λακεδαιμονίων γεγενημένοις δεδογμένον ὑμῖν
ἐστὶ βοηθεῖν, ἤν τι παράσπονδον αὐτοῖς ἐκεῖνοι
προστάττωσιν, ἡμᾶς δ' οἳ τὸν μὲν πλεῖστον χρόνον
μεθ' ὑμῶν ὄντες διατετελέκαμεν, τὸν δὲ τελευταῖον
μόνον πόλεμον ὑπὸ Λακεδαιμονίοις ἠναγκάσθημεν
γενέσθαι, διὰ ταύτην τὴν πρόφασιν ἀθλιώτατα πάν-
46 των ἀνθρώπων περιόψεσθε διακειμένους. τίνας γὰρ
ἂν ἡμῶν εὕροι τις δυστυχεστέρους, οἵτινες καὶ
πόλεως καὶ χώρας καὶ χρημάτων ἐν μιᾷ στερηθέν-
τες ἡμέρᾳ, πάντων τῶν ἀναγκαίων ὁμοίως ἐνδεεῖς
ὄντες ἀλῆται καὶ πτωχοὶ καθέσταμεν, ἀποροῦντες
ὅποι τραπώμεθα, καὶ πάσας τὰς οἰκήσεις δυσχε-
ραίνοντες· ἤν τε γὰρ δυστυχοῦντας καταλάβωμεν,
ἀλγοῦμεν ἀναγκαζόμενοι πρὸς τοῖς οἰκείοις κακοῖς
47 καὶ τῶν ἀλλοτρίων κοινωνεῖν· ἤν θ' ὡς εὖ πράττοντας ἔλθωμεν, ἔτι χαλεπώτερον ἔχομεν, οὐ ταῖς
ἐκείνων φθονοῦντες εὐπορίαις, ἀλλὰ μᾶλλον ἐν τοῖς
τῶν πέλας ἀγαθοῖς τὰς ἡμετέρας αὐτῶν συμφορὰς
καθορῶντες, ἐφ' αἷς ἡμεῖς οὐδεμίαν ἡμέραν ἀδακρυ-
τὶ διάγομεν ἀλλὰ πενθοῦντες τὴν πατρίδα καὶ
θρηνοῦντες τὴν μεταβολὴν τὴν γεγενημένην ἅπαντα
48 τὸν χρόνον διατελοῦμεν. τίνα γὰρ ἡμᾶς οἴεσθε
γνώμην ἔχειν ὁρῶντας καὶ τοὺς γονέας αὐτῶν
ἀναξίως γηροτροφουμένους καὶ τοὺς παῖδας οὐκ

are making war on the Lacedaemonians on behalf of
the same obligations ? Or again, if you abandoned
your own possessions in your desire to strengthen
the alliance as much as possible, yet are about to
permit the Thebans to keep the territory of others
and act in such fashion as to injure your reputation
with all the world ?

But this would be the crowning outrage—if you
have determined to stand by those who have been
the constant allies of the Lacedaemonians when the
Lacedaemonians demand of them an action which
violates the treaty, and yet shall permit us, who have
been your allies for the longest time, and were subservient to the Lacedaemonians under compulsion
in the last war only, to become for that reason the
most miserable of all mankind. For who could be
found to be more unhappy than we are who, in one
day deprived of our city, our lands, and our possessions, and being destitute of all necessities alike,
have become wanderers and beggars, not knowing
whither to turn and, whatever our habitation, finding
no happiness there ? For if we fall in with the
unfortunate, we grieve that we must be compelled,
in addition to our own ills, to share in the ills of
others ; and if we encounter those who fare well,
our lot is even harder to bear, not because we envy
them their prosperity, but because amid the blessings
of our neighbours we see more clearly our own
miseries—miseries so great that we spend no day
without tears, but spend all our time mourning the
loss of our fatherland and bewailing the change in
our fortunes. What, think you, is our state of mind
when we see our own parents unworthily cared for
in their old age, and our children, instead of being

161

ISOCRATES

ἐπὶ ταῖς ἐλπίσιν αἷς ἐποιησάμεθα παιδευομένους,
ἀλλὰ πολλοὺς μὲν μικρῶν ἕνεκα συμβολαίων δου-
[306] λεύοντας, ἄλλους δ᾽ ἐπὶ θητείαν ἰόντας, τοὺς δ᾽
ὅπως ἕκαστοι δύνανται τὰ καθ᾽ ἡμέραν ποριζο-
μένους, ἀπρεπῶς καὶ τοῖς τῶν προγόνων ἔργοις
καὶ ταῖς αὐτῶν ἡλικίαις καὶ τοῖς φρονήμασι τοῖς
49 ἡμετέροις; ὃ δὲ πάντων ἄλγιστον, ὅταν τις ἴδῃ
χωριζομένους ἀπ᾽ ἀλλήλων μὴ μόνον πολίτας ἀπὸ
πολιτῶν ἀλλὰ καὶ γυναῖκας ἀπ᾽ ἀνδρῶν καὶ θυγα-
τέρας ἀπὸ μητέρων καὶ πᾶσαν τὴν συγγένειαν
διαλυομένην, ὃ πολλοῖς τῶν ἡμετέρων πολιτῶν διὰ
τὴν ἀπορίαν συμβέβηκεν· ὁ γὰρ κοινὸς βίος ἀπο-
λωλὼς ἰδίας τὰς ἐλπίδας ἕκαστον ἡμῶν ἔχειν πεποί-
50 ηκεν. οἶμαι δ᾽ ὑμᾶς οὐδὲ τὰς ἄλλας αἰσχύνας
ἀγνοεῖν τὰς διὰ πενίαν καὶ φυγὴν γιγνομένας, ἃς
ἡμεῖς τῇ μὲν διανοίᾳ χαλεπώτερον τῶν ἄλλων
φέρομεν, τῷ δὲ λόγῳ παραλείπομεν, αἰσχυνόμενοι
λίαν ἀκριβῶς τὰς ἡμετέρας αὐτῶν ἀτυχίας ἐξετάζειν.

51 Ὧν αὐτοὺς ὑμᾶς ἀξιοῦμεν ἐνθυμουμένους ἐπι-
μέλειάν τινα ποιήσασθαι περὶ ἡμῶν. καὶ γὰρ οὐδ᾽
ἀλλότριοι τυγχάνομεν ὑμῖν ὄντες, ἀλλὰ ταῖς μὲν
εὐνοίαις ἅπαντες οἰκεῖοι, τῇ δὲ συγγενείᾳ τὸ πλῆθος
ἡμῶν· διὰ γὰρ τὰς ἐπιγαμίας τὰς δοθείσας ἐκ
πολιτίδων ὑμετέρων γεγόναμεν· ὥστ᾽ οὐχ οἷόν θ᾽
ὑμῖν ἀμελῆσαι περὶ ὧν ἐληλύθαμεν δεησόμενοι.
52 καὶ γὰρ ἂν πάντων εἴη δεινότατον, εἰ πρότερον μὲν
ἡμῖν μετέδοτε τῆς πατρίδος τῆς ὑμετέρας αὐτῶν,

ᵃ Cf. Lysias, *Against Eratosthenes* 98.
ᵇ The unhappy lot of the exile is a commonplace in Greek
poetry and prose ; cf. Tyrtaeus, *frag.* 10.

educated as we had hoped when we begat them, often because of petty debts reduced to slavery,[a] others working for hire, and the rest procuring their daily livelihood as best each one can, in a manner that accords with neither the deeds of their ancestors, nor their own youth, nor our own self-respect? But our greatest anguish of all is when one sees separated from each other, not only citizens from citizens, but also wives from husbands, daughters from mothers, and every tie of kinship severed; and this has befallen many of our fellow-citizens because of poverty. For the destruction of our communal life has compelled each of us to cherish hopes for himself alone. I presume that you yourselves are not ignorant of the other causes of shame that poverty and exile bring in their train,[b] and although we in our hearts bear these with greater difficulty than all the rest, yet we forbear to speak of them since we are ashamed to enumerate one by one our own misfortunes.

All these things we ask you to bear in mind and to take some measure of consideration for us. For indeed we are not aliens to you; on the contrary, all of us are akin to you in our loyalty and most of us in blood also; for by the right of intermarriage [c] granted to us we are born of mothers who were of your city. You cannot, therefore, be indifferent to the pleas we have come to make. For it would be the cruellest blow of all, if you, having long ago bestowed upon us the right of a common citizenship with yourselves, should now decide not even to

---

[a] The Plataeans were granted Athenian citizenship after the destruction of their city in 427 B.C. This honour included the right of intermarriage.

νῦν δε μηδὲ τὴν ἡμετέραν ἀποδοῦναι δόξειεν ὑμῖν.
ἔπειτ' οὐδ' εἰκὸς ἕνα μὲν ἕκαστον ἐλεεῖσθαι τῶν
παρὰ τὸ δίκαιον δυστυχούντων, ὅλην δὲ πόλιν
οὕτως ἀνόμως διεφθαρμένην μηδὲ κατὰ μικρὸν
οἴκτου δυνηθῆναι τυχεῖν, ἄλλως τε καὶ παρ' ὑμᾶς
καταφυγοῦσαν, οἷς οὐδὲ τὸ πρότερον αἰσχρῶς οὐδ'
53 ἀκλεῶς ἀπέβη τοὺς ἱκέτας ἐλεήσασιν. ἐλθόντων
γὰρ Ἀργείων ὡς τοὺς προγόνους ὑμῶν καὶ δεη-
θέντων ἀνελέσθαι τοὺς ὑπὸ τῇ Καδμείᾳ τελευτήσαντας, πεισθέντες ὑπ' ἐκείνων καὶ Θηβαίους
ἀναγκάσαντες βουλεύσασθαι νομιμώτερον οὐ μόνον
αὐτοὶ κατ' ἐκείνους τοὺς καιροὺς εὐδοκίμησαν,
ἀλλὰ καὶ τῇ πόλει δόξαν ἀείμνηστον εἰς ἅπαντα τὸν
χρόνον κατέλιπον, ἧς οὐκ ἄξιον προδότας γενέσθαι.
[307] καὶ γὰρ αἰσχρὸν φιλοτιμεῖσθαι μὲν ἐπὶ τοῖς τῶν
προγόνων ἔργοις, φαίνεσθαι δ' ἐκείνοις τἀναντία
περὶ τῶν ἱκετῶν πράττοντας.
54 Καίτοι πολὺ περὶ μειζόνων καὶ δικαιοτέρων
ἥκομεν ποιησόμενοι τὰς δεήσεις· οἱ μὲν γὰρ ἐπὶ
τὴν ἀλλοτρίαν στρατεύσαντες ἱκέτευον ὑμᾶς, ἡμεῖς
δὲ τὴν ἡμετέραν αὐτῶν ἀπολωλεκότες, κἀκεῖνοι
μὲν παρεκάλουν ἐπὶ τὴν τῶν νεκρῶν ἀναίρεσιν,
55 ἡμεῖς δ' ἐπὶ τὴν τῶν λοιπῶν σωτηρίαν. ἔστι δ'
οὐκ ἴσον κακὸν οὐδ' ὅμοιον τοὺς τεθνεῶτας ταφῆς
εἴργεσθαι καὶ τοὺς ζῶντας πατρίδος ἀποστερεῖσθαι
καὶ τῶν ἄλλων ἀγαθῶν ἁπάντων, ἀλλὰ τὸ μὲν
δεινότερον τοῖς κωλύουσιν ἢ τοῖς ἀτυχοῦσι, τὸ δὲ
μηδεμίαν ἔχοντα καταφυγὴν ἀλλ' ἄπολιν γενόμενον

ᵃ See *Panegyr.* 55 (Vol. I, p. 153).

restore to us our own. Furthermore, it is not reasonable that, while every individual who is the victim of injustice receives pity at your hands, yet an entire city so lawlessly destroyed should be unable in the slightest degree to win commiseration from you, especially when it has taken refuge with you who in former times incurred neither shame nor infamy when you showed pity for suppliants. For when the Argives came to your ancestors and implored them to take up for burial the bodies of the dead at the foot of the Cadmea,*a* your forefathers yielded to their persuasion and compelled the Thebans to adopt measures more conformable to our usage, and thus not only gained renown for themselves in those times, but also bequeathed to your city a glory never to be forgotten for all time to come, and this glory it would be unworthy of you to betray. For it is disgraceful that you should pride yourselves on the glorious deeds of your ancestors and then be found acting concerning your suppliants in a manner the very opposite of theirs.

And yet the entreaties that we have come here to make are of far more weight and are more just ; for the Argives came to you as suppliants after they had invaded an alien territory, whereas we have come after having lost our own ; they called upon you to take up the bodies of their dead, but we do it for the rescue of the survivors. But it is not an equal or even similar evil that the dead should be denied burial and that the living should be despoiled of their fatherland and all their goods besides : nay, in the former case it is a greater disgrace for those who prevent the burial than for those who suffer the misfortune, but in the latter, to have no refuge, to be

καθ' ἑκάστην τὴν ἡμέραν κακοπαθεῖν καὶ τοὺς
αὐτοῦ περιορᾶν μὴ δυνάμενον ἐπαρκεῖν, τί δεῖ
λέγειν ὅσον τὰς ἄλλας συμφορὰς ὑπερβέβληκεν;

56 Ὑπὲρ ὧν ἅπαντας ὑμᾶς ἱκετεύομεν ἀποδοῦναι
τὴν χώραν ἡμῖν καὶ τὴν πόλιν, τοὺς μὲν πρεσβυτέρους ὑπομιμνήσκοντες, ὡς οἰκτρὸν τοὺς τηλικούτους ὁρᾶσθαι δυστυχοῦντας καὶ τῶν καθ' ἡμέραν
ἀποροῦντας, τοὺς δὲ νεωτέρους ἀντιβολοῦντες καὶ
δεόμενοι βοηθῆσαι τοῖς ἡλικιώταις καὶ μὴ περιιδεῖν
57 ἔτι πλείω κακὰ τῶν εἰρημένων παθόντας. ὀφείλετε
δὲ μόνοι τῶν Ἑλλήνων τοῦτον τὸν ἔρανον, ἀνα-
στάτοις ἡμῖν γεγενημένοις ἐπαμῦναι. καὶ γὰρ τοὺς
ἡμετέρους προγόνους φασὶν ἐκλιπόντων τῶν ὑμετέρων πατέρων ἐν τῷ Περσικῷ πολέμῳ ταύτην τὴν
χώραν μόνους τῶν ἔξω Πελοποννήσου κοινωνοὺς
ἐκείνοις τῶν κινδύνων γενομένους συνανασῶσαι τὴν
πόλιν αὐτοῖς· ὥστε δικαίως ἂν τὴν αὐτὴν εὐεργεσίαν ἀπολάβοιμεν ἥνπερ αὐτοὶ τυγχάνομεν εἰς
ὑμᾶς ὑπάρξαντες.

58 Εἰ δ' οὖν καὶ μηδὲν ὑμῖν τῶν σωμάτων τῶν
ἡμετέρων δέδοκται φροντίζειν, ἀλλὰ τήν γε χώραν
οὐ πρὸς ὑμῶν ἐστιν ἀνέχεσθαι πεπορθημένην, ἐν ᾗ
μέγιστα σημεῖα τῆς ἀρετῆς τῆς ὑμετέρας καὶ τῶν
59 ἄλλων τῶν συναγωνισαμένων καταλείπεται· τὰ μὲν
γὰρ ἄλλα τρόπαια πόλει πρὸς πόλιν γέγονεν, ἐκεῖνα
δ' ὑπὲρ ἁπάσης τῆς Ἑλλάδος πρὸς ὅλην τὴν ἐκ τῆς
[308] Ἀσίας δύναμιν ἕστηκεν. ἃ Θηβαῖοι μὲν εἰκότως
ἀφανίζουσι, τὰ γὰρ μνημεῖα τῶν τότε γενομένων
αἰσχύνη τούτοις ἐστίν, ὑμῖν δὲ προσήκει διασώζειν·
ἐξ ἐκείνων γὰρ τῶν ἔργων ἡγεμόνες κατέστητε τῶν

---

^a Cf. Panath. 93.

166

without a fatherland, daily to suffer hardships and to watch without having the power to succour the suffering of one's own, why need I say how far this has exceeded all other calamities ?

For these reasons we supplicate you one and all, Athenians, to restore to us our land and city, reminding the older men among you how piteous a thing it is that men of their age should be seen in misfortune and in lack of their daily bread ; and the younger men we beg and implore to succour their equals in age and not to let them suffer still more evils than those I have described. Alone of the Greeks you Athenians owe us this contribution of succour, to rescue us now that we have been driven from our homes. It is a just request, for our ancestors, we are told, when in the Persian War your fathers had abandoned this land, alone of those who lived outside of the Peloponnesus shared in their perils and thus helped them to save their city.[a] It is but just, therefore, that we should receive in return the same benefaction which we first conferred upon you.

If, however, you have determined to have no regard for our persons, yet it is not in your interest to let our country at any rate be ravaged, a country in which are left the most solemn memorials of your own valour and of that of all the others who fought at your side. For while all other trophies have been erected by one city victorious over another, those were in commemoration of the victory of all Greece pitted against all the power of Asia. Although the Thebans have good reason for destroying these trophies, since memorials of the events of that time bring shame to them, yet it is proper that you should preserve them ; for the deeds done there gave you

60 Ἑλλήνων. ἄξιον δὲ καὶ τῶν θεῶν καὶ τῶν ἡρώων
μνησθῆναι τῶν ἐκεῖνον τὸν τόπον κατεχόντων καὶ
μὴ περιορᾶν τὰς τιμὰς αὐτῶν καταλυομένας, οἷς
ὑμεῖς καλλιερησάμενοι τοιοῦτον ὑπέστητε κίνδυνον,
ὃς καὶ τούτους καὶ τοὺς ἄλλους ἅπαντας Ἕλληνας
ἠλευθέρωσεν. χρὴ δὲ καὶ τῶν προγόνων ποιήσα-
σθαί τινα πρόνοιαν καὶ μὴ παραμελῆσαι μηδὲ τῆς
61 περὶ ἐκείνους εὐσεβείας, οἳ πῶς ἂν διατεθεῖεν, εἴ
τις ἄρα τοῖς ἐκεῖ φρόνησίς ἐστι περὶ τῶν ἐνθάδε
γιγνομένων, εἰ κυρίων ὑμῶν ὄντων αἴσθοιντο τοὺς
μὲν δουλεύειν τοῖς βαρβάροις ἀξιώσαντας δεσπότας
τῶν ἄλλων καθισταμένους, ἡμᾶς δὲ τοὺς ὑπὲρ τῆς
ἐλευθερίας συναγωνισαμένους μόνους τῶν Ἑλλήνων
ἀναστάτους γεγενημένους, καὶ τοὺς μὲν τῶν συγ-
κινδυνευσάντων τάφους μὴ τυγχάνοντας τῶν νομιζομένων σπάνει τῶν ἐποισόντων, Θηβαίους δὲ τοὺς
τἀναντία παραταξαμένους κρατοῦντας τῆς χώρας
62 ἐκείνης; ἐνθυμεῖσθε δ' ὅτι Λακεδαιμονίων μεγίστην ἐποιεῖσθε κατηγορίαν, ὅτι Θηβαίοις χαριζό-
μενοι τοῖς τῶν Ἑλλήνων προδόταις ἡμᾶς τοὺς
εὐεργέτας διέφθειραν. μὴ τοίνυν ἐάσητε ταύτας
τὰς βλασφημίας περὶ τὴν ὑμετέραν γενέσθαι πόλιν,
μηδὲ τὴν ὕβριν τὴν τούτων ἀντὶ τῆς παρούσης
ἕλησθε δόξης.

63 Πολλῶν δ' ἐνόντων εἰπεῖν ἐξ ὧν ἄν τις ὑμᾶς
ἐπαγάγοι μᾶλλον φροντίσαι τῆς ἡμετέρας σωτηρίας
οὐ δύναμαι πάντα περιλαβεῖν, ἀλλ' αὐτοὺς χρὴ

the leadership of the Greeks. And it is right that you should remember both the gods and the heroes who haunt that place and not permit the honours due them to be suppressed ; for it was after favourable sacrifice to them that you took upon yourselves a battle so decisive that it established the freedom of both the Thebans and all the other Greeks besides. You must also take some thought of your ancestors and not be negligent of the piety due to them. Pray what would be their feelings—if we may assume that the dead yonder possess any perception of what takes place here *—if they should perceive that, although you are masters, those who saw fit to be the slaves of barbarians had become despots over all the other Greeks and that we, who fought at your side for freedom, alone of the Greeks, have been driven from our homes, and that the graves of their companions in peril do not receive the customary funereal offerings through the lack of those to bring them, and that the Thebans, who were drawn up in battle array with the enemy, hold sway over that land ? Remember, too, that you used to bring bitter reproach against the Lacedaemonians because, to gratify the Thebans who were the betrayers of Greece, they destroyed us, its benefactors. Do not, therefore, allow your city to incur these foul accusations and do not prefer the insolence of the Thebans to your own fair fame.

Although many things remain to be said which might induce you to have greater regard for our safety, I cannot include them all in my discourse ; but it is proper that you yourselves, having not only

* This proviso is frequently found in Greek literature ; *cf.* Isocrates, *Aegin.* 42 ; *Evag.* 2.

καὶ τὰ παραλελειμμένα συνιδόντας καὶ μνησθέντας μάλιστα μὲν τῶν ὅρκων καὶ τῶν συνθηκῶν, ἔπειτα δὲ καὶ τῆς ἡμετέρας εὐνοίας καὶ τῆς τούτων ἔχθρας, ψηφίσασθαί τι περὶ ἡμῶν δίκαιον.[1]

[1] τι περὶ ἡμῶν δίκαιον ΓΕ : τὰ δίκαια περὶ ἡμῶν vulg.

observed all that I have passed over but also having recalled especially your oaths and your treaties, and then our devotion to you and the hostility of the Thebans, should give a righteous judgement in our cause.

XVI. CONCERNING THE TEAM OF HORSES (*DE BIGIS*)

INTRODUCTION

THIS discourse, one of the six extant forensic speeches of Isocrates, was written for a defendant in an action for damage (δίκη βλάβης) for the sum of five talents. The speaker is the younger Alcibiades, son of the famous Alcibiades, who, on reaching his majority (about 397 B.C.), was sued by Teisias, an Athenian citizen, on the ground that the elder Alcibiades had robbed him of a team of four race-horses.

Alcibiades had entered seven four-horse chariots at the Olympic festival (probably in 416 B.C.). The city of Argos had originally owned one of these teams and the alleged robbery of this team by Alcibiades is the subject of this suit.

Plutarch in his *Life of Alcibiades* gives an account of the affair. He says that Alcibiades had been commissioned by an Athenian citizen named Diomedes to buy a chariot and team of Argos. This team was bought by Alcibiades and was entered at Olympia as his own. The suit followed, and Isocrates, according to Plutarch, wrote a speech for the defence. Slightly different versions are given by the historian Diodorus xiii. 74.[a]

The confusion of names (Diomedes in Diodorus and Plutarch, and Teisias in our speech) is accounted

---

[a] Cf. Jebb, *Attic Orators* ii. p. 228 and Andoc. *Against Alcibiades*.

for by Blass (*Die attische Beredsamkeit* ii. p. 205) as being an error on the part of Ephorus, the source of Diodorus. It may well be, however, that two individuals, Diomedes and Teisias, had joined in furnishing the money for the purchase of the team and that the suit, which had been delayed until after the death of the elder Alcibiades, was brought by Teisias as the survivor.

The first part of the extant speech, the part which contained the statement of facts and the citation of evidence, is missing. The part which we have is largely a defence by the younger Alcibiades of his father's life and a eulogy of his character and deeds.

Some critics have thought that the speech, because of its nature and style and its extravagant praise of an unpopular and scandalous person, was not written for a genuine occasion in court, but is a mere display-piece, or a model for pupils. This view, however, lacks convincing proof. As for the conjectural date of the speech, Blass gives 397 B.C.

16. ΠΕΡΙ ΤΟΥ ΖΕΥΓΟΥΣ

Περὶ μὲν οὖν τοῦ ζεύγους τῶν ἵππων, ὡς οὐκ
ἀφελόμενος ὁ πατὴρ Τεισίαν εἶχεν, ἀλλὰ πριάμενος
παρὰ τῆς πόλεως τῆς Ἀργείων, τῶν τε πρέσβεων
τῶν ἐκεῖθεν ἡκόντων καὶ τῶν ἄλλων τῶν εἰδότων
ἀκηκόατε μαρτυρούντων· τὸν αὐτὸν δὲ τρόπον ἅπαν-
2 τές εἰσιν εἰθισμένοι με συκοφαντεῖν. τὰς μὲν γὰρ
δίκας ὑπὲρ τῶν ἰδίων ἐγκλημάτων λαγχάνουσι, τὰς
δὲ κατηγορίας ὑπὲρ τῶν τῆς πόλεως πραγμάτων
ποιοῦνται, καὶ πλείω χρόνον διατρίβουσι τὸν πατέρα μου διαβάλλοντες ἢ περὶ ὧν ἀντώμοσαν διδά-
σκοντες, καὶ τοσοῦτον καταφρονοῦσι τῶν νόμων
ὥστε περὶ ὧν ὑμᾶς ὑπ' ἐκείνου φασὶν ἠδικῆσθαι,
τούτων αὐτοὶ δίκην παρ' ἐμοῦ λαβεῖν ἀξιοῦσιν.
3 ἐγὼ δ' ἡγοῦμαι μὲν οὐδὲν προσήκειν τὰς κοινὰς
αἰτίας τοῖς ἰδίοις ἀγῶσιν· ἐπειδὴ δὲ Τεισίας πολλάκις ὀνειδίζει μοι τὴν φυγὴν τὴν τοῦ πατρὸς καὶ
μᾶλλον ὑπὲρ τῶν ὑμετέρων ἢ τῶν αὐτοῦ σπουδάζει
πραγμάτων, ἀνάγκη πρὸς ταῦτα τὴν ἀπολογίαν
ποιεῖσθαι· καὶ γὰρ ἂν αἰσχυνοίμην, εἴ τῳ δόξαιμι

---

[a] It should be noted that we have only the second part of
this speech, the eulogy of Alcibiades the elder; the first

176

XVI. CONCERNING THE TEAM OF HORSES [a]

. . . . . .

So then, concerning the team of horses [b]—that my father was in possession of them, not by having taken them away from Teisias, but by having purchased them from the Argive state—you have heard both the Argive ambassadors and the others conversant with the facts testify. But in just this same fashion all are accustomed maliciously to accuse me. For they obtain leave to bring actions against me on private complaints, but make their accusations on behalf of the interests of the state, and they spend more time in slandering my father than they do in informing you with respect to their sworn charges; and so great is their contempt of the law that they claim personal satisfaction from me for the wrongs which, as they say, you suffered at my father's hands. But it is my opinion that charges involving the public interest have nothing to do with private suits; but as Teisias often reproaches me with my father's banishment, and is more zealous concerning your affairs than he is regarding his own, I must address my defence to these matters. Certainly I should be

part must have presented the statement of facts and the citation of evidence.

[b] The "team" consisted of *four* race-horses.

τῶν πολιτῶν ἧττον φροντίζειν τῆς ἐκείνου δόξης ἢ
τῶν ἐμαυτοῦ κινδύνων.

4 Πρὸς μὲν οὖν τοὺς πρεσβυτέρους βραχὺς ἂν
ἐξήρκει λόγος· ἅπαντες γὰρ ἴσασιν ὅτι διὰ τοὺς
αὐτοὺς ἄνδρας ἥ τε δημοκρατία κατελύθη κἀκεῖνος
ἐκ τῆς πόλεως ἐξέπεσεν· τῶν δὲ νεωτέρων ἕνεκα,
οἳ τῶν μὲν πραγμάτων ὕστεροι γεγόνασι τῶν δὲ
διαβαλλόντων πολλάκις ἀκηκόασι, πορρωτέρωθεν
ἄρξομαι διδάσκειν.

5 Οἱ γὰρ τὸ πρῶτον ἐπιβουλεύσαντες τῷ δήμῳ
καὶ καταστήσαντες τοὺς τετρακοσίους, ἐπειδὴ
παρακαλούμενος ὁ πατὴρ οὐκ ἤθελε γενέσθαι μετ᾽
αὐτῶν, ὁρῶντες αὐτὸν καὶ πρὸς τὰς πράξεις ἐρ-
ρωμένως ἔχοντα καὶ πρὸς τὸ πλῆθος πιστῶς διακείμενον, οὐχ ἡγοῦντ᾽ οὐδὲν οἷοί τ᾽ εἶναι κινεῖν τῶν
καθεστώτων, πρὶν ἐκποδὼν ἐκεῖνος αὐτοῖς γένοιτο.

6 εἰδότες δὲ τὴν πόλιν τῶν μὲν περὶ τοὺς θεοὺς
μάλιστ᾽ ἂν ὀργισθεῖσαν, εἴ τις εἰς τὰ μυστήρια
φαίνοιτ᾽ ἐξαμαρτάνων, τῶν δ᾽ ἄλλων εἴ τις τὴν
[348] δημοκρατίαν τολμῴη καταλύειν, ἀμφοτέρας ταύτας
συνθέντες τὰς αἰτίας εἰσήγγελλον εἰς τὴν βουλήν,
λέγοντες ὡς ὁ πατὴρ μὲν συνάγοι τὴν ἑταιρείαν
ἐπὶ νεωτέροις πράγμασιν, οὗτοι δ᾽ ἐν τῇ Πουλυ-
τίωνος οἰκίᾳ συνδειπνοῦντες τὰ μυστήρια ποιή-
7 σειαν. ὀρθῆς δὲ τῆς πόλεως γενομένης διὰ τὸ
μέγεθος τῶν αἰτιῶν καὶ διὰ ταχέων συλλεγείσης
ἐκκλησίας οὕτω σαφῶς ἐπέδειξεν αὐτοὺς ψευδο-

---

[a] The Revolution of the Four Hundred in 411 b.c. conducted the Athenian government for only a few months.

[b] The Eleusinian Mysteries were celebrated annually at
Eleusis in Attica and were performed in honour of Demeter
and her daughter Persephonê.

ashamed, if I were to seem to any of my fellow-citizens to have less concern for my father's good name than for my own peril.

Now so far as the older men are concerned, a brief statement could have sufficed : for they all know that the same men were responsible for the destruction of the democracy and for my father's exile ; but for the benefit of the younger men, who have lived after the events and have often heard the slanderers, I will begin my exposition from an earlier time.

Now the persons who first plotted against the democracy and established the Four Hundred,[a] inasmuch as my father, although he was repeatedly invited to join them would not do so, seeing that he was a vigorous opponent of their activities and a loyal supporter of the people, judged that they were powerless to upset the established order until he was removed out of their way. And since they knew that in matters pertaining to the gods the city would be most enraged if any man should be shown to be violating the Mysteries,[b] and that in other matters if any man should dare to attempt the overthrow of the democracy, they combined both these charges and tried to bring an action of impeachment before the senate. They asserted that my father was holding meetings of his political club with a view to revolution, and that these members of the club, when dining together in the house of Pulytion,[c] had given a performance of the Mysteries. The city was greatly excited by reason of the gravity of the charges, and a meeting of the Assembly was hastily called at which my father so clearly proved that the

* Cf. Andoc. On the Mysteries 12.

μένους, ὥστε παρὰ μὲν τῶν κατηγόρων ἡδέως ἂν
ὁ δῆμος δίκην ἔλαβε, τὸν δ' εἰς Σικελίαν στρατηγὸν
ἐχειροτόνησεν. μετὰ δὲ ταῦθ' ὁ μὲν ἐξέπλευσεν
ὡς ἀπηλλαγμένος ἤδη τῆς διαβολῆς, οἱ δὲ συστή-
σαντες τὴν βουλὴν καὶ τοὺς ῥήτορας ὑφ' αὑτοῖς
ποιησάμενοι πάλιν ἤγειρον τὸ πρᾶγμα καὶ μηνυτὰς
8 εἰσέπεμπον. καὶ τί δεῖ μακρολογεῖν; οὐ γὰρ
πρότερον ἐπαύσαντο, πρὶν τόν τε πατέρ' ἐκ τοῦ
στρατοπέδου μετεπέμψαντο, καὶ τῶν φίλων αὐτοῦ
τοὺς μὲν ἀπέκτειναν, τοὺς δ' ἐκ τῆς πόλεως ἐξέβαλον. πυθόμενος δὲ τήν τε τῶν ἐχθρῶν δύναμιν
καὶ τὰς τῶν ἐπιτηδείων συμφοράς, καὶ νομίζων
δεινὰ πάσχειν ὅτι παρόντα μὲν αὐτὸν οὐκ ἔκρινον,
ἀπόντος δὲ κατεγίγνωσκον, οὐδ' ὡς ἀπελθεῖν
9 ἠξίωσεν εἰς τοὺς πολεμίους· ἀλλ' ἐκεῖνος μὲν
τοσαύτην πρόνοιαν ἔσχεν ὑπὲρ τοῦ μηδὲ φεύγων
μηδὲν ἐξαμαρτεῖν εἰς τὴν πόλιν, ὥστ' εἰς Ἄργος
ἐλθὼν ἡσυχίαν εἶχεν, οἱ δ' εἰς τοσοῦτον ὕβρεως
ἦλθον, ὥστ' ἔπεισαν ὑμᾶς ἐλαύνειν αὐτὸν ἐξ ἁπάσης τῆς Ἑλλάδος καὶ στηλίτην ἀναγράφειν καὶ
πρέσβεις πέμποντας ἐξαιτεῖν παρ' Ἀργείων. ἀπορῶν δ' ὅ τι χρήσαιτο τοῖς παροῦσι κακοῖς καὶ
πανταχόθεν εἰργόμενος καὶ σωτηρίας οὐδεμιᾶς ἄλλης αὐτῷ φαινομένης τελευτῶν ἐπὶ Λακεδαιμονίους
ἠναγκάσθη καταφυγεῖν.

10 Καὶ τὰ μὲν γενόμενα ταῦτ' ἐστίν· τοσοῦτον δὲ
τοῖς ἐχθροῖς τῆς ὕβρεως περίεστιν, ὥσθ' οὕτως ἀ-
νόμως τοῦ πατρὸς ἐκπεσόντος ὡς δεινὰ δεδρακότος
αὐτοῦ κατηγοροῦσι, καὶ διαβάλλειν ἐπιχειροῦσιν

---

* The ill-fated Sicilian Expedition, 415–413 B.C.

accusers were lying that the people would have been glad to punish them, and furthermore elected him general for the Sicilian expedition.[a]   Thereupon he sailed away, judging that he had been already cleared of their calumnies ; but his accusers, having united the Council and having made the public speakers subservient to themselves, again revived the matter and suborned informers.   Why need I say more ?   They did not cease until they had recalled my father from the expedition and had put to death some of his friends and had banished others from the city.   But when he had learned the power of his enemies and the misfortunes of his friends, although he was of opinion that he was being grossly wronged because they would not try him when he was in Athens but were for condemning him in his absence, not even in these circumstances did my father see fit to desert to the enemy ; on the contrary, even in exile he was so scrupulous to avoid injuring his city that he went to Argos and remained quietly there.   But his enemies reached such a pitch of insolence that they persuaded you to banish him from Greece entirely, to inscribe his name on a column as a traitor, and to send envoys to demand his surrender by the Argives.   And he, being at a loss to know what to do in the misfortunes which encompassed him and everywhere hemmed him in, as he saw no other means of safety, was compelled at last to take refuge with the Lacedaemonians.

These are the actual facts ; but such an excess of insolence have my father's enemies that they accuse him, who was exiled in so illegal a manner as if he had committed outrageous crimes, and try to ruin his reputation by saying that he caused the

ὡς Δεκέλειάν τ᾽ ἐπετείχισε καὶ τὰς νήσους ἀπέστη-
11 σε καὶ τῶν πολεμίων διδάσκαλος κατέστη. καὶ
ἐνίοτε μὲν αὐτοῦ προσποιοῦνται καταφρονεῖν, λέγοντες ὡς οὐδὲν διέφερε τῶν ἄλλων, νυνὶ δ᾽ ἁπάντων αὐτὸν τῶν γεγενημένων αἰτιῶνται καί φασι
παρ᾽ ἐκείνου μαθεῖν Λακεδαιμονίους ὡς χρὴ πολε-
[349] μεῖν, οἳ καὶ τοὺς ἄλλους διδάσκειν τέχνην ἔχουσιν.
ἐγὼ δ᾽ εἴ μοι χρόνος ἱκανὸς γένοιτο, ῥᾳδίως ἂν
αὐτὸν ἐπιδείξαιμι τὰ μὲν δικαίως πράξαντα, τῶν
δ᾽ ἀδίκως αἰτίαν ἔχοντα. πάντων δ᾽ ἂν εἴη δεινότατον, εἰ τοῦ πατρὸς μετὰ τὴν φυγὴν δωρεὰν
λαβόντος ἐγὼ διὰ τὴν ἐκείνου φυγὴν ζημιωθείην.
12 Ἡγοῦμαι δ᾽ αὐτὸν παρ᾽ ὑμῶν δικαίως ἂν πλείστης συγγνώμης τυγχάνειν· ὑπὸ γὰρ τῶν τριάκοντ᾽
ἐκπεσόντες ταῖς αὐταῖς ἐκείνῳ συμφοραῖς ἐχρή-
σασθε. ἐξ ὧν ἐνθυμεῖσθαι χρή, πῶς ἕκαστος ὑμῶν
διέκειτο καὶ τίνα γνώμην εἶχε καὶ ποῖον κίνδυνον
οὐκ ἂν ὑπέμεινεν ὥστε παύσασθαι μὲν μετοικῶν,
κατελθεῖν δ᾽ εἰς τὴν πατρίδα, τιμωρήσασθαι δὲ
13 τοὺς ἐκβαλόντας. ἐπὶ τίνα δ᾽ ἢ πόλιν ἢ φίλον ἢ
ξένον οὐκ ἤλθετε δεησόμενοι συγκαταγαγεῖν ὑμᾶς;
τίνος δ᾽ ἀπέσχεσθε πειρώμενοι κατελθεῖν; οὐ
καταλαβόντες τὸν Πειραιᾶ καὶ τὸν σῖτον τὸν ἐν τῇ
χώρᾳ διεφθείρετε καὶ τὴν γῆν ἐτέμνετε καὶ τὰ
προάστεια ἐνεπρήσατε καὶ τελευτῶντες τοῖς τείχεσι
14 προσεβάλετε; καὶ ταῦθ᾽ οὕτω σφόδρ᾽ ἐνομίζετε

ᵃ Decelea was a fort on Mt. Parnes, fourteen miles N.E.
from Athens. The Lacedaemonians occupied it in 413 B.C.
Cf. Lysias, *Against Alcibiades* 30, and for the facts Thucydides vi. 91. 6.
ᵇ Cf. Lysias, *Against Alcibiades* 35-38.
ᵉ After the capture of Athens by the Spartans in 404 B.C.

fortification of Decelea,[a] and the revolt of the islands, and that he became the enemy's counsellor. And sometimes they pretend to despise him,[b] saying that in no respect did he excel his contemporaries; yet at the present time they blame him for all that has happened and say that the Lacedaemonians have learned from him the art of war—they who can teach the rest of the world this accomplishment! As for me, if I had sufficient time, I could easily prove that some of those things he did justly, but that others are unjustly imputed to him. Yet the most shocking thing that could happen would be this—if, while after his exile my father was recompensed, I, because he was exiled, should be penalized.

I think, however, that in justice he should obtain from you a full pardon; for you, when banished by the Thirty Tyrants,[c] experienced the same misfortunes as he. Wherefore you should reflect how each of you was affected, what thoughts you each had, and what peril each would not have undergone so as to bring his own banishment to an end and to return to his native land, and to be avenged on those who banished him. To what city, or friend, or stranger did you not apply, to entreat them to help you to get back to your country? From what effort did you abstain in your endeavours to be restored? Did you not seize the Piraeus and destroy the crops in the fields and harry the land and set fire to the suburbs and finally assault the walls? And so vehemently did you believe that these actions

an oligarchy known as the Thirty Tyrants was established. The cruelty of their government caused many of the democratic party to go into exile. Led by Thrasybulus these exiles were restored when the Thirty were overthrown in 403 B.C.

χρῆναι ποιεῖν, ὥστε τοῖς ἡσυχίαν ἄγουσι τῶν συμφυγάδων μᾶλλον ὠργίζεσθε ἢ τοῖς αἰτίοις τῶν συμφορῶν γεγενημένοις. ὥστ' οὐκ εἰκὸς ἐπιτιμᾶν τοῖς τῶν αὐτῶν ὑμῖν ἐπιθυμοῦσιν, οὐδὲ κακοὺς ἄνδρας νομίζειν, ὅσοι φεύγοντες κατελθεῖν ἐζήτησαν, ἀλλὰ πολὺ μᾶλλον ὅσοι μένοντες φυγῆς ἄξι' ἐποίησαν· οὐδ' ἐντεῦθεν ἀρξαμένους κρίνειν, ὁποῖός τις ἦν ὁ πατὴρ πολίτης, ὅτ' οὐδὲν αὐτῷ τῆς πόλεως προσ-
15 ῆκεν, ἀλλ' ἐπ' ἐκείνου τοῦ χρόνου σκοπεῖν οἷος ἦν πρὶν φυγεῖν περὶ τὸ πλῆθος, καὶ ὅτι διακοσίους ὁπλίτας ἔχων τὰς μεγίστας πόλεις τῶν ἐν Πελοποννήσῳ Λακεδαιμονίων μὲν ἀπέστησεν, ὑμῖν δὲ συμμάχους ἐποίησε, καὶ εἰς οἵους κινδύνους αὐτοὺς κατέστησε, καὶ ὡς περὶ Σικελίαν ἐστρατήγησεν. τούτων μὲν γὰρ ἐκείνῳ προσήκει χάριν ὑμᾶς ἔχειν· τῶν δ' ἐν τῇ συμφορᾷ γενομένων τοὺς ἐκβαλόντας αὐτὸν δικαίως ἂν αἰτίους νομίζοιτε.

16 Ἀναμνήσθητε δὲ πρὸς ὑμᾶς αὐτούς, ἐπειδὴ
[350] κατῆλθεν, ὡς πόλλ' ἀγαθὰ τὴν πόλιν ἐποίησεν, ἔτι δὲ πρότερον, ὡς ἐχόντων τῶν πραγμάτων αὐτὸν κατεδέξασθε, καταλελυμένου μὲν τοῦ δήμου, στασιαζόντων δὲ τῶν πολιτῶν, διαφερομένων δὲ τῶν στρατιωτῶν πρὸς τὰς ἀρχὰς τὰς ἐνθάδε καθεστηκυίας, εἰς τοῦτο δὲ μανίας ἀμφοτέρων ἀφιγμένων ὥστε μηδετέροις μηδεμίαν ἐλπίδ' εἶναι σωτηρίας·
17 οἱ μὲν γὰρ τοὺς ἔχοντας τὴν πόλιν ἐχθροὺς ἐνόμιζον μᾶλλον ἢ Λακεδαιμονίους, οἱ δὲ τοὺς ἐκ Δεκελείας

---

[a] 419 b.c. *Cf.* Thucydides v. 52. 2.
[b] By the Revolution of the Four Hundred.
[c] The Athenian army and fleet, sympathetic to the democracy, were at the island of Samos (Thucydides viii. 82 and 86). [d] The oligarchs in Athens.

were justifiable that you were more indignant with those of your fellow-exiles who were inactive than with those who had been the authors of your misfortunes. It is not fair, therefore, to censure those who wanted the same things which you desired, nor yet to regard all those men as base who, when they were exiles, sought to return, but much more should you condemn those oligarchs who, remaining in Athens, did deeds which deserved the penalty of exile ; nor is it fair that you, in judging what sort of citizen my father was, should begin at the time when he had no part in the city's affairs ; on the contrary, you should look to that earlier time and observe how he served the people before his exile, and call to mind that with two hundred heavy-armed soldiers he caused the most powerful cities in the Peloponnesus to revolt from the Lacedaemonians,[a] and brought them into alliance with you, and in what perils he involved the Lacedaemonians themselves, and how he behaved as general in Sicily. For these services he is deserving of your gratitude ; but for that which happened when he was in misfortune it is those who banished him whom you would justly hold responsible.

Remember, too, I beg you, the many benefits he conferred upon the city after his return from exile, and, even before that time, the state of affairs here when you received him back : the democracy had been overthrown,[b] the citizens were in a state of civil war, the army was disaffected toward the government established here, and both parties had reached such a state of madness that neither had any hope of salvation. For the one party [c] regarded those who were in possession of the city as greater enemies than the Lacedaemonians ; and the other [d]

μετεπέμποντο, ἡγούμενοι κρεῖττον εἶναι τοῖς πολεμίοις τὴν πατρίδα παραδοῦναι μᾶλλον ἢ τοῖς ὑπὲρ
τῆς πόλεως στρατευομένοις τῆς πολιτείας μετα-
18 δοῦναι. τοιαύτην μὲν οὖν τῶν πολιτῶν γνώμην
ἐχόντων, κρατούντων δὲ τῶν πολεμίων καὶ τῆς γῆς
καὶ τῆς θαλάττης, ἔτι δὲ χρημάτων ὑμῖν μὲν οὐκ
ὄντων, ἐκείνοις δὲ βασιλέως παρέχοντος, πρὸς δὲ
τούτοις ἐνενήκοντα νεῶν ἐκ Φοινίκης εἰς Ἄσπεν-
δον ἡκουσῶν καὶ παρεσκευασμένων Λακεδαιμονίοις
βοηθεῖν, ἐν τοσαύταις συμφοραῖς καὶ τοιούτοις
19 κινδύνοις τῆς πόλεως οὔσης, μεταπεμψαμένων αὐτὸν τῶν στρατιωτῶν οὐκ ἐσεμνύνατ' ἐπὶ τοῖς παροῦσιν, οὐδ' ἐμέμψατο περὶ τῶν γεγενημένων, οὐδ'
ἐβουλεύσατο περὶ τῶν μελλόντων, ἀλλ' εὐθὺς
εἵλετο μετὰ τῆς πόλεως ὁτιοῦν πάσχειν μᾶλλον
ἢ μετὰ Λακεδαιμονίων εὐτυχεῖν, καὶ πᾶσι φανερὸν ἐποίησεν ὅτι τοῖς ἐκβαλοῦσιν ἀλλ' οὐχ ὑμῖν
ἐπολέμει, καὶ ὅτι κατελθεῖν ἀλλ' οὐκ ἀπολέσαι τὴν
20 πόλιν ἐπεθύμει. γενόμενος δὲ μεθ' ὑμῶν ἔπεισε
μὲν Τισσαφέρνην μὴ παρέχειν χρήματα Λακεδαιμονίοις, ἔπαυσε δὲ τοὺς συμμάχους ὑμῶν ἀφ-
ισταμένους, διέδωκε δὲ παρ' αὑτοῦ μισθὸν τοῖς
στρατιώταις, ἀπέδωκε δὲ τῷ δήμῳ τὴν πολιτείαν, διήλλαξε δὲ τοὺς πολίτας, ἀπέστρεψε δὲ τὰς
21 ναῦς τὰς Φοινίσσας. καὶ μετὰ ταῦτα καθ' ἕκαστον
μέν, ὅσας τριήρεις ἔλαβεν ἢ μάχας ἐνίκησεν ἢ
πόλεις κατὰ κράτος εἷλεν ἢ λόγῳ πείσας φίλας

―――――――――
[a] The Persian king depended largely upon Phoenicia for
ships of war.

were making overtures to the Spartan forces in
Decelea, judging that it was preferable to hand over
their country to its enemies rather than to give a
share in the rights of citizenship to those who were
fighting for the city. Such was the state of mind
of the citizens : the enemy was in control of land
and sea ; your financial resources were exhausted,
while the Persian king was supplying them with
funds ; furthermore, ninety ships had come from
Phoenicia *a* to Aspendus *b* and were prepared to aid
the Lacedaemonians. By so many misfortunes and
such perils was the city beset when the army summoned my father, and he did not treat them with
disdain in their plight, nor did he rebuke them for
the past, nor did he deliberate about the future ;
on the contrary, he chose at once to suffer any misfortune with his country rather than to enjoy prosperity with the Lacedaemonians, and he made it
manifest to all that he was warring on those who
had banished him and not on you, and that his heart
was set on a return to Athens and not on her ruin.
Having thrown in his lot with you, he persuaded
Tissaphernes *c* not to furnish the Lacedaemonians
with money, checked the defection of your allies,
distributed pay from his own resources to the soldiers,
restored political power to the people, reconciled the
citizens, and turned back the Phoenician fleet. As
to his later services, it would be an arduous task
to enumerate them one by one—all the ships of
war that he subsequently captured, or the battles
that he won, or the cities he took by storm or by

b Aspendus, a town in Asia Minor, in Pamphylia, was
situated on the river Eurymedon.
    c Persian satrap of western Asia Minor from 414 B.C.

ὑμῖν ἐποίησε, πολὺ ἂν ἔργον εἴη λέγειν· πλείστων
δὲ κινδύνων τῇ πόλει κατ᾽ ἐκεῖνον τὸν καιρὸν
γενομένων οὐδεπώποτε τοῦ πατρὸς ἡγουμένου τρόπαιον ὑμῶν ἔστησαν οἱ πολέμιοι.

22
[351]
    Περὶ μὲν οὖν τῶν ἐστρατηγημένων οἶδα μὲν ὅτι
πολλὰ παραλείπω, διὰ τοῦτο δ᾽ οὐκ ἀκριβῶς εἴρηκα
περὶ αὐτῶν, ὅτι σχεδὸν ἅπαντες μνημονεύετε τὰ
πραχθέντα. λοιδοροῦσι δὲ λίαν ἀσελγῶς καὶ θρασέως καὶ τὸν ἄλλον βίον τὸν τοῦ πατρός, καὶ οὐκ
αἰσχύνονται τοιαύτῃ παρρησίᾳ χρώμενοι περὶ τοῦ
τεθνεῶτος, ἣν ἔδεισαν ἂν ποιήσασθαι περὶ ζῶντος,
23 ἀλλ᾽ εἰς τοσοῦτον ἀνοίας ἐληλύθασιν, ὥστ᾽ οἴονται
καὶ παρ᾽ ὑμῖν καὶ παρὰ τοῖς ἄλλοις εὐδοκιμήσειν,
ἢν ὡς ἂν δύνωνται πλεῖστα περὶ αὐτοῦ βλασφη-
μήσωσιν, ὥσπερ οὐ πάντας εἰδότας ὅτι καὶ τοῖς
φαυλοτάτοις τῶν ἀνθρώπων ἔξεστιν οὐ μόνον περὶ
τῶν ἀνδρῶν τῶν ἀρίστων ἀλλὰ καὶ περὶ τῶν θεῶν
24 ὑβριστικοὺς λόγους εἰπεῖν. ἴσως μὲν οὖν ἀνόητόν
ἐστιν ἁπάντων τῶν εἰρημένων φροντίζειν· ὅμως δ᾽
οὐχ ἥκιστ᾽ ἐπιθυμῶ περὶ τῶν ἐπιτηδευμάτων τῶν
τοῦ πατρὸς διελθεῖν πρὸς ὑμᾶς, μικρὸν προλαβὼν
καὶ τῶν προγόνων ἐπιμνησθείς, ἵν᾽ ἐπίστησθ᾽ ὅτι
πόρρωθεν ἡμῖν ὑπάρχει μέγιστα καὶ κάλλιστα
τῶν πολιτῶν.

25 Ὁ γὰρ πατὴρ πρὸς μὲν ἀνδρῶν ἦν Εὐπατριδῶν,[a]
ὧν τὴν εὐγένειαν ἐξ αὐτῆς τῆς ἐπωνυμίας ῥᾴδιον
γνῶναι, πρὸς γυναικῶν δ᾽ Ἀλκμεωνιδῶν, οἳ τοῦ
μὲν πλούτου μέγιστον μνημεῖον κατέλιπον, ἵππων
γὰρ ζεύγει πρῶτος Ἀλκμέων τῶν πολιτῶν Ὀλυμπίασιν ἐνίκησε, τὴν δ᾽ εὔνοιαν ἣν εἶχον εἰς τὸ

---

[a] The Eupatrids (*sons of noble sires*) were the nobles, or
patricians, in Athens of the early time.

persuasion made your friends. But although innumerable dangers beset the city at that time, never did the enemy erect a trophy of victory over you while my father was your leader.

I am aware that I am omitting many of my father's exploits as your general; I have not recounted them in detail because nearly all of you recall the facts. But my father's private life they revile with excessive indecency and audacity, and they are not ashamed, now that he is dead, to use a licence of speech concerning him which they would have feared to employ while he lived. Nay, they have come to such a pitch of folly that they think they will win repute with both you and with the world at large if they indulge in the wildest possible abuse of him; as if all did not know that it is in the power of the vilest of men to abuse with insulting words, not only the best of men, but even the gods. Perhaps it is foolish for me to take to heart all that has been said; nevertheless, I desire very much to recount to you my father's private pursuits, going back a little to make mention of his ancestors, that you may know that from early times our standing and services have been the greatest and most honourable among the citizens of Athens.

My father on the male side belonged to the Eupatrids,[a] whose noble birth is apparent from the very name. On the female side he was of the Alcmeonidae,[b] who left behind a glorious memorial of their wealth; for Alcmeon[c] was the first Athenian to win at Olympia with a team of horses, and the

[b] Descendants of Alcmeon, one of the greatest families in early Athens, expelled from the city in 595 B.C.

[c] Son of Megacles.

πλῆθος, ἐν τοῖς τυραννικοῖς ἐπεδείξαντο· συγγενεῖς
γὰρ ὄντες Πεισιστράτου καὶ πρὶν εἰς τὴν ἀρχὴν
καταστῆναι μάλιστ' αὐτῷ χρώμενοι τῶν πολιτῶν,
οὐκ ἠξίωσαν μετασχεῖν τῆς ἐκείνου τυραννίδος,
ἀλλ' εἵλοντο φυγεῖν μᾶλλον ἢ τοὺς πολίτας ἰδεῖν
26 δουλεύοντας. τετταράκοντα δ' ἔτη τῆς στάσεως
γενομένης ὑπὸ μὲν τῶν τυράννων τοσούτῳ μᾶλλον
τῶν ἄλλων ἐμισήθησαν, ὥσθ' ὁπότε τἀκείνων κρα-
τήσειεν, οὐ μόνον τὰς οἰκίας αὐτῶν κατέσκαπτον
ἀλλὰ καὶ τοὺς τάφους ἀνώρυττον, ὑπὸ δὲ τῶν
συμφυγάδων οὕτω σφόδρ' ἐπιστεύθησαν, ὥσθ'
ἅπαντα τοῦτον τὸν χρόνον ἡγούμενοι τοῦ δήμου
διετέλεσαν. καὶ τὸ τελευταῖον Ἀλκιβιάδης καὶ
Κλεισθένης, ὁ μὲν πρὸς πατρός, ὁ δὲ πρὸς μητρὸς
[352] ὧν πρόπαππος τοῦ πατρὸς τοὐμοῦ, στρατηγή-
σαντες τῆς φυγῆς κατήγαγον τὸν δῆμον καὶ τοὺς
27 τυράννους ἐξέβαλον, καὶ κατέστησαν ἐκείνην τὴν
δημοκρατίαν, ἐξ ἧς οἱ πολῖται πρὸς μὲν ἀνδρίαν
οὕτως ἐπαιδεύθησαν ὥστε τοὺς βαρβάρους τοὺς
ἐπὶ πᾶσαν ἐλθόντας τὴν Ἑλλάδα μόνοι νικᾶν μαχόμενοι, περὶ δὲ δικαιοσύνης τοσαύτην δόξαν ἔλαβον
ὥσθ' ἑκόντας αὐτοῖς τοὺς Ἕλληνας ἐγχειρίσαι τὴν
ἀρχὴν τῆς θαλάττης, τὴν δὲ πόλιν τηλικαύτην τὸ
μέγεθος ἐποίησαν καὶ τῇ δυνάμει καὶ ταῖς ἄλλαις
κατασκευαῖς ὥστε τοὺς φάσκοντας αὐτὴν ἄστυ τῆς
Ἑλλάδος εἶναι καὶ τοιαύταις ὑπερβολαῖς εἰθισμένους χρῆσθαι δοκεῖν ἀληθῆ λέγειν.
28 Τὴν μὲν οὖν φιλίαν τὴν πρὸς τὸν δῆμον οὕτω

---

[a] Pisistratus was tyrant of Athens in the sixth century B.C.
[b] Roughly speaking the period of the rule of Pisistratus
and his sons, 560–510 B.C.
[c] Cf. Herodotus v. 71.

goodwill which they had toward the people they displayed in the time of the tyrants. For they were kinsmen of Pisistratus [a] and before he came to power were closest to him of all the citizens, but they refused to share his tyranny; on the contrary, they preferred exile rather than to see their fellow-citizens enslaved. And during the forty years [b] of civic discord the Alcmeonidae were hated so much more bitterly than all other Athenians by the tyrants that whenever the tyrants had the upper hand they not only razed their dwellings, but even dug up their tombs [c]; and so completely were the Alcmeonidae trusted by their fellow-exiles that they continued during all that time to be leaders of the people. At last, Alcibiades and Cleisthenes [d]—the former my great-grandfather on my father's side, the latter my father's maternal great-grandfather—assuming the leadership of those in exile, restored the people to their country, and drove out the tyrants. And they established that democratic form of government which so effectively trained the citizens in bravery that single-handed they conquered in battle [e] the barbarians who had attacked all Greece; and they won so great renown for justice that the Greeks voluntarily put in their hands the dominion of the sea; and they made Athens so great in her power and her other resources that those who allege that she is the capital of Greece [f] and habitually apply to her similar exaggerated expressions appear to be speaking the truth.

Now this friendship with the people, which was,

[d] Cleisthenes was the reformer of the Athenian constitution and founder of the democracy.
[e] Marathon, 490 B.C.　　[f] Cf. Isocrates, Antid. 299.

παλαιὰν καὶ γνησίαν καὶ διὰ τὰς μεγίστας εὐεργεσίας γεγενημένην παρὰ τῶν προγόνων παρέλαβεν·
αὐτὸς δὲ κατελείφθη μὲν ὀρφανός, ὁ γὰρ πατὴρ
αὐτοῦ μαχόμενος ἐν Κορωνείᾳ τοῖς πολεμίοις ἀπέθανεν, ἐπετροπεύθη δ᾽ ὑπὸ Περικλέους, ὃν πάντες
ἂν ὁμολογήσειαν καὶ σωφρονέστατον καὶ δικαιότατον καὶ σοφώτατον γενέσθαι τῶν πολιτῶν. ἡγοῦμαι γὰρ καὶ τοῦτ᾽ εἶναι τῶν καλῶν, ἐκ τοιούτων
γενόμενον ὑπὸ τοιούτοις ἤθεσιν ἐπιτροπευθῆναι καὶ
29 τραφῆναι καὶ παιδευθῆναι.   δοκιμασθεὶς δ᾽ οὐκ
ἐνδεέστερος ἐγένετο τῶν προειρημένων, οὐδ᾽ ἠξίωσεν αὐτὸς μὲν ῥᾳθύμως ζῆν, σεμνύνεσθαι δ᾽ ἐπὶ
ταῖς τῶν προγόνων ἀρεταῖς, ἀλλ᾽ εὐθὺς οὕτω μέγ᾽
ἐφρόνησεν, ὥστ᾽ ᾠήθη δεῖν δι᾽ αὐτὸν καὶ τἀκείνων
ἔργα μνημονεύεσθαι.   καὶ πρῶτον μέν, ὅτε Φορ-
μίων ἐξήγαγεν ἐπὶ Θρᾴκης χιλίους Ἀθηναίων,
ἐπιλεξάμενος τοὺς ἀρίστους, μετὰ τούτων στρατευσάμενος τοιοῦτος ἦν ἐν τοῖς κινδύνοις ὥστε
στεφανωθῆναι καὶ πανοπλίαν λαβεῖν παρὰ τοῦ
30 στρατηγοῦ.   καίτοι τί χρὴ[1] τὸν τῶν μεγίστων
ἐπαίνων ἄξιον; οὐ μετὰ μὲν τῶν βελτίστων ἐκ
τῆς πόλεως στρατευόμενον ἀριστείων ἀξιοῦσθαι,
πρὸς δὲ τοὺς κρατίστους τῶν Ἑλλήνων ἀντιστρα-
τηγοῦντ᾽ ἐν ἅπασι τοῖς κινδύνοις αὐτῶν φαίνεσθαι
περιγιγνόμενον; ἐκεῖνος τοίνυν τῶν μὲν νέος ὢν
ἔτυχε, τὰ δ᾽ ἐπειδὴ πρεσβύτερος ἦν ἔπραξεν.

---

[1] χρὴ ΓΕ : χρὴ νομίζειν ποιεῖν vulg.

---

[a] Cleinias.
[b] A town in Boeotia where the Athenians were defeated
by the Boeotians in 446 B.C.
[c] A famous Athenian general.

as I have shown, so ancient, genuine, and based upon services of the greatest importance, my father inherited from his ancestors. My father himself was left an orphan (for his father [a] died in battle at Coronea [b]) and became the ward of Pericles, whom all would acknowledge to have been the most moderate, the most just, and the wisest of the citizens. For I count this also among his blessings that, being of such origin, he was fostered, reared, and educated under the guardianship of a man of such character. When he was admitted to citizenship, he showed himself not inferior to those whom I have mentioned, nor did he think it fitting that he should lead a life of ease, pluming himself upon the brave deeds of his ancestors ; on the contrary, from the beginning he was so fired with ambition that he thought that even their great deeds should be held in remembrance through his own. And first of all, when Phormio [c] led a thousand of the flower of Athenian soldiers to Thrace,[d] my father served with this expedition, and so distinguished himself in the perilous actions of the campaign that he was crowned and received a full suit of armour from his general. Really what is required of the man who is thought worthy of the highest praise ? Should he not, when serving with the bravest of the citizens, be thought worthy of the prize of valour, and when leading an army against the best of the Greeks in all the battles show his superiority to them ? My father, then, in his youth did win that prize of valour and in later life did achieve the latter.

[d] Expedition to recover the city of Potidaea in 432 B.C. Thucydides (i. 64. 2) speaks of 1600 hoplites. *Cf.* Plato, *Symp.* 220 E for the award of valour given to Alcibiades.

ISOCRATES

31
[353] Μετὰ δὲ ταῦτα τὴν μητέρα τὴν ἐμὴν ἔγημεν·
ἡγοῦμαι γὰρ καὶ ταύτην ἀριστεῖον αὐτὸν λαβεῖν. ὁ
γὰρ πατὴρ αὐτῆς Ἱππόνικος, πλούτῳ μὲν πρῶτος
ὢν τῶν Ἑλλήνων, γένει δ' οὐδενὸς ὕστερος τῶν
πολιτῶν, τιμώμενος δὲ καὶ θαυμαζόμενος μάλιστα
τῶν ἐφ' αὑτοῦ, μετὰ προικὸς δὲ πλείστης καὶ δόξης
μεγίστης ἐκδιδοὺς τὴν θυγατέρα, καὶ τοῦ γάμου
τυχεῖν εὐχομένων μὲν ἁπάντων, ἀξιούντων δὲ τῶν
πρώτων, τὸν πατέρα τὸν ἐμὸν ἐξ ἁπάντων ἐκλεξάμενος κηδεστὴν ἐπεθύμησε ποιήσασθαι.

32 Περὶ δὲ τοὺς αὐτοὺς χρόνους ὁρῶν τὴν ἐν
Ὀλυμπίᾳ πανήγυριν ὑπὸ πάντων ἀνθρώπων
ἀγαπωμένην καὶ θαυμαζομένην, καὶ τοὺς Ἕλληνας
ἐπίδειξιν ἐν αὐτῇ ποιουμένους πλούτου καὶ ῥώμης
καὶ παιδεύσεως, καὶ τούς τ' ἀθλητὰς ζηλουμένους
καὶ τὰς πόλεις ὀνομαστὰς γιγνομένας τὰς τῶν
νικώντων, καὶ πρὸς τούτοις ἡγούμενος τὰς μὲν
ἐνθάδε λῃτουργίας ὑπὲρ τῶν ἰδίων πρὸς τοὺς πολίτας εἶναι, τὰς δ' εἰς ἐκείνην τὴν πανήγυριν ὑπὲρ τῆς
33 πόλεως εἰς ἅπασαν τὴν Ἑλλάδα γίγνεσθαι, ταῦτα
διανοηθείς, οὐδενὸς ἀφυέστερος οὐδ' ἀρρωστότερος
τῷ σώματι γενόμενος τοὺς μὲν γυμνικοὺς ἀγῶνας
ὑπερεῖδεν, εἰδὼς ἐνίους τῶν ἀθλητῶν καὶ κακῶς γεγονότας καὶ μικρὰς πόλεις οἰκοῦντας καὶ ταπεινῶς
πεπαιδευμένους, ἱπποτροφεῖν δ' ἐπιχειρήσας, ὃ τῶν
εὐδαιμονεστάτων ἔργον ἐστί, φαῦλος δ' οὐδεὶς
ἂν ποιήσειεν, οὐ μόνον τοὺς ἀνταγωνιστὰς ἀλλὰ
34 καὶ τοὺς πώποτε νικήσαντας ὑπερεβάλετο. ζεύγη
γὰρ καθῆκε τοσαῦτα μὲν τὸν ἀριθμὸν ὅσοις οὐδ' αἱ
μέγισται τῶν πόλεων ἠγωνίσαντο, τοιαῦτα δὲ τὴν

---

[a] Hipparetê.   [b] Son of Callias, noted for his wealth.

194

After this he married my mother *a* ; and I believe that in her he also won a glorious prize of valour. For her father was Hipponicus,*b* first in wealth of all the Greeks and second in birth to none of the citizens, most honoured and admired of his contemporaries. The richest dowry and fairest reputation went with his daughter's hand ; and although all coveted union with her, and only the greatest thought themselves worthy, it was my father whom Hipponicus chose from among them all and desired to make his son-in-law.

About the same time my father, seeing that the festival assembly at Olympia was beloved and admired by the whole world and that in it the Greeks made display of their wealth, strength of body, and training, and that not only the athletes were the objects of envy but that also the cities of the victors became renowned, and believing moreover that while the public services performed in Athens redound to the prestige, in the eyes of his fellow-citizens, of the person who renders them, expenditures in the Olympian Festival, however, enhance the city's reputation throughout all Greece, reflecting upon these things, I say, although in natural gifts and in strength of body he was inferior to none, he disdained the gymnastic contests, for he knew that some of the athletes were of low birth, inhabitants of petty states, and of mean education, but turned to the breeding of race-horses, which is possible only for those most blest by Fortune and not to be pursued by one of low estate, and not only did he surpass his rivals, but also all who had ever before won the victory. For he entered a larger number of teams in competition than even the mightiest cities had

ἀρετὴν ὥστε καὶ πρῶτος καὶ δεύτερος γενέσθαι καὶ
τρίτος. χωρὶς δὲ τούτων ἐν ταῖς θυσίαις καὶ ταῖς
ἄλλαις ταῖς περὶ τὴν ἑορτὴν δαπάναις οὕτως ἀφει-
δῶς διέκειτο καὶ μεγαλοπρεπῶς ὥστε φαίνεσθαι τὰ
κοινὰ τὰ τῶν ἄλλων ἐλάττω τῶν ἰδίων τῶν ἐκείνου.
κατέλυσε δὲ τὴν θεωρίαν, τὰς μὲν τῶν προτέρων
εὐτυχίας μικρὰς πρὸς τὰς αὑτοῦ δόξαι ποιήσας,
[354] τοὺς δ' ἐφ' αὑτοῦ νικήσαντας παύσας ζηλουμένους,
τοῖς δὲ μέλλουσιν ἱπποτροφεῖν οὐδεμίαν ὑπερβολὴν
35 καταλιπών. περὶ δὲ τῶν ἐνθάδε χορηγιῶν καὶ
γυμνασιαρχιῶν καὶ τριηραρχιῶν αἰσχύνομαι λέγειν·
τοσοῦτον γὰρ ἐν τοῖς ἄλλοις διήνεγκεν, ὥσθ' οἱ μὲν
ἐνδεεστέρως ἐκείνου λῃτουργήσαντες ἐκ τούτων
σφᾶς αὐτοὺς ἐγκωμιάζουσιν, ὑπὲρ ἐκείνου δ' εἴ τις
καὶ τῶν τηλικούτων χάριν ἀπαιτοίη, περὶ μικρῶν
ἂν δόξειε τοὺς λόγους ποιεῖσθαι.

36 Πρὸς δὲ τὴν πολιτείαν, οὐδὲ γὰρ[1] τοῦτο παραλειπτέον, ὥσπερ οὐδ'[2] ἐκεῖνος αὐτῆς ἠμέλησεν,
ἀλλὰ τοσούτω τῶν μάλιστ' εὐδοκιμησάντων ἀμεί-

---

[1] οὐδὲ γὰρ Λ: οὐδέ γε Γ.
[2] ὥσπερ οὐδ' Λ: οὐδὲ γὰρ Γ. Kayser proposed to delete
ἀλλὰ and περὶ τὸν δῆμον to correct the anacoluthon, which
may well be intentional.

---

[a] *Cf.* Thucydides vi. 16. 2 and Plutarch, *Alcibiades* 11,
who give the same testimony; Alcibiades entered seven
teams. *Cf.* Plutarch, *Alcibiades* : " His horse-breeding was
famous, among other things, for the number of his racing-
chariots. He was the only man, not excluding kings, who
ever entered at Olympia as many as seven. And his winning
not only first place but second and fourth according to
Thucydides—second and third according to Euripides—is
the highest and most honourable distinction ever won in this
field. Euripides' Ode contains the following passage :
" ' But I will sing thy praises, son of Cleinias. A noble

done, and they were of such excellence that he came out first, second, and third.[a] Besides this, his generosity in the sacrifices and in the other expenses connected with the festival was so lavish and magnificent that the public funds of all the others [b] were clearly less than the private means of Alcibiades alone. And when he brought his mission to an end he had caused the successes of his predecessors to seem petty in comparison with his own and those who in his own day had been victors to be no longer objects of emulation, and to future breeders of racing-steeds he left behind no possibility of surpassing him. With regard to my father's services here in Athens as choregus and gymnasiarch and trierarch [c] I am ashamed to speak ; for so greatly did he excel in all the other public duties that, although those who have served the state in less splendid fashion sing their own praises therefor, if anyone should on my father's behalf ask for a vote of thanks even in recognition of services as great as his, he would seem to be talking about petty things.

As regards his behaviour as a citizen—for neither should this be passed over in silence—just as he on his part did not neglect his civic duties, but on the contrary, to so great a degree had proved himself

thing is victory, noblest of the noble to do what no Greek had ever done, be first and second and third in the chariot-race, and go unwearied yet, wreathed in the olive of Zeus, to make the herald cry you.' "—(Edmonds, *Lyra Graeca* ii. p. 241.) [b] *i.e.*, the Θεωροί, representing the other states.
  [c] These public services (referred to in § 32) were the *liturgies*, discharged by the wealthier citizens, *e.g.*, the *choregia* (expenses of the public choruses) ; the *gymnasiarchia* (defraying of expenses of training athletes for the contests) ; and the *trierarchia* (the cost of equipping a warship and keeping it in service for a year).

νων περὶ τὸν δῆμον γέγονεν, ὅσον τοὺς μὲν ἄλλους
εὑρήσεθ' ὑπὲρ αὑτῶν στασιάσαντας, ἐκεῖνον δ' ὑπὲρ
ὑμῶν κινδυνεύοντα. οὐ γὰρ ἀπελαυνόμενος ἀπὸ
τῆς ὀλιγαρχίας ἀλλὰ παρακαλούμενος ἦν δημοτικός·
καὶ πολλάκις ἐκγενόμενον αὐτῷ μὴ μόνον μετ'
ὀλίγων τῶν ἄλλων ἄρχειν ἀλλὰ καὶ τούτων αὐτῶν
πλέον ἔχειν, οὐκ ἠθέλησεν, ἀλλ' εἵλεθ' ὑπὸ τῆς
πόλεως ἀδικηθῆναι μᾶλλον ἢ τὴν πολιτείαν προ-
37 δοῦναι. καὶ ταῦθ' ἕως μὲν συνεχῶς ἐδημοκρατεῖσθ'
οὐδεὶς ἂν ὑμᾶς λέγων ἔπεισεν· νῦν δ' αἱ στάσεις αἱ
γενόμεναι σαφῶς ἐπέδειξαν καὶ τοὺς δημοτικοὺς
καὶ τοὺς ὀλιγαρχικοὺς καὶ τοὺς οὐδετέρων ἐπιθυμοῦντας καὶ τοὺς ἀμφοτέρων μετέχειν ἀξιοῦντας.
ἐν αἷς δὶς ὑπὸ τῶν ἐχθρῶν τῶν ὑμετέρων ἐξέπεσεν·
καὶ τὸ μὲν πρότερον, ἐπειδὴ τάχιστ' ἐκεῖνον ἐκποδὼν ἐποιήσαντο, τὸν δῆμον κατέλυσαν, τὸ δ'
ὕστερον οὐκ ἔφθασαν ὑμᾶς καταδουλωσάμενοι, καὶ
πρῶτου τῶν πολιτῶν αὐτοῦ φυγὴν κατέγνωσαν·
οὕτω σφόδρ' ἥ τε πόλις τῶν τοῦ πατρὸς κακῶν
38 ἀπέλαυσε κἀκεῖνος τῶν τῆς πόλεως συμφορῶν ἐκοι-
νώνησεν. καίτοι πολλοὶ τῶν πολιτῶν πρὸς αὐτὸν
δυσκόλως εἶχον ὡς πρὸς τυραννεῖν ἐπιβουλεύοντα,
οὐκ ἐκ τῶν ἔργων σκοποῦντες, ἀλλ' ἡγούμενοι
τὸ μὲν πρᾶγμ' ὑπὸ πάντων ζηλοῦσθαι, δύνασθαι
[355] δ' ἂν ἐκεῖνον μάλιστα διαπράξασθαι. διὸ καὶ
δικαίως ἂν αὐτῷ πλείω χάριν ἔχοιτε, ὅτι τὴν μὲν
αἰτίαν μόνος τῶν πολιτῶν ἄξιος ἦν ταύτην ἔχειν,

---

a i.e., of plotting to become tyrant.

a more loyal friend of the people than those who had gained the highest repute, that while, as you will find, the others stirred up sedition for selfish advantage, he was incurring danger on your behalf. For his devotion to the democracy was not that of one who was excluded from the oligarchy, but of one who was invited to join it : indeed, time and again when it was in his power as one of a small group, not only to rule the rest, but even to dominate them, he refused, choosing rather to suffer the city's unjust penalties rather than to be traitor to our form of government. Of the truth of these statements no one would have convinced you as long as you still continued to be governed as a democracy ; but as it was, the civil conflicts which arose clearly showed who were the democrats and who the oligarchs, as well as those who desired neither régime, and those who laid claim to a share in both. In these uprisings your enemies twice exiled my father : on the first occasion, no sooner had they got him out of the way than they abolished the democracy ; on the second, hardly had they reduced you to servitude than they condemned him to exile before any other citizen ; so exactly did my father's misfortunes affect the city and he share in her disasters. And yet many of the citizens were ill disposed toward him in the belief that he was plotting a tyranny ; they held this opinion, not on the basis of his deeds, but in the thought that all men aspire to this power and that he would have the best chance of attaining it. Wherefore you would justly feel the greater gratitude to him because, while he alone of the citizens was powerful enough to have this charge [a] brought against him, he was of opinion that as regards politi-

τῆς δὲ πολιτείας ἴσον ᾤετο δεῖν καὶ τοῖς ἄλλοις
μετεῖναι.

39 Διὰ δὲ τὸ πλῆθος τῶν ἐνόντων εἰπεῖν ὑπὲρ τοῦ
πατρὸς ἀπορῶ, τίνος ἐν τῷ παρόντι πρέπει μνησθῆναι καὶ ποῖ᾽ αὐτῶν χρὴ παραλιπεῖν· ἀεὶ γάρ μοι
δοκεῖ μεῖζον εἶναι τὸ μήπω πεφρασμένον τῶν ἤδη
πρὸς ὑμᾶς εἰρημένων. ἐπεὶ καὶ τοῦθ᾽ ἡγοῦμαι
πᾶσιν εἶναι φανερὸν ὅτι τοῦτον ἀναγκαῖόν ἐστιν
εὐνούστατον εἶναι ταῖς τῆς πόλεως εὐτυχίαις, ὅτῳ
πλεῖστον μέρος καὶ τῶν ἀγαθῶν καὶ τῶν κακῶν
40 μέτεστιν. ἐκείνου τοίνυν εὖ μὲν πραττούσης τῆς
πόλεως τίς εὐδαιμονέστερος ἢ θαυμαστότερος ἢ
ζηλωτότερος ἦν τῶν πολιτῶν, δυστυχησάσης δὲ τίς
ἐλπίδων μειζόνων ἢ χρημάτων πλειόνων ἢ δόξης
καλλίονος ἐστερήθη; οὐ τὸ τελευταῖον ἐπειδὴ
κατέστησαν οἱ τριάκονθ᾽ οἱ μὲν ἄλλοι τὴν πόλιν
ἔφυγον, ἐκεῖνος δ᾽ ἐξ ἁπάσης τῆς Ἑλλάδος ἐξέπε-
σεν; οὐ Λακεδαιμόνιοι καὶ Λύσανδρος ὁμοίως
ἔργον ἐποιήσαντ᾽ ἐκεῖνον ἀποκτεῖναι καὶ τὴν ὑμετέραν καταλῦσαι δύναμιν, οὐδεμίαν ἡγούμενοι πίστιν
ἕξειν παρὰ τῆς πόλεως, εἰ τὰ τείχη καταβάλοιεν, εἰ
41 μὴ καὶ τὸν ἀναστῆσαι δυνάμενον ἀπολέσαιεν; ὥστ᾽
οὐ μόνον ἐξ ὧν ὑμᾶς εὖ πεποίηκεν ἀλλὰ καὶ ἐξ
ὧν δι᾽ ὑμᾶς κακῶς πέπονθε ῥάδιον γνῶναι τὴν
εὔνοιαν τὴν ἐκείνου. φαίνεται γὰρ τῷ δήμῳ βοη-
θῶν, τῆς αὐτῆς πολιτείας ὑμῖν ἐπιθυμῶν, ὑπὸ τῶν

<hr />

ᵃ Spartan general, victorious over the Athenians at Aegospotami (405 B.C.).
ᵇ The Long Walls, uniting Athens and its harbour

cal power he should be on an equality with his fellow-citizens.

Because of the multitude of things that might be said on my father's behalf I am at a loss which of them it is appropriate to mention on the present occasion and which should be omitted. For always the plea that has not yet been spoken seems to me of greater importance than the arguments which have already been presented to you. And I believe that it is obvious to everyone that he must needs be most devoted to the welfare of the city who has the greatest share in her evil fortunes as well as in her good. Well then, when Athens was prosperous, who of the citizens was more prosperous, more admired, or more envied than my father? And when she suffered ill-fortune, who was deprived of brighter hopes, or of greater wealth, or of fairer repute? Finally, when the Thirty Tyrants established their rule, while the others merely suffered exile from Athens, was he not banished from all Greece? Did not the Lacedaemonians and Lysander [a] exert themselves as much to cause his death as to bring about the downfall of your dominion, in the belief that they could not be sure of the city's loyalty if they demolished her walls [b] unless they should also destroy the man who could rebuild them? Thus it is not only from his services to you, but also from what he suffered on your account, that you may easily recognize his loyalty. For it is self-evident that it was the people he was aiding, that he desired the same form of government as yourselves, that he suffered at the hands of the same persons, that he was unfortunate when the

Piraeus, were destroyed in 404 B.C. (Xenophon, *Hell.* ii. 2. 20) and were rebuilt by Conon in 394 B.C.

αὐτῶν κακῶς πάσχων, ἅμα τῇ πόλει δυστυχῶν,
τοὺς αὐτοὺς ἐχθροὺς καὶ φίλους ὑμῖν νομίζων, ἐκ
παντὸς τρόπου κινδυνεύων τὰ μὲν ὑφ' ὑμῶν, τὰ
42 δὲ δι' ὑμᾶς, τὰ δ' ὑπὲρ ὑμῶν, τὰ δὲ μεθ' ὑμῶν,
ἀνόμοιος πολίτης Χαρικλεῖ τῷ τούτου κηδεστῇ
γεγενημένος, ὃς τοῖς μὲν πολεμίοις δουλεύειν ἐπεθύμει, τῶν δὲ πολιτῶν ἄρχειν ἠξίου, καὶ φεύγων
μὲν ἡσυχίαν εἶχε, κατελθὼν δὲ κακῶς ἐποίει τὴν
πόλιν. καίτοι πῶς ἂν γένοιτ' ἢ φίλος πονηρότερος
43 ἢ ἐχθρὸς ἐλάττονος ἄξιος; εἶτα σὺ κηδεστὴς μὲν
ὢν ἐκείνου, βεβουλευκὼς δ' ἐπὶ τῶν τριάκοντα
τολμᾷς ἑτέροις μνησικακεῖν, καὶ οὐκ αἰσχύνει τὰς
συνθήκας παραβαίνων δι' ἃς αὐτὸς οἰκεῖς τὴν πόλιν,
οὐδ' ἐνθυμεῖ διότι, ὁπόταν δόξῃ τῶν παρεληλυθό-
[356] των τιμωρίαν ποιεῖσθαι, σοὶ καὶ προτέρῳ καὶ μᾶλ-
44 λον ἢ 'μοὶ κινδυνεύειν ὑπάρχει; οὐ γὰρ δήπου παρ'
ἐμοῦ μὲν ὑπὲρ ὧν ὁ πατὴρ ἔπραξε δίκην λήψονται,
σοὶ δὲ καὶ ὧν αὐτὸς ἡμάρτηκας συγγνώμην ἕξουσιν. ἀλλὰ μὴν οὐδ' ὁμοίας ἐκείνῳ φανήσει τὰς
προφάσεις ἔχων· οὐ γὰρ ἐκπεσὼν ἐκ τῆς πατρίδος
ἀλλὰ συμπολιτευόμενος, οὐδ' ἀναγκασθεὶς ἀλλ'
ἑκών, οὐδ' ἀμυνόμενος ἀλλ' ὑπάρχων ἠδίκεις αὐτούς, ὥστ' οὐδ' ἀπολογίας σοι προσήκει τυχεῖν
παρ' αὐτῶν.

45 Ἀλλὰ γὰρ περὶ μὲν τῶν Τεισίᾳ πεπολιτευμένων

ᵃ Charicles was one of the most cruel of the Thirty Tyrants.
Cf. Lysias, *Against Eratosthenes* 55 ; Xenophon, *Hell.* ii. 3. 2.

202

state was unfortunate, that he considered the same persons as you his enemies and friends, that in every way he exposed himself to danger either at your hands, or on your account, or on your behalf, or in partnership with you, being as a citizen quite unlike Charicles,[a] my opponent's brother-in-law, who chose to be a slave to the enemy, yet claimed the right to rule his fellow-citizens ; who, when in exile, was inactive, but on his return was ever injuring the city. And yet how could one prove himself to be a baser friend or a viler enemy ? And then do you, Teisias, his brother-in-law and a member of the Council in the time of the Thirty Tyrants, have the hardihood to rake up old grudges against those of the other side, and are you not ashamed to be violating the terms of the amnesty which permits you to reside in the city, nor do you even reflect that, whenever the decision shall be made to exact punishment for past crimes, it is you who are menaced by danger more speedy and greater than mine ? For surely they will not inflict punishment on me for my father's acts and at the same time pardon you for the crimes you yourself have committed ! No, assuredly it will not be found that your pleas in extenuation are anything like his ! For you were not banished from your native land, but on the contrary you were a member of the government ; you did not act under compulsion, but you were a willing agent ; it was not in self-defence, but on your own initiative, that you were wronging your fellow-citizens, so that it is not fitting that you should be permitted by them even to enter a plea in your defence.

But on the subject of the political misdeeds of

ἴσως πότ' ἐν τοῖς τούτου κινδύνοις ἐγγενήσεται καὶ
διὰ μακροτέρων εἰπεῖν· ὑμᾶς δ' ἀξιῶ μὴ προέσθαι
με τοῖς ἐχθροῖς μηδ' ἀνηκέστοις συμφοραῖς περι-
βαλεῖν. ἱκανῶς γὰρ καὶ νῦν πεπείραμαι κακῶν, ὃς
εὐθὺς μὲν γενόμενος ὀρφανὸς κατελείφθην, τοῦ μὲν
πατρὸς φυγόντος, τῆς δὲ μητρὸς τελευτησάσης,
οὔπω δὲ τέτταρ' ἔτη γεγονὼς διὰ τὴν τοῦ πατρὸς
φυγὴν περὶ τοῦ σώματος εἰς κίνδυνον κατέστην,
46 ἔτι δὲ παῖς ὢν ὑπὸ τῶν τριάκοντ' ἐκ τῆς πόλεως
ἐξέπεσον. κατελθόντων δὲ τῶν ἐκ Πειραιῶς καὶ
τῶν ἄλλων κομιζομένων τὰς οὐσίας ἐγὼ μόνος τὴν
γῆν, ἣν ἡμῖν ἀπέδωκεν ὁ δῆμος ἀντὶ τῶν δημευ-
θέντων χρημάτων, διὰ τὴν τῶν ἐχθρῶν δύναμιν
ἀπεστερήθην. τοσαῦτα δὲ προδεδυστυχηκὼς καὶ δὶς
τὴν οὐσίαν ἀπολωλεκὼς νυνὶ πέντε ταλάντων φεύγω
δίκην. καὶ τὸ μὲν ἔγκλημ' ἐστὶ περὶ χρημάτων,
ἀγωνίζομαι δ' εἰ χρὴ μετεῖναί μοι τῆς πόλεως.
47 τῶν γὰρ αὐτῶν τιμημάτων ἐπιγεγραμμένων οὐ
περὶ τῶν αὐτῶν ἅπασιν ὁ κίνδυνός ἐστιν, ἀλλὰ
τοῖς μὲν χρήματα κεκτημένοις περὶ ζημίας, τοῖς
δ' ἀπόρως ὥσπερ ἐγὼ διακειμένοις περὶ ἀτιμίας,
ἣν ἐγὼ φυγῆς μείζω συμφορὰν νομίζω· πολὺ γὰρ
ἀθλιώτερον παρὰ τοῖς αὐτοῦ πολίταις ἠτιμωμένον
48 οἰκεῖν ἢ παρ' ἑτέροις μετοικεῖν. δέομαι δ' οὖν
ὑμῶν βοηθῆσαί μοι καὶ μὴ περιιδεῖν ὑπὸ τῶν

---

[a] The democratic party, led by Thrasybulus, in 403 B.C.
had taken Piraeus and made it their headquarters.

[b] After Alcibiades' condemnation as participant in the
violation of the Eleusinian Mysteries. Large portions of the
list of these confiscated goods are preserved in inscriptions.

[c] 414 B.C. and 404 B.C.

Teisias, very likely some day at his trial I shall have the opportunity of speaking at greater length. But as for you, men of the jury, I beg you not to abandon me to my enemies nor entangle me in the net of irremediable misfortunes. For even now I have had sufficient experience of evils, since at my birth I was left an orphan through my father's exile and my mother's death ; and I was not yet four years of age when I was brought into peril of my life owing to my father's exile ; and while still a boy I was banished from the city by the Thirty. And when the men of the Piraeus ^a were restored, and all the rest recovered their possessions, I alone by the influence of my personal enemies was deprived of the land which the people gave us as compensation for the confiscated property.^b And after having already suffered so many misfortunes and having twice lost my property,^c I am now the defendant in an action involving five talents.^d And although the complaint involves money, the real issue is my right to continue to enjoy citizenship. For although the same penalties are prescribed for all by our laws, yet the legal risk is not the same for all ; on the contrary, the wealthy risk a fine, but those who are in straitened circumstances, as is the case with me, are in danger of disfranchisement, and this is a misfortune greater, in my opinion, than exile ; for it is a far more wretched fate to live among one's fellow-citizens deprived of civic rights than to dwell an alien among foreigners. I entreat you, therefore, to aid me and not to suffer me to be despitefully

^d The talent was not a coin, but a sum of money roughly equivalent (although it would purchase much more) to $1000 (over £200).

ἐχθρῶν ὑβρισθέντα μηδὲ τῆς πατρίδος στερηθέντα
μηδ' ἐπὶ τοιαύταις τύχαις περίβλεπτον γενόμενον.
[357] δικαίως δ' ἂν ὑφ' ὑμῶν ἐξ αὐτῶν τῶν ἔργων ἐλεη-
θείην, εἰ καὶ τῷ λόγῳ τυγχάνω μὴ δυνάμενος ἐπὶ
τοῦθ' ὑμᾶς ἄγειν, εἴπερ χρὴ τούτους ἐλεεῖν, τοὺς
ἀδίκως μὲν κινδυνεύοντας, περὶ δὲ τῶν μεγίστων ἀγωνιζομένους, ἀναξίως δ' αὑτῶν καὶ τῶν
προγόνων πράττοντας, πλείστων δὲ χρημάτων
ἀπεστερημένους καὶ μεγίστῃ μεταβολῇ τοῦ βίου
κεχρημένους.

49 Πολλὰ δ' ἔχων ἐμαυτὸν ὀδύρασθαι μάλιστ' ἐπὶ
τούτοις ἀγανακτῶ, πρῶτον μὲν εἰ τούτῳ δώσω
δίκην παρ' οὗ λαβεῖν μοι προσήκει, δεύτερον δ' εἰ
διὰ τὴν τοῦ πατρὸς νίκην τὴν Ὀλυμπίασιν ἀτι-
μωθήσομαι, δι' ἣν τοὺς ἄλλους ὁρῶ δωρεὰς λαμβά-
50 νοντας, πρὸς δὲ τούτοις εἰ Τεισίας μὲν μηδὲν
ἀγαθὸν ποιήσας τὴν πόλιν καὶ ἐν δημοκρατίᾳ καὶ
ἐν ὀλιγαρχίᾳ μέγα δυνήσεται, ἐγὼ δ' εἰ μηδετέρους
ἀδικήσας ὑπ' ἀμφοτέρων κακῶς πείσομαι, καὶ περὶ
μὲν τῶν ἄλλων τἀναντία τοῖς τριάκοντα πράξετε,
περὶ δ' ἐμοῦ τὴν αὐτὴν ἐκείνοις γνώμην ἕξετε, καὶ
τότε μὲν μεθ' ὑμῶν, νῦν δ' ὑφ' ὑμῶν τῆς πόλεως
στερήσομαι.

---

[a] For the rewards of victory at Olympia cf. Plato, Apol.
36 D-E.

treated by my personal enemies, or to be deprived of my fatherland, or to be made notorious by such misfortunes. The facts in the case would of themselves justly win for me your pity, even if I have not the power by my words to evoke it, since pity truly should be felt for those who are unjustly brought to trial, who are fighting for the greatest stakes, whose present condition is not in accordance with their own worth or with that of their ancestors, seeing that they have been deprived of immense wealth and have experienced life's greatest vicissitudes.

Although I have many reasons for lamenting my fate, I am especially indignant for these reasons : first, if I must be punished by this man, who should justly be punished by me ; second, if I shall lose my civic rights by reason of my father's victory at Olympia, when I see other men richly rewarded for such a victory [a] ; and, in addition, if Teisias, a man who never did the city any good, is to remain powerful in the democracy just as he was in the oligarchy, whereas I, who injured neither party, am to be ill-treated by both ; and finally, if, while in all other matters your actions are to be the opposite of those of the Thirty, you shall in regard to me show the same spirit as they, and if I, who then lost my fatherland in company with you, shall now be deprived of it by you.

207

XVII. TRAPEZITICUS

INTRODUCTION

THE discourse *Trapeziticus*, or the " Speech pertaining
to the Banker " as the title might be fully rendered,
is a composition of considerable importance as it gives
information about banking in ancient Athens [a] and
throws light on the relations existing between Athens
and the Kingdom of Bosporus. The banker involved
in the case is one of the best known to us of his profession in Athens, since information concerning him
is found in several of the orations of Demosthenes
(*e.g.*, *For Phormio*).

The career of Pasion is of interest. He had been
a slave of the bankers Antisthenes and Archestratus,
but was given his freedom because of his services
and succeeded them in the bank. One of his clients
was the father of Demosthenes. Because of services
rendered to the state Pasion was given the rights
of citizenship by the Athenians.

The *Trapeziticus* was written by Isocrates for a
young man, a subject of Satyrus, king of Bosporus
(the Crimea of to-day), who accuses the banker Pasion
of having appropriated a deposit of money which had
been entrusted to him by the complainant. The
interesting facts of the case are given in detail by
the speaker.

[a] On banking in ancient Athens see Calhoun, *Business
Life in Ancient Athens*, pp. 81-131.

TRAPEZITICUS

The date of the discourse may be placed about the year 393 B.C. for two reasons : the Spartan hegemony of the sea is referred to as in the past (§ 36) and the battle of Cnidus, where the Spartan fleet was defeated by the Athenians under Conon, took place in August, 394 B.C., and Satyrus I of Bosporus is still living, as seen from the reference in § 57 of the speech. According to Diodorus (xiv. 93) Satyrus died in 393 B.C.

The issue of this case, like that of so many other trials of antiquity, is unknown. In any case the business of Pasion, who enjoyed an excellent reputation as a banker in Athens, continued to prosper and at his death, in 370–369 B.C., he left his bank to his freedman Phormio to be carried on.

There is no reason to doubt the authenticity of this discourse ; on the contrary, its genuineness is attested by the famous literary critic Dionysius of Halicarnassus in his critical essay on Isocrates (19-20). In fact, Dionysius quotes and criticizes the first twelve sections of the *Trapeziticus* in Chapter 19 of his essay.[a]

[a] Benseler thought the speech spurious because of the frequency of hiatus. All recent authorities accept its authenticity : *cf.* Blass, *Die attische Beredsamkeit* ii. p. 234 ; Jebb, *Attic Orators* ii. p. 227 ; Mathieu et Brémond, *Isocrate* i. pp. 68-69.

17. ΤΡΑΠΕΖΙΤΙΚΟΣ

Ὁ μὲν ἀγών μοι μέγας ἐστίν, ὦ ἄνδρες δικασταί.
οὐ γὰρ μόνον περὶ πολλῶν χρημάτων κινδυνεύω,
ἀλλὰ καὶ περὶ τοῦ μὴ δοκεῖν ἀδίκως τῶν ἀλλοτρίων
ἐπιθυμεῖν· ὃ ἐγὼ περὶ πλείστου ποιοῦμαι. οὐσία
μὲν γὰρ ἱκανή μοι καταλειφθήσεται καὶ τούτων
στερηθέντι· εἰ δὲ δόξαιμι μηδὲν προσῆκον τοσαῦτα
χρήματ' ἐγκαλέσαι, διαβληθείην ἂν τὸν ἅπαντα
βίον.

2 Ἔστι δ', ὦ ἄνδρες δικασταί, πάντων χαλεπώτατον τοιούτων ἀντιδίκων τυχεῖν. τὰ μὲν γὰρ
συμβόλαια τὰ πρὸς τοὺς ἐπὶ ταῖς τραπέζαις ἄνευ
μαρτύρων γίγνεται, τοῖς ἀδικουμένοις δὲ πρὸς
τοιούτους ἀνάγκη κινδυνεύειν, οἳ καὶ φίλους πολλοὺς κέκτηνται καὶ χρήματα πολλὰ διαχειρίζουσι
καὶ πιστοὶ διὰ τὴν τέχνην δοκοῦσιν εἶναι. ὅμως
δὲ καὶ τούτων ὑπαρχόντων ἡγοῦμαι φανερὸν πᾶσι
ποιήσειν ὅτι ἀποστεροῦμαι τῶν χρημάτων ὑπὸ
Πασίωνος.

3 Ἐξ ἀρχῆς οὖν ὑμῖν, ὅπως ἂν δύνωμαι, διηγήσομαι τὰ πεπραγμένα. ἐμοὶ γάρ, ὦ ἄνδρες δικασταί, πατὴρ μέν ἐστι Σωπαῖος, ὃν οἱ πλέοντες εἰς

212

XVII. TRAPEZITICUS

THIS trial, men of the jury, is an important one for me. For I have at stake, not only a large sum of money, but also my reputation—for I risk being thought to covet what justly belongs to another ; and that is what gives me the greatest concern. For sufficient property will be left to me even if I am defrauded of this sum ; but if I should be thought to be laying claim to so large a sum of money without just cause, I should have an evil reputation as long as I live.[a]

The greatest difficulty of all, men of the jury, is that I have adversaries of the character of the defendants here. For contracts with the managers of banks are entered into without witnesses, and any who are wronged by them are obliged to bring suit against men who have many friends, handle much money, and have a reputation for honesty because of their profession. In spite of these considerations I think I shall make it clear to all that I have been defrauded of my money by Pasion.

I shall relate the facts to you from the beginning as well as I can. My father, men of the jury, is Sopaeus ; all who sail to the Pontus know that his

---

[a] The plea that the litigant's reputation is at stake is a commonplace in the forensic orations ; *cf.* the speeches of Lysias.

τὸν Πόντον ἅπαντες ἴσασιν οὕτως οἰκείως πρὸς
[359] Σάτυρον διακείμενον, ὥστε πολλῆς μὲν χώρας ἄρχειν, ἁπάσης δὲ τῆς δυνάμεως ἐπιμελεῖσθαι τῆς
4 ἐκείνου. πυνθανόμενος δὲ καὶ περὶ τῆσδε τῆς
πόλεως καὶ περὶ τῆς ἄλλης Ἑλλάδος ἐπεθύμησ᾽
ἀποδημῆσαι. γεμίσας οὖν ὁ πατήρ μου δύο ναῦς
σίτου καὶ χρήματα δοὺς ἐξέπεμψεν ἅμα κατ᾽ ἐμπο-
ρίαν καὶ κατὰ θεωρίαν· συστήσαντος δέ μοι Πυθο-
δώρου τοῦ Φοίνικος Πασίωνα ἐχρώμην τῇ τούτου
5 τραπέζῃ. χρόνῳ δ᾽ ὕστερον διαβολῆς πρὸς Σάτυρον
γενομένης ὡς καὶ ὁ πατὴρ οὑμὸς ἐπιβουλεύοι τῇ
ἀρχῇ κἀγὼ τοῖς φυγάσι συγγιγνοίμην, τὸν μὲν
πατέρα μου συλλαμβάνει, ἐπιστέλλει δὲ τοῖς ἐνθάδ᾽
ἐπιδημοῦσιν ἐκ τοῦ Πόντου τά τε χρήματα παρ᾽
ἐμοῦ παραλαβεῖν καὶ αὐτὸν εἰσπλεῖν κελεύειν· ἐὰν
6 δὲ τούτων μηδὲν ποιῶ, παρ᾽ ὑμῶν ἐξαιτεῖν. ἐν
τοσούτοις δὲ κακοῖς ὤν, ὦ ἄνδρες δικασταί, λέγω
πρὸς Πασίωνα τὰς ἐμαυτοῦ συμφοράς· οὕτω γὰρ
οἰκείως πρὸς αὐτὸν διεκείμην ὥστε μὴ μόνον περὶ
χρημάτων ἀλλὰ καὶ περὶ τῶν ἄλλων τούτῳ μάλιστα
πιστεύειν. ἡγούμην[1] δ᾽ εἰ μὲν προοίμην ἅπαντα τὰ
χρήματα, κινδυνεύειν, εἴ τι πάθοι ᾽κεῖνος, στερηθεὶς καὶ τῶν ἐνθάδε καὶ τῶν ἐκεῖ, πάντων ἐνδεὴς
γενήσεσθαι· εἰ δ᾽ ὁμολογῶν εἶναι ἐπιστείλαντος
Σατύρου μὴ παραδοίην, εἰς τὰς μεγίστας διαβολὰς
ἐμαυτὸν καὶ τὸν πατέρα καταστήσειν πρὸς Σά-
7 τυρον.[1] βουλευομένοις οὖν ἡμῖν ἐδόκει βέλτιστον

---

[1] ἡγούμην . . . πρὸς Σάτυρον: these lines, not found in the
mss., are cited from this speech by the critic Dionysius of
Halicarnassus. Blass brackets them.

[a] Satyrus was king of Bosporus (407-393 B.C.) ; cf. Lysias,
In Defence of Mantitheus 4.

relations with Satyrus [a] are so intimate that he is
ruler of an extensive territory and has charge of that
ruler's entire forces. Having heard reports both of
this state and of the other lands where Greeks live,
I desired to travel abroad. And so my father loaded
two ships with grain,[b] gave me money, and sent me
off on a trading expedition and at the same time to
see the world.[c] Pythodorus, the Phoenician, introduced Pasion to me and I opened an account at his
bank. Later on, as a result of slander which reached
Satyrus to the effect that my father was plotting
against the throne and that I was associating with
the exiles, Satyrus arrested my father and sent orders
to citizens of Pontus in residence here in Athens to
take possession of my money and to bid me to return
and, if I refused to obey, to demand of you my
extradition. When I found myself in difficulties so
embarrassing, men of the jury, I related my troubles
to Pasion ; for I was on such intimate terms with
him that I had the greatest confidence in him, not
only in matters of money, but in everything else as
well. I thought that, if I should yield control of all
my money, I should run the risk, in case my father
met with misfortune, after having been deprived of
my money both here in Athens and at home, of becoming utterly destitute ; and that, if I should
acknowledge the existence of money here, yet fail
to surrender it at Satyrus' command, I should create
the most serious grounds of complaint against myself
and my father in the mind of Satyrus. On delibera-

[b] Athens imported great quantities of grain from the
Pontus ; cf. Demosthenes, *Against Leptines* 31-35.

[c] Cf. Herodotus i. 29 where Solon leaves Athens " to see
the world " (κατὰ θεωρίαν).

εἶναι προσομολογεῖν[1] πάντα ποιεῖν, ὅσα Σάτυρος
προσέταττε, καὶ[1] τὰ μὲν φανερὰ τῶν χρημάτων
παραδοῦναι, περὶ δὲ τῶν παρὰ τούτῳ κειμένων μὴ
μόνον ἔξαρνον εἶναι ἀλλὰ καὶ ὀφείλοντά με καὶ
τούτῳ καὶ ἑτέροις ἐπὶ τόκῳ φαίνεσθαι καὶ πάντα
ποιεῖν ἐξ ὧν ἐκεῖνοι μάλιστ' ἤμελλον πεισθήσεσθαι
μὴ εἶναί μοι χρήματα.

8 Τότε μὲν οὖν, ὦ ἄνδρες δικασταί, ἐνόμιζόν μοι
Πασίωνα δι' εὔνοιαν ἅπαντα ταῦτα συμβουλεύειν·
ἐπειδὴ δὲ πρὸς τοὺς παρὰ Σατύρου διεπραξάμην,
ἔγνων αὐτὸν ἐπιβουλεύοντα τοῖς ἐμοῖς. βουλομέ-
νου γὰρ ἐμοῦ κομίσασθαι τἀμαυτοῦ καὶ πλεῖν εἰς
Βυζάντιον, ἡγησάμενος οὗτος κάλλιστον αὐτῷ και-
[360] ρὸν παραπεπτωκέναι—τὰ μὲν γὰρ χρήματα πόλλ'
εἶναι τὰ παρ' αὑτῷ κείμενα καὶ ἄξι' ἀναισχυντίας, ἐμὲ δὲ πολλῶν ἀκουόντων ἔξαρνον γεγενῆσθαι
μηδὲν κεκτῆσθαι, πᾶσί τε φανερὸν ἀπαιτούμενον
9 καὶ ἑτέροις προσομολογοῦντα ὀφείλειν—καὶ πρὸς
τούτοις, ὦ ἄνδρες δικασταί, ἐνόμιζεν, εἰ μὲν αὐτοῦ
μένειν ἐπιχειροίην, ἐκδοθήσεσθαί μ' ὑπὸ τῆς πόλεως Σατύρῳ, εἰ δ' ἄλλοσέ ποι τραποίμην, οὐδὲν
μελήσειν αὐτῷ τῶν ἐμῶν λόγων, εἰ δ' εἰσπλευσοί-
μην εἰς τὸν Πόντον, ἀποθανεῖσθαί με μετὰ τοῦ
πατρός· ταῦτα διαλογιζόμενος διενοεῖτό μ' ἀποστερεῖν τὰ χρήματα. καὶ πρὸς μὲν ἐμὲ προσεποιεῖτ'
ἀπορεῖν ἐν τῷ παρόντι καὶ οὐκ ἂν ἔχειν ἀποδοῦναι·
ἐπειδὴ δὲ βουλόμενος εἰδέναι σαφῶς τὸ πρᾶγμα
προσπέμπω Φιλόμηλον αὐτῷ καὶ Μενέξενον ἀπαιτή-

---

[1] προσομολογεῖν . . . καί : these words are not found in the
best mss., nor in Dionysius. It is probable that they are a
gloss.

tion we decided that it would be best to agree to comply with all of Satyrus' demands and to surrender the money whose existence was known, but with respect to the funds on deposit with Pasion we should not only deny their existence but also make it appear that I had borrowed at interest both from Pasion and from others,[a] and to do everything which was likely to make them believe that I had no money.

At that time, men of the jury, I thought that Pasion was giving me all this advice because of goodwill toward me ; but when I had arranged matters with the representatives of Satyrus, I perceived that he had designs on my property. For when I wished to recover my money and sail to Byzantium, Pasion thought a most favourable opportunity had come his way ; for the sum of money on deposit with him was large and of sufficient value to warrant a shameless act, and I, in the presence of many listeners, had denied that I possessed anything, and everybody had seen that money was being demanded of me and that I was acknowledging that I was indebted to others also. Besides this, men of the jury, he was of opinion that if I attempted to remain here, I should be handed over by Athens to Satyrus, and if I should go anywhere else, he would be indifferent to my complaints, and if I should sail to the Pontus, I should be put to death along with my father ; it was on the strength of these calculations that Pasion decided to defraud me of my money. And although to me he pretended that for the moment he was short of funds and would not be able to repay me, yet when I, wishing to ascertain exactly the truth, sent Philomelus and Menexenus to him to demand

* *e.g.*, Stratocles, *cf.* §§ 35-36.

σοντας, ἔξαρνος γίγνεται πρὸς αὐτοὺς μηδὲν ἔχειν
10 τῶν ἐμῶν. πανταχόθεν δέ μοι τοσούτων κακῶν
προσπεπτωκότων τίν' οἴεσθέ με γνώμην ἔχειν, ᾧ γ'
ὑπῆρχε σιγῶντι μὲν ὑπὸ τούτου ἀπεστερῆσθαι τῶν
χρημάτων, λέγοντι δὲ ταῦτα μὲν μηδὲν μᾶλλον
κομίσασθαι, πρὸς Σάτυρον δ' εἰς τὴν μεγίστην
διαβολὴν καὶ ἐμαυτὸν καὶ τὸν πατέρα καταστῆσαι;
κράτιστον οὖν ἡγησάμην ἡσυχίαν ἄγειν.

11 Μετὰ δὲ ταῦτ', ὦ ἄνδρες δικασταί, ἀφικνοῦνταί
μοι οἱ ἀπαγγέλλοντες ὅτι ὁ πατὴρ ἀφεῖται, καὶ
Σατύρῳ οὕτως ἁπάντων μεταμέλει τῶν πεπραγμένων, ὥστε πίστεις τὰς μεγίστας αὐτῷ δεδωκὼς εἴη,
καὶ τὴν ἀρχὴν ἔτι μείζω πεποιηκὼς ἧς εἶχε πρότερον, καὶ τὴν ἀδελφὴν τὴν ἐμὴν εἰληφὼς γυναῖκα
τῷ αὑτοῦ υἱεῖ. πυθόμενος δὲ ταῦτα Πασίων καὶ
εἰδὼς ὅτι φανερῶς ἤδη πράξω περὶ τῶν ἐμαυτοῦ,
ἀφανίζει Κίττον τὸν παῖδα, ὃς συνῄδει περὶ τῶν
12 χρημάτων. ἐπειδὴ δ' ἐγὼ προσελθὼν ἐξήτουν
αὐτόν, ἡγούμενος ἔλεγχον ἂν τοῦτον σαφέστατον
γενέσθαι περὶ ὧν ἐνεκάλουν, λέγει λόγον πάντων
δεινότατον, ὡς ἐγὼ καὶ Μενέξενος διαφθείραντες
καὶ πείσαντες αὐτὸν ἐπὶ τῇ τραπέζῃ καθήμενον ἓξ
τάλαντ' ἀργυρίου λάβοιμεν παρ' αὐτοῦ· ἵνα δὲ
μηδεὶς ἔλεγχος μηδὲ βάσανος γένοιτο περὶ αὐτῶν,
ἔφασκεν ἡμᾶς ἀφανίσαντας τὸν παῖδ' ἀντεγκαλεῖν
[361] αὐτῷ καὶ ἐξαιτεῖν τοῦτον, ὃν αὐτοὶ ἠφανίσαμεν.
καὶ ταῦτα λέγων καὶ ἀγανακτῶν καὶ δακρύων
εἷλκέ με πρὸς τὸν πολέμαρχον, ἐγγυητὰς αἰτῶν,

ᵃ The Polemarch was one of the nine archons of Athens.
He had supervision of the affairs of foreigners and resident-
aliens.

my property, he denied to them that he had anything belonging to me. Thus beset on every side by misfortunes so dire, what, think you, was my state of mind ? If I kept silent I should be defrauded of my money by Pasion here ; if I should make this complaint, I was none the more likely to recover it and I should bring myself and my father into the greatest disrepute with Satyrus. The wisest course, therefore, as I thought, was to keep silent.

After this, men of the jury, messengers arrived with the news that my father had been released and that Satyrus was so repentant of all that had occurred that he had bestowed upon my father pledges of his confidence of the most sweeping kind, and had given him authority even greater than he formerly possessed and had chosen my sister as his son's wife. When Pasion learned this and understood that I would now bring action openly about my property, he spirited away his slave Cittus, who had knowledge of our financial transactions. And when I went to him and demanded the surrender of Cittus, because I believed that this slave could furnish the clearest proof of my claim, Pasion made the most outrageous charge, that I and Menexenus had bribed and corrupted Cittus as he sat at his banking-table and received six talents of silver from him. And that there might be neither examination nor testimony under torture on these matters, he asserted that it was we who had spirited away the slave and had brought a counter-charge against himself with a demand that this slave, whom we ourselves had spirited away, be produced. And while he was making this plea and protesting and weeping, he dragged me before the Polemarch ^a with a demand

219

καὶ οὐ πρότερον ἀφῆκεν, ἕως αὐτῷ κατέστησ᾽ ἐξ
ταλάντων ἐγγυητάς.

Καί μοι κάλει τούτων μάρτυρας.

ΜΑΡΤΥΡΕΣ

13 Τῶν μὲν μαρτύρων ἀκηκόατε, ὦ ἄνδρες δικασταί·
ἐγὼ δὲ τὰ μὲν ἀπολωλεκὼς ἤδη, περὶ δὲ τῶν
αἰσχίστας αἰτίας ἔχων, αὐτὸς μὲν εἰς Πελοπόννησον
ᾠχόμην ζητήσων, Μενέξενος δ᾽ εὑρίσκει τὸν παῖδ᾽
ἐνθάδε, καὶ ἐπιλαβόμενος ἠξίου αὐτὸν βασανίζεσθαι
καὶ περὶ τῆς παρακαταθήκης καὶ περὶ ὧν οὗτος
14 ἡμᾶς ᾐτιάσατο. Πασίων δ᾽ εἰς τοῦτο τόλμης ἀφί-
κεθ᾽ ὥστ᾽ ἀφῃρεῖτ᾽ αὐτὸν ὡς ἐλεύθερον ὄντα, καὶ
οὐκ ᾐσχύνετ᾽ οὐδ᾽ ἐδεδοίκει, ὃν ἔφασκεν ὑφ᾽ ἡμῶν
ἠνδραποδίσθαι καὶ παρ᾽ οὗ τοσαῦτα χρήμαθ᾽ ἡμᾶς
ἔχειν, τοῦτον ἐξαιρούμενος εἰς ἐλευθερίαν καὶ
κωλύων βασανίζεσθαι. ὃ δὲ πάντων δεινότατον·
κατεγγυῶντος γὰρ Μενεξένου πρὸς τὸν πολέμαρχον
τὸν παῖδα, Πασίων αὐτὸν ἑπτὰ ταλάντων διηγ-
γυήσατο.

Καί μοι τούτων ἀνάβητε μάρτυρες.

ΜΑΡΤΥΡΕΣ

15 Τούτων τοίνυν αὐτῷ πεπραγμένων, ὦ ἄνδρες
δικασταί, ἡγούμενος περὶ μὲν τῶν παρεληλυθότων
φανερῶς ἡμαρτηκέναι, οἰόμενος δ᾽ ἐκ τῶν λοιπῶν
ἐπανορθώσεσθαι, προσῆλθεν ἡμῖν φάσκων ἕτοιμος
εἶναι παραδοῦναι βασανίζειν τὸν παῖδα. ἑλόμενοι
δὲ βασανιστὰς ἀπηντήσαμεν εἰς τὸ Ἡφαιστεῖον.

ᵃ The evidence of slaves could only be given under
torture; cf. § 54.

for bondsmen, and he did not release me until I had furnished bondsmen in the sum of six talents.

(*To the Clerk*) Please summon for me witnesses to these facts.

WITNESSES

You have heard the witnesses, men of the jury ; and I, who had already lost part of my money and with regard to the rest was under the most infamous charges, left Athens for the Peloponnesus to investigate for myself. But Menexenus found the slave here in the city, and having seized him demanded that he give testimony under torture ª about both the deposit and the charge brought by his master. Pasion, however, reached such a pitch of audacity that he secured the release of the slave on the ground that he was a freeman and, utterly devoid of shame and of fear, he claimed as a freeman and prevented the torture of a person who, as he alleged, had been stolen from him by us and had given us all that money. But the crowning impudence of all was this —that when Menexenus compelled Pasion to give security for the slave before the Polemarch, he gave bond for him in the sum of seven talents.

(*To the Clerk*) Let witnesses to these facts take the stand.

WITNESSES

After he had acted in this way, men of the jury, Pasion, believing that his past conduct had clearly been in error and thinking he could rectify the situation by his subsequent acts, came to us and asserted that he was ready to surrender the slave for torture. We chose questioners and met in the temple of

221

κἀγὼ μὲν ἠξίουν αὐτοὺς μαστιγοῦν τὸν ἐκδοθέντα
καὶ στρεβλοῦν, ἕως τἀληθῆ δόξειεν αὐτοῖς λέγειν·
Πασίων δ' οὑτοσὶ οὐ δημοκοίνους ἔφασκεν αὐτοὺς
ἐλέσθαι, ἀλλ' ἐκέλευε λόγῳ πυνθάνεσθαι παρὰ τοῦ
16 παιδός, εἴ τι βούλοιντο. διαφερομένων δ' ἡμῶν οἱ
βασανισταὶ αὐτοὶ μὲν οὐκ ἔφασαν βασανιεῖν, ἔγνωσαν δὲ Πασίων· ἐμοὶ παραδοῦναι τὸν παῖδα. οὗτος
δ' οὕτω σφόδρ' ἔφευγε τὴν βάσανον, ὥστε περὶ μὲν
τῆς παραδόσεως οὐκ ἤθελεν αὐτοῖς πείθεσθαι, τὸ
δ' ἀργύριον ἕτοιμος ἦν ἀποτίνειν, εἰ καταγνοῖεν
αὐτοῦ.

Καί μοι κάλει τούτων μάρτυρας.

ΜΑΡΤΥΡΕΣ

[362]
17 Ἐπειδὴ τοίνυν ἐκ τῶν συνόδων, ὦ ἄνδρες δικασταί, πάντες αὐτοῦ κατεγίγνωσκον ἀδικεῖν καὶ
δεινὰ ποιεῖν, ὅστις τὸν παῖδα, ὃν ἔφασκον ἐγὼ
συνειδέναι περὶ τῶν χρημάτων, πρῶτον μὲν αὐτὸς
ἀφανίσας ὑφ' ἡμῶν αὐτὸν ᾐτιᾶτ' ἠφανίσθαι, ἔπειτα
δὲ συλληφθέντα ὡς ἐλεύθερον ὄντα διεκώλυσε
βασανίζεσθαι, μετὰ δὲ ταῦθ' ὡς δοῦλον ἐκδοὺς καὶ
βασανιστὰς ἑλόμενος λόγῳ μὲν ἐκέλευσε βασανίζειν, ἔργῳ δ' οὐκ εἴα, διὰ ταῦθ' ἡγούμενος οὐδεμίαν
αὐτῷ σωτηρίαν εἶναι, ἐάνπερ εἰς ὑμᾶς εἰσέλθῃ,
προσπέμπων ἐδεῖτό μου εἰς ἱερὸν ἐλθόνθ' ἑαυτῷ
18 συγγενέσθαι. καὶ ἐπειδὴ ἤλθομεν εἰς ἀκρόπολιν,

---

[a] The Hephaisteion, in Athens, which has long been popu-
larly but erroneously called the Theseum.

Hephaestus.[a] And I demanded that they flog and rack the slave, who had been surrendered, until they were of opinion that he was telling the truth. But Pasion here asserted that they had not been chosen as torturers, and bade them make oral interrogation of the slave if they wished any information. Because of our disagreement the examiners refused to put the slave to torture themselves, but decreed that Pasion should surrender him to me. But Pasion was so anxious to avoid the employment of torture that he refused to obey them in respect to the surrender of the slave, but declared that he was ready to restore to me the money if they should pronounce judgement against him.

(*To the Clerk*) Please call for me witnesses to these facts.

WITNESSES

When, as a result of these meetings, men of the jury, all declared that Pasion was guilty of wrongdoing and of scandalous conduct (since, in the first place, it was Pasion himself who had spirited away the slave who, so I had asserted, had knowledge of the money-dealings, although he accused us of having concealed him, and next, when the slave was arrested, had prevented him from giving testimony under torture on the ground that he was a freeman, and finally, after this, having surrendered him as a slave and having chosen questioners, he nominally gave orders that he be tortured but in point of fact forbade it), Pasion, I say, understanding that there was no possibility of escape for himself if he came before you, sent a messenger to beg me to meet him in a sanctuary. And when we had come to the Acropolis, he

ἐγκαλυψάμενος ἔκλαε καὶ ἔλεγεν, ὡς ἠναγκάσθη
μὲν δι' ἀπορίαν ἔξαρνος γενέσθαι, ὀλίγου δὲ χρόνου
πειράσοιτο τὰ χρήματ' ἀποδοῦναι· ἐδεῖτο δέ μου
συγγνώμην ἔχειν αὐτῷ καὶ συγκρύψαι τὴν συμφοράν, ἵνα μὴ παρακαταθήκας δεχόμενος φανερὸς
γένηται τοιαῦτ' ἐξημαρτηκώς. ἡγούμενος δ' αὐτῷ
μεταμέλειν τῶν πεπραγμένων συνεχώρουν καὶ ἐκέ-
λευον αὐτὸν ἐξευρεῖν, ὅντιν' ἂν βούληται τρόπον,
ὅπως τούτῳ τε καλῶς ἕξει κἀγὼ τἀμαυτοῦ κο-
μιοῦμαι.

19 Τρίτῃ δ' ἡμέρᾳ συνελθόντες πίστιν τ' ἔδομεν
ἀλλήλοις ἦ μὴν σιωπήσεσθαι τὰ πραχθέντα, ἣν
οὗτος ἔλυσεν, ὡς ὑμεῖς αὐτοὶ προϊόντος τοῦ λόγου
γνώσεσθε, καὶ ὡμολόγησεν εἰς τὸν Πόντον μοι
συμπλευσεῖσθαι κἀκεῖ τὸ χρυσίον ἀποδώσειν, ἵν'
ὡς πορρωτάτω ἀπὸ τῆσδε τῆς πόλεως διαλύσειε
τὸ συμβόλαιον, καὶ τῶν μὲν ἐνθάδε μηδεὶς εἰδείη
τὸν τρόπον τῆς ἀπαλλαγῆς, ἐκπλεύσαντι δ' αὐτῷ
ἐξείη λέγειν ὅ τι αὐτὸς βούλοιτο· εἰ δὲ μὴ ταῦτα
ποιήσειε, δίαιταν ἐπὶ ῥητοῖς ἐπέτρεπε Σατύρῳ,
ἐφ' ᾧτε καταγιγνώσκειν ἡμιόλι' αὐτοῦ τὰ χρή-
20 ματα. ταῦτα δὲ συγγράψαντες καὶ ἀναγαγόντες
εἰς ἀκρόπολιν Πύρωνα Φεραῖον ἄνδρα, εἰθισμένον
εἰσπλεῖν εἰς τὸν Πόντον, δίδομεν αὐτῷ φυλάττειν
τὰς συνθήκας, προστάξαντες αὐτῷ, ἐὰν μὲν διαλλαγῶμεν πρὸς ἡμᾶς αὐτούς, κατακαῦσαι τὸ γραμματεῖον, εἰ δὲ μή, Σατύρῳ ἀποδοῦναι.

21 Τὰ μὲν οὖν ἡμέτερ', ὦ ἄνδρες δικασταί, οὕτω

---

* For arbitration *under terms* or *on certain conditions* cf.
also Isocrates, *Against Callimachus* 10. In such cases the
arbitrator had no discretionary power. *Cf.* Jebb's *Attic
Orators* ii. p. 234.

covered his head and wept, saying that he had been
compelled to deny the debt because of lack of funds,
but that he would try to repay me in a short time.
He begged me to forgive him and to keep his misfortune secret, in order that he, as a receiver of
deposits, might not be shown to have been culpable
in such matters. In the belief that he repented of
his past conduct I yielded, and bade him to devise
a method, of any kind he wished, that his affairs might
be in order and I receive back my money.

Two days later we met again and solemnly pledged
each other to keep the affair secret, a pledge which he
failed to keep, as you yourselves will learn as my
story proceeds, and he agreed to sail with me to the
Pontus and there pay me back the gold, in order
that he might settle our contract at as great a distance as possible from Athens, and that no one here
might know the nature of our settlement, and also
that on his return from the Pontus he might say
anything he pleased ; but in the event that he
should not fulfil these obligations, he proposed to
entrust to Satyrus an arbitration on stated terms [a]
which would permit Satyrus to condemn Pasion to
pay the original sum, and half as much in addition.
When he had drawn up this agreement in writing,
we brought to the Acropolis Pyron, of Pherae,[b] who
frequently sailed to the Pontus, and placed the
agreement in his custody, stipulating that if we
should come to a satisfactory settlement with each
other, he should burn the memorandum ; otherwise,
he was to deliver it to Satyrus.

The questions in dispute between ourselves, men
of the jury, had been settled in this manner ; but

[b] In Thessaly.

διεπέπρακτο· Μενέξενος δ' ὀργιζόμενος ὑπὲρ τῆς αἰτίας ἧς κἀκεῖνον Πασίων[1] ἠτιάσατο, λαχὼν δίκην [363] ἐξῄτει τὸν Κίττον, ἀξιῶν τὴν αὐτὴν Πασίωνι ψευδομένῳ γίγνεσθαι ζημίαν ἥσπερ ἂν αὐτὸς ἐτύγχανεν, εἴ τι τούτων ἐφαίνετο ποιήσας. καὶ οὗτος, ὦ ἄνδρες δικασταί, ἐδεῖτό μου ἀπαλλάττειν Μενέξενον, λέγων ὅτι οὐδὲν αὐτῷ πλέον ἔσται, εἰ τὰ μὲν χρήματ' ἐκ τῶν συγγεγραμμένων εἰς τὸν Πόντον εἰσπλεύσας ἀποδώσει, αὐτὸς δ' ὁμοίως ἐνθάδε καταγέλαστος ἔσοιτο· ὁ γὰρ παῖς, ἐὰν βασανίζηται, 22 περὶ πάντων τἀληθῆ κατερεῖ. ἐγὼ δ' ἠξίουν πρὸς μὲν Μενέξενον πράττειν ὅ τι βούλοιτο, πρὸς δ' ἐμὲ ποιεῖν αὐτὸν τὰ συγκείμενα. ἐν ἐκείνῳ μὲν οὖν τῷ χρόνῳ ταπεινὸς ἦν, οὐκ ἔχων ὅ τι χρήσαιτο τοῖς αὑτοῦ κακοῖς. καὶ γὰρ οὐ μόνον περὶ τῆς βασάνου καὶ τῆς δίκης ἐκείνης ἐδεδοίκει τῆς εἰλημμένης, ἀλλὰ καὶ περὶ τοῦ γραμματείου, ὅπως μὴ ὑπὸ τοῦ 23 Μενεξένου συλληφθήσοιτο. ἀπορῶν δὲ καὶ οὐδεμίαν ἄλλην εὑρίσκων ἀπαλλαγήν, πείσας τοῦ ξένου τοὺς παῖδας διαφθείρει τὸ γραμματεῖον, ὃ ἔδει Σάτυρον λαβεῖν, εἰ μή μ' ἀπαλλάξειεν οὗτος. καὶ οὐκ ἔφθη διαπραξάμενος ταῦτα καὶ θρασύτατος ἁπάντων ἀνθρώπων ἐγένετο, καὶ οὔτ' εἰς τὸν Πόντον ἔφη μοι συμπλευσεῖσθαι οὔτ' εἶναι πρὸς ἔμ' αὐτῷ συμβόλαιον οὐδέν, ἀνοίγειν τ' ἐκέλευε τὸ γραμματεῖον ἐναντίον μαρτύρων. τί ἂν ὑμῖν τὰ πολλὰ λέγοιμι, ὦ ἄνδρες δικασταί; εὑρέθη γὰρ ἐν τῷ γραμματείῳ γεγραμμένος[2] ἀφειμένος ἁπάντων τῶν ἐγκλημάτων ὑπ' ἐμοῦ.

---

[1] Πασίων, omitted by LE, is bracketed by Blass.
[2] γεγραμμένος Benseler: γεγραμμένον MSS.: ἐν τῷ γραμματείῳ γεγραμμένον is bracketed by Blass.

Menexenus was so enraged because of the charge
which Pasion had brought against him also, that he
brought an action for libel against him and demanded
the surrender of Cittus, asking that Pasion, if guilty
of falsification, should suffer the same penalty which
he himself would have incurred for the same acts.
And Pasion, men of the jury, begged me to appease
Menexenus, saying it would be of no advantage
to himself if, after having sailed to the Pontus,
he should pay the money in accordance with
the terms of the agreement, and then should all the
same be made a laughing-stock in Athens ; for the
slave, if put to the torture, would testify to the truth
of everything. I for my part, however, asked him
to take any action he pleased as to Menexenus, but
to carry out his agreements with me. At that time
he was in a humble mood, for he did not know what
to do in his plight. For not only was he in a state
of fear in regard to the torture and the impending
suit, but also with respect to the memorandum, lest
Menexenus should obtain possession of it. And
being embarrassed and finding no other means of
relief, he bribed the slaves of the alien Pyron and
falsified the memorandum which Satyrus was to
receive in case he did not come to an agreement
with me. No sooner had he accomplished this than
he became the most impudent of all men and declared
that he would not sail with me to the Pontus and
that no contract at all existed between us, and he
demanded that the memorandum be opened in the
presence of witnesses. Why need I say more to you,
men of the jury ? For it was discovered to have
been written in the memorandum that Pasion was
released of all claims on my part !

24 Τὰ μὲν οὖν γεγενημένα, ὡς ἀκριβέστατα οἷός τ'
ἦν, ἅπανθ' ὑμῖν εἴρηκα. ἡγοῦμαι δὲ Πασίων', ὦ
ἄνδρες δικασταί, ἐκ τοῦ διεφθαρμένου γραμματείου
τὴν ἀπολογίαν ποιήσεσθαι καὶ τούτοις ἰσχυριεῖσθαι
μάλιστα. ὑμεῖς οὖν μοι τὸν νοῦν προσέχετε· οἶμαι
γὰρ ἐξ αὐτῶν τούτων φανερὰν ὑμῖν ποιήσειν τὴν
τούτου πονηρίαν.

25 Πρῶτον δ' ἐκ τούτου σκοπεῖσθε. ὅτε γὰρ ἐδίδο-
μεν τῷ ξένῳ τὴν συνθήκην, καθ' ἣν οὗτος μὲν
ἀφεῖσθαί φησι τῶν ἐγκλημάτων, ἐγὼ δ' ὡς ἔδει με
παρὰ τούτου κομίσασθαι τὸ χρυσίον, ἐκελεύομεν
τὸν ξένον, ἐὰν μὲν διαλλαγῶμεν πρὸς ἡμᾶς αὐτούς,
κατακαῦσαι τὸ γραμματεῖον, εἰ δὲ μή, Σατύρῳ
ἀποδοῦναι· καὶ ταῦτα ῥηθῆναι ὑπ' ἀμφοτέρων
26 ἡμῶν ὁμολογεῖται. καίτοι τί μαθόντες, ὦ ἄνδρες
[364] δικασταί, προσετάττομεν ἀποδοῦναι Σατύρῳ τὸ
γραμματεῖον, ἂν μὴ διαλλαγῶμεν, εἴπερ ἀπηλλαγμένος ἤδη Πασίων ἦν τῶν·ἐγκλημάτων καὶ τέλος
εἶχεν ἡμῖν τὸ πρᾶγμα; ἀλλὰ δῆλον ὅτι ταύτας τὰς
συνθήκας ἐποιησάμεθ' ὡς ὑπολοίπων ὄντων ἡμῖν
ἔτι πραγμάτων, περὶ ὧν ἔδει τοῦτον πρὸς ἐμὲ κατὰ
27 τὸ γραμματεῖον διαλύσασθαι. ἔπειτ' ἐγὼ μέν, ὦ
ἄνδρες δικασταί, ἔχω τὰς αἰτίας εἰπεῖν δι' ἃς
οὗτος ὡμολόγησεν ἀποδώσειν τὸ χρυσίον· ἐπεὶ γὰρ
ἡμεῖς τε τῶν πρὸς Σάτυρον διαβολῶν ἀπηλλάγημεν
καὶ τὸν Κίττον οὐχ οἷός τ' ἐγένετ' ἀφανίσαι, τὸν
συνειδότα περὶ τῆς παρακαταθήκης, ἡγησάμενος,
28 εἰ μὲν ἐκδοίη τὸν παῖδα βασανίσαι, φανερὸς γενήσεσθαι πανουργῶν, εἰ δὲ μὴ ποιήσειε ταῦτ', ὀφλήσειν

ᵃ The refusal by an accused master to submit his slave
for testimony under torture was used by an adversary as
228

Well, all the facts in the case I have told you as accurately as I could. But I think, men of the jury, that Pasion will base his defence on the falsified memorandum, and will especially rely on its contents. Do you, therefore, give your attention to me ; for I think that from these very contents I shall reveal to you his rascality.

Consider the matter first in this way. When we gave to the alien, Pyron, the agreement by which Pasion, as he claims, is released from my demands, but as I contend, I was to have received back the gold from him, we bade the alien, in case we arrived at an understanding with each other, to burn the memorandum ; otherwise, to give it to Satyrus, and that this was stated both of us agree. And yet, men of the jury, what possessed us to stipulate that the memorandum should be given to Satyrus in case of our failure to come to terms, if Pasion had already been freed of my claims and our business had been concluded ? On the contrary, it is clear that we had made this agreement because there yet remained matters which Pasion had to settle with me in accordance with the memorandum. In the next place, men of the jury, I can give you the reasons why he agreed to repay me the gold ; for when we had been cleared of the false accusations lodged with Satyrus, and Pasion had been unable to spirit away Cittus, who had knowledge of my deposit, he understood that if he should deliver his slave to torture, he would be convicted of an act of rascality, and, on the other hand, if he failed to do so, he would lose his case [a] ; he wished, therefore,

practically a confession of guilt; *cf.* Antiphon, *On the Murder of Herodes* 38 and *On the Choreutes* 27.

τὴν δίκην, ἐβουλήθη πρὸς αὐτὸν ἐμὲ τὴν ἀπαλλαγὴν
ποιήσασθαι. τοῦτον δὲ κελεύσατ' ἀποδεῖξαι, τί
κερδαίνων ἢ τίνα κίνδυνον φοβηθεὶς ἀφῆκ' αὐτὸν
τῶν ἐγκλημάτων; ἐὰν δὲ μηδὲν ἔχῃ τούτων ὑμῖν
ἀποφαίνειν, πῶς οὐκ ἂν δικαίως ἐμοὶ μᾶλλον ἢ
τούτῳ περὶ τοῦ γραμματείου πιστεύοιτε;

29   Καὶ μὲν δή, ὦ ἄνδρες δικασταί, καὶ τόδε ῥᾴδιον
πᾶσι γνῶναι, ὅτι ἐμοὶ μέν, ὃς ἐνεκάλουν, εἰ τοὺς
ἐλέγχους ἐφοβούμην, ἐξῆν καὶ μηδεμίαν συνθήκην
ποιησάμενον χαίρειν ἐᾶν τὸ πρᾶγμα· τούτῳ δὲ διά
τε τὴν βάσανον καὶ τους ἀγῶνας τοὺς ἐν ὑμῖν οὐχ
οἷόν τ' ἦν ὁπότε βούλοιτ' ἀπηλλάχθαι τῶν κινδύνων, εἰ μὴ πείσειεν ἐμὲ τὸν ἐγκαλοῦντα. ὥστ' οὐκ
ἐμὲ περὶ τῆς ἀφέσεως ἀλλὰ τοῦτον περὶ τῆς ἀπο-
δόσεως τῶν χρημάτων ἔδει τὰς συνθήκας ποιεῖσθαι.

30 ἔτι δὲ κἀκεῖν' ὑπερφυές, εἰ πρὶν μὲν συγγράψασθαι
τὸ γραμματεῖον οὕτω σφόδρ' ἠπίστησα τοῖς πράγμασιν ὥστε μὴ μόνον ἀφεῖναι Πασίωνα τῶν ἐγκλημάτων ἀλλὰ καὶ συνθήκας περὶ αὐτῶν ποιήσασθαι,
ἐπειδὴ δὲ τοιοῦτον ἔλεγχον κατ' ἐμαυτοῦ συνε-
γραψάμην, τηνικαῦτ' ἐπεθύμησ' εἰς ὑμᾶς εἰσελθεῖν.
καίτοι τίς ἂν οὕτω περὶ τῶν αὑτοῦ πραγμάτων

31 βουλεύσαιτο; ὃ δὲ πάντων μέγιστον τεκμήριον
ὡς οὐκ ἀφειμένος ἦν Πασίων ἐν ταῖς συνθήκαις
ἀλλ' ὡμολογηκὼς ἀποδώσειν τὸ χρυσίον· ὅτε γὰρ
Μενέξενος ἔλαχεν αὐτῷ τὴν δίκην, οὔπω διεφθαρμένου τοῦ γραμματείου, προσπέμπων Ἀγύρριον,
[365] ὄντ' ἀμφοτέροις ἡμῖν ἐπιτήδειον, ἠξίου μ' ἢ Μενέξενον ἀπαλλάττειν ἢ τὰς συνθήκας τὰς γεγενημένας

___

a An influential man in public affairs ; cf. Andoc. On the
Mysteries 133.

to reach a settlement with me in person. Bid him show you what gain I had in view, or what danger I feared, that I dropped my charges against him. But if he can show you nothing of the kind, would you not with greater justice trust me rather than him in the matter of the memorandum?

Furthermore, men of the jury, this too is easy for all to see—that whereas I, the plaintiff, if I distrusted the sufficiency of my proofs, could drop the prosecution even without entering into any agreement, yet Pasion, on account both of the examination of his slave under torture and the suits lodged with you, could not possibly free himself from his risks when he wished except by gaining the consent of me, the complainant. In consequence, I was not obliged to make an agreement about the dismissal of my charges, but it was necessary for him to do so about the repayment of my money. Besides, it would have been a preposterous state of affairs if, before the memorandum had been drawn up, I should have had so little confidence in my case as not only to drop the charges against Pasion, but also to make an agreement concerning these charges and, after I had drawn up such written proof against myself, should then have desired to bring the case before you. And yet who would plan so foolishly in regard to his own interests? But here is the strongest proof of all that in the agreement Pasion was not absolved from his debt, but on the contrary had agreed to repay the gold: when Menexenus lodged his suit against him, which was before the memorandum had been tampered with, Pasion sent Agyrrhius,[a] a friend of both of us, to beg that I either appease Menexenus or annul the agreement

231

32 πρὸς αὑτὸν ἀναιρεῖν. καίτοι, ὦ ἄνδρες δικασταί,
οἴεσθ' ἂν αὐτὸν ἐπιθυμεῖν ἀναιρεθῆναι ταύτας τὰς
συνθήκας, ἐξ ὧν ψευδομένους ἡμᾶς ἔμελλεν ἐξε-
λέγξειν; οὔκουν ἐπειδή γε μετεγράφησαν, τούτους
ἔλεγε τοὺς λόγους, ἀλλὰ περὶ ἁπάντων εἰς ἐκείνας
κατέφευγε καὶ ἀνοίγειν ἐκέλευε τὸ γραμματεῖον.
ὡς οὖν τὸ πρῶτον ἀναιρεῖν ἐζήτει τὰς συνθήκας,
αὐτὸν Ἀγύρριον μαρτυροῦντα παρέξομαι.

Καί μοι ἀνάβηθι.

ΜΑΡΤΥΡΙΑ

33 Ὅτι μὲν τοίνυν τὰς συνθήκας ἐποιησάμεθ' οὐχ
ὡς Πασίων ἐπιχειρήσει λέγειν, ἀλλ' ὡς ἐγὼ πρὸς
ὑμᾶς εἴρηκα, ἱκανῶς ἐπιδεδεῖχθαι νομίζω. οὐκ
ἄξιον δὲ θαυμάζειν, ὦ ἄνδρες δικασταί, εἰ τὸ γραμματεῖον διέφθειρεν, οὐ μόνον διὰ τοῦτο, ὅτι πολλὰ
τοιαῦτ' ἤδη γέγονεν, ἀλλ' ὅτι καὶ τῶν χρωμένων
τινὲς Πασίωνι πολὺ δεινότερα τούτων πεποιήκασι.
Πυθόδωρον γὰρ τὸν σκηνίτην καλούμενον, ὃς ὑπὲρ
Πασίωνος ἅπαντα καὶ λέγει καὶ πράττει, τίς οὐκ
οἶδεν ὑμῶν πέρυσιν ἀνοίξαντα τὰς ὑδρίας καὶ τοὺς
κριτὰς ἐξελόντα τοὺς ὑπὸ τῆς βουλῆς εἰσβληθέντας;
34 καίτοι ὅστις μικρῶν ἕνεκα καὶ περὶ τοῦ σώματος
κινδυνεύων ταύτας ὑπανοίγειν ἐτόλμησεν, αἳ σεση-
μασμέναι μὲν ἦσαν ὑπὸ τῶν πρυτάνεων, κατ-
εσφραγισμέναι δ' ὑπὸ τῶν χορηγῶν, ἐφυλάττοντο

---

^a Cf. Demosthenes, Against Conon 7.
^b These contained the names of those who had been
nominated as possible judges of the dramatic contests of the
festival of Dionysus.
^c The Prytanes (Presidents), a committee of 50, one-tenth

I had made with himself. And yet, men of the jury, do you think that he would desire the annulment of this agreement, which he could use to convict us of falsehood ? At any rate, this was not what he was saying after they had altered the memorandum ; on the contrary, in all details he appealed to the agreement and ordered the memorandum to be opened. In proof that Pasion at first was eager for the suppression of the agreement I will produce Agyrrhius himself as witness.

(*To the witness*) Please take the stand.

TESTIMONY

So then, the fact that we made the agreement, not as Pasion will try to explain, but as I have related to you, I think has been sufficiently established. And it should not occasion surprise, men of the jury, that he falsified the memorandum, not only for the reason that there have been numerous frauds of such nature, but because some of Pasion's friends have been guilty of conduct far worse. For instance, is there anyone who is ignorant that Pythodorus, called the " shop-keeper," [a] whose words and acts are all in Pasion's interest, last year opened the voting-urns [b] and removed the ballots naming the judges which had been cast by the Council ? And yet when a man who, for petty gain and at the peril of his life, has the effrontery to open secretly the urns that had been stamped by the prytanes [c] and sealed by the choregi,[d]

part of the Council of 500, managed for one-tenth of the year the affairs of the Council and of the Assembly.

[d] The Choregi were well-to-do Athenians, who were chosen to defray the costs of bringing out the choruses in the dramatic festivals.

δ' ὑπὸ τῶν ταμιῶν, ἔκειντο δ' ἐν ἀκροπόλει, τί δεῖ
θαυμάζειν, εἰ γραμματείδιον παρ' ἀνθρώπῳ ξένῳ
κείμενον τοσαῦτα μέλλοντες χρήματα κερδαίνειν
μετέγραψαν, ἢ τοὺς παῖδας αὐτοῦ πείσαντες ἢ ἄλλῳ
τρόπῳ, ᾧ ἠδύναντο, μηχανησάμενοι; περὶ μὲν οὖν
τούτων οὐκ οἶδ' ὅ τι δεῖ πλείω λέγειν.

35 Ἤδη δέ τινας Πασίων ἐπεχείρησε πείθειν, ὡς
τὸ παράπαν οὐδ' ἦν ἐνθάδε μοι χρήματα, λέγων
ὡς παρὰ Στρατοκλέους ἐδανεισάμην τριακοσίους
στατῆρας. ἄξιον οὖν καὶ περὶ τούτων ἀκοῦσαι, ἵν'
ἐπίστησθ', οἵοις τεκμηρίοις ἐπαρθεὶς ἀποστερεῖ με
τῶν χρημάτων. ἐγὼ γάρ, ὦ ἄνδρες δικασταί,
μέλλοντος Στρατοκλέους εἰσπλεῖν εἰς τὸν Πόντον,
βουλόμενος ἐκεῖθεν ὡς πλεῖστ' ἐκκομίσασθαι τῶν
χρημάτων, ἐδεήθην Στρατοκλέους τὸ μὲν αὐτοῦ
[366] χρυσίον ἐμοὶ καταλιπεῖν, ἐν δὲ τῷ Πόντῳ παρὰ τοῦ
36 πατρὸς τοὐμοῦ κομίσασθαι, νομίζων μεγάλα κερδαίνειν, εἰ κατὰ πλοῦν μὴ κινδυνεύοι τὰ χρήματα,
ἄλλως τε καὶ Λακεδαιμονίων ἀρχόντων κατ' ἐκεῖνον τὸν χρόνον τῆς θαλάττης. τούτῳ μὲν οὖν
οὐδὲν ἡγοῦμαι τοῦτ' εἶναι σημεῖον, ὡς οὐκ ἦν
ἐνθάδε μοι χρήματα. ἐμοὶ δὲ μέγιστ' ἔσται τεκ-
μήρια τὰ πρὸς Στρατοκλέα πραχθέντα, ὡς ἦν μοι
37 παρὰ τούτῳ χρυσίον. ἐρωτῶντος γὰρ Στρατοκλέους, ὅστις αὐτῷ ἀποδώσει τὰ χρήματα, ἐὰν ὁ
πατὴρ οὑμὸς μὴ ποιήσῃ τὰ ἐπεσταλμένα, αὐτὸς δ'
ἐκπλεύσας ἐνθάδ' ἐμὲ μὴ καταλάβῃ, Πασίων' αὐτῷ
συνέστησα, καὶ ὡμολόγησεν οὗτος αὐτῷ καὶ τὸ
ἀρχαῖον καὶ τοὺς τόκους τοὺς γιγνομένους ἀπο-

ᵃ The *stater* was a coin of a certain weight. The Persian

urns that were guarded by the treasurers and kept on the Acropolis, why should there be surprise that men, who hoped to make so great a profit, falsified an insignificant written agreement in the possession of a foreigner, gaining their ends either by the bribery of his slaves or by some other means in their power? On this point, however, I do not know what more I need say.

Already Pasion has tried to persuade certain persons that I had no money at all here, asserting that I had borrowed three hundred staters [a] from Stratocles. It is worth while, therefore, that you should hear me also on these matters, in order that you may understand how flimsy is the proof which encourages him to try to defraud me of my money. Now, men of the jury, when Stratocles was about to sail for Pontus, I, wishing to get as much of my money out of that country as possible, asked Stratocles to leave with me his own gold and on his arrival in Pontus to collect its equivalent from my father there, as I thought it would be highly advantageous not to jeopardize my money by the risks of a voyage, especially as the Lacedaemonians were then masters of the sea. For Pasion, then, I do not think that this is any indication that I had no money here; but for me my dealings with Stratocles will constitute the strongest proof that I had gold on deposit with Pasion. For when Stratocles inquired of me who would repay him in case my father failed to carry out my written instructions, and if, on his return, he should not find me here, I introduced Pasion to him, and Pasion himself agreed to repay him both the principal and

gold stater, or *daric*, was worth a little more than a pound sterling. These were probably Cyzicene staters of Asia Minor.

δώσειν. καίτοι εἰ μηδὲν ἔκειτο παρ' αὐτῷ τῶν
ἐμῶν, οἴεσθ' ἂν αὐτὸν οὕτω ῥαδίως τοσούτων
χρημάτων ἐγγυητήν μου γενέσθαι;
Καί μοι ἀνάβητε, μάρτυρες.

38 Ἴσως τοίνυν, ὦ ἄνδρες δικασταί, καὶ τούτων
ὑμῖν μάρτυρας παρέξεται, ὡς ἔξαρνος ἐγενόμην
πρὸς τοὺς ὑπὲρ Σατύρου πράττοντας μηδὲν κεκτῆσθαι πλὴν ὧν ἐκείνοις παρεδίδουν, καὶ ὡς αὐτὸς
ἐπελαμβάνετο τῶν χρημάτων τῶν ἐμῶν ὁμολο-
γοῦντος ἐμοῦ ὀφείλειν τριακοσίας δραχμάς, καὶ ὅτι
Ἱππολαΐδαν, ξένον ὄντ' ἐμαυτοῦ καὶ ἐπιτήδειον,
39 περιεώρων παρὰ τούτου δανειζόμενον. ἐγὼ δ', ὦ
ἄνδρες δικασταί, καταστὰς εἰς συμφορὰς οἵας ὑμῖν
διηγησάμην, καὶ τῶν μὲν οἴκοι πάντων ἀπεστερημένος, τὰ δ' ἐνθάδ' ἀναγκαζόμενος παραδιδόναι
τοῖς ἥκουσιν, ὑπολοίπου δ' οὐδενὸς ὄντος μοι, πλὴν
εἰ δυνηθείην λαθεῖν περιποιησάμενος τὸ χρυσίον τὸ
παρὰ τούτῳ κείμενον, ὁμολογῶ καὶ τούτῳ προσ-
ομολογῆσαι τριακοσίας δραχμὰς καὶ περὶ τῶν
ἄλλων τοιαῦτα πράττειν καὶ λέγειν ἐξ ὧν ἐκείνους
40 μάλιστ' ἂν πείθειν ᾠόμην μηδὲν εἶναί μοι. καὶ
ταῦθ' ὡς οὐ δι' ἀπορίαν ἐγίγνετο, ἀλλ' ἵνα πιστευ-
θείην ὑπ' ἐκείνων, ῥαδίως γνώσεσθε. πρῶτον μὲν
γὰρ ὑμῖν μάρτυρας παρέξομαι τοὺς εἰδότας πολλά
μοι χρήματ' ἐκ τοῦ Πόντου κομισθέντα, ἔπειτα δὲ
τοὺς ὁρῶντάς με τῇ τούτου τραπέζῃ χρώμενον, ἔτι
δὲ παρ' ὧν ἐχρυσώνησ' ὑπ' ἐκεῖνον τὸν χρόνον
236

the accrued interest. And yet if Pasion had not had on deposit some money belonging to me, do you think he would so readily have become my guarantor for so large a sum ?

(*To the witnesses*) Witnesses, please take the stand.

WITNESSES

Perhaps, men of the jury, he will present witnesses to you who will testify that I also denied, in the presence of the agents of Satyrus, that I possessed any money except that which I surrendered to them, and that he himself was laying claim to my money on my own confession that I owed him three hundred drachmas, and also that I had allowed Hippolaïdas, my guest and friend, to borrow from him.ᵃ As for me, men of the jury, since I was involved in the difficulties which I have related to you, deprived of all I had at home and under compulsion to surrender what I had here to the envoys from Pontus, and finding myself without any means unless I could secretly retain in my possession the money on deposit with Pasion, I did, I admit, acknowledge a debt due him of three hundred drachmas and that in other respects I behaved and spoke in a manner which I thought would best persuade them that I possessed nothing. And that these things were done by me, not because of lack of funds, but that the parties in Pontus might believe that to be the case, you will readily learn. I will present to you first those who knew that I had received much money from Pontus ; next, those who saw me as a patron of Pasion's bank, and, besides, the persons from whom

ᵃ This is cited to indicate that the speaker had no means himself from which to make the loan to his friend.

41
[367] πλέον ἢ χιλίους στατῆρας. πρὸς δὲ τούτοις εἰσ-
φορᾶς ἡμῖν προσταχθείσης καὶ ἑτέρων ἐπιγραφέων
γενομένων ἐγὼ πλεῖστον εἰσήνεγκα τῶν ξένων, αὐτός θ' αἱρεθεὶς ἐμαυτῷ μὲν ἐπέγραψα τὴν μεγίστην
εἰσφοράν, ὑπὲρ Πασίωνος δ' ἐδεόμην τῶν συνεπι-
γραφέων, λέγων ὅτι τοῖς ἐμοῖς χρήμασι τυγχάνει
χρώμενος.

Καί μοι ἀνάβητε μάρτυρες.

ΜΑΡΤΥΡΕΣ

42 Αὐτὸν τοίνυν Πασίων' ἔργῳ παρέξομαι τούτοις
συμμαρτυροῦντα. ὁλκάδα γάρ, ἐφ' ᾗ πολλὰ χρήματ' ἦν ἐγὼ δεδωκώς, ἔφηνέ τις ὡς οὖσαν ἀνδρὸς
Δηλίου. ἀμφισβητοῦντος δ' ἐμοῦ καὶ καθέλκειν
ἀξιοῦντος οὕτω τὴν βουλὴν διέθεσαν οἱ βουλόμενοι
συκοφαντεῖν, ὥστε τὸ μὲν πρῶτον παρὰ μικρὸν
ἦλθον ἄκριτος ἀποθανεῖν, τελευτῶντες δ' ἐπείσθη-
43 σαν ἐγγυητὰς παρ' ἐμοῦ δέξασθαι. καὶ Φίλιππος
μὲν ὤν μοι ξένος πατρικός, κληθεὶς καὶ ὑπακούσας,
δείσας τὸ μέγεθος τοῦ κινδύνου ἀπιὼν ᾤχετο·
Πασίων δ' Ἀρχέστρατόν μοι τὸν ἀπὸ τῆς τραπέζης ἑπτὰ ταλάντων ἐγγυητὴν παρέσχεν. καίτοι
εἰ μικρῶν ἀπεστερεῖτο καὶ μηδὲν ᾔδει μ' ἐνθάδε
κεκτημένον, οὐκ ἂν δήπου τοσούτων χρημάτων
44 ἐγγυητής μου κατέστη. ἀλλὰ δῆλον ὅτι τὰς μὲν
τριακοσίας δραχμὰς ἐνεκάλεσεν ἐμοὶ χαριζόμενος,
τῶν δ' ἑπτὰ ταλάντων ἐγγυητής μοι ἐγένεθ' ἡγούμενος πίστιν ἔχειν ἱκανὴν τὸ χρυσίον τὸ παρ' αὐτῷ

---

[a] The speaker had lent money on the cargo of the merchant-
man, which apparently was denounced as being contraband
for some reason.

at that time I bought more than a thousand gold staters. In addition to this, when a special tax was imposed upon us and other men than I were appointed registrars, I contributed more than any other foreigner ; and when I was myself chosen registrar, I subscribed the largest contribution, but I pleaded with my fellow-registrars on behalf of Pasion, explaining that it was my money that he was using.

(*To the witnesses*) Witnesses, please take the stand.

WITNESSES

Pasion himself, moreover—in effect, at least—I will present as corroborating these statements. An information had been laid by a certain party against a trading-ship, upon which I had lent a large sum of money, as belonging to a man of Delos.[a] When I disputed this claim and demanded that the ship put to sea, those who make a business of blackmail so influenced the Council that at first I almost was put to death without a trial ; finally, however, they were persuaded to accept bondsmen from me. And Philip, who was my father's guest-friend, was summoned and appeared, but took to flight in alarm at the magnitude of the danger ; Pasion, however, furnished for me Archestratus,[b] the banker, as surety for seven talents. And yet if he stood to lose but a small sum and had known that I possessed no funds here, surely he would not have become my surety for so large an amount. But it is obvious that Pasion called in the three hundred drachmas as a favour to me, and that he became my surety for seven talents because he judged that the gold on deposit with him was a

[b] The banker Archestratus was the former master of Pasion.

κειμενον. ὡς μὲν τοίνυν ἦν τέ μοι πολλὰ χρήματ'
ἐνθάδε καὶ ταῦτ' ἐπὶ τῇ τούτου τραπέζῃ κεῖταί μοι,
καὶ ἐκ τῶν ἔργων τῶν Πασίωνος ὑμῖν δεδήλωκα
καὶ παρὰ τῶν ἄλλων τῶν εἰδότων ἀκηκόατε.

45 Δοκεῖτε δέ μοι, ὦ ἄνδρες δικασταί, ἄριστ' ἂν
γνῶναι περὶ ὧν ἀμφισβητοῦμεν, ἀναμνησθέντες
ἐκεῖνον τὸν χρόνον, καὶ τὰ πράγματα πῶς εἶχεν
ἡμῖν, ὅτ' ἐγὼ Μενέξενον καὶ Φιλόμηλον προσ-
έπεμψ' ἀπαιτήσοντας τὴν παρακαταθήκην, καὶ
Πασίων τὸ πρῶτον ἐτόλμησεν ἔξαρνος γενέσθαι.
εὑρήσετε γὰρ τὸν μὲν πατέρα μου συνειλημμένον
καὶ τὴν οὐσίαν ἅπασαν ἀφῃρημένον, ἐμοὶ δ' οὐχ οἷόν
τ' ὂν διὰ τὰς παρούσας τύχας οὔτ' αὐτοῦ μένειν
46 οὔτ' εἰς τὸν Πόντον εἰσπλεῖν. καίτοι πότερον εἰκὸς
[368] ἔμ' ἐν τοσούτοις ὄντα κακοῖς ἀδίκως ἐγκαλεῖν, ἢ
Πασίωνα καὶ διὰ τὸ μέγεθος τῶν ἡμετέρων συμφορῶν καὶ διὰ τὸ πλῆθος τῶν χρημάτων ἐπαρθῆναι
τὴν ἀποστέρησιν ποιήσασθαι; τίς δὲ πώποτ' εἰς
τοσοῦτον συκοφαντίας ἀφίκετο ὥστε αὐτὸς περὶ τοῦ
σώματος κινδυνεύων τοῖς ἀλλοτρίοις ἐπιβουλεύειν;
μετὰ ποίας δ' ἂν ἐλπίδος ἢ τί διανοηθεὶς ἀδίκως
ἦλθον ἐπὶ τοῦτον; πότερον ὡς δείσας τὴν δύναμιν
τὴν ἐμὴν ἤμελλεν εὐθύς μοι δώσειν ἀργύριον; ἀλλ'
47 οὐχ οὕτως ἑκάτερος ἡμῶν ἔπραττεν. ἀλλ' εἰς
ἀγῶνα καταστὰς ᾤμην καὶ παρὰ τὸ δίκαιον πλέον
ἕξειν Πασίωνος παρ' ὑμῖν; ὃς οὐδὲ μένειν ἐνθάδε
παρεσκευαζόμην, δεδιὼς μή μ' ἐξαιτήσειε Σάτυρος
παρ' ὑμῶν. ἀλλ' ἵνα μηδὲν διαπραττόμενος ἐχθρὸς

---

* For the same argument *cf.* Isocrates, *Against Euthynus* 14.

sufficient guarantee. That, therefore, I had a large sum of money here and that it was deposited in his bank I have not only proved to you from Pasion's acts but you have also heard it from the others who know the facts.

It seems to me, men of the jury, that you would best decide upon the questions at issue if you should call to mind that period and the situation in which our affairs stood when I sent Menexenus and Philomelus to claim the deposit and Pasion for the first time had the hardihood to deny its existence. You will find, in fact, that my father had been arrested and deprived of all his property, and that I was unable, because of the embarrassment in which I found myself, either to remain here or to sail to the Pontus. And yet, which is the more reasonable supposition —that I, involved in misfortunes so great brought unjust charges against Pasion or that he, because of the magnitude of our misfortunes and the large sum of money involved, was tempted to defraud us? But what man ever went so far in chicanery as, with his own life in jeopardy, to plot against the possessions of others?[a] With what hope or with what intent would I have unjustly proceeded against Pasion? Was it my thought that, in fear of my influence, he would forthwith give me money? But neither the one nor the other of us was in such a situation. Or was I of opinion that by bringing the matter to issue in court I should have greater influence with you than Pasion, even contrary to justice—I, who was not even preparing to remain in Athens, since I feared that Satyrus would demand of you my extradition? Or was I going to act so that, without accomplishing anything, I should

τούτῳ κατασταίην, ᾧ μάλιστ' ἐτύγχανον πάντων
τῶν ἐν τῇ πόλει χρώμενος; καὶ τίς ἂν ὑμῶν
ἀξιώσειε καταγνῶναί μου τοσαύτην μανίαν καὶ
ἀμαθίαν;

48 Ἐνθυμηθῆναι δ' ἄξιόν ἐστιν, ὦ ἄνδρες δικασταί,
τὴν ἀτοπίαν καὶ τὴν ἀπιστίαν ὧν ἑκάστοτε Πασίων
ἐπεχείρει λέγειν. ὅτε μὲν γὰρ οὕτως ἔπραττον,
ὥστ' οὐδ' ἄν, εἰ προσωμολόγει μ' ἀποστερεῖν τῶν
χρημάτων, οἷός τ' ἂν ἦν παρ' αὐτοῦ δίκην λαβεῖν,
τότε μὲν αἰτιᾶταί μ' ἀδίκως ἐγκαλεῖν ἐπιχειρῆσαι·
ἐπειδὴ δ' ἐγώ τε τῶν πρὸς Σάτυρον διαβολῶν
ἀπηλλάγην καὶ τοῦτον ἅπαντες ὀφλήσειν τὴν δίκην
ἐνόμιζον, τηνικαῦτά μέ φησιν ἀφεῖναι πάντων τῶν
ἐγκλημάτων αὐτόν. καίτοι πῶς ἂν τούτων ἀλογώ-
τερα γένοιτο;

49 Ἀλλὰ γὰρ ἴσως περὶ τούτων μόνον ἀλλ' οὐ καὶ
περὶ τῶν ἄλλων ἐναντί' αὐτὸς αὑτῷ καὶ λέγων καὶ
πράττων φανερός ἐστιν· ὃς τὸν μὲν παῖδα, ὃν αὐτὸς
ἠφάνισεν, ὑφ' ἡμῶν ἔφασκεν ἀνδραποδισθῆναι, τὸν
αὐτὸν δὲ τοῦτον ἀπεγράψατο μὲν ἐν τοῖς τιμήμασιν
ὡς δοῦλον μετὰ τῶν οἰκετῶν τῶν ἄλλων, ἐπεὶ
δ' αὐτὸν ἠξίου Μενέξενος βασανίζειν, ἀφῃρεῖθ' ὡς
50 ἐλεύθερον ὄντα. πρὸς δὲ τούτοις ἀποστερῶν αὐτὸς
τὴν παρακαταθήκην, ἐτόλμησεν ἡμῖν ἐγκαλεῖν, ὡς
ἔχομεν ἓξ τάλαντ' ἀπὸ τῆς τούτου τραπέζης.
καίτοι ὅστις περὶ πραγμάτων οὕτω φανερῶν ἐπ-
[369] εχείρει ψεύδεσθαι, πῶς χρὴ πιστεύειν αὐτῷ περὶ
ὧν μόνος πρὸς μόνον ἔπραξεν;

51 Τὸ τελευταῖον τοίνυν, ὦ ἄνδρες δικασταί, ὁμο-
242

make a personal enemy of the man with whom, as
it happened, of all the inhabitants of Athens, I was
on terms of greatest intimacy? Who of you, I ask,
would think it right to condemn me as being guilty
of such folly and stupidity?

It is also right, men of the jury, that you should note
the absurdity and the incredibility of the arguments
which Pasion on each occasion undertook to present.
For when my situation was such that, even if he
acknowledged that he was defrauding me of my
money, I could not have exacted the penalty from
him, it is then that he accuses me of trying to make
unjust claims; but when I had been declared innocent of the slanderous charges lodged with Satyrus
and all thought that he would lose his suit, it is then
that he says I renounced all claims against him. And
yet how could anything be more illogical than this?

But, you may say, perhaps it is on these matters
only, and not on the others, that he obviously con-
tradicts himself in both words and deeds. Yet he is
the man who, though he alleged that the slave whom
he himself had spirited away had been enslaved by
us, yet listed this same person in his property-
schedule as a slave along with his other servants,
and then when Menexenus demanded that this slave
give testimony under torture, Pasion brought about
his release on the ground that he was a freeman!
Furthermore, while he himself was defrauding me
of my deposit, he had the impudence to accuse us of
having six talents from his bank. And yet when a
man did not hesitate to lie in matters so obvious
to everybody, how can he be believed about matters
transacted between us two alone?

Finally, men of the jury, although he had agreed

λογήσας ὡς Σάτυρον εἰσπλευσεῖσθαι καὶ ποιήσειν
ἅττ' ἂν ἐκεῖνος γνῷ, καὶ ταῦτ' ἐξηπάτησε, καὶ αὐτὸς μὲν οὐκ ἤθελεν εἰσπλεῦσαι πολλάκις ἐμοῦ προ-
καλεσαμένου, εἰσέπεμψε δὲ τὸν Κίττον· ὃς ἐλθὼν
ἐκεῖσ' ἔλεγεν ὅτι ἐλεύθερος εἴη καὶ τὸ γένος Μιλή-
σιος, εἰσπέμψειε δ' αὐτὸν Πασίων διδάξοντα περὶ
52 τῶν χρημάτων. ἀκούσας δὲ Σάτυρος ἀμφοτέρων
ἡμῶν δικάζειν μὲν οὐκ ἠξίου περὶ τῶν ἐνθάδε
γενομένων συμβολαίων, ἄλλως τε καὶ μὴ παρόντος
τούτου μηδὲ μέλλοντος ποιήσειν ἃ ἐκεῖνος δικά-
σειεν, οὕτω δὲ σφόδρ' ἐνόμιζεν ἀδικεῖσθαί με, ὥστε
συγκαλέσας τοὺς ναυκλήρους ἐδεῖτ' αὐτῶν βοηθεῖν
ἐμοὶ καὶ μὴ περιορᾶν ἀδικούμενον, καὶ πρὸς τὴν
πόλιν συγγράψας ἐπιστολὴν ἔδωκε φέρειν Ξενο-
τίμῳ τῷ Καρκίνου.

Καί μοι ἀνάγνωθι αὐτοῖς.

ΕΠΙΣΤΟΛΗ

53 Οὕτω τοίνυν, ὦ ἄνδρες δικασταί, πολλῶν μοι τῶν
δικαίων ὑπαρχόντων, ἐκεῖν' ἡγοῦμαι μέγιστον εἶναι
τεκμήριον ὡς ἀποστερεῖ με Πασίων τῶν χρημάτων, ὅτι τὸν παῖδ' οὐκ ἠθέλησε βασανίζειν ἐκδοῦναι
τὸν συνειδότα περὶ τῆς παρακαταθήκης. καίτοι
περὶ τῶν πρὸς τοὺς ἐπὶ ταῖς τραπέζαις συμβολαίων
τίς ἂν ἔλεγχος ἰσχυρότερος τούτου γένοιτο; οὐ γὰρ
54 δὴ μάρτυράς γ' αὐτῶν ποιούμεθα. ὁρῶ δὲ καὶ ὑμᾶς
καὶ περὶ τῶν ἰδίων καὶ περὶ τῶν δημοσίων οὐδὲν
πιστότερον οὐδ' ἀληθέστερον βασάνου νομίζοντας,
καὶ μάρτυρας μὲν ἡγουμένους[1] οἷόν τ' εἶναι καὶ τῶν

---

[1] ἡγουμένους ΓΕ : μὴ γενομένους Blass.

to sail to the country of Satyrus and to do whatever he decreed, he deceived me even in this ; he refused to sail himself in spite of my frequent solicitations, but sent Cittus instead. On his arrival Cittus alleged that he was a freeman, a Milesian by birth, and that Pasion had sent him to furnish information about the money. When Satyrus had heard us both, he did not wish to render a decision concerning contracts made in Athens, especially since Pasion was absent and not likely to comply with his decision ; but he believed so strongly that I was being wronged that he called together the shipowners [a] and asked them to assist me and not suffer me to be wronged. And he wrote a letter to the city of Athens and gave it to Xenotimus, son of Carcinus, for delivery.

(*To the Clerk*) Please read the letter to the jury.

LETTER

Although, men of the jury, my claims to justice are so many, I think that the strongest proof that Pasion defrauded me of my money is this—that he refused to surrender for torture the slave who knew about the deposit. And yet, in respect to contracts where banks are concerned, what stronger proof could there be than this ? For witnesses certainly we do not use in contracts with banks.[b] I see that in private and public causes you judge that nothing is more deserving of belief, or truer, than testimony given under torture, and that while you think it possible to suborn witnesses even for acts which

---

[a] Of the Athenian colony at Bosporus.
[b] *Cf.* § 2.

μὴ γενομένων¹ παρασκευάσασθαι, τὰς δὲ βασάνους
φανερῶς ἐπιδεικνύναι, ὁπότεροι τἀληθῆ λέγουσιν.
ἃ οὗτος εἰδὼς ἠβουλήθη εἰκάζειν ὑμᾶς περὶ τοῦ
πράγματος μᾶλλον ἢ σαφῶς εἰδέναι. οὐ γὰρ δὴ
τοῦτό γ' ἂν εἰπεῖν ἔχοι, ὡς ἔλαττον ἔμελλεν ἕξειν
ἐν τῇ βασάνῳ, καὶ διὰ τοῦτ' οὐκ εἰκὸς ἦν αὐτὸν
55 ἐκδοῦναι. πάντες γὰρ ἐπίστασθ' ὅτι κατειπὼν μὲν
ἤμελλε τὸν ἐπίλοιπον χρόνον ὑπὸ τούτου κάκιστ'
ἀνθρώπων ἀπολεῖσθαι, διακαρτερήσας δὲ καὶ ἐλεύθερος ἔσεσθαι καὶ μεθέξειν ὧν οὗτός μ' ἀπεστέρη-
σεν. ἀλλ' ὅμως τοσούτῳ μέλλων πλέον ἕξειν,
[370] συνειδὼς αὑτῷ τὰ πεπραγμένα, ὑπέμεινε καὶ δίκας
φεύγειν καὶ τὰς ἄλλας αἰτίας ἔχειν, ὥστε μηδεμίαν
βάσανον περὶ τοῦ πράγματος τούτου γενέσθαι.

56 Ἐγὼ οὖν ὑμῶν δέομαι μεμνημένους τούτων
καταψηφίσασθαι Πασίωνος, καὶ μὴ τοσαύτην πονηρίαν ἐμοῦ καταγνῶναι, ὡς οἰκῶν ἐν τῷ Πόντῳ
καὶ τοσαύτην οὐσίαν κεκτημένος ὥστε καὶ ἑτέρους
εὖ ποιεῖν δύνασθαι, Πασίων' ἦλθον συκοφαντήσων
καὶ ψευδεῖς αὐτῷ παρακαταθήκας ἐγκαλῶν.

57 Ἄξιον δὲ καὶ Σατύρου καὶ τοῦ πατρὸς ἐνθυμηθῆναι, οἳ πάντα τὸν χρόνον περὶ πλείστου τῶν
Ἑλλήνων ὑμᾶς ποιοῦνται, καὶ πολλάκις ἤδη διὰ
σπάνιν σίτου τὰς τῶν ἄλλων ἐμπόρων ναῦς κενὰς
ἐκπέμποντες ὑμῖν ἐξαγωγὴν ἔδοσαν· καὶ ἐν τοῖς
ἰδίοις συμβολαίοις, ὧν ἐκεῖνοι κριταὶ γίγνονται,

¹ γενομένων Drerup : παραγενομένων ΓΕ : πεπραγμένων Fuhr,
Blass.

ᵃ A commonplace ; cf. Antiphon, On the Choreutes 25
ᵇ Cf. Demosthenes, Against Leptines 31.

never occurred at all, yet that testimony under torture clearly shows which party is telling the truth.[a]
Pasion, being aware of this, wished that in this affair
you should judge by conjecture rather than know
the exact truth. For he certainly would not be able
to say that he was likely to be at a disadvantage
if torture should be used and that for this reason
the surrender of his slave could not reasonably be
expected of him. For you all know that if Cittus
spoke against his master, he would likely suffer for
the remainder of his life in the most cruel manner
at the hands of his master, but that if he held firm
in his denials, he would be free and have a share of
my money which his master had taken. In spite of
the fact that he was to have so great an advantage
Pasion, conscious of his guilty deeds, submitted to
stand suit and to rest under the other charges, all
to prevent any testimony under torture being given
in this case !

I therefore ask of you that, keeping these facts
in mind, you cast your votes against Pasion and not
judge me guilty of a villainy so great, that I, who
live in Pontus and possess so large an estate that I
am able even to assist others, have come here maliciously to prosecute Pasion and to accuse him of
dishonesty in the matter of a deposit made with his
bank.

It is right also that you keep in mind both Satyrus
and my father, who have always esteemed you above
all the other Greeks and frequently in past times,
when there was a scarcity of grain and they were
sending away empty the ships of other merchants,
granted to you the right of export [b] ; also, in the
private contracts in which they are arbiters, you

οὐ μόνον ἴσον ἀλλὰ καὶ πλέον ἔχοντες ἀπέρχεσθε.
58 ὥστ' οὐκ ἂν εἰκτόως περὶ ὀλίγου ποιήσαισθε τὰς
ἐκείνων ἐπιστολάς. δέομαι οὖν ὑμῶν καὶ ὑπὲρ
ἐμαυτοῦ καὶ ὑπὲρ ἐκείνων τὰ δίκαια ψηφίσασθαι
καὶ μὴ τοὺς Πασίωνος λόγους ψευδεῖς ὄντας
πιστοτέρους ἡγεῖσθαι τῶν ἐμῶν.

come off not only on even terms but even at an advantage. You would not reasonably, therefore, consider their letters of little importance. I ask of you, then, both on their behalf and on my own, that you vote in accordance with justice and not count the false assertions of Pasion to be more worthy of belief than my own words.

XVIII. SPECIAL PLEA AGAINST CALLIMACHUS

INTRODUCTION

ISOCRATES wrote this forensic speech for a client who was defending himself against an Action for Damages brought by a person named Callimachus. The defendant in reply entered a Special Plea of Exception, or Demurrer, denying the admissibility of the suit. In a case of this kind the positions of plaintiff and defendant were reversed, so that the defendant, contrary to the usual procedure, spoke first.

The facts of the case, related in the speech, are briefly as follows : Patrocles, Archon Basileus (King-Archon) of Athens in 403 B.C. during the brief period when the Ten held power in succession to the Thirty Tyrants, denounced Callimachus for illegally having in his possession a sum of money which belonged to one of the exiled members of the democratic party who had assembled at Piraeus. The case was referred by the Ten to the Council, which decreed that the money should be confiscated. After the citizens at Piraeus had been restored to power in Athens, Callimachus brought successful actions against several defendants : Patrocles was compelled to pay ten minas *a* ; one Lysimachus two minas ; and the defendant compromised the case by the payment of two minas. This last payment was sanctioned by an arbitrator, which action estopped further litigation.

---

a A *mina* = 100 drachmae, about $18 or £4.

AGAINST CALLIMACHUS

In spite of this, Callimachus again brought suit for one hundred minas, whereupon the defendant produced a witness of the previous arbitration. Callimachus, after an interval, brought a new action. The client of Isocrates then appealed to the new law of Archinus. This was a law which Archinus, in an endeavour to bring to an end civic discord and enmities in accordance with the spirit and the terms of the general amnesty which had been declared following the restoration of the democracy, had succeeded in having passed. The law provided that when an action was brought in violation of the Amnesty, the defendant could enter an Exception or Special Plea and this Special Plea should precede a regular trial ; further, if either party failed to receive one-fifth of the votes of the tribunal, he was liable to the fine of one-sixth of the sum in litigation.

This case occurred soon after the Amnesty of 403 B.C. The trial, for which this speech was written, may be assigned with probability to the year 402 B.C. and early in the career of Isocrates.

The plainness and simplicity of the style of the speech and the detailed argumentation, which reminds the student of the Attic orator Isaeus, are in keeping with the subject, the occasion, and the speaker.[a]

[a] For a discussion of the speech see Blass, *Die attische Beredsamkeit* ii. p. 213 ; Jebb, *Attic Orators* ii. pp. 233 ff. ; and Mathieu et Brémond, *Isocrate* i. pp. 15 ff.

18. ΠΑΡΑΓΡΑΦΗ ΠΡΟΣ ΚΑΛΛΙΜΑΧΟΝ

[371] Εἰ μὲν καὶ ἄλλοι τινὲς ἦσαν ἠγωνισμένοι τοιαύτην παραγραφήν, ἀπ᾽ αὐτοῦ τοῦ πράγματος ἠρχόμην ἂν τοὺς λόγους ποιεῖσθαι· νῦν δ᾽ ἀνάγκη περὶ τοῦ νόμου πρῶτον εἰπεῖν καθ᾽ ὃν εἰσεληλύθαμεν, ἵν᾽ ἐπιστάμενοι περὶ ὧν ἀμφισβητοῦμεν, τὴν ψῆφον φέρητε, καὶ μηδεὶς ὑμῶν θαυμάσῃ διότι φεύγων τὴν δίκην πρότερος λέγω τοῦ διώκοντος.

2 Ἐπειδὴ γὰρ ἐκ Πειραιέως κατελθόντες ἐνίους ἑωρᾶτε τῶν πολιτῶν συκοφαντεῖν ὡρμημένους καὶ τὰς συνθήκας λύειν ἐπιχειροῦντας, βουλόμενοι τούτους τε παῦσαι καὶ τοῖς ἄλλοις ἐπιδεῖξαι ὅτι οὐκ ἀναγκασθέντες ἐποιήσασθ᾽ αὐτὰς ἀλλ᾽ ἡγούμενοι τῇ πόλει συμφέρειν, εἰπόντος Ἀρχίνου νόμον ἔθεσθε, ἄν τις δικάζηται παρὰ τοὺς ὅρκους, ἐξεῖναι τῷ φεύγοντι παραγράψασθαι, τοὺς δ᾽ ἄρχοντας περὶ τούτου πρῶτον εἰσάγειν, λέγειν δὲ πρότερον τὸν

3 παραγραψάμενον, ὁπότερος δ᾽ ἂν ἡττηθῇ, τὴν ἐπωβελίαν ὀφείλειν, ἵν᾽ οἱ τολμῶντες μνησικακεῖν

---

^a A reference to the citizens of the democratic party who returned from exile to Athens in 403 B.C. after the defeat of the Thirty Tyrants. They had taken their stand under Thrasybulus in the harbour-city, Piraeus.

^b An act passed in 403 B.C. by the citizens, after the expulsion of the Thirty Tyrants, to put an end to civic discord and to re-establish the democracy.

XVIII. SPECIAL PLEA AGAINST
CALLIMACHUS

If any others had employed in litigation such a special plea of exception, I should have begun my discourse with the facts themselves ; but as the situation is, I am compelled first to speak of the law in accordance with which we have come before the court, that you may cast your votes with an understanding of the issues in our dispute and that no one of you may be surprised that I, although defendant in the case, am speaking prior to the plaintiff.

Now after your return to the city from Piraeus,[a] you saw that some of the citizens were bent upon bringing malicious prosecutions and were attempting to violate the Amnesty[b] ; so, wishing to restrain these persons and to show to all others that you had not made these agreements under compulsion, but because you thought them of advantage to the city, you enacted a law, on the motion of Archinus, to the effect that, if any person should commence a lawsuit in violation of the oaths, the defendant should have the power to enter a plea of exception, the magistrates should first submit this question to the tribunal, and that the defendant who had entered the plea should speak first ; and further, that the loser should pay a penalty of one-sixth of the sum at stake. The purpose of the penalty was this—that persons who

μὴ μόνον ἐπιορκοῦντες ἐξελέγχοιντο μηδὲ τὴν
παρὰ τῶν θεῶν τιμωρίαν ὑπομένοιεν ἀλλὰ καὶ
παραχρῆμα ζημιοῖντο. δεινὸν οὖν ἡγησάμην, εἰ
τῶν νόμων οὕτως ἐχόντων ἐγὼ περιόψομαι τὸν μὲν
συκοφάντην ἐν τριάκοντα δραχμαῖς κινδυνεύοντα,
ἐμαυτὸν δὲ περὶ τῆς οὐσίας ἁπάσης ἀγωνιζόμενον.

4 Ἀποδείξω δὲ Καλλίμαχον οὐ μόνον παρὰ τὰς
συνθήκας δικαζόμενον, ἀλλὰ καὶ περὶ τῶν ἐγκλημάτων ψευδόμενον, καὶ προσέτι δίαιταν ἡμῖν γεγενημένην περὶ αὐτῶν. βούλομαι δ' ἐξ ἀρχῆς ὑμῖν
διηγήσασθαι τὰ πραχθέντα· ἂν γὰρ τοῦτο μάθητε
ὡς οὐδὲν ὑπ' ἐμοῦ κακὸν πέπονθεν, ἡγοῦμαι ταῖς
τε συνθήκαις ὑμᾶς ἥδιον βοηθήσειν καὶ τούτῳ
μᾶλλον ὀργιεῖσθαι.

5
[372] Ἦρχον μὲν γὰρ οἱ δέκα οἱ μετὰ τοὺς τριάκοντα
καταστάντες, ὄντος δέ μοι Πατροκλέους ἐπιτη-
δείου, τοῦ τότε βασιλεύοντος, ἔτυχον μετ' αὐτοῦ
βαδίζων. ἐκεῖνος δ' ἐχθρὸς ὢν Καλλιμάχῳ τῷ
νῦν ἐμὲ διώκοντι τὴν δίκην, ἀπήντησεν ἀργύριον
φέροντι. λαβόμενος δ' αὐτοῦ Πάμφιλον ἔφασκεν
αὐτὸ καταλιπεῖν καὶ δημόσιον γίγνεσθαι· ἐκεῖνον
6 γὰρ εἶναι τῶν ἐν Πειραιεῖ. ἀμφισβητοῦντος δὲ
τούτου καὶ λοιδορίας αὐτοῖς γενομένης ἄλλοι τε
πολλοὶ συνέδραμον, καὶ κατὰ τύχην Ῥίνων εἷς τῶν
δέκα γενόμενος προσῆλθεν. εὐθὺς οὖν πρὸς αὐτὸν
τὴν φάσιν τῶν χρημάτων ὁ Πατροκλῆς ἐποιεῖτο· ὁ
δ' ὡς τοὺς συνάρχοντας ἦγεν ἀμφοτέρους. ἐκεῖνοι

ᵃ The most important of the Athenian nine archons was
not the King-Archon, as the name might suggest, but the
Archon Eponymus, who gave his name to the year in which
he held office. The King-Archon had charge of public worship and the conduct of certain criminal processes.

had the effrontery to rake up old grudges should not only be convicted of perjury but also, not awaiting the vengeance of the gods, should suffer immediate punishment. I thought, therefore, that it was absurd if, under the existing laws, I was to permit my calumniator to risk only thirty drachmas, while I myself am contesting a suit in which my whole property is at stake.

I intend to prove that Callimachus not only is bringing a suit in violation of the terms of the Amnesty agreement, but that he is also guilty of falsehood in his charges, and furthermore, that we have already resorted to arbitration in the matter at issue. But I wish to relate the facts to you from the beginning; for if you learn that he has suffered no wrong at my hands, I think that you will be more inclined to defend the Amnesty and be more incensed with him.

The government of the Ten, who had succeeded the Thirty, was then in control when Patrocles, a friend of mine, was the King-Archon,[a] and with him one day I happened to be walking. Patrocles, an enemy of Callimachus who is now prosecuting me in this suit, met him as he was carrying a sum of money, laid hold of him, and claimed that this money had been left by Pamphilus and belonged to the government; for Pamphilus was a member of the party of the Piraeus.[b] Callimachus denied this and as a violent quarrel ensued many others came running up; among them by chance Rhinon, who had become one of the Ten, approached. So Patrocles immediately laid information with him concerning the money and Rhinon led them both before his colleagues.

[b] Cf. § 2 note a.

δ' εἰς τὴν βουλὴν περὶ αὐτῶν ἀπέδοσαν· κρίσεως δὲ γενομένης ἔδοξε τὰ χρήματα δημόσι' εἶναι.
7 μετὰ δὲ ταῦτ', ἐπειδὴ κατῆλθον οἱ φεύγοντες ἐκ Πειραιέως, οὗτος[1] ἐνεκάλει τῷ Πατροκλεῖ καὶ δίκας ἐλάγχανεν ὡς αἰτίῳ τῆς συμφορᾶς γεγενημένῳ· διαλλαγεὶς δὲ πρὸς ἐκεῖνον καὶ πραξάμενος αὐτὸν δέκα μνᾶς ἀργυρίου Λυσίμαχον ἐσυκοφάντει· λαβὼν δὲ καὶ παρὰ τούτου διακοσίας δραχμὰς ἐμοὶ πράγματα παρεῖχεν. καὶ τὸ μὲν πρῶτον ἐνεκάλει φάσκων με συμπράττειν ἐκείνοις, τελευτῶν δ' εἰς τοῦτ' ἀναιδείας ἦλθεν ὥσθ' ἁπάντων με τῶν γεγενημένων ᾐτιᾶτο· ἅπερ ἴσως καὶ νῦν τολμήσει
8 κατηγορεῖν. ἐγὼ δ' ὑμῖν παρέξομαι μάρτυρας πρῶτον μὲν τοὺς ἐξ ἀρχῆς παραγενομένους, ὡς οὔτ' ἐπελαβόμην οὔτ' ἐφηψάμην τῶν χρημάτων, ἔπειτα 'Ρίνωνα[2] καὶ τοὺς συνάρχοντας, ὡς οὐκ ἐγὼ τὴν φάσιν ἀλλὰ Πατροκλῆς ἐποιήσατο πρὸς αὐτούς, ἔτι δὲ τοὺς βουλευτάς, ὡς ἐκεῖνος ἦν ὁ κατηγορῶν.

Καί μοι κάλει τούτων μάρτυρας.

ΜΑΡΤΥΡΕΣ

9 Οὕτω τοίνυν πολλῶν παραγενομένων τοῖς πραχθεῖσιν, ὥσπερ οὐδενὸς συνειδότος αὐτὸς μὲν οὗτος ἐφιστάμενος εἰς τοὺς ὄχλους καὶ καθίζων ἐπὶ τοῖς ἐργαστηρίοις λόγους ἐποιεῖτο ὡς δεινὰ πεπονθὼς

---

[1] οὗτος added by Blass.　　[2] 'Ρίνωνα added by Sauppe.

---

[a] During the rule of the Thirty, and of their successors the Ten, the judicial functions of the Athenian juries were usurped by the Council.

These officials referred the matter to the Council *a* ;
after an adjudication, the money was declared the
property of the state. Later, after the return of the
citizen-exiles from Piraeus, Callimachus brought a
charge against Patrocles and instituted proceedings
against him on the ground that he was responsible
for his loss. And when he had effected with him a
settlement of the matter and had exacted from him
ten minas of silver, Callimachus maliciously accused
Lysimachus. Having obtained two hundred drachmas
from him, he began to make trouble for me. At first
he charged me with being the accomplice of the
others ; in the end, he came to such a pitch of
impudence that he accused me as responsible for
everything that had been done, and it may be that
even now he will have the effrontery to make just
such an accusation. In rebuttal, however, I will present to you as witnesses, first, those who were present
at the beginning of the affair, who will testify that
I did not arrest Callimachus nor did I touch the
money ; second, Rhinon and his colleagues, who
will tell you that it was Patrocles, and not I, who
denounced him to them ; and finally, the members
of the Council, who will attest that Patrocles was
the accuser.

(*To the Clerk*) Please call witnesses of these facts.

Witnesses

Although so many persons had been present when
the events took place, Callimachus here, as if no one
had any knowledge of the matter, himself mixed
with the crowds, sat in the workshops, and related
again and again his story, how he had suffered out-

ISOCRATES

ὑπ' ἐμοῦ καὶ τῶν χρημάτων ἀπεστερημένος, τῶν
δὲ χρωμένων τινὲς τούτῳ προσιόντες μοι συνεβούλευον ἀπαλλάττεσθαι τῆς πρὸς τοῦτον διαφορᾶς καὶ
μὴ βούλεσθαι κακῶς ἀκούειν μηδὲ κινδυνεύειν περὶ
[373] πολλῶν χρημάτων, μηδ' εἰ σφόδρα πιστεύω τῷ
πράγματι, λέγοντες ὡς πολλὰ παρὰ γνώμην ἐν τοῖς
10 δικαστηρίοις ἀποβαίνει, καὶ ὅτι τύχῃ μᾶλλον ἢ τῷ
δικαίῳ κρίνεται τὰ παρ' ὑμῖν, ὥστε λυσιτελεῖν μοι
μίκρ' ἀναλώσαντι μεγάλων ἐγκλημάτων ἀπαλλαγῆναι μᾶλλον ἢ μηδὲν ἀποτείσαντι κινδυνεύειν περὶ
τηλικούτων. τί δ' ἂν ὑμῖν τὰ πολλὰ καθ' ἕκαστον
διηγοίμην;[1] οὐδὲν γὰρ[2] παρέλιπον τῶν εἰθισμένων
περὶ τῶν τοιούτων λέγεσθαι. τελευτῶν δ' οὖν ἐπείσ-
θην, ἅπαντα γὰρ εἰρήσεται τἀληθῆ πρὸς ὑμᾶς,
δοῦναι τούτῳ διακοσίας δραχμάς. ἵνα δὲ μὴ πάλιν
ἐξείη συκοφαντεῖν αὐτῷ, δίαιταν ἐπὶ ῥητοῖς ἐπετρέψαμεν Νικομάχῳ Βατῆθεν. . . .

ΜΑΡΤΥΡΕΣ

11 Τὸ μὲν τοίνυν πρῶτον ἐνέμεινε τοῖς ὡμολογη-
μένοις, ὕστερον δ' ἐπιβουλεύσας μετὰ Ξενοτίμου,
τοῦ τοὺς νόμους διαφθείροντος καὶ τὰ δικαστήρια
δεκάζοντος καὶ τὰς ἀρχὰς λυμαινομένου καὶ πάντων κακῶν αἰτίου, λαγχάνει μοι δίκην μυρίων
δραχμῶν. προβαλλομένου δ' ἐμοῦ μάρτυρα, ὡς
οὐκ εἰσαγώγιμος ἦν ἡ δίκη διαίτης γεγενημένης,

[1] τί δ' ἂν ὑμῖν τὰ πολλὰ καθ' ἕκαστον διηγοίμην vulg. Blass
omits δ' and καθ' ἕκαστον.
[2] οὐδὲν γὰρ added by Blass.

[a] A similar example of arbitration *under stated terms* (*i.e.*,
limited arbitration, where the arbitrator had no discretionary

260

rageous treatment at my hands and had been
defrauded of his money. And some of his friends
came to me and advised me to settle the dispute
with him, and not deliberately to risk defamation
and great financial loss, even though I had the
greatest confidence in my cause ; and they went on
to say that many decisions rendered in the tribunals
were contrary to the expectation of litigants, and
that chance rather than justice determined the issue
in your courts. Consequently, they asserted, it was
in my interest to be freed of serious charges by
paying a petty sum, rather than by paying nothing
to run the risk of penalties of such gravity. Why
need I relate to you all the details ? They omitted
none of the arguments which are customarily urged
in such cases. In any case I was finally prevailed
upon (for I will tell you the whole truth) to give him
two hundred drachmas. But in order that it might
not be in his power to blackmail me again, we
committed the arbitration under stated terms [a] to
Nicomachus of Batê. . . .[b]

WITNESSES

At first Callimachus kept his agreement, but later
in complicity with Xenotimus—that falsifier of the
laws, corrupter of our tribunals, vilifier of the authorities, and author of every evil—he brought suit against
me for the sum of ten thousand drachmas. But when
I brought forward in my defence a witness to show
that the suit was not within the jurisdiction of the

power) is found in *Trapez.* 19. *Cf.* Jebb, *Attic Orators*
ii. p. 234.

[b] A lacuna is here indicated by Blass, perhaps καί μοι
κάλει τούτων μάρτυρας (" please call witnesses to these facts ").

12 ἐκείνῳ μὲν οὐκ ἐπεξῆλθεν, εἰδὼς ὅτι, εἰ μὴ μεταλάβοι τὸ πέμπτον μέρος τῶν ψήφων, τὴν ἐπωβελίαν ὀφλήσει, πείσας δὲ τὴν ἀρχὴν πάλιν τὴν αὐτὴν δίκην ἐγράψατο, ὡς ἐν τοῖς πρυτανείοις μόνον κινδυνεύσων. ἀπορῶν δ' ὅ τι χρησαίμην τοῖς κακοῖς, ἡγησάμην εἶναι κράτιστον ἐξ ἴσου καταστήσαντ' ἀμφοτέροις τὸν κίνδυνον εἰσελθεῖν εἰς ὑμᾶς. καὶ τὰ μὲν γενόμενα ταῦτ' ἐστίν.

13 Πυνθάνομαι δὲ Καλλίμαχον οὐ μόνον περὶ τῶν ἐγκλημάτων διανοεῖσθαι ψευδῆ λέγειν, ἀλλὰ καὶ τὴν δίαιταν μέλλειν ἔξαρνον εἶναι καὶ παρεσκευάσθαι λέγειν τοιούτους λόγους, ὡς οὐκ ἄν ποτ' ἐπέτρεψε Νικομάχῳ δίαιταν, ὃν ἠπίστατο πάλαι χρώμενον ἡμῖν, καὶ ὡς οὐκ εἰκὸς ἦν αὐτὸν ἀντὶ μυρίων

14 δραχμῶν διακοσίας ἐθελῆσαι λαβεῖν. ὑμεῖς δ' ἐνθυμεῖσθε πρῶτον μὲν ὅτι τὴν δίαιταν οὐκ ἀμφισβητοῦντες ἀλλ' ἐπὶ ῥητοῖς ἐπετρέψαμεν, ὥστ' οὐδὲν

[374] ἄτοπον ἐποίησεν, εἰ Νικόμαχον εἵλετο διαιτητήν, ἀλλὰ πολὺ μᾶλλον εἰ περὶ τῶν πραγμάτων ὡμολογηκὼς περὶ τοῦ διαιτητοῦ διεφέρετο. ἔπειτ' ὀφειλομένων μὲν αὐτῷ μυρίων δραχμῶν οὐκ εἰκὸς ἦν αὐτὸν ἐπὶ δυοῖν μναῖν ποιήσασθαι τὴν διαλλαγήν· ἀδίκως δ' αἰτιώμενον καὶ συκοφαντοῦντα οὐδὲν θαυμαστὸν τοσοῦτον ἐθελῆσαι λαβεῖν. ἔτι δ', εἰ μεγάλ' ἐγκαλῶν ὀλίγ' ἐπράξατο, οὐ τούτῳ τοῦτο τεκμήριόν ἐστιν, ὡς ἡ δίαιτα οὐ γέγονεν, ἀλλὰ

---

[a] See Introduction to this speech.

[b] 10,000 drachmas=about $1800 or approximately £360 sterling ; two minas (200 drachmas)=about $36 or between seven and eight pounds.

court by reason of the previous arbitration, he did not attack my witness—for he knew that, if he did not receive the fifth of the votes cast, he would be assessed a penalty of one-sixth of the amount demanded—but having won over the magistrate, he again brought the same suit, in the belief that he risked only his court deposit-fee. And since I was at a loss how to cope with my difficulties, I judged that it was best to make the hazard equal for us both *a* and to come before you. And these are the facts.

I learn that Callimachus not only intends to speak falsely in the matter of his complaint, but will also deny that the arbitration took place, and that he is prepared to go so far as to assert that he never would have entrusted an arbitration to Nicomachus, whom he knew to be an old friend of ours, and further, that it is improbable that he was willing to accept two hundred drachmas instead of ten thousand. You must reflect, however, first, that we were not in dispute in the matter of the arbitration, but we committed it as an arbitration under stated terms, so that it is not at all strange that Callimachus chose Nicomachus as arbiter ; it would have been far stranger if, after he had come to an agreement about the matter, he had then made difficulty about the choice of arbiter. In the next place, it is not reasonable to assume that, if ten thousand drachmas had been owing to him, he would have settled for two minas *b* ; but since his charges were unjust and in the nature of blackmail, it is not astonishing that he was willing to take so little. Furthermore, if, after exorbitant demands, he exacted little, this is no proof in favour of his contention that the arbitration did not take place ; on the contrary, it confirms

πολὺ μᾶλλον ἡμῖν, ὡς καὶ τὴν ἀρχὴν οὐ δικαίως
15 ἐνεκάλεσεν. θαυμάζω δ' εἰ αὐτὸν μὲν ἱκανὸν γνῶναι νομίζει ὅτι οὐκ εἰκὸς ἀντὶ μυρίων δραχμῶν διακοσίας ἐθελῆσαι λαβεῖν, ἐμὲ δ' οὐκ ἂν οἴεται τοῦτ'
ἐξευρεῖν, εἴπερ ἠβουλόμην ψευδῆ λέγειν, ὅτι πλέον
ἔδει φάσκειν τούτων δεδωκέναι. ἀξιῶ δ', ὅσον περ
ἂν τούτῳ σημεῖον ἦν ὡς ἡ δίαιτα οὐ γέγονεν,
ἑλόντι τὰ διαμαρτυρηθέντα, τοσοῦτον ἐμοὶ γενέσθαι
τεκμήριον ὡς ἀληθῆ λέγω περὶ αὐτῆς, ἐπειδὴ τῷ
μάρτυρι φανερός ἐστιν οὐδ' ἐπεξελθεῖν ἀξιώσας.
16 Ἡγοῦμαι δ', εἰ μήθ' ἡ δίαιτα ἐγεγόνει μήτε τῶν
πεπραγμένων ἦσαν μάρτυρες, ἔδει δ' ἐκ τῶν εἰκότων σκοπεῖν, οὐδ' οὕτω χαλεπῶς ἂν ὑμᾶς γνῶναι
τὰ δίκαια. εἰ μὲν γὰρ καὶ τοὺς ἄλλους ἀδικεῖν
ἐτόλμων, εἰκότως ἄν μου κατεγιγνώσκετε καὶ περὶ
τοῦτον ἐξαμαρτάνειν· νῦν δ' οὐδένα φανήσομαι τῶν
πολιτῶν οὔτε χρήμασι ζημιώσας οὔτε περὶ τοῦ
σώματος εἰς κίνδυνον καταστήσας, οὔτ' ἐκ μὲν τῶν
μετεχόντων τῆς πολιτείας ἐξαλείψας, εἰς δὲ τὸν
17 μετὰ Λυσάνδρου κατάλογον ἐγγράψας. καίτοι
πολλοὺς ἐπῆρεν ἡ τῶν τριάκοντα πονηρία τοιαῦτα
ποιεῖν· οὐ γὰρ ὅτι τοὺς ἀδικοῦντας ἐκόλαζον, ἀλλ'
ἐνίοις καὶ προσέταττον ἐξαμαρτάνειν. ἐγὼ μὲν
τοίνυν οὐδ' ἐπὶ τῆς ἐκείνων ἀρχῆς οὐδὲν εὑρεθή-
σομαι τοιοῦτον ἐργασάμενος· οὗτος δ' ἀδικηθῆναί

---

[a] A list of citizens who were deprived of their civic rights;
cf. *Against Euthynus* 2 and Xenophon, *Hell.* ii. 3. 17-19.
[b] For the crimes of the Thirty see the vivid account by
Lysias in his speech *Against Eratosthenes.*

all the more our contention that his claim was unjust in the first place. I am astonished that, while he judges himself capable of recognizing that it was not probable that he was willing to take two hundred drachmas instead of the ten thousand, yet believes that I am incapable of discovering, if I had wished to lie, that I ought to have asserted that I had given him more. But this I ask—that in so far as it would have been an indication in his favour that the arbitration did not take place, if he had proved the falsity of the testimony, to that same extent it shall be proof in favour of my contention that I tell the truth concerning the arbitration, inasmuch as it is clearly shown that he did not dare to proceed against my witness.

I think, however, that even if there had been neither arbitration nor witnesses to the actual facts and you were under the necessity of considering the case in the light of the probabilities, not even in this event would you have difficulty in arriving at a just verdict. For if I were so audacious a man as to wrong others, you would with good reason condemn me as doing wrong to him also ; but as it is, I shall be found innocent of having harmed any citizen in regard to his property, or of jeopardizing his life, or of having expunged his name from the list of active citizens, or of having inscribed his name on Lysander's list.ᵃ And yet the wickedness of the Thirty ᵇ impelled many to act in this way ; for they not only did not punish the evil-doers but they even commanded some persons to do wrong. So as for me, not even when they had control of the government, shall I be found guilty of any such misdeed ; yet Callimachus says that he was wronged after the

φησιν, ὅτ' ἐξεβέβληντο μὲν οἱ τριάκοντα, ὁ δὲ
Πειραιεὺς ἦν κατειλημμένος, ἐκράτει δ' ὁ δῆμος,
18 περὶ διαλλαγῶν δ' ἦσαν οἱ λόγοι. καίτοι δοκεῖ
ἂν ὑμῖν, ὅστις ἐπὶ τῶν τριάκοντα κόσμιον αὑτὸν
[375] παρέσχεν, εἰς τοῦτον ἀποθέσθαι τὸν χρόνον ἀδικεῖν,
ἐν ᾧ καὶ τοῖς πρότερον ἡμαρτηκόσι μετέμελεν; ὁ
δὲ πάντων δεινότατον, εἰ τῶν μὲν ὑπαρχόντων
ἐχθρῶν μηδ' ἀμύνεσθαι μηδέν' ἠξίωσα, τοῦτον δὲ
κακῶς ποιεῖν ἐπεχείρουν, πρὸς ὃν οὐδὲν πώποτέ μοι
συμβόλαιον ἐγένετο.

19 Ὡς μὲν οὖν οὐκ αἴτιός εἰμι Καλλιμάχῳ τῆς τῶν
χρημάτων δημεύσεως, ἱκανῶς ἀποδεδεῖχθαί μοι
νομίζω· ὡς δ' οὐκ ἐξῆν αὐτῷ δικάζεσθαι περὶ τῶν
τότε γεγενημένων, οὐδ' εἰ πάντα ταῦτ' ἦν πεποιηκὼς ἅ φησιν αὐτός, ἐκ τῶν συνθηκῶν γνώσεσθε.

Καί μοι λαβὲ τὸ βιβλίον.

20 Ἆρα μικρῷ τῷ δικαίῳ πιστεύων τὴν παραγρα-
φὴν ἐποιησάμην, ἀλλ' οὐ τῶν μὲν συνθηκῶν διαρ-
ρήδην ἀφιεισῶν τοὺς ἐνδείξαντας ἢ φήναντας ἢ
τῶν ἄλλων τι τῶν τοιούτων πράξαντας, ἐμαυτὸν
δ' ἔχων ἀποφαίνειν, ὡς οὔτε ταῦτα πεποίηκα οὔτ'
ἄλλ' οὐδὲν ἐξήμαρτον;

Ἀνάγνωθι δή μοι καὶ τοὺς ὅρκους.

21 Οὐκ οὖν δεινόν, ὦ ἄνδρες δικασταί, οὕτω μὲν τῶν
συνθηκῶν ἐχουσῶν, τοιούτων δὲ τῶν ὅρκων γενομένων, τοσοῦτον φρονεῖν Καλλίμαχον ἐπὶ τοῖς

ᵃ Cf. § 2 note a.

Thirty had been expelled, the Piraeus had been taken, and when the democracy was in power, and the terms of reconciliation were being discussed. And yet do you think that a man who was well-behaved under the Thirty put off his wrongdoing until that period when even those who had formerly transgressed were repentant ? But the most absurd thing of all would be this—that although I never saw fit to avenge myself on anyone of my existing enemies, I was attempting to injure this man with whom I have never had any business dealings at all !

That I am not responsible for the confiscation of the money of Callimachus I think I have sufficiently proved. But that it was not legally in his power to bring a suit pertaining to events which occurred then, not even if I had done everything he says I did, you will learn from the covenant of Amnesty.[a]

(*To the Clerk*) Please take the document.

COVENANT OF AMNESTY

Was it, then, a weak defence of my rights I trusted in when I entered this demurrer ? On the contrary, do not the terms of the Amnesty explicitly exculpate any who have laid information against or denounced any person or have done any similar thing, and am I not able to prove that I have neither committed these acts nor transgressed in any other way ?

(*To the Clerk*) Please read the Oaths also.

OATHS

Is it not outrageous, men of the jury, that, although such were the terms of the covenant and the oaths which were sworn were of such nature, Callimachus

λόγοις τοῖς αὑτοῦ ὥσθ᾿ ἡγεῖσθαι πείσειν ὑμᾶς
ἐναντία τούτοις ψηφίσασθαι; καὶ εἰ μὲν ἑώρα
μεταμέλον τῇ πόλει τῶν πεπραγμένων, οὐκ ἄξιον
ἦν θαυμάζειν αὐτοῦ· νῦν δ᾿ οὐ μόνον ἐν τῇ θέσει
τῶν νόμων ἐπεδείξασθε περὶ πολλοῦ ποιούμενοι
22 τὰς συνθήκας, ἀλλὰ καὶ Φίλωνα τὸν ἐκ Κοίλης
ἐνδειχθέντα παραπρεσβεύεσθαι, καὶ περὶ μὲν τοῦ
πράγματος οὐδὲν ἔχοντ᾿ ἀπολογήσασθαι, τὰς δὲ
συνθήκας παρεχόμενον, ἔδοξεν ὑμῖν ἀφεῖναι καὶ
μηδὲ κρίσιν περὶ αὐτοῦ ποιήσασθαι. καὶ ἡ μὲν
πόλις οὐδὲ παρὰ τῶν ὁμολογούντων ἐξαμαρτάνειν
ἀξιοῖ δίκην λαβεῖν, οὗτος δὲ καὶ τοὺς οὐδὲν ἠδικη-
23 κότας τολμᾷ συκοφαντεῖν. καὶ μὴν οὐδὲ τάδ᾿
αὐτὸν λέληθεν, ὅτι Θρασύβουλος καὶ Ἄνυτος μέγιστον μὲν δυνάμενοι τῶν ἐν τῇ πόλει, πολλῶν
δ᾿ ἀπεστερημένοι χρημάτων, εἰδότες δὲ τοὺς ἀπο-
γράψαντας, ὅμως οὐ τολμῶσιν αὐτοῖς δίκας λαγ-
χάνειν οὐδὲ μνησικακεῖν, ἀλλ᾿ εἰ καὶ περὶ τῶν
[376] ἄλλων μᾶλλον ἑτέρων δύνανται διαπράττεσθαι,
24 ἀλλ᾿ οὖν περί γε τῶν ἐν ταῖς συνθήκαις ἴσον
ἔχειν τοῖς ἄλλοις ἀξιοῦσιν. καὶ οὐχ οὗτοι μόνοι
ταῦτ᾿ ἠξιώκασιν, ἀλλ᾿ οὐδ᾿ ὑμῶν οὐδεὶς τοιαύτην
δίκην εἰσελθεῖν τετόλμηκεν. καίτοι δεινόν, εἰ ἐπὶ
μὲν τοῖς ὑμετέροις αὐτῶν πράγμασιν ἐμμένετε τοῖς
ὅρκοις, ἐπὶ δὲ τῇ τούτου συκοφαντίᾳ παραβαίνειν
ἐπιχειρήσετε, καὶ τὰς μὲν ἰδίας ὁμολογίας δημο-
σίᾳ κυρίας ἀναγκάζετ᾿ εἶναι, τὰς δὲ τῆς πόλεως
268

is so convinced of his own eloquence that he believes
he will persuade you to vote in opposition to them ?
If he saw that the city regretted its past action, his
conduct should not occasion surprise ; but as a matter
of fact you have shown the importance you attach
to the covenant, not only in the enactment of the
laws, but when Philon of Coelê was indicted for mal-
versation on an embassy, and although he could offer
no defence but merely cited the covenant in exonera-
tion, you decided to dismiss his case and not even hold
him for trial. And although the city does not think
it proper to punish even confessed transgressors, yet
this man has the effrontery to bring malicious charges
against those who have done no wrong at all.
Furthermore, he is certainly not unaware of this
either—that Thrasybulus and Anytus, men of the
greatest influence in the city, although they have
been robbed of large sums of money and know who
gave in lists of their goods, nevertheless are not so
brazen as to bring suit against them or to bring up
old grudges against them ; on the contrary, even if,
in respect to all other claims, they have greater
power than others to accomplish their ends, yet in
matters covered by the covenant at least they see
fit to put themselves on terms of equality with the
other citizens. And it is not these men alone who
have accepted this point of view ; no, not even
one of you has dared to bring such an action. And
yet it would be outrageous if you, while honouring
your oaths where your own affairs are concerned,
shall attempt to violate them in connexion with the
calumnious charges of Callimachus, and if, while
insisting that private agreements must be held valid
by public authority, shall allow anyone who so

25 συνθήκας ἰδίᾳ τὸν βουλόμενον λύειν ἐάσετε. ὃ δὲ
πάντων ἄν τις μάλιστα θαυμάσειεν, εἰ, ὅτε μὲν
ἄδηλον ἦν, εἰ συνοίσουσιν αἱ διαλλαγαὶ τῇ πόλει,
τοιούτους ὅρκους ἐποιήσασθε περὶ αὐτῶν, ὥστ’
εἰ καὶ μὴ συνέφερεν ἀναγκαῖον εἶναι τοῖς ὡμο-
λογημένοις ἐμμένειν, ἐπειδὴ δ’ οὕτω καλῶς ὑμῖν
συμβέβηκεν ὥστε καὶ μηδεμιᾶς πίστεως γεγενημένης ἄξιον εἶναι τὴν παροῦσαν πολιτείαν[a] διαφυ-
26 λάττειν, τηνικαῦτα τοὺς ὅρκους παραβήσεσθε· καὶ
τοῖς μὲν εἰρηκόσιν ὡς χρὴ τὰς συνθήκας ἐξαλεί-
φειν ὠργίζεσθε, τουτονὶ δ’, ὃς γεγραμμένας αὐτὰς
τολμᾷ παραβαίνειν, ἀζήμιον ἀφήσετε. ἀλλ’ οὔτ’
ἂν δίκαια οὔτ’ ἄξι’ ὑμῶν αὐτῶν οὔτ’ ἂν πρέποντα
τοῖς πρότερον ἐγνωσμένοις ποιήσαιτε.

27 Ἐνθυμεῖσθε δ’ ὅτι περὶ τῶν μεγίστων ἥκετε
δικάσοντες· περὶ γὰρ συνθηκῶν τὴν ψῆφον οἴσετε,
ἃς οὐδὲ πώποτ’ οὔθ’ ὑμῖν πρὸς ἑτέρους οὔτ’ ἄλλοις
πρὸς ὑμᾶς ἐλυσιτέλησε παραβῆναι, τοσαύτην δ’
ἔχουσι δύναμιν ὥστε τὰ πλεῖστα τοῦ βίου καὶ τοῖς
Ἕλλησι καὶ τοῖς βαρβάροις διὰ συνθηκῶν εἶναι.
28 ταύταις γὰρ πιστεύοντες ὡς ἀλλήλους ἀφικνούμεθα
καὶ ποριζόμεθα ὧν ἕκαστοι τυγχάνομεν δεόμενοι·
μετὰ τούτων καὶ τὰ συμβόλαια τὰ πρὸς ἡμᾶς αὐτοὺς ποιούμεθα καὶ τὰς ἰδίας ἔχθρας καὶ τοὺς
κοινοὺς πολέμους διαλυόμεθα· τούτῳ μόνῳ κοινῷ

---

[a] *i.e.*, the Democracy.

desires, on his own private authority, to break the covenants of the state. But it would be the most astounding outcome of all if, while it was still uncertain whether or not the reconciliation would be of advantage to the city, you strengthened it with such oaths that, even if it proved disadvantageous, you were forced to abide by your agreements, yet now, when the results have been so happy for you that, even if you had not given any solemn pledge to do so, it is right for you scrupulously to preserve the existing government,[a] you are going to seize that moment to violate your oaths! And although you were incensed with those who have said that the covenant of Amnesty should be repealed, yet this man, who has the effrontery to transgress it after its official promulgation, you are going to discharge without a penalty! No, should you do so, you would neither be rendering justice nor acting in a manner worthy of yourselves or consistent with your former decisions.

I beg you, however, to bear in mind that you have come to pass judgement on matters of the highest importance; for you are going to cast your votes on the question of a covenant, and covenants have never been violated to the advantage of either yourselves in relation to the other parties or of others in relation to you; and they have such binding force that almost all the daily activities of Greeks and of barbarians are governed by covenants. For it is through our reliance on them that we visit one another's lands and procure those things of which we both have need; with the aid of these we make our contracts with each other and put an end to both our private animosities and our common wars. This

πάντες ἄνθρωποι διατελοῦμεν χρώμενοι. ὥσθ᾽
ἅπασι μὲν προσήκει βοηθεῖν αὐταῖς, μάλιστα δ᾽
ὑμῖν.

29 Ὑπόγυιον γάρ ἐστιν, ἐξ οὗ καταπολεμηθέντες,
ἐπὶ τοῖς ἐχθροῖς γενόμενοι, πολλῶν ἐπιθυμησάντων
διαφθεῖραι τὴν πόλιν, εἰς ὅρκους καὶ συνθήκας
κατεφύγομεν, ἃς εἰ Λακεδαιμόνιοι τολμῷεν παραβαίνειν, σφόδρ᾽ ἂν ἕκαστος ὑμῶν ἀγανακτήσειεν.
30
[377] καίτοι πῶς οἷόν τ᾽ ἐστὶν ἑτέρων κατηγορεῖν οἷς
αὐτός τις ἔνοχός ἐστιν; τῷ δ᾽ ἂν δόξαιμεν ἀδικεῖ-
σθαι παρὰ τὰς συνθήκας κακῶς πάσχοντες, εἰ μηδ᾽
αὐτοὶ φαινοίμεθ᾽ αὐτὰς περὶ πολλοῦ ποιούμενοι;
τίνας δὲ πίστεις πρὸς τοὺς ἄλλους εὑρήσομεν, εἰ
τὰς πρὸς ἡμᾶς αὐτοὺς γεγενημένας οὕτως εἰκῇ
31 λύσομεν; ἄξιον δὲ καὶ τῶνδε μνησθῆναι, διότι
πολλῶν καὶ καλῶν τοῖς προγόνοις ἐν τῷ πολέμῳ
πεπραγμένων οὐχ ἥκισθ᾽ ἡ πόλις ἐκ τούτων τῶν
διαλλαγῶν εὐδοκίμησεν. πρὸς μὲν γὰρ τὸν πόλεμον
πολλαὶ πόλεις ἂν εὑρεθεῖεν καλῶς ἠγωνισμέναι,
περὶ δὲ στάσεως οὐκ ἔστιν ἣν ἄν τις ἐπιδείξειεν
32 ἄμεινον τῆς ἡμετέρας βεβουλευμένην. ἔτι δὲ τῶν
μὲν τοιούτων ἔργων, ὅσα μετὰ κινδύνων πέπρακται, τὸ πλεῖστον ἄν τις μέρος τῇ τύχῃ μεταδοίη·
τῆς δ᾽ εἰς ἡμᾶς αὐτοὺς μετριότητος οὐδεὶς ἂν ἄλλ᾽
ἢ τὴν ἡμετέραν γνώμην αἰτιάσαιτο. ὥστ᾽ οὐκ
ἄξιον προδότας ταύτης τῆς δόξης γενέσθαι.

33 Καὶ μηδεὶς ἡγείσθω μ᾽ ὑπερβάλλειν μηδὲ μείζω
λέγειν, ὅτι δίκην ἰδίαν φεύγων τούτους εἴρηκα τοὺς
λόγους. οὐ γὰρ μόνον περὶ τῶν ἐπιγεγραμμένων

is the only universal institution which all we of the human race constantly employ. It is, therefore, the duty of all men to uphold them, and, above all, yours.

It is your duty, I say, for recently, when we had been conquered and had fallen into the power of enemies at home and many wished to destroy the city, we took refuge in the oaths and covenants ; and if the Lacedaemonians should dare to violate these, every man of you would be exceedingly indignant. And yet how can one accuse the other party of transgressions of which he is himself guilty ? Who would regard us as victims of injustice when suffering injury through a violation of covenants, if even we ourselves were manifestly holding them in slight esteem ? What pledges shall we find binding in our relations with other peoples if we so lightly disregard those which we have made among ourselves ? This, too, is worthy of our remembrance that, although our forefathers performed many glorious deeds in war, yet not the least of its glory our city has won through these treaties of reconciliation. For whereas many cities might be found which have waged war gloriously, in dealing with civil discord there is none which could be shown to have taken wiser measures than ours. Furthermore, the great majority of all those achievements that have been accomplished by fighting may be attributed to Fortune ; but for the moderation we showed towards one another no one could find any other cause than our good judgement. Consequently it is not fitting that we should prove false to this glorious reputation.

And let no one think that I exaggerate or pass due bounds, because I, a defendant in a private suit, have spoken in this fashion. For this law-suit is con-

χρημάτων ἐστὶν οὗτος ὁ ἀγών, ἀλλ' ἐμοὶ μὲν περὶ
τούτων, ὑμῖν δὲ περὶ τῶν ὀλίγῳ πρότερον εἰρη-
μένων· ὑπὲρ ὧν οὐδεὶς οὔτ' ἂν εἰπεῖν ἀξίως δύναιτο
34 οὔτ' ἂν τίμημ' ἱκανὸν ἐπιγράψαιτο. τοσοῦτον γὰρ
αὕτη διαφέρει τῶν ἄλλων δικῶν, ὥστε τῶν μὲν τοῖς
ἀγωνιζομένοις μόνον προσήκει, ταύτῃ δὲ τὸ κοινὸν
τῆς πόλεως συγκινδυνεύει. περὶ ταύτης δύ' ὅρκους
ὀμόσαντες δικάζετε, τὸν μέν, ὅνπερ ἐπὶ ταῖς ἄλλαις
εἴθισθε, τὸν δ' ὃν ἐπὶ ταῖς συνθήκαις ἐποιήσασθε.
ταύτην ἀδίκως γνόντες οὐ τοὺς τῆς πόλεως μόνον
νόμους ἀλλὰ καὶ τοὺς ἁπάντων κοινοὺς παραβή-
σεσθε. ὥστ' οὐκ ἄξιον οὔτε κατὰ χάριν οὔτε κατ'
ἐπιείκειαν οὔτε κατ' ἄλλ' οὐδὲν ἢ κατὰ τοὺς ὅρκους
περὶ αὐτῶν ψηφίσασθαι.

35 Ὡς μὲν οὖν[1] χρὴ καὶ συμφέρει καὶ δίκαιον
ὑμᾶς ἐστιν οὕτω περὶ τῶν συνθηκῶν γιγνώσκειν,
οὐδ' αὐτὸν ἡγοῦμαι Καλλίμαχον ἀντερεῖν· οἶμαι δ'
αὐτὸν ὀδυρεῖσθαι τὴν παροῦσαν πενίαν καὶ τὴν
[378] γεγενημένην αὐτῷ συμφοράν, καὶ λέξειν ὡς δεινὰ
καὶ σχέτλια πείσεται, εἰ τῶν χρημάτων, ὧν ἐπὶ τῆς
ὀλιγαρχίας ἀφῃρέθη, τούτων ἐν δημοκρατίᾳ τὴν
ἐπωβελίαν ὀφλήσει, καὶ εἰ τότε μὲν διὰ τὴν οὐσίαν
τὴν αὐτοῦ φυγεῖν ἠναγκάσθη, νυνὶ δ' ἐν ᾧ χρόνῳ
προσῆκεν αὐτὸν δίκην λαβεῖν, ἄτιμος γενήσεται.
36 κατηγορήσει δὲ καὶ τῶν ἐν τῇ μεταστάσει γενομένων, ὡς ἐκ τούτων μάλισθ' ὑμᾶς εἰς ὀργὴν κατα-

---

[1] μὲ νοῦν χρὴ mss. : μὲν οὖν οὐ χρή Dobree, accepted by Blass.

---

[a] If Callimachus lost the suit, he would be liable to a fine
(ἡ ἐπωβελία) of one-sixth of the sum at which the damages
were laid.

[c] If the fine should not be paid within the appointed period
of time, Callimachus would lose his rights as a citizen.

274

cerned not merely with the sum of money specified in the indictment ; for me, it is true, this is the issue, but for you it is that of which I have just spoken ; and on this subject no one would be able to speak in fitting fashion nor could he fix an adequate penalty. For this law-suit differs so greatly from other private suits in this respect that, while the latter are of concern to the litigants only, in this private law-suit the common interests of the city are likewise at stake. In trying this case you are bound by two oaths : one is the customary judicial oath which you take in all ordinary cases, and the other is that oath which you swore when you ratified the covenant of Amnesty. If you render an unjust verdict in this case, you will be violating not only the laws of the city, but also the laws common to all men. Consequently, it is not fitting that your votes should be based upon favour, or upon mere equity, nor upon anything else than upon the oaths you took when you made the covenant of Amnesty.

Now that it is right, and is expedient and just that you should decide thus concerning the covenant of Amnesty not even Callimachus himself, I think, will gainsay ; but he intends, I suppose, to bewail his present poverty and the misfortune which has befallen him, and to say that his fate will be dreadful and cruel if now under the democracy he must pay the assessed fine for the money of which under the oligarchy he was deprived,[a] and also if then because he possessed property he was forced to go into exile, yet now, at a time when he ought to get satisfaction for wrongs done him, he is to be deprived of his civic rights.[b] And he will accuse also those who took part in the revolution, in the hope that in this way especi-

στήσων· ἴσως γάρ τινος ἀκήκοεν, ὡς ὑμεῖς, ὅταν
μὴ τοὺς ἀδικοῦντας λάβητε, τοὺς ἐντυγχάνοντας
κολάζετε. ἐγὼ δ' οὔθ' ὑμᾶς ταύτην ἔχειν τὴν
γνώμην ἡγοῦμαι, πρός τε τοὺς ὑπειρημένους λόγους
37 ῥᾴδιον ἀντειπεῖν νομίζω. πρὸς μὲν οὖν τοὺς ὀδυρ-
μούς, ὅτι προσήκει βοηθεῖν ὑμᾶς, οὐχ οἵτινες ἂν
δυστυχεστάτους σφᾶς αὐτοὺς ἀποδείξωσιν, ἀλλ'
οἵτινες ἂν περὶ ὧν ἀντωμόσαντο δικαιότερα λέγοντες φαίνωνται. περὶ δὲ τῆς ἐπωβελίας, εἰ μὲν
ἐγὼ τούτων τῶν πραγμάτων αἴτιος ἦν, εἰκότως
ἂν αὐτῷ μέλλοντι ζημιώσεσθαι συνήχθεσθε· νῦν δ'
οὗτός ἐστιν ὁ συκοφαντῶν, ὥστ' οὐδὲν ἂν δικαίως
38 αὐτοῦ λέγοντος ἀποδέχοισθε. ἔπειτα κἀκεῖνο χρὴ
σκοπεῖν, ὅτι πάντες οἱ κατελθόντες ἐκ Πειραιέως
ἔχοιεν ἂν τοὺς αὐτοὺς λόγους εἰπεῖν, οὕσπερ οὗτος,
ὧν οὐδεὶς ἄλλος τετόλμηκε τοιαύτην δίκην εἰσελθεῖν. καίτοι χρὴ μισεῖν ὑμᾶς τοὺς τοιούτους καὶ
κακοὺς πολίτας νομίζειν, οἵτινες ταῖς μὲν συμφοραῖς ὁμοίαις τῷ πλήθει κέχρηνται, τὰς δὲ τιμωρίας
39 διαφόρους τῶν ἄλλων ἀξιοῦσι ποιεῖσθαι. πρὸς δὲ
τούτοις ἔτι καὶ νῦν ἔξεστιν αὐτῷ, πρὶν ἀποπειρα-
θῆναι τῆς ὑμετέρας γνώμης, ἀφέντι τὴν δίκην
ἀπηλλάχθαι πάντων τῶν πραγμάτων. καίτοι πῶς
οὐκ ἄλογόν ἐστιν ἐν τούτῳ τῷ κινδύνῳ ζητεῖν
αὐτὸν ἐλέου παρ' ὑμῶν τυγχάνειν, οὗ κύριος αὐτός
ἐστι, καὶ εἰς ὃν αὐτὸς αὐτὸν καθίστησι, καὶ ὃν ἔτι
40 καὶ νῦν ἔξεστιν αὐτῷ μὴ κινδυνεύειν; ἂν δ' ἄρα
μεμνῆται τῶν ἐπὶ τῆς ὀλιγαρχίας γεγενημένων,
ἀξιοῦτε αὐτὸν μὴ 'κείνων κατηγορεῖν, ὑπὲρ ὧν

ally he will arouse you to wrath ; for perhaps he
has heard it said that whenever you fail to apprehend
the guilty, you punish any who cross your path.
But I for my part do not think that you are so disposed, and I believe that it is easy to controvert the
pleas just suggested. As for his lamentations, it is
fitting that you give aid, not to those who try to
show that they are the most miserable of men, but
to those whose statements concerning the facts to
which they have sworn in their affidavits are manifestly the more just. And in regard to the penalty
assessed against the loser, if I were responsible for
this action, you might reasonably sympathize with
him as about to be penalized ; but the truth is, it is
he who brings in a calumnious accusation and therefore you cannot in justice accept anything he says.
In the second place, you should consider this point—
that all the exiles who returned to the city from the
Peiraeus would be able to use the very same arguments as he ; but no one except Callimachus has had
the audacity to introduce such a suit. And yet you
ought to hate such persons and regard them as bad
citizens who, although they have suffered the same
misfortunes as the party of the people, think fit to
exact exceptional punishments. Furthermore, it is
possible for him even now, before he has made trial
of your decision, to drop the suit and to be entirely
rid of all his troubles. And yet is it not stupid of
him to seek to win your pity while in this jeopardy,
for which he himself is responsible, and in which he
has involved himself, a jeopardy which even now it
is possible for him to avoid ? And if he does mention
events which occurred under the oligarchy, demand
of him that, instead of accusing persons whom no

οὐδεὶς ἀπολογήσεται, ἀλλ' ὡς ἐγὼ τὰ χρήματα
εἴληφα διδάσκειν, περὶ οὗπερ ὑμᾶς δεῖ ψηφίζε-
σθαι, μηδ' ὡς αὐτὸς δεινὰ πέπονθεν ἀποφαίνειν,
[379] ἀλλ' ὡς ἐγὼ πεποίηκα ἐξελέγχειν, παρ' οὗπερ
41 ἀξιοῖ τἀπολωλότα κομίζεσθαι· ἐπεὶ κακῶς γ' αὐτὸν πράττοντα ἐπιδεῖξαι καὶ πρὸς ἄλλον ὁντινοῦν
ἀγωνιζόμενος τῶν πολιτῶν δύναται. καίτοι χρὴ
μέγα παρ' ὑμῖν δύνασθαι τῶν κατηγοριῶν, οὐχ
αἷς ἔξεστι χρῆσθαι καὶ πρὸς τοὺς μηδὲν ἡμαρτη-
κότας, ἀλλ' ἃς οὐχ οἷόν τ' εἰπεῖν ἀλλ' ἢ κατὰ τῶν
ἠδικηκότων. πρὸς μὲν οὖν τούτους τοὺς λόγους
καὶ ταῦτ' ἴσως ἀρκέσει καὶ τάχ' ἀντειπεῖν ἐξέσται.

42 Ἐνθυμεῖσθε δ', εἰ καί τῳ δόξω δὶς περὶ τῶν
αὐτῶν λέγειν, ὅτι πολλοὶ προσέχουσι ταύτῃ τῇ
δίκῃ τὸν νοῦν, οὐ τῶν ἡμετέρων πραγμάτων φροντίζοντες, ἀλλ' ἡγούμενοι περὶ τῶν συνθηκῶν εἶναι
τὴν κρίσιν. οὓς ὑμεῖς τὰ δίκαια γνόντες ἀδεῶς
οἰκεῖν ἐν τῇ πόλει ποιήσετε· εἰ δὲ μή, πῶς οἴεσθε
διακείσεσθαι τοὺς ἐν ἄστει μείναντας, ἢν ὁμοίως
ἅπασιν ὀργιζόμενοι φαίνησθε τοῖς μετασχοῦσι τῆς
43 πολιτείας; τίνα δὲ γνώμην ἕξειν τοὺς καὶ μικρὸν
ἁμάρτημα σφίσιν αὐτοῖς συνειδότας, ὅταν ὁρῶσι
μηδὲ τοὺς κοσμίως πεπολιτευμένους τῶν δικαίων
τυγχάνοντας; πόσην δὲ χρὴ προσδοκᾶν ἔσεσθαι
ταραχήν, ὅταν οἱ μὲν ἐπαρθῶσι συκοφαντεῖν ὡς
ὑμῶν αὐτοῖς ἤδη ταῦτ' ἐγνωκότων, οἱ δὲ δεδίωσι

ᵃ i.e., the oligarchs.   ᵇ The former oligarchs.
ᶜ Those of democratic principles.

278

one will defend,[a] he prove that it was I who took his money; for this is the issue upon which you must cast your votes. And demand that he, instead of showing that he has suffered cruel wrongs, prove that it is I who have committed them, I, from whom he seeks to recover what he has lost; since the fact of his evil plight he can readily establish in a suit brought against any other citizen whatever. And yet the accusations which should have great weight with you are not those which may be made even against those who are entirely guiltless, but those only which cannot be brought against any persons except those who have committed an act of injustice. To these allegations, this will perhaps be a sufficient reply and a further rebuttal soon will be possible.

Also bear in mind, I ask you—even though I may be thought by someone to be repeating myself— that many persons are attentively watching the outcome of this case; not because they are interested in our affairs, but because they believe that the covenant of Amnesty is on trial. Such persons, if your decision is just, you will enable to dwell in the city without fear; otherwise, how do you expect those who remained in the city to feel, if you show that you are angry with all alike who obtained the rights of citizenship? And what will those think who are conscious of even slight error on their part, when they see that not even persons whose conduct as citizens has been decent obtain justice? What confusion must be expected to ensue when some [b] are encouraged to bring malicious accusations in the belief that your sentiments are now the same as theirs, and when others [c] fear the present form of

τὴν παροῦσαν πολιτείαν ὡς οὐδεμιᾶς αὐτοῖς ἔτι
44 καταφυγῆς ὑπαρχούσης; ἆρ' οὐκ ἄξιον φοβεῖσθαι
μὴ συγχυθέντων τῶν ὅρκων πάλιν εἰς ταὐτὰ κατα-
στῶμεν ἐξ ὧνπερ ἠναγκάσθημεν τὰς συνθήκας
ποιήσασθαι; καὶ μὴν οὐ δεῖ γ' ὑμᾶς παρ' ἑτέρων
μαθεῖν, ὅσον ἐστὶν ὁμόνοια ἀγαθὸν ἢ στάσις κα-
κόν· οὕτω γὰρ ἀμφοτέρων σφόδρα πεπείρασθε,
ὥστε καὶ τοὺς ἄλλους ὑμεῖς ἄριστ' ἂν διδάξαιτε
περὶ αὐτῶν.

45 Ἵνα δὲ μὴ δοκῶ διὰ τοῦτο πολὺν χρόνον περὶ τὰς
συνθήκας διατρίβειν, ὅτι ῥᾴδιόν ἐστι περὶ αὐτῶν
πολλὰ καὶ δίκαια εἰπεῖν, τοσοῦτον ὑμῖν ἔτι διακελεύομαι μνημονεύειν, ὅταν φέρητε τὴν ψῆφον,
ὅτι πρὶν μὲν ποιήσασθαι ταύτας ἐπολεμοῦμεν, οἱ
μὲν τὸν κύκλον ἔχοντες, οἱ δὲ τὸν Πειραιᾶ κατειλη-
φότες, μᾶλλον ἀλλήλους μισοῦντες ἢ τοὺς ὑπὸ τῶν
46 προγόνων πολεμίους ἡμῖν καταλειφθέντας, ἐπειδὴ
[380] δὲ τὰς πίστεις ἀλλήλοις ἔδομεν εἰς ταὐτὸν συνελθόντες, οὕτω καλῶς καὶ κοινῶς πολιτευόμεθα,
ὥσπερ οὐδεμιᾶς ἡμῖν συμφορᾶς γεγενημένης. καὶ
τότε μὲν ἀμαθεστάτους καὶ δυστυχεστάτους πάντες
ἡμᾶς ἐνόμιζον· νῦν δ' εὐδαιμονέστατοι καὶ σω-
47 φρονέστατοι τῶν Ἑλλήνων δοκοῦμεν εἶναι. ὥστ'
ἄξιον οὐ μόνον τηλικαύταις ζημίαις κολάζειν τοὺς
παραβαίνειν τολμῶντας τὰς συνθήκας ἀλλὰ ταῖς
ἐσχάταις, ὡς τῶν μεγίστων κακῶν αἰτίους ὄντας,
ἄλλως τε καὶ τοὺς ὥσπερ Καλλίμαχος βεβιωκότας.

ᵃ The oligarchs were in power in the city; the democratic

government on the ground that no place of refuge is any longer left to them ? May we not rightly fear that, once your oaths have been violated, we shall again be brought to the same state of affairs which compelled us to make the covenant of Amnesty ? Certainly you do not need to learn from others how great is the blessing of concord or how great a curse is civil war ; for you have experienced both in so extreme a form that you yourselves would be best qualified to instruct all others regarding them.

But lest it be thought that the reason I am dwelling long on the covenant of Amnesty is merely because it is easy when speaking on that subject to make many just observations, I urge you to remember when you cast your votes only one thing more—that before we entered into those agreements we Athenians were in a state of war, some of us occupying the circle enclosed by the city's walls, others Piraeus after we had captured it,[a] and we hated each other more than we did the enemies bequeathed to us by our ancestors. But after we came together and exchanged the solemn pledges, we have lived so uprightly and so like citizens of one country that it seemed as if no misfortune had ever befallen us. At that time all looked upon us as the most foolish and ill-fated of mankind ; now, however, we are regarded as the happiest and wisest of the Greeks. Therefore it is incumbent upon us to inflict upon those who dare to violate the covenant, not merely the heavy penalties prescribed by the treaty, but the most extreme, on the ground that these persons are the cause of the greatest evils, especially those who have lived as Callimachus has

party, after their occupation of Phylê (the fort on Mt. Parnes in Attica), captured and held Piraeus.

ὃς δέκα μὲν ἔτη συνεχῶς ὑμῖν Λακεδαιμονίων
πολεμησάντων οὐδὲ μίαν παρέσχεν αὑτὸν ἡμέραν
48 τάξαι τοῖς στρατηγοῖς, ἀλλ' ἐκεῖνον μὲν τὸν χρόνον
διετέλεσεν ἀποδιδράσκων καὶ τὴν οὐσίαν ἀπο-
κρυπτόμενος, ἐπειδὴ δ' οἱ τριάκοντα κατέστησαν,
τηνικαῦτα κατέπλευσεν εἰς τὴν πόλιν. καὶ φησὶ
μὲν εἶναι δημοτικός, τοσούτῳ δὲ μᾶλλον τῶν ἄλλων
ἐπεθύμει μετασχεῖν ἐκείνης τῆς πολιτείας, ὥστ'
οὐδ' εἰ κακῶς ἔπαθεν, ἠξίωσεν ἀπελθεῖν, ἀλλ'
ᾑρεῖτο μετὰ τῶν ἡμαρτηκότων εἰς αὑτὸν πολιορ-
κεῖσθαι μᾶλλον ἢ μεθ' ὑμῶν τῶν συνηδικημένων
49 πολιτεύεσθαι. καὶ μέχρι τῆς ἡμέρας ἐκείνης παρ-
έμεινε μετέχων τῆς πολιτείας, ἐν ᾗ προσβαλεῖν
ἠμέλλετε πρὸς τὸ τεῖχος· τότε δ' ἐξῆλθεν, οὐ τὰ
παρόντα μισήσας ἀλλὰ δείσας τὸν ἐπιόντα κίνδυνον,
ὡς ὕστερον ἐδήλωσεν. ἐπειδὴ γὰρ Λακεδαιμονίων
ἐλθόντων ὁ δῆμος ἐν τῷ Πειραιεῖ κατεκλείσθη,
πάλιν ἐκεῖθεν διαδρὰς ἐν Βοιωτοῖς διῃτᾶτο· ὥστ'
αὐτῷ προσήκει μετὰ τῶν αὐτομόλων ἀναγεγράφθαι
50 πολὺ μᾶλλον ἢ τῶν φυγόντων ὀνομάζεσθαι. καὶ
τοιοῦτος γεγενημένος καὶ περὶ τοὺς ἐκ Πειραιέως
καὶ περὶ τοὺς ἐν ἄστει μείναντας καὶ περὶ πᾶσαν
τὴν πόλιν, οὐκ ἀγαπᾷ τῶν ἴσων τυγχάνειν τοῖς
ἄλλοις ἀλλὰ ζητεῖ πλέον ἔχειν ὑμῶν, ὥσπερ ἢ
μόνος ἀδικηθεὶς ἢ βέλτιστος ὢν τῶν πολιτῶν ἢ

---

* A reference to the so-called Decelean War (413–404 b.c.)
when the Spartans occupied Decelea in Attica.

lived. For during the ten years *a* when the **Lace-**
daemonians warred upon you uninterruptedly, not
for one single day's service did he present himself
to the generals ; on the contrary, all through that
period he continued to evade service and to keep
his property in concealment. But when the Thirty
came to power, then it was that he sailed back to
Athens. And although he professes to be a friend
of the people, yet he was so much more eager than
anybody else to participate in the oligarchical government that, even though it meant hardship, he saw
fit not to depart, but preferred to be besieged in
company with those who had injured him rather than
to live as a citizen with you, who likewise had been
wronged by them. And he remained as a participant
in their government until that day on which you
were on the point of attacking the walls of Athens ;
then he left the city, not because he had come to hate
the present régime, but because he was afraid of the
danger which threatened, as he later made evident.
For when the Lacedaemonians came and the democracy was shut up in the Piraeus,*b* again he fled
from there and resided among the Boeotians ; it is
far more fitting, therefore, that his name should
be enrolled in the list of the deserters than that he
should be called one of the " exiles." And although
he has proved to be a man of such character by his
conduct toward the people who occupied the Piraeus,
toward those who remained in the city, and toward
the whole state, he is not content to be on equal
terms with the others, but seeks to be treated better
than you, as if either he alone had suffered injury,
or was the best of the citizens, or had met with the

* By Pausanias, king of Sparta and his general, Lysander.

μεγίσταις συμφοραῖς δι' ὑμᾶς κεχρημένος ἢ πλείστων ἀγαθῶν αἴτιος τῇ πόλει γεγενημένος.

51 Ἐβουλόμην δ' ἂν ὑμᾶς ὁμοίως ἐμοὶ γιγνώσκειν αὐτόν, ἵν' αὐτῷ μὴ τῶν ἀπολωλότων συνήχθεσθε ἀλλὰ τῶν ὑπολοίπων ἐφθονεῖτε. νῦν δὲ περὶ μὲν τῶν ἄλλων ὅσοις ἐπιβεβούλευκε, καὶ δίκας οἵας

[381] δεδίκασται καὶ γραφὰς ἃς¹ εἰσελήλυθε, καὶ μεθ' ὧν συνέστηκε καὶ καθ' ὧν τὰ ψευδῆ μεμαρτύρηκεν, οὐδ' ἂν δὶς τοσοῦτον ὕδωρ ἱκανὸν διηγήσασθαι

52 γένοιτο· ἐν δὲ μόνον ἀκούσαντες τῶν τούτῳ πεπραγμένων ῥᾳδίως καὶ τὴν ἄλλην αὐτοῦ πονηρίαν γνώσεσθε.

Κρατῖνος γὰρ ἠμφισβήτησε χωρίου τῷ τούτου κηδεστῇ. μάχης δ' αὐτοῖς γενομένης, ὑποκρυψάμενοι θεράπαιναν ᾐτιῶντο τὸν Κρατῖνον συντρῖψαι τῆς κεφαλῆς αὐτῆς, ἐκ δὲ τοῦ τραύματος φάσκοντες ἀποθανεῖν τὴν ἄνθρωπον λαγχάνουσιν αὐτῷ φόνου

53 δίκην ἐπὶ Παλλαδίῳ. πυθόμενος δ' ὁ Κρατῖνος τὰς τούτων ἐπιβουλὰς τὸν μὲν ἄλλον χρόνον ἡσυχίαν ἦγεν, ἵνα μὴ μεταθεῖντο τὸ πρᾶγμα μηδ' ἑτέρους λόγους ἐξευρίσκοιεν, ἀλλ' ἐπ' αὐτοφώρῳ ληφθεῖεν κακουργοῦντες· ἐπειδὴ δ' ὁ κηδεστὴς μὲν ἦν ὁ τούτου κατηγορηκώς, οὗτος δὲ μεμαρτυρηκὼς ἦ

54 μὴν τεθνάναι τὴν ἄνθρωπον, ἐλθόντες εἰς τὴν

---

¹ ἃς after γραφὰς added by Corais.

ᵃ The time allotted to the litigant for his speech in the Athenian law-courts was regulated by an official water-clock (the *klepsydra*). One has been found; *cf. Hesperia* viii., 1939.

gravest misfortunes on your account, or had been the cause of the most numerous benefits to the city.

I could wish that you knew him as well as I do, in order that, instead of commiserating with him over his losses, you might bear him a grudge for what he has left. The fact is, though, that if I should try to tell of all the others who have been the objects of his plots, of the private law-suits in which he has been involved, of the public suits which he has entered, of the persons with whom he has conspired or against whom he has borne false witness, not even twice as much water *a* as has been allotted me would prove sufficient. But when you have heard only one of the acts which he has committed you will readily recognize the general run of his villainy.

Cratinus once had a dispute over a farm with the brother-in-law of Callimachus. A personal encounter ensued. Having concealed a female slave, they accused Cratinus of having crushed her head, and asserting that she had died as a result of the wound, they brought suit against him in the court of the Palladium *b* on the charge of murder. Cratinus, learning of their plots, remained quiet for a long time in order that they might not change their plans and concoct another story, but instead might be caught in the very act of committing a crime. When the brother-in-law of Callimachus had made accusation and Callimachus had testified on oath that the woman was actually dead, Cratinus and his friends

b The tribunal for cases of unpremeditated homicide; also for trials involving the murder of slaves, resident-aliens, and foreigners. *Cf.* Arist. *Ath. Pol.* 57. 3.

οἰκίαν ἵν᾽ ἦν κεκρυμμένη, βίᾳ λαβόντες αὐτὴν καὶ
ἀγαγόντες ἐπὶ τὸ δικαστήριον ζῶσαν ἅπασι τοῖς
παροῦσιν ἐπέδειξαν. ὥσθ᾽ ἑπτακοσίων μὲν δικαζ-
όντων, τεττάρων δὲ καὶ δέκα μαρτυρησάντων
ἅπερ οὗτος, οὐδεμίαν ψῆφον μετέλαβε.[1]

Καί μοι κάλει τούτων μάρτυρας.

ΜΑΡΤΥΡΕΣ

55 Τίς οὖν ἂν ἀξίως δύναιτο κατηγορῆσαι τῶν
τούτῳ πεπραγμένων; ἢ τίς ἂν εὑρεῖν ἔχοι παρά-
δειγμα μεῖζον ἀδικίας καὶ συκοφαντίας καὶ πονηρίας; ἔνια μὲν γὰρ τῶν ἀδικημάτων οὐκ ἂν ὅλον
τὸν τρόπον δηλώσειε τῶν ἀδικησάντων, ἐκ δὲ τῶν
τοιούτων ἔργων ἅπαντα τὸν βίον τῶν ἐξαμαρτανόν-
56 των ῥᾴδιον κατιδεῖν ἐστίν. ὅστις γὰρ τοὺς ζῶντας
τεθνάναι μαρτυρεῖ, τίνος ἂν ὑμῖν ἀποσχέσθαι δοκεῖ;
ἢ ὅστις ἐπὶ τοῖς ἀλλοτρίοις πράγμασιν οὕτω πονη-
ρός ἐστι, τί οὐκ ἂν ἐπὶ τοῖς αὑτοῦ τολμήσειεν;
πῶς δὲ χρὴ τούτῳ πιστεύειν ὑπὲρ αὑτοῦ λέγοντι,
ὃς ὑπὲρ ἑτέρων ἐπιορκῶν ἐξελέγχεται; τίς δὲ
πώποτε φανερώτερον ἐπεδείχθη τὰ ψευδῆ μαρτυ-
ρῶν; τοὺς μὲν γὰρ ἄλλους ἐκ τῶν λεγομένων
κρίνετε, τὴν δὲ τούτου μαρτυρίαν, ὅτι ψευδὴς ἦν,
57 εἶδον οἱ δικάζοντες. καὶ τοιαῦθ᾽ ἡμαρτηκὼς ἐπι-
[382] χειρήσει λέγειν, ὡς ἡμεῖς ψευδόμεθα, ὅμοιον ἐργα-
ζόμενος, ὥσπερ ἂν εἴ τῳ Φρυνώνδας πανουργίαν

---

[1] μετέλαβε Λ and editions : Blass μετέλαβον referring to
Cratinus and his friends.

went to the house where she had been hidden, seized her by force and, bringing her into court, presented her alive to all present. The result was that, in a tribunal of seven hundred judges, after fourteen witnesses had given the same testimony as that of Callimachus, he failed to receive a single vote.

(*To the Clerk*) Please call witnesses to these facts.

WITNESSES

Who, therefore, would be able to condemn his acts as they deserve ? Or who would be able to find a more flagrant example of wrongdoing, of malicious prosecution, and of villainy ? Some misdeeds, it is true, do not reveal in its entirety the character of the evil-doers, but from acts such as his it is easy to discern the whole life of the culprits. For any man who testifies that the living are dead, from what villainy do you think that he would abstain ? What outrageous deed would a man not have the effrontery to commit in his own interest who is so knavish a villain in the interest of others ? How is it right to trust this man when he speaks in his own behalf, who is proved guilty of perjury in his testimony on behalf of another ? Who was ever more convincingly proved to be a giver of false testimony ? You judge all other defendants by what is said of them, but this man's testimony the jurors themselves saw was false. And after the commission of such crimes he will dare to say that it is we who are lying. Why that would be as if Phrynondas [a] should reproach a

---

[a] A notorious swindler ; *cf.* Aristophanes, *Thesm.* 861 and Aeschines, *Ctes.* 137.

ὀνειδίσειεν ἢ Φιλουργὸς ὁ τὸ Γοργόνειον ὑφελό-
μενος τοὺς ἄλλους ἱεροσύλους ἔφασκεν εἶναι. τίνα
δὲ προσήκει τῶν μὴ γενομένων παρασχέσθαι
μάρτυρας μᾶλλον ἢ τοῦτον, ὃς αὐτὸς ἑτέροις τὰ
ψευδῆ τολμᾷ μαρτυρεῖν;

58 Ἀλλὰ γὰρ Καλλιμάχου μὲν ἐξέσται πολλάκις
κατηγορεῖν, οὕτω γὰρ παρεσκεύασται πολιτεύεσθαι, περὶ δ' ἐμαυτοῦ τὰς μὲν ἄλλας ἁπάσας παρα-
λείψω λειτουργίας, ἧς δ' οὐ μόνον ἄν μοι δικαίως
ἔχοιτε χάριν ἀλλὰ καὶ τεκμηρίῳ χρήσαισθε περὶ τοῦ
παντὸς πράγματος, ταύτης δὲ μνησθήσομαι πρὸς
59 ὑμᾶς. ὅτε γὰρ ἡ πόλις ἀπώλεσε τὰς ναῦς τὰς ἐν
Ἑλλησπόντῳ καὶ τῆς δυνάμεως ἐστερήθη, τῶν μὲν
πλείστων τριηράρχων τοσοῦτον διήνεγκον, ὅτι μετ'
ὀλίγων ἔσωσα τὴν ναῦν, αὐτῶν δὲ τούτων, ὅτι
καταπλεύσας εἰς τὸν Πειραιᾶ μόνος οὐ κατέλυσα
60 τὴν τριηραρχίαν, ἀλλὰ τῶν ἄλλων ἀσμένως ἀπαλ-
λαττομένων τῶν λῃτουργιῶν καὶ πρὸς τὰ παρόντ'
ἀθύμως διακειμένων, καὶ τῶν μὲν ἀνηλωμένων
αὐτοῖς μεταμέλον, τὰ δὲ λοιπὰ ἀποκρυπτομένων,
καὶ νομιζόντων τὰ μὲν κοινὰ διεφθάρθαι, τὰ δ' ἴδια
σκοπουμένων, οὐ τὴν αὐτὴν ἐκείνοις γνώμην ἔσχον,
ἀλλὰ πείσας τὸν ἀδελφὸν συντριηραρχεῖν, παρ'
ἡμῶν αὐτῶν μισθὸν διδόντες τοῖς ναύταις κακῶς
61 ἐποιοῦμεν τοὺς πολεμίους. τὸ δὲ τελευταῖον προ-

---

a The golden relief of this head, the work of Pheidias, was

man with villainy, or as if Philurgos, who stole the
Gorgon's head,[a] had called everybody else temple-
robbers ! Who is more likely to present witnesses
of events which have not occurred than my antagonist
here, who himself has the hardihood to testify falsely
for others ?

But against Callimachus it will be possible to bring
accusations time and again, for he has contrived his
life as a citizen that way ; but as for myself, I shall
say nothing of all my other contributions to the state,
but I will merely remind you of that one, a service
for which, if you would do me justice, you would not
only be grateful, but you would take it even as evidence bearing upon the case as a whole. Now when
the city had lost its ships in the Hellespont [b] and was
shorn of its power, I so far surpassed the majority
of the trierarchs that I was one of the very few who
saved their ships : and of these few I alone brought
back my ship to the Piraeus and did not resign my
duties as trierarch ; but when the other trierarchs
were glad to be relieved of their duties and were
discouraged over the situation, and not only regretted the loss of what they had already spent, but
were trying to conceal the remainder and, judging
that the commonwealth was completely ruined, were
looking out for their private interests, my decision
was not the same as theirs ; but after persuading my
brother to be joint-trierarch with me, we paid the
crew out of our own means and proceeded to harass
the enemy. And finally, when Lysander [c] pro-

---

affixed to the shield of the gold and ivory statue of Athena
in the Parthenon.
  [b] At Aegospotami, 405 B.C.
    [c] The general of the victorious Spartan army of occupation.

εἰπόντος Λυσάνδρου, εἴ τις εἰσάγοι σῖτον ὡς ὑμᾶς,
θάνατον τὴν ζημίαν, οὕτω φιλοτίμως εἴχομεν πρὸς
τὴν πόλιν, ὥστε τῶν ἄλλων οὐδὲ τὸν σφέτερον
αὐτῶν εἰσάγειν τολμώντων ἡμεῖς τὸν ὡς ἐκείνους
εἰσπλέοντα λαμβάνοντες εἰς τὸν Πειραιᾶ κατήγο-
μεν. ἀνθ' ὧν ὑμεῖς ἐψηφίσασθ' ἡμᾶς στεφανῶσαι
καὶ πρόσθε τῶν ἐπωνύμων ἀνειπεῖν ὡς μεγάλων
62 ἀγαθῶν αἰτίους ὄντας. καίτοι χρὴ τούτους δημοτικοὺς νομίζειν, οὐχ ὅσοι κρατοῦντος τοῦ δήμου
μετασχεῖν τῶν πραγμάτων ἐπεθύμησαν, ἀλλ' οἳ
δυστυχησάσης τῆς πόλεως προκινδυνεύειν ὑμῶν
ἠθέλησαν, καὶ χάριν ἔχειν, οὐκ εἴ τις αὐτὸς κακῶς
[383] πέπονθεν, ἀλλ' εἴ τις ὑμᾶς εὖ πεποίηκε, καὶ πένητας
γενομένους ἐλεεῖν οὐ τοὺς ἀπολωλεκότας τὴν οὐσίαν
63 ἀλλὰ τοὺς εἰς ὑμᾶς ἀνηλωκότας. ὧν εἷς ἐγὼ
φανήσομαι γεγενημένος, ὃς πάντων ἂν εἴην δυστυ-
χέστατος, εἰ πολλὰ τῶν ἐμαυτοῦ δεδαπανημένος εἰς
τὴν πόλιν εἶτα δόξαιμι τοῖς ἀλλοτρίοις ἐπιβουλεύειν
καὶ περὶ μηδενὸς ποιεῖσθαι τὰς παρ' ὑμῖν διαβολάς,
ὃς οὐ μόνον τὴν οὐσίαν ἀλλὰ καὶ τὴν ψυχὴν τὴν
ἐμαυτοῦ περὶ ἐλάττονος φαίνομαι ποιούμενος τοῦ
64 παρ' ὑμῖν εὐδοκιμεῖν. τῷ δ' οὐκ ἂν ὑμῶν μετα-
μελήσειεν, εἰ καὶ μὴ παραχρῆμα ἀλλ' ὀλίγον
ὕστερον, εἰ τὸν μὲν συκοφάντην ἴδοιτε πλούσιον
γεγενημένον, ἐμὲ δ' ἐξ ὧν ὑπέλιπον λῃτουργῶν,

---

a These were statues of those heroes who gave their names
to the ten Attic tribes. The probable site of these statues
is near the north-centre of the Agora, near the statues of
290

claimed that if anyone should import grain to you he would be punished with death, we were so zealous for the city's welfare that, although no one else dared to bring in even his own, we intercepted the grain that was being brought in to them and discharged it at the Piraeus. In recognition of these services you voted that we should be honoured with crowns, and that in front of the statues of the eponymous heroes [a] we should be proclaimed as the authors of great blessings. Yet surely men who should now be regarded as friends of the people are not those who, when the people were in power, were eager to participate in affairs, but those who, when the state was suffering misfortune, were willing to brave the first dangers in your behalf, and gratitude is due, not to him who has suffered personal hardships, but to him who has conferred benefits upon you ; and in the case of those who have become poor, pity should be felt, not for those who have lost their property, but for those who have spent their fortune for your good. Of these last named it will be found that I have been one ; and I should be the most miserable of all men, if, after I have spent much of my fortune for the good of the city, it should be thought that I plot against the property of others, and that I care naught for your poor opinion of me; when it is obvious that I set less store, not merely on my property, but even on my life, than on your good opinion. Who among you would not feel remorse, even if not immediately, yet soon hereafter, if you should see the calumniator enriched, but me despoiled even of that which I left remaining when serving you as

Harmodius and Aristogeiton and in the neighbourhood of the temple of Ares.

καὶ τούτων ἐκπεπτωκότα; καὶ τὸν μὲν μηδὲ πώποτε ὑπὲρ ὑμῶν κινδυνεύσαντα μεῖζον καὶ τῶν
65 νόμων καὶ τῶν συνθηκῶν δυνάμενον, ἐμὲ δὲ τὸν
οὕτω πρόθυμον περὶ τὴν πόλιν γεγενημένον μηδὲ
τῶν δικαίων ἀξιούμενον τυγχάνειν; τίς δ' οὐκ ἂν
ὑμῖν ἐπιτιμήσειεν, εἰ πεισθέντες ὑπὸ τῶν Καλλιμάχου λόγων τοσαύτην πονηρίαν ἡμῶν καταγνοίητε,
οὓς ἐκ τῶν ἔργων κρίναντες δι' ἀνδραγαθίαν ἐστε-
φανώσατε, ὅτ' οὐδ' οὕτω ῥᾴδιον ἦν ὥσπερ νῦν
τυχεῖν ταύτης τῆς τιμῆς;

66   Τοὐναντίον δ' ἡμῖν συμβέβηκεν ἢ τοῖς ἄλλοις· οἱ
μὲν γὰρ ἄλλοι τοὺς εἰληφότας τὰς δωρεὰς ὑπο-
μιμνήσκουσιν, ἡμεῖς δ' ὑμᾶς τοὺς δεδωκότας ἀξιοῦμεν μνημονεύειν, ἵν' ὑμῖν τεκμήριον τῶν εἰρημένων
ἁπάντων καὶ τῶν ἐπιτηδευμάτων τῶν ἡμετέρων
67 γένηται.   δῆλον δ' ὅτι ταύτης τῆς τιμῆς ἀξίους
ἡμᾶς αὐτοὺς παρείχομεν, οὐχ ἵν' ὀλιγαρχίας γενομένης τἀλλότρια διαρπάζοιμεν, ἀλλ' ἵνα σωθείσης
τῆς πόλεως οἵ τ' ἄλλοι τὰ σφέτερ' αὐτῶν ἔχοιεν,
ἡμῖν τε παρὰ τῷ πλήθει τῶν πολιτῶν χάρις
ὀφείλοιτο· ἣν ὑμᾶς[1] νῦν ἀπαιτοῦμεν, οὐ πλέον ἔχειν
τοῦ δικαίου ζητοῦντες, ἀλλ' ἀποφαίνοντες μὲν ὡς
οὐδὲν ἀδικοῦμεν, ἀξιοῦντες δὲ[2] τοῖς ὅρκοις καὶ
68 ταῖς συνθήκαις ἐμμένειν.[3]   καὶ γὰρ ἂν εἴη δεινὸν
εἰ τοὺς μὲν ἠδικηκότας τιμωρίας ἀφεῖναι κύριαι
γένοιντο,[4] ἐφ' ἡμῖν δὲ τοῖς εὖ πεποιηκόσιν ἄκυροι
κατασταθεῖεν.   ἄξιον δὲ τὴν παροῦσαν τύχην δια-

---

[1] ὑμᾶς Blass : ἡμεῖς.
[2] ἀξιοῦντες δὲ added by Blass, the mss. indicating a lacuna
of 8 or 9 letters.

292

trierarch ; and if you should see this man, who never even ran a risk on your behalf, influential enough to override both the laws and the covenant of Amnesty, and me, who have been so zealous in serving the state, adjudged unworthy of obtaining even my just rights ? And who would not reproach you, if, cajoled by the words of Callimachus, you should find me guilty of such baseness, you who, when you judged us on the strength of our deeds, crowned us for our bravery at a time when it was not so easy as it is now to win that honour ?

It has come to pass that our appeal is the opposite of that which other litigants generally make ; for everybody else reminds the recipients of the bene-factions they have received, whereas we ask you, the donors, to bear your gifts in mind, that they may serve you as corroboration of all I have said and of our principles of conduct. And it is evident that we showed ourselves worthy of this honour, not for the purpose of plundering the property of others after the oligarchy had been established, but in order that, after the city had been saved, not only all the citizens might keep their own possessions, but also that in the hearts of our fellow-citizens at large there might be a feeling of gratitude to us as a debt to be paid. It is this that we beg of you now, not seeking to have more than is just, but offering proof that we are guilty of no wrongdoing and asking you to abide by the oaths and the covenant of Amnesty. For it would be outrageous if those covenants should be held valid for the exculpation of the evil-doers, but should be made invalid for us, your benefactors ! And it is prudent for you to guard well your present

---

[3] ἐμμένειν Blass : ἐμμένοντες.   [4] γένοιντο Aldus : ἐγένοντο Λ.

[384] φυλάττειν, ἐνθυμουμένους, ὅτι ἑτέρας μὲν πόλεις
ἐποίησαν ἤδη συνθῆκαι μᾶλλον¹ στασιάσαι, τὴν δ᾽
ἡμετέραν μᾶλλον ὁμονοεῖν. ὧν χρὴ μεμνημένους
ἅμα τά τε δίκαια καὶ τὰ συμφέροντα ψηφίσασθαι.

---

¹ μᾶλλον στασιάσαι Blass, who transfers μᾶλλον from before
ὁμονοεῖν and indicates unnecessarily a lacuna there : Drerup
μηκέτι στασιάσαι.

fortune, remembering that while in the past such agreements have increased civic discord in other cities, yet to ours they have brought a greater degree of concord.[a] So you, keeping these considerations in mind, should cast your votes for that which is at the same time just and also expedient.

[a] In §§ 67-68 the manuscripts offer a text both illegible in places and corrupt otherwise ; see the critical notes.

XIX. AEGINETICUS

INTRODUCTION

THE speech called *Aegineticus* is a *Claim to an Inherit-ance* (ἐπιδικασία) and is probably the best of the six forensic speeches written by Isocrates in the first period of his literary activity (403–393 B.C.) when he practised the profession of a *logographos*, or writer of speeches for litigants.

Thrasylochus, a citizen of the little island of Siphnos in the Aegean Sea, had at his death bequeathed his property to the speaker, his adopted son, to whom he also gave his sister as wife. A half-sister of Thrasylochus disputed the right of the speaker to receive the estate and herself laid claim to the inheritance. This discourse, composed by Isocrates, is the defence of the heir.

The speaker and Thrasylochus, political exiles from their island Siphnos, had settled at Aegina, where the testator died. At Aegina the case was tried ; in fact, this is the only extant Greek forensic speech which is concerned with a law-suit outside of Attica.

The speech is composed with great care and may be regarded as a model of its kind. The narrative part of the discourse, in which the history of the family is given, is vividly presented and the defend-ant's relations with the testator and his devotion to him are attested by convincing proofs. Cogent argu-ments are employed to persuade the Aeginetan jury

that the will of Thrasylochus and the claims of the speaker are entirely justified on the basis of law, morality, and religion.

Although the exact date [a] of the speech is uncertain, it must be not long after 394 B.C., when the power of Sparta, supporter of oligarchies in the Cyclades, was overthrown at Cnidus. This is shown by the facts of the speech related in §§ 18-20 ; the aristocrats of Siphnos (including Thrasylochus and the speaker) were driven from their island by democratic exiles.

[a] *Cf.* Mathieu et Brémond, *Isocrate* i. p. 92, who plausibly suggest 391 or 390 B.C. Blass, *Die attische Beredsamkeit* ii. p. 236, assigns the speech to the period after 393 B.C. and before 390 B.C.

19. ΑΙΓΙΝΗΤΙΚΟΣ

Ἐνόμιζον μέν, ὦ ἄνδρες Αἰγινῆται, οὕτω καλῶς βεβουλεῦσθαι περὶ τῶν αὑτοῦ Θρασύλοχον ὥστε μηδέν' ἄν ποτ' ἐλθεῖν ἐναντία πράξοντα ταῖς διαθήκαις αἷς ἐκεῖνος κατέλιπεν· ἐπειδὴ δὲ τοῖς ἀντιδίκοις τοιαύτη γνώμη παρέστηκεν ὥστε καὶ πρὸς οὕτως ἐχούσας αὐτὰς ἀμφισβητεῖν, ἀναγκαίως ἔχει 2 παρ' ὑμῶν πειρᾶσθαι τῶν δικαίων τυγχάνειν. τοὐναντίον δὲ πέπονθα τοῖς πλείστοις τῶν ἀνθρώπων. τοὺς μὲν γὰρ ἄλλους ὁρῶ χαλεπῶς φέροντας, ὅταν ἀδίκως περί τινος κινδυνεύωσιν, ἐγὼ δ' ὀλίγου δέω χάριν ἔχειν τούτοις, ὅτι μ' εἰς τουτονὶ τὸν ἀγῶνα [385] κατέστησαν. ἀκρίτου μὲν γὰρ ὄντος τοῦ πράγματος οὐκ ἂν ἠπίστασθ' ὁποῖός τις γεγενημένος περὶ τὸν τετελευτηκότα κληρονόμος εἰμὶ τῶν ἐκείνου· πυθόμενοι δὲ τὰ πραχθέντα πάντες εἴσεσθ' ὅτι δικαίως ἂν καὶ μείζονος ἢ τοσαύτης δωρεᾶς ἠξι- 3 ώθην. χρῆν μέντοι καὶ τὴν ἀμφισβητοῦσαν τῶν χρημάτων μὴ παρ' ὑμῶν πειρᾶσθαι λαμβάνειν τὴν οὐσίαν, ἣν Θρασύλοχος κατέλιπεν, ἀλλὰ περὶ ἐκεῖνον χρηστὴν οὖσαν οὕτως ἀξιοῦν αὐτῆς ἐπιδικάζεσθαι. νῦν δ' αὐτῇ τοσούτου δεῖ μεταμέλειν ὧν εἰς ζῶντ' ἐξήμαρτεν, ὥστε καὶ τεθνεῶτος αὐτοῦ πειρᾶται τήν τε διαθήκην ἄκυρον ἅμα καὶ τὸν

300

XIX. AEGINETICUS

I was of opinion, citizens of Aegina, that Thrasylochus had arranged his affairs so prudently that no one would ever come before a court to bring a suit in opposition to the will which he left. But since my adversaries have determined to contest a testament so purposefully drawn, I am compelled to try to obtain my rights from you. My feeling is unlike that of most men. For I see that others are indignant when they are unjustly involved in a law-suit, whereas I am almost grateful to my opponents for bringing me into this trial.[a] For if the matter had not been brought before a tribunal you would not have known of my devotion to the deceased, which led to my being made his heir ; but when you learn the facts you will all perceive that I might justly have been thought worthy of even a greater reward. The proper course, however, for the woman who is laying claim to the property would have been, not to try to obtain from you the estate left by Thrasylochus, but to show that she also was devoted to him and on that ground thought fit to bring suit for it. But the truth is, she is so far from repenting of her misconduct towards Thrasylochus in his life-time, that now too that he is dead she is trying to annul his

---

[a] A commonplace ; cf. Lysias, In Defence of Mantitheus 1-2 ; On the Refusal of a Pension 1.

4 οἶκον ἔρημον ποιῆσαι. θαυμάζω δὲ καὶ τῶν πρατ-
τόντων ὑπὲρ αὐτῆς, εἰ διὰ τοῦτ' οἴονται καλὸν εἶναι
τὸν κίνδυνον, ὅτι μὴ κατορθώσαντες οὐδὲν μέλλουσιν ἀποτείσειν. ἐγὼ μὲν γὰρ ἡγοῦμαι μεγάλην
εἶναι καὶ ταύτην ζημίαν, ἂν ἐξελεγχθέντες ὡς
ἀδίκως ἀμφισβητοῦσιν, ἔπειθ' ὑμῖν δόξωσι χείρους
εἶναι. τὴν μὲν οὖν τούτων κακίαν ἐξ αὐτῶν τῶν
ἔργων γνώσεσθ', ἐπειδὰν διὰ τέλους ἀκούσητε τῶν
πεπραγμένων· ὅθεν δ', οἶμαι, τάχιστ' ἂν ὑμᾶς
μαθεῖν περὶ ὧν ἀμφισβητοῦμεν, ἐντεῦθεν ἄρξομαι
διηγεῖσθαι.

5 Θράσυλλος γὰρ ὁ πατὴρ τοῦ καταλιπόντος τὴν
διαθήκην παρὰ μὲν τῶν προγόνων οὐδεμίαν οὐσίαν
παρέλαβεν, ξένος δὲ Πολεμαινέτῳ τῷ μάντει γενόμενος οὕτως οἰκείως διετέθη πρὸς αὐτὸν ὥστ'
ἀποθνῄσκων ἐκεῖνος τάς τε βίβλους τὰς περὶ τῆς
μαντικῆς αὐτῷ κατέλιπε καὶ τῆς οὐσίας μέρος τι
6 τῆς νῦν οὔσης ἔδωκεν. λαβὼν δὲ Θράσυλλος ταύτας ἀφορμὰς ἐχρῆτο τῇ τέχνῃ· πλάνης δὲ γενόμενος
καὶ διαιτηθεὶς ἐν πολλαῖς πόλεσιν ἄλλαις τε γυναιξὶ
συνεγένετο, ὧν ἔνιαι καὶ παιδάρι' ἀπέδειξαν ἃ
'κεῖνος οὐδὲ πώποτε γνήσι' ἐνόμισε, καὶ δὴ καὶ
τὴν ταύτης μητέρ' ἐν τούτοις τοῖς χρόνοις ἔλαβεν.
7 ἐπειδὴ δ' οὐσίαν τε πολλὴν ἐκτήσατο καὶ τὴν
πατρίδ' ἐπόθεσεν, ἐκείνης μὲν καὶ τῶν ἄλλων ἀπηλ-
λάγη, καταπλεύσας δ' εἰς Σίφνον ἔγημεν ἀδελφὴν
τοῦ πατρὸς τοὐμοῦ, πλούτῳ μὲν αὐτὸς πρῶτος ὢν
τῶν πολιτῶν, γένει δὲ καὶ τοῖς ἄλλοις ἀξιώμασιν
8 εἰδὼς τὴν ἡμετέραν οἰκίαν προέχουσαν. οὕτω δὲ
[386] σφόδρ' ἠγάπησε τὴν τοῦ πατρὸς φιλίαν, ὥστ' ἀπο-
θανούσης ἐκείνης ἄπαιδος αὖθις ἠγάγετ' ἀνεψιὰν

will and to leave the home without heirs. And I am astonished that those who are acting in her behalf think this action is reputable, just because, if they fail to win, they will need to pay no penalty. For my part, I think that it will be a severe penalty, if, having been convicted of making a wrongful claim, they shall thereafter suffer in your esteem. However, you will know the baseness of these men from their very acts when you have heard to the end what they have done ; and I shall begin the recital of them at the point from which, in my opinion, you will be able to learn most quickly the matters at issue.

Thrasyllus, the father of the testator, had inherited nothing from his parents ; but having become the guest-friend of Polemaenetus, the soothsayer, he became so intimate with him that Polemaenetus at his death left to him his books on divination and gave him a portion of the property which is now in question. Thrasyllus, with these books as his capital, practised the art of divination. He became an itinerant soothsayer, lived in many cities, and was intimate with several women, some of whom had children whom he never even recognized as legitimate, and, in particular, during this period he lived with the mother of the complainant. When he had acquired a large fortune and yearned for his fatherland, he left this woman and the others as well, and debarking at Siphnos married a sister of my father. Thrasyllus himself was indeed the leading citizen in wealth, but he knew that our family was likewise pre-eminent in lineage and in general standing ; and he cherished so warmly my father's affection for him that at the death of his wife, who was without children, he remarried, taking as wife my father's

τοῦ πατρός, οὐ βουλόμενος διαλύσασθαι τὴν πρὸς
ἡμᾶς οἰκειότητα. οὐ πολὺν δὲ χρόνον συνοικήσας
ταῖς αὐταῖς τύχαις ἐχρήσατο καὶ περὶ ταύτην,
9 αἶσπερ καὶ περὶ τὴν προτέραν. μετὰ δὲ ταῦτ᾽
ἔγημεν ἐκ Σερίφου παρ᾽ ἀνθρώπων πολὺ πλείονος
ἀξίων ἢ κατὰ τὴν αὐτῶν πόλιν, ἐξ ἧς ἐγένετο
Σώπολις καὶ Θρασύλοχος καὶ θυγάτηρ ἡ νῦν ἐμοὶ
συνοικοῦσα. Θράσυλλος μὲν οὖν τούτους μόνους
παῖδας γνησίους καταλιπὼν καὶ κληρονόμους τῶν
αὐτοῦ καταστήσας τὸν βίον ἐτελεύτησεν.

10 Ἐγὼ δὲ καὶ Θρασύλοχος τοσαύτην φιλίαν παρὰ
τῶν πατέρων παραλαβόντες ὅσην ὀλίγῳ πρότερον
διηγησάμην, ἔτι μείζω τῆς ὑπαρχούσης αὐτὴν
ἐποιήσαμεν. ἕως μὲν γὰρ παῖδες ἦμεν, περὶ πλείονος ἡμᾶς αὐτοὺς ἡγούμεθα ἢ τοὺς ἀδελφούς, καὶ
οὔτε θυσίαν οὔτε θεωρίαν οὔτ᾽ ἄλλην ἑορτὴν οὐδεμίαν χωρὶς ἀλλήλων ἤγομεν· ἐπειδὴ δ᾽ ἄνδρες
ἐγενόμεθα, οὐδὲν πώποτ᾽ ἐναντίον ἡμῖν αὐτοῖς
ἐπράξαμεν, ἀλλὰ καὶ τῶν ἰδίων ἐκοινωνοῦμεν καὶ
πρὸς τὰ τῆς πόλεως ὁμοίως διεκείμεθα καὶ φίλοις
11 καὶ ξένοις τοῖς αὐτοῖς ἐχρώμεθα. καὶ τί δεῖ λέγειν
τὰς οἴκοι χρήσεις; ἀλλ᾽ οὐδὲ φυγόντες ἀπ᾽ ἀλλήλων ἠξιώσαμεν γενέσθαι. τὸ δὲ τελευταῖον φθόη
σχόμενον αὐτὸν καὶ πολὺν χρόνον ἀσθενήσαντα,
καὶ τοῦ μὲν ἀδελφοῦ Σωπόλιδος αὐτῷ πρότερον
τετελευτηκότος, τῆς δὲ μητρὸς καὶ τῆς ἀδελφῆς
οὔπω παρουσῶν, μετὰ τοσαύτης ἐρημίας γενόμενον
οὕτως ἐπιπόνως καὶ καλῶς αὐτὸν ἐθεράπευσα,
ὥστ᾽ ἐκεῖνον μὴ νομίζειν ἀξίαν μοι δύνασθαι χάριν

cousin, as he did not wish to dissolve the affinity with us. But after he had lived with her for only a short time, he suffered the same bereavement as with his former wife. After this he married a woman of Seriphos, belonging to a family of greater consequence than might be expected of a native of their island.[a] Of this marriage were born Sopolis, Thrasylochus, and a daughter, who is my wife. These were the only legitimate children left by Thrasyllus and he made these his heirs when he died.

Thrasylochus and I, having inherited from our fathers a friendship the intimacy of which I have recently mentioned, made the bond still closer. For during our childhood we were fonder of each other than of our brothers, and we would perform no sacrifice, make no pilgrimage, and celebrate no festival except in one another's company ; and when we reached manhood we never opposed one another in any action undertaken, for we not only shared our private concerns but also held similar sentiments regarding public affairs, and we had the same intimates and guest-friends. And why need I speak further of our intimacy at home ?[b] In truth, not even in exile did we care to be apart. Finally, when Thrasylochus was striken with the wasting disease and suffered a long illness—his brother Sopolis had previously died[c] and his mother and sister had not yet arrived[d]—seeing him so completely destitute of companionship I nursed him with such unremitting care and devotion that he thought he could never

---

[a] The insignificance of Seriphos was proverbial ; cf. Plato, Rep. 329 E.   [b] That is, at Siphnos.
[c] Sopolis died in Lycia (cf. § 40).
[d] At Aegina.

12 ἀποδοῦναι τῶν πεπραγμένων. ὅμως δ' οὐδὲν ἐνέλιπεν, ἀλλ' ἐπειδὴ πονήρως διέκειτο καὶ οὐδεμίαν ἐλπίδ' εἶχε τοῦ βίου, παρακαλέσας μάρτυρας υἱόν μ' ἐποιήσατο καὶ τὴν ἀδελφὴν τὴν αὑτοῦ καὶ τὴν οὐσίαν ἔδωκεν.

Καί μοι λαβὲ τὰς διαθήκας.

ΔΙΑΘΗΚΑΙ

Ἀνάγνωθι δή μοι καὶ τὸν νόμον τὸν Αἰγινητῶν· κατὰ γὰρ τοῦτον ἔδει ποιεῖσθαι τὰς διαθήκας· ἐνθάδε γὰρ μετῳκοῦμεν.

ΝΟΜΟΣ

13 Κατὰ τουτονὶ τὸν νόμον, ὦ ἄνδρες Αἰγινῆται, υἱόν μ' ἐποιήσατο Θρασύλοχος, πολίτην μὲν αὑτοῦ
[387] καὶ φίλον ὄντα, γεγονότα δ' οὐδενὸς χεῖρον Σιφνίων, πεπαιδευμένον δ' ὁμοίως αὑτῷ καὶ τεθραμμένον. ὥστ' οὐκ οἶδ' ὅπως ἂν μᾶλλον κατὰ τὸν νόμον ἔπραξεν, ὃς τοὺς ὁμοίους κελεύει παῖδας εἰσποιεῖσθαι.

Λαβὲ δή μοι καὶ τὸν Κείων νόμον, καθ' ὃν ἡμεῖς ἐπολιτευόμεθα.

ΝΟΜΟΣ

14 Εἰ μὲν τοίνυν, ὦ ἄνδρες Αἰγινῆται, τούτοις μὲν τοῖς νόμοις ἠναντιοῦντο, τὸν δὲ παρ' αὑτοῖς κείμενον σύνδικον εἶχον, ἧττον ἄξιον ἦν θαυμάζειν αὐτῶν· νῦν δὲ κἀκεῖνος ὁμοίως τοῖς ἀνεγνωσμένοις κεῖται.

Καί μοι λαβὲ τὸ βιβλίον.

---

* The law of Ceos was valid also in Siphnos.

repay me with a gratitude adequate to my services
Nevertheless he left nothing undone to reward me,
and when he was in a grievous condition and had
given up all hope of life, he summoned witnesses,
made me his adoptive son, and gave me his sister
and his fortune.

(*To the Clerk*) Please take the will.

The Will

Read to me also the law of Aegina ; for it was
necessary that the will be drawn in accordance with
this law, since we were alien residents of this island.

Law

It was in accordance with this law, citizens of
Aegina, that Thrasylochus adopted me as his son,
for I was his fellow-citizen and friend, in birth inferior
to no one of the Siphnians, and had been reared and
educated very much as he himself had been. I
therefore do not see how he could have acted more
consistently with the law, since the law insists that
only persons of the same status may be adopted.

(*To the Clerk*) Please take also the law of Ceos,[a]
under which we were living.

Law

If, therefore, citizens of Aegina, my opponents
were refusing to recognize the validity of these laws,
but were able to produce in support of their case the
law of their own country, their conduct would have
been less astonishing. But the truth is that their
own law is in agreement with those already read.

(*To the Clerk*) Please take this document.

NOMOΣ

15 Τί οὖν ὑπόλοιπόν ἐστιν αὐτοῖς, ὅπου τὰς μὲν διαθήκας αὐτοὶ προσομολογοῦσι Θρασύλοχον καταλιπεῖν, τῶν δὲ νόμων τούτοις μὲν οὐδείς, ἐμοὶ δὲ πάντες βοηθοῦσι, πρῶτον μὲν ὁ παρ' ὑμῖν τοῖς μέλλουσι διαγνώσεσθαι περὶ τοῦ πράγματος, ἔπειθ' ὁ Σιφνίων, ὅθεν ἦν ὁ τὴν διαθήκην καταλιπών, ἔτι δ' ὁ παρ' αὐτοῖς τοῖς ἀμφισβητοῦσι κείμενος; καίτοι τίνος ἂν ὑμῖν ἀποσχέσθαι δοκοῦσιν, οἵτινες ζητοῦσι πείθειν ὑμᾶς, ὡς χρὴ τὰς διαθήκας ἀκύρους ποιῆσαι τῶν μὲν νόμων οὕτως ἐχόντων, ὑμῶν δὲ κατ' αὐτοὺς ὀμωμοκότων ψηφιεῖσθαι;

16 Περὶ μὲν οὖν αὐτοῦ τοῦ πράγματος ἱκανῶς ἀποδεδεῖχθαι νομίζω· ἵνα δὲ μηδεὶς οἴηται μήτ' ἐμὲ διὰ μικρὰς προφάσεις ἔχειν τὸν κλῆρον μήτε ταύτην ἐπιεικῆ γεγενημένην περὶ Θρασύλοχον ἀποστερεῖσθαι τῶν χρημάτων, βούλομαι καὶ περὶ τούτων εἰπεῖν. αἰσχυνθείην γὰρ ἂν ὑπὲρ τοῦ τετελευτηκότος, εἰ μὴ πάντες πεισθείητε, μὴ μόνον ὡς κατὰ τοὺς νόμους ἀλλ' ὡς καὶ δικαίως ταῦτ' ἔπραξεν.

17 ῥᾳδίας δ' ἡγοῦμαι τὰς ἀποδείξεις εἶναι. τοσοῦτον γὰρ διηνέγκαμεν ὥσθ' αὕτη μὲν ἡ κατὰ γένος ἀμφισβητοῦσα πάντα τὸν χρόνον διετέλεσε καὶ πρὸς αὐτὸν ἐκεῖνον καὶ πρὸς Σώπολιν καὶ πρὸς τὴν μητέρ' αὐτῶν διαφερομένη καὶ δυσμενῶς ἔχουσα, ἐγὼ δ' οὐ μόνον περὶ Θρασύλοχον καὶ τὸν ἀδελφὸν ἀλλὰ καὶ περὶ αὐτὴν τὴν οὐσίαν, ἧς ἀμφισβητοῦμεν, φανήσομαι πλείστου τῶν φίλων ἄξιος γεγενημένος.

What argument is left to them, therefore, since they themselves admit that Thrasylochus left the will and that they can cite no law in their favour, whereas all support my case—first, the law which is valid among you who are to adjudge the case, next, the law of Siphnos, the fatherland of the testator, and finally the law of the country of my opponents ? And yet from what illegal act do you think these persons would abstain, inasmuch as they seek to persuade you that you should declare this will invalid, although the laws read as you have heard and you have taken oath to cast your votes in conformity with them ?

On the issue itself I consider that I have adduced sufficient proof ; but that no one may think that my possession of the inheritance rests upon feeble grounds, or that this woman had been kindly in her behaviour toward Thrasylochus and is being defrauded of his fortune, I wish also to discuss these matters. For I should be ashamed in behalf of the deceased unless you were all convinced that his actions were strictly in accordance, not only with the law, but also with justice. And I believe that proof of this is easy. There was, in truth, this great difference between us—that this woman, who bases her contention on the ground of relationship, never ceased to be at variance with the testator and evilly-disposed toward him and toward Sopolis and their mother, whereas I shall be shown to have been the most deserving of all his friends, not only in my relations with Thrasylochus and his brother, but also with regard to the estate in controversy.

18 Καὶ περὶ μὲν τῶν παλαιῶν πολὺ ἂν ἔργον εἴη
λέγειν· ὅτε δὲ Πασῖνος Πάρον κατέλαβεν, ἔτυχεν
αὐτοῖς ὑπεκκείμενα τὰ πλεῖστα τῆς οὐσίας παρὰ
[388] τοῖς ξένοις τοῖς ἐμοῖς· ᾠόμεθα γὰρ μάλιστα ταύτην
τὴν νῆσον ἀσφαλῶς ἔχειν. ἀπορούντων δ᾽ ἐκείνων
καὶ νομιζόντων αὔτ᾽ ἀπολωλέναι, πλεύσας ἐγὼ τῆς
νυκτὸς ἐξεκόμισ᾽ αὐτοῖς τὰ χρήματα, κινδυνεύσας
19 περὶ τοῦ σώματος· ἐφρουρεῖτο μὲν γὰρ ἡ χώρα,
συγκατειληφότες δ᾽ ἦσάν τινες τῶν ἡμετέρων
φυγάδων τὴν πόλιν, οἳ μιᾶς ἡμέρας ἀπέκτειναν
αὐτόχειρες γενόμενοι τόν τε πατέρα τὸν ἐμὸν καὶ
τὸν θεῖον καὶ τὸν κηδεστὴν καὶ πρὸς τούτοις
ἀνεψιοὺς τρεῖς. ἀλλ᾽ ὅμως οὐδέν με τούτων
ἀπέτρεψεν, ἀλλ᾽ ᾠχόμην πλέων, ἡγούμενος ὁμοίως
με δεῖν ὑπὲρ ἐκείνων κινδυνεύειν ὥσπερ ὑπὲρ ἐμαυ-
20 τοῦ. μετὰ δὲ ταῦτα φυγῆς ἡμῖν γενομένης ἐκ
τῆς πόλεως μετὰ τοιούτου θορύβου καὶ δέους ὥστ᾽
ἐνίους καὶ τῶν σφετέρων αὐτῶν ἀμελεῖν, οὐδ᾽ ἐν
τούτοις τοῖς κακοῖς ἠγάπησα, εἰ τοὺς οἰκείους τοὺς
ἐμαυτοῦ διασῶσαι δυνηθείην, ἀλλ᾽ εἰδὼς Σώπολιν
μὲν ἀποδημοῦντα, αὐτὸν δ᾽ ἐκεῖνον ἀρρώστως
διακείμενον, συνεξεκόμισ᾽ αὐτῷ καὶ τὴν μητέρα
καὶ τὴν ἀδελφὴν καὶ τὴν οὐσίαν ἅπασαν. καίτοι
τίνα δικαιότερον αὐτὴν ἔχειν προσήκει ἢ[1] τὸν τότε
μὲν συνδιασώσαντα, νῦν δὲ παρὰ τῶν κυρίων
εἰληφότα;
21 Τὰ μὲν τοίνυν εἰρημέν᾽ ἐστὶν ἐν οἷς ἐκινδύνευσα
μέν, φλαῦρον δ᾽ οὐδὲν ἀπέλαυσα· ἔχω δὲ καὶ τοιαῦτ᾽
εἰπεῖν, ἐξ ὧν ἐκείνῳ χαριζόμενος αὐτὸς ταῖς μεγίσταις συμφοραῖς περιέπεσον. ἐπειδὴ γὰρ ἤλθομεν
εἰς Μῆλον, αἰσθόμενος, ὅτι μέλλομεν αὐτοῦ κατα-

---

[1] ἔχειν προσήκει ἢ Ξ vulg.: ἔχειν ἢ Λς: Blass.

It would be a long story to tell of the events
of long ago ; but when Pasinus ᵃ took Paros, it
chanced that my friends had the greatest part of
their fortune deposited as a pledge with my guest-
friends there ; for we thought that this island was
by far the safest. When they were at their wits'
end and believed that their property was lost, I
sailed thither by night and got their money out at
the risk of my life ; for the country was occupied
by a garrison, and some of the exiles from our island
had participated in the seizure of the city, and these,
in one day and with their own hands, had slain my
father, my uncle, my brother-in-law and, in addition,
three cousins. However, I was deterred by none
of these risks, but I took ship, thinking I ought
to run the risk as much for my friends' sake as for
my own. Afterwards when a general flight from the
city ᵇ ensued, accompanied by such confusion and
fear that some persons were indifferent even to the
fate of their own relations, I was not content, even
in these misfortunes, merely to be able to save the
members of my own household, but knowing that
Sopolis was absent and Thrasylochus was in feeble
health, I helped him to convey from the country his
mother, his sister, and all his fortune. And yet who
with greater justice should possess this fortune than
the person who then helped to save it and now has
received it from its legitimate owners ?

I have related the adventures in which I incurred
danger indeed, yet suffered no harm ; but I have
also to speak of friendly services I rendered him
which involved me in the greatest misfortunes. For
when we had arrived at Melos, and Thrasylochus

ᵃ An unknown person.   ᵇ Siphnos.

μένειν, ἐδεῖτό μου συμπλεῖν εἰς Τροιζῆνα καὶ μη-
δαμῶς αὐτὸν ἀπολιπεῖν, λέγων τὴν ἀρρωστίαν τοῦ
σώματος καὶ τὸ πλῆθος τῶν ἐχθρῶν, καὶ ὅτι χωρὶς
ἐμοῦ γενόμενος οὐδὲν ἕξοι χρῆσθαι τοῖς αὐτοῦ
22 πράγμασιν. φοβουμένης δὲ τῆς μητρός, ὅτι τὸ
χωρίον ἐπυνθάνετο νοσῶδες εἶναι, καὶ τῶν ξένων
συμβουλευόντων αὐτοῦ μένειν, ὅμως ἔδοξεν ἡμῖν
ἐκείνῳ χαριστέον εἶναι. καὶ μετὰ ταῦτ' οὐκ ἔφθη-
μεν εἰς Τροιζῆν' ἐλθόντες καὶ τοιαύταις νόσοις
ἐλήφθημεν, ἐξ ὧν αὐτὸς μὲν παρὰ μικρὸν ἦλθον
ἀποθανεῖν, ἀδελφὴν δὲ κόρην τετρακαιδεκέτιν γε-
γονυῖαν ἐντὸς τριάκονθ' ἡμερῶν κατέθαψα, τὴν δὲ
[389] μητέρ' οὐδὲ πένθ' ἡμέραις ἐκείνης ὕστερον. καίτοι
τίν' οἴεσθέ με γνώμην ἔχειν τοσαύτης μοι μετα-
23 βολῆς τοῦ βίου γεγενημένης; ὃς τὸν μὲν ἄλλον
χρόνον ἀπαθὴς ἦν κακῶν, νεωστὶ δ' ἐπειρώμην
φυγῆς καὶ τοῦ παρ' ἑτέροις μὲν μετοικεῖν, στέρε-
σθαι δὲ τῶν ἐμαυτοῦ, πρὸς δὲ τούτοις ὁρῶν τὴν
μητέρα τὴν αὐτοῦ καὶ τὴν ἀδελφὴν ἐκ μὲν τῆς
πατρίδος ἐκπεπτωκυίας, ἐπὶ δὲ ξένης καὶ παρ'
ἀλλοτρίοις τὸν βίον τελευτώσας. ὥστ' οὐδεὶς ἂν
μοι δικαίως φθονήσειεν, εἴ τι τῶν Θρασυλόχου
πραγμάτων ἀγαθὸν ἀπολέλαυκα· καὶ γὰρ ἵνα
χαρισαίμην ἐκείνῳ, κατοικισάμενος ἐν Τροιζῆνι
τοιαύταις ἐχρησάμην συμφοραῖς, ὧν οὐδέποτ' ἂν
ἐπιλαθέσθαι δυνηθείην.

24 Καὶ μὴν οὐδὲ τοῦθ' ἕξουσιν εἰπεῖν ὡς εὖ μὲν
πράττοντος Θρασυλόχου πάντα ταῦθ' ὑπέμενον,
δυστυχήσαντα δ' αὐτὸν ἀπέλιπον· ἐν αὐτοῖς γὰρ
τούτοις ἔτι σαφέστερον καὶ μᾶλλον ἐνεπεδειξάμην
τὴν εὔνοιαν ἣν εἶχον εἰς ἐκεῖνον. ἐπειδὴ γὰρ εἰς

perceived that we were likely to remain there, he begged me to sail with him to Troezen*a* and by all means not to abandon him, mentioning his bodily infirmity and the multitude of his enemies, saying that without me he would not know how to manage his own affairs. And although my mother was afraid because she had heard that Troezen was unhealthy and our guest-friends advised us to remain where we were, nevertheless we decided that we ought to gratify his wish. No sooner had we arrived at Troezen than we were attacked by illnesses of such severity that I barely escaped with my own life, and within thirty days I buried my young sister, fourteen years of age, and my mother not five days thereafter. In what state of mind do you think I was after such a change in my life ? I had previously been inexperienced in misfortune and I had only recently suffered exile and living an alien among foreigners, and had lost my fortune ; in addition, I saw my mother and my sister driven from their native land and ending their lives in a foreign land among strangers. No one could justly begrudge it me, therefore, if I have received some benefit from the troublesome affairs of Thrasylochus ; for it was to gratify him that I went to live in Troezen, where I experienced misfortunes so dire that I shall never be able to forget them.

Furthermore, there is one thing my opponents cannot say of me—that when Thrasylochus was prosperous I suffered all these woes, but that I abandoned him in his adversity. For it was precisely then that I gave clearer and stronger proof of my devotion to

---

a On the southern coast of the Saronic Gulf, in the north-eastern part of the Peloponnese, near Epidaurus.

Αἴγιναν κατοικισάμενος ἠσθένησε ταύτην τὴν νόσον
ἐξ ἧσπερ ἀπέθανεν, οὕτως αὐτὸν ἐθεράπευσα ὡς
οὐκ οἶδ' ὅστις πώποθ' ἕτερος ἕτερον, τὸν μὲν
πλεῖστον τοῦ χρόνου πονήρως μὲν ἔχοντα, περιιέναι
δ' ἔτι δυνάμενον, ἐξ μῆνας δὲ συνεχῶς ἐν τῇ κλίνῃ
25 κείμενον. καὶ τούτων τῶν ταλαιπωριῶν οὐδεὶς τῶν
συγγενῶν μετασχεῖν ἠξίωσεν, ἀλλ' οὐδ' ἐπισκεψό-
μενος ἀφίκετο πλὴν τῆς μητρὸς καὶ τῆς ἀδελφῆς,
αἳ πλέον θάτερον ἐποίησαν· ἀσθενοῦσαι γὰρ ἦλθον
ἐκ Τροιζῆνος, ὥστ' αὐταὶ θεραπείας ἐδέοντο. ἀλλ'
ὅμως ἐγώ, τοιούτων τῶν ἄλλων περὶ αὐτὸν γεγενημένων, οὐκ ἀπεῖπον οὐδ' ἀπέστην ἀλλ' ἐνοσήλευον
26 αὐτὸν μετὰ παιδὸς ἑνός· οὐδὲ γὰρ τῶν οἰκετῶν
οὐδεὶς ὑπέμεινεν. καὶ γὰρ φύσει χαλεπὸς ὢν ἔτι
δυσκολώτερον διὰ τὴν νόσον διέκειτο, ὥστ' οὐκ
ἐκείνων ἄξιον θαυμάζειν, εἰ μὴ παρέμενον, ἀλλὰ
πολὺ μᾶλλον, ὅπως ἐγὼ τοιαύτην νόσον θεραπεύων
ἀνταρκεῖν ἠδυνάμην· ὃς ἔμπυος μὲν ἦν πολὺν
χρόνον, ἐκ δὲ τῆς κλίνης οὐκ ἠδύνατο κινεῖσθαι,
27 τοιαῦτα δ' ἔπασχεν ὥσθ' ἡμᾶς μηδεμίαν ἡμέραν
ἀδακρύτους διάγειν, ἀλλὰ θρηνοῦντες διετελοῦμεν
καὶ τοὺς πόνους τοὺς ἀλλήλων καὶ τὴν φυγὴν καὶ
τὴν ἐρημίαν τὴν ἡμετέραν αὐτῶν. καὶ ταῦτ' οὐδένα χρόνον διέλειπεν· οὐδὲ γὰρ ἀπελθεῖν οἷόν τ'
[390] ἦν ἢ δοκεῖν ἀμελεῖν, ὅ μοι πολὺ δεινότερον ἦν τῶν
κακῶν τῶν παρόντων.
28 Ἐβουλόμην δ' ἂν ὑμῖν οἷός τ' εἶναι ποιῆσαι
φανερὸν οἷος περὶ αὐτὸν ἐγενόμην· οἶμαι γὰρ οὐδ'
ἂν τὴν φωνὴν ὑμᾶς ἀνασχέσθαι τῶν ἀντιδίκων.
νῦν δὲ τὰ χαλεπώτατα τῶν ἐν τῇ θεραπείᾳ καὶ

---

[a] *Cf. Plataicus* 47 for the same expression.

314

him. When, for instance, he settled in Aegina and fell ill of the malady which resulted in his death, I nursed him with a care such as no one else I know of has ever bestowed upon another. Most of the time he was very ill, yet still able to go about; finally he lay for six months bedridden. And no one of his relations saw fit to share with me the drudgery of caring for him; no one even came to see him with the exception of his mother and sister; and they made the task more difficult; for they were ill when they came from Troezen, so that they themselves were in need of care. But although the others were thus indifferent, I did not grow weary nor did I leave the scene, but I nursed him with the help of one slave boy; for no one of the domestics could stand it. For being by nature irascible, he became, because of his malady, still more difficult to handle. It should not occasion surprise, therefore, that these persons would not remain with him, but it is much more a cause for wonder that I was able to hold out in caring for a man sick of such a malady; for he was filled with pus for a long time, and was unable to leave his bed; and his suffering was so great that we did not pass a single day without tears,[a] but kept up our lamentations both for the hardships we both had to endure, and for our exile and our isolation. And there was no intermission at any time; for it was impossible to leave him or to seem to neglect him— for to me this would have seemed more dreadful than the woes which afflicted us.

I wish I could make clearly apparent to you my conduct with respect to him; for in that case I think that you would not endure even a word from my opponents. The truth is, it is not easy to describe the

315

δυσχερέστατα καὶ πόνους ἀηδεστάτους ἔχοντα καὶ
πλείστης ἐπιμελείας δεηθέντ' οὐκ εὐδιήγητ' ἐστίν.
ἀλλ' ὑμεῖς αὐτοὶ σκοπεῖτε, μετὰ πόσων ἄν τις
ἀγρυπνιῶν καὶ ταλαιπωριῶν τοιοῦτον νόσημα τοσ-
29 οῦτον χρόνον θεραπεύσειεν. ἐγὼ μὲν γὰρ οὕτω κακῶς διετέθην, ὥσθ' ὅσοι περ εἰσῆλθον τῶν φίλων,
ἔφασαν δεδιέναι, μὴ κἀγὼ προσαπόλωμαι, καὶ συν-
εβούλευόν μοι φυλάττεσθαι, λέγοντες ὡς οἱ πλεῖστοι τῶν θεραπευσάντων ταύτην τὴν νόσον αὐτοὶ
προσδιεφθάρησαν. πρὸς οὓς ἐγὼ τοιαῦτ' ἀπεκρινά-
μην ὅτι πολὺ ἂν θᾶττον ἑλοίμην ἀποθανεῖν ἢ
'κεῖνον περιδεῖν δι' ἔνδειαν τοῦ θεραπεύσοντος
πρὸ μοίρας τελευτήσαντα.

30 Καὶ τοιούτῳ μοι γεγενημένῳ τετόλμηκεν ἀμφισβητεῖν τῶν χρημάτων ἡ μηδ' ἐπισκέψασθαι
πώποτ' αὐτὸν ἀξιώσασα, τοσοῦτον μὲν χρόνον
ἀσθενήσαντα, πυνθανομένη δὲ καθ' ἑκάστην τὴν
ἡμέραν, ὡς διέκειτο, ῥᾳδίας δ' οὔσης αὐτῇ τῆς
πορείας. εἶτα νῦν αὐτὸν ἀδελφίζειν ἐπιχειρήσουσιν,
ὥσπερ οὐχ ὅσῳ περ ἂν οἰκειότερον προσείπωσι
τὸν τεθνεῶτα, τοσούτῳ δόξουσιν αὐτὴν μείζω
31 καὶ δεινότερ' ἐξαμαρτεῖν· ἥτις οὐδ' ἐπειδὴ τελευ-
τᾶν ἤμελλε τὸν βίον, ὁρῶσα τοὺς πολίτας τοὺς
ἡμετέρους, ὅσοι περ ἦσαν ἐν Τροιζῆνι, διαπλέον-
τας εἰς Αἴγιναν, ἵν' αὐτὸν συγκαταθάψειαν, οὐδ'
εἰς τοῦτον τὸν καιρὸν ἀπήντησεν, ἀλλ' οὕτως
ὠμῶς καὶ σχετλίως εἶχεν, ὥστ' ἐπὶ μὲν τὸ κῆδος
οὐκ ἠξίωσεν ἀφικέσθαι, τῶν δὲ καταλειφθέντων
οὐδὲ δέχ' ἡμέρας διαλιποῦσ' ἦλθεν ἀμφισβητοῦσα,
ὥσπερ τῶν χρημάτων ἀλλ' οὐκ ἐκείνου συγγενὴς
32 οὖσα. καὶ εἰ μὲν ὁμολογήσει τοσαύτην ἔχθραν
ὑπάρχειν αὐτῇ πρὸς ἐκεῖνον ὥστ' εἰκότως ταῦτα

duties involved in my care of the invalid, duties that
were very hard, very difficult to endure, most dis-
agreeably toilsome, and exacting an unremitting care.
But do you yourselves consider what loss of sleep,
what miseries are the inevitable accompaniment of
a prolonged nursing of a malady like his. In truth,
in my own case, I was reduced to such a condition
that all my friends who visited me expressed fear
that I too would perish with the dying man and they
advised me to take care, saying that the majority
of those who had nursed this disease themselves fell
victims to it also. My reply to them was this—that
I would much prefer to die than to see him perish
before his fated day for lack of a friend to nurse him.

And although my behaviour was as I have described,
this woman has had the hardihood to contest with me
his fortune, she who never even saw fit to visit him
during his long illness, though she had daily information about his condition, and though the journey was
easy for her. To think that they will now attempt to
" brother " him,[a] as if the effect of calling the dead
man by a name of closer kinship would not be to
make her shortcomings seem worse and more shocking ! Why, when he was at the point of death,
and when she saw all our fellow-citizens who were
in Troezen sailing to Aegina to take part in his
funeral, she did not even at that moment come, but
was so cruel and heartless in conduct that while she
did not see fit to come to his funeral, yet, less than
ten days thereafter she arrived to claim the property
he had left, as if she were related to his money and
not to him ! And if she will admit that her hatred
for him was so bitter that this conduct was reason-

* ἀδελφίζειν, a rare word, " to call brother."

ποιεῖν, οὐκ ἂν κακῶς εἴη βεβουλευμένος, εἰ τοῖς
[391] φίλοις ἠβουλήθη μᾶλλον ἢ ταύτῃ τὴν οὐσίαν κατα-
λιπεῖν· εἰ δὲ μηδεμιᾶς διαφορᾶς οὔσης οὕτως
ἀμελὴς καὶ κακὴ περὶ αὐτὸν ἐγένετο, πολὺ ἂν
δήπου δικαιότερον στερηθείη τῶν αὐτῆς ἢ τῶν
33 ἐκείνου κληρονόμος γίγνοιτο. ἐνθυμεῖσθε δ' ὅτι
τὸ μὲν ταύτης μέρος οὔτ' ἐν τῇ νόσῳ θεραπείας
ἔτυχεν οὔτ' ἀποθανὼν τῶν νομιζομένων ἠξιώθη,
δι' ἐμὲ δ' ἀμφότερα ταῦτ' αὐτῷ γεγένηται. καίτοι
δίκαιόν ἐστιν ὑμᾶς τὴν ψῆφον φέρειν, οὐκ εἴ τινες
γένει μέν φασι προσήκειν, ἐν δὲ τοῖς ἔργοις ὅμοιοι
τοῖς ἐχθροῖς γεγόνασιν, ἀλλὰ πολὺ μᾶλλον ὅσοι
μηδὲν ὄνομα συγγενείας ἔχοντες οἰκειοτέρους σφᾶς
αὐτοὺς ἐν ταῖς συμφοραῖς τῶν ἀναγκαίων παρέσχον.
34 Λέγουσι δ' ὡς τὰς μὲν διαθήκας οὐκ ἀπιστοῦσι
Θρασύλοχον καταλιπεῖν, οὐ μέντοι καλῶς οὐδ'
ὀρθῶς φασὶν αὐτὰς ἔχειν. καίτοι, ὦ ἄνδρες Αἰγινῆται, πῶς ἄν τις ἄμεινον ἢ μᾶλλον συμφερόντως
περὶ τῶν αὑτοῦ πραγμάτων ἐβουλεύσατο; ὃς οὔτ'
ἔρημον τὸν οἶκον κατέλιπε τοῖς τε φίλοις χάριν
ἀπέδωκεν, ἔτι δὲ τὴν μητέρα καὶ τὴν ἀδελφὴν οὐ
μόνον τῶν αὑτοῦ κυρίας ἀλλὰ καὶ τῶν ἐμῶν κατέστησε, τὴν μὲν ἐμοὶ συνοικίσας, τῇ δ' υἱὸν μ'
35 εἰσποιήσας; ἆρ' ἂν ἐκείνως ἄμεινον ἔπραξεν, εἰ
μήτε τῆς μητρὸς τὸν ἐπιμελησόμενον κατέστησε,
μήτ' ἐμοῦ μηδεμίαν μνείαν ἐποιήσατο, τὴν δ'
ἀδελφὴν ἐπὶ τῇ τύχῃ κατέλιπε, καὶ τὸν οἶκον
ἀνώνυμον τὸν αὑτοῦ περιεῖδε γενόμενον;

able, then Thrasylochus would be considered not to have been ill-advised in preferring to leave his property to his friends rather than to this woman ; but if there existed no variance between them and yet she was so neglectful of him and so unkind toward him, surely with greater justice would she be deprived of her own possessions than become heir to his. Bear in mind that, so far as she was concerned, he had no care during his illness, nor when he died was he thought worthy of the customary funeral rites, whereas it was through me that he obtained both. Surely you will justly cast your votes in favour, not of those who claim blood-relationship yet in their conduct have acted like enemies, but with much greater propriety you will side with those who, though having no title of relationship, yet showed themselves, when the deceased was in misfortune, more nearly akin than the nearest relatives.

My opponents say that they do not doubt that Thrasylochus left the will, but they assert that it is not honourable and proper. And yet, citizens of Aegina, how could anyone have given better or greater evidence of interest in the disposal of his own property ? He did not leave his home without heirs and he has shown due gratitude to his friends and, further, he made his mother and his sister possessors, not only of their own property, but of mine also by giving the latter to me as wife and by making me, by adoption, the son of the former. Would he have acted more wisely if he had taken the alternative course—if he had failed to appoint a protector for his mother, and if he had made no mention of me, but had abandoned his sister to chance and permitted the name of his family to perish ?

36 Ἀλλὰ γὰρ ἴσως ἀνάξιος ἦν υἱὸς εἰσποιηθῆναι Θρασυλόχῳ καὶ λαβεῖν αὐτοῦ τὴν ἀδελφήν. ἀλλὰ πάντες ἂν μαρτυρήσειαν Σίφνιοι τοὺς προγόνους τοὺς ἐμοὺς καὶ γένει καὶ πλούτῳ καὶ δόξῃ καὶ τοῖς ἄλλοις ἅπασι πρώτους εἶναι τῶν πολιτῶν. τίνες γὰρ ἢ μειζόνων ἀρχῶν ἠξιώθησαν ἢ πλείω χρήματ' εἰσήνεγκαν ἢ κάλλιον ἐχορήγησαν ἢ μεγαλοπρεπέστερον τὰς ἄλλας λῃτουργίας ἐλῃτούργησαν; ἐκ ποίας δ' οἰκίας τῶν ἐν Σίφνῳ πλείους βασιλεῖς

37 γεγόνασιν; ὥστε Θρασύλοχός τ' εἰ καὶ μηδὲ πώποτ' αὐτῷ διελέχθην, εἰκότως ἂν ἠβουλήθη μοι διὰ ταῦτα δοῦναι τὴν ἀδελφήν, ἐγώ τ' εἰ καὶ μηδέν μοι τούτων ὑπῆρχεν, ἀλλὰ φαυλότατος ἦν τῶν πολιτῶν, δικαίως ἂν παρ' αὐτοῦ διὰ τὰς εὐεργεσίας

[392] τὰς εἰς ἐκεῖνον τῶν μεγίστων ἠξιώθην.

38 Οἶμαι τοίνυν αὐτὸν καὶ Σωπόλιδι τἀδελφῷ μάλιστα κεχαρίσθαι ταῦτα διαθέμενον. καὶ γὰρ ἐκεῖνος ταύτην μὲν ἐμίσει καὶ κακόνουν τοῖς αὑτοῦ πράγμασιν ἡγεῖτο, ἐμὲ δὲ περὶ πλείστου τῶν αὑτοῦ φίλων ἐποιεῖτο. ἐδήλωσε δ' ἐν ἄλλοις τε πολλοῖς καὶ ὅτ' ἔδοξε τοῖς συμφυγάσιν ἐπιχειρεῖν τῇ πόλει μετὰ τῶν ἐπικούρων. αἱρεθεὶς γὰρ ἄρχειν αὐτοκράτωρ ἐμὲ καὶ γραμματέα προσείλετο καὶ τῶν χρημάτων ταμίαν ἁπάντων κατέστησε, καὶ ὅτ' ἠμέλλομεν κινδυνεύειν, αὐτὸς αὑτῷ με παρετάξατο.

39 καὶ σκέψασθ' ὡς σφόδρ' αὐτῷ συνήνεγκεν· δυστυχησάντων γὰρ ἡμῶν ἐν τῇ προσβολῇ τῇ πρὸς τὴν

---

[a] A *choregus* was a citizen who defrayed the expenses of bringing out a chorus. It is of interest to learn that the institution of the *choregia* was in effect on the island of Siphnos, as it was also at Ceos.

320

But perhaps I was unworthy of being adopted as a son by Thrasylochus and of receiving his sister in marriage. All the Siphnians would bear witness, however, that my ancestors were foremost of the citizens there in birth, in wealth, in reputation, and in general standing. For who were thought worthy of higher offices, or made greater contributions, or served as choregi [a] more handsomely, or discharged the other special public services with greater magnificence ? What family in Siphnos has furnished more kings ? [b] Thrasylochus, therefore, even if I had never spoken to him, would reasonably have wished to give his sister to me just for these reasons ; and I, even if I had not possessed any of these advantages, but had been the lowest of the citizens, would justly have been esteemed by him as deserving of the greatest recompenses by reason of the services I had rendered him.

I believe, moreover, that in making this disposition of his estate he did what was most pleasing to his brother Sopolis also. For Sopolis also hated this woman and regarded her as ill-disposed toward his interests, whereas he valued me above all his friends. He showed this feeling for me in many ways and in particular when our companions in exile determined, with the help of their auxiliary troops, to capture the city. For when he was designated leader with full powers he both chose me as secretary and appointed me treasurer of all funds, and when we were about to engage in battle, he placed me next to himself. And consider how greatly he profited thereby ; for when our attack on the city met with ill success,

---

[b] These " kings " probably had only religious functions ; cf. the Archon Basileus at Athens.

πόλιν καὶ τῆς ἀναχωρήσεως οὐχ οἵας ἠβουλόμεθα
γενομένης, τετρωμένον αὐτὸν καὶ βαδίζειν οὐ
δυνάμενον ἀλλ᾿ ὀλιγοψυχοῦντα ἀπεκόμισ᾿ ἐπὶ τὸ
πλοῖον μετὰ τοῦ θεράποντος τοὐμαυτοῦ, φέρων ἐπὶ
τῶν ὤμων, ὥστ᾿ ἐκεῖνον πολλάκις καὶ πρὸς πολλοὺς εἰπεῖν ὅτι μόνος ἀνθρώπων αἴτιος εἴην αὐτῷ
40 τῆς σωτηρίας. καίτοι τίς ἂν μείζων ταύτης εὐερ-
γεσία γένοιτο; ἐπειδὴ τοίνυν εἰς Λυκίαν ἐκπλεύσας
ἀπέθανεν, αὕτη μὲν οὐ πολλαῖς ἡμέραις ὕστερον
μετὰ τὴν ἀγγελίαν ἔθυε καὶ ἑώρταζε καὶ οὐδὲ τὸν
ἀδελφὸν ᾐσχύνετο τὸν ἔτι ζῶντα, οὕτως ὀλίγον
φροντίζουσα τοῦ τεθνεῶτος, ἐγὼ δ᾿ ἐπένθησ᾿ αὐτόν,
41 ὥσπερ τοὺς οἰκείους νόμος ἐστίν. καὶ ταῦτα πάντ᾿
ἐποίουν διὰ τὸν τρόπον τὸν ἐμαυτοῦ καὶ τὴν φιλίαν
τὴν πρὸς ἐκείνους ἀλλ᾿ οὐ ταυτησὶ τῆς δίκης ἕνεκα·
οὐ γὰρ ᾤμην αὐτοὺς οὕτω δυστυχήσειν ὥστ᾿
ἄπαιδας ἀμφοτέρους τελευτήσαντας εἰς ἔλεγχον
καταστήσειν, ὁποῖός τις ἕκαστος ἡμῶν περὶ αὐτοὺς
ἐγένετο.

42 Πρὸς μὲν οὖν Θρασύλοχόν τε καὶ Σώπολιν ὡς
αὕτη τε κἀγὼ διεκείμεθα, σχεδὸν ἀκηκόατε· τρέψ-
ονται δ᾿ ἴσως ἐπ᾿ ἐκεῖνον τὸν λόγον ὅσπερ αὐτοῖς
λοιπός ἐστιν, ὡς Θράσυλλος ὁ πατὴρ ὁ ταύτης
ἡγοῖτ᾿ ἂν δεινὰ πάσχειν, εἴ τίς ἐστιν αἴσθησις τοῖς
τεθνεῶσι περὶ τῶν ἐνθάδε γιγνομένων, ὁρῶν τὴν
μὲν θυγατέρ᾿ ἀποστερουμένην τῶν χρημάτων, ἐμὲ
δὲ κληρονόμον ὧν αὐτὸς ἐκτήσατο γιγνόμενον.
43 ἐγὼ δ᾿ ἡγοῦμαι μὲν οὐ περὶ τῶν πάλαι τεθνεώτων,
[393] ἀλλὰ περὶ τῶν ἔναγχος τὸν κλῆρον καταλιπόντων

---

[a] A frequent sentiment in Greek literature ; cf. Isocrates,
Plat. 61 and *Evag.* 2.

and the retreat did not succeed as we desired, and
when he was wounded, unable to walk and in a faint-
ing condition, I and my servant carried him off on our
shoulders to the ship. Consequently he often said
to many persons that I was solely responsible for his
coming through alive. Yet what greater benefaction
than this could a man receive? Moreover, when he
had sailed to Lycia and died there, this woman, a
few days after the news of his death, was sacrificing
and holding festival, and had no shame before his
surviving brother, so little regard did she have for
the dead man, but I instituted mourning for him
in the custom prescribed for relatives. And it was
my character and my affection for the two brothers
that moved me to do all this and not any expectation of this trial; for I did not think that both
would come to such an unhappy end that by dying
without children they were going to oblige us to
prove how each one of us had felt and acted toward
them.

How this woman and myself conducted ourselves
toward Thrasylochus and Sopolis you have, in the
main, heard; but perhaps they will have recourse
to the one argument which remains to them—that
Thrasyllus, the father of this woman, will feel that
he is being dishonoured (if the dead have any perception of happenings in this world) [a] when he sees
his daughter being deprived of her fortune and me
becoming the heir of what he had acquired.[b] But
I am of opinion that it is proper for us to speak here,
not concerning those who died long ago, but of those

[b] This passage is interesting as an example of an orator's
anticipation (*anticipatio* or προκατάληψις) of an opponent's
argument.

προσήκειν ἡμῖν τοὺς λόγους ποιεῖσθαι. Θράσυλλος
μὲν γάρ, οὗσπερ ἠβούλετο, τούτους κυρίους τῶν
αὑτοῦ κατέλιπεν· δίκαιον δὲ καὶ Θρασυλόχῳ ταὐτὰ
ταῦτ' ἀποδοθῆναι παρ' ὑμῶν, καὶ γενέσθαι δια-
δόχους τῆς κληρονομίας μὴ ταύτην, ἀλλ' οἷς ἐκεῖνος
διέθετο· οὐ μέντ' ἄν μοι δοκῶ φυγεῖν οὐδὲ τὴν
44 Θρασύλλου γνώμην. οἶμαι γὰρ ἂν αὐτὸν πάντων
γενέσθαι ταύτῃ χαλεπώτατον δικαστήν, εἴπερ αἴσ-
θοιτο, οἷα περὶ τοὺς παῖδας αὐτοῦ γεγένηται. πολλοῦ γ' ἂν δεήσειεν ἀχθεσθῆναι κατὰ τοὺς νόμους
ὑμῶν ψηφισαμένων, ἀλλὰ πολὺ ἂν μᾶλλον, εἰ τὰς
τῶν παίδων διαθήκας ἀκύρους ἴδοι γενομένας. καὶ
γὰρ εἰ μὲν εἰς τὸν οἶκον τὸν ἐμὸν δεδωκὼς ἦν
Θρασύλοχος τὴν οὐσίαν, τοῦτ' ἂν ἐπιτιμᾶν εἶχον
αὐτῷ· νῦν δ' εἰς τὸν αὑτῶν μ'[1] εἰσεποιήσατο, ὥστ'
οὐκ ἐλάττω τυγχάνουσιν εἰληφότες ὧν δεδώκασιν.
45 χωρὶς δὲ τούτων, οὐδένα μᾶλλον εἰκός ἐστιν ἢ
Θράσυλλον εὔνουν εἶναι τοῖς κατὰ δόσιν ἀμφισβη-
τοῦσιν· καὶ γὰρ αὐτὸς καὶ τὴν τέχνην ἔμαθε παρὰ
Πολεμαινέτου τοῦ μάντεως καὶ τὰ χρήματ' ἔλαβεν
οὐ κατὰ γένος ἀλλὰ δι' ἀρετήν, ὥστ' οὐκ ἂν δήπου
φθονήσειεν, εἴ τις περὶ τοὺς παῖδας αὐτοῦ χρηστὸς
γενόμενος τῆς αὐτῆς δωρεᾶς ἧσπερ ἐκεῖνος ἠξιώθη.
46 μεμνῆσθαι δὲ χρὴ καὶ τῶν ἐν ἀρχῇ ῥηθέντων.
ἐπέδειξα γὰρ ὑμῖν αὐτὸν οὕτω περὶ πολλοῦ τὴν
ἡμετέραν οἰκειότητα ποιησάμενον ὥστε γῆμαι καὶ
τὴν ἀδελφὴν τὴν τοῦ πατρὸς καὶ τὴν ἀνεψιάν.
καίτοι τίσιν ἂν θᾶττον τὴν αὑτοῦ θυγατέρ' ἐξέδωκεν

___

[1] μ' after αὑτῶν added by Blass.

___

[a] i.e., all the property has been kept in the family since

who recently left their heritage. As to Thrasyllus, he left as possessors of his estate the persons of his choice; and it is only just, then, that to Thrasylochus also the same privilege should be granted by you, and that not this woman, but those whom he designated in his will, should become the successors to the inheritance. However, I do not believe that I need evade the judgement of Thrasyllus. He would be, I think, the most harsh judge of all for her, if he knows how she has treated his children. If you should vote in accordance with the laws, he would be far from taking offence, but he would be far more incensed if he should see the testaments of his children annulled. If, for instance, Thrasylochus had given his property to my family, they would have had reason to lay that up against him; as it is, he adopted me into his own family, so that the plaintiffs have not received less than they gave.[a] Apart from this, it is reasonable to suppose that Thrasyllus, more than anyone else, was friendly toward those whose claims are based upon a testamentary gift. For he himself learned his art from Polemaenetus the soothsayer, and received his fortune, not through family relationship but through merit; surely, therefore, he would not complain if a man who had acted honourably toward his children should be regarded as deserving of the same reward as himself. You should call to mind also what I said in the beginning. For I pointed out to you that he esteemed relationship with our family so highly that he married the sister and then the cousin of my father. And yet to whom would he more willingly have given his own daughter in marriage than

the continuity of the family had been assured by the adoption of the speaker.

325

ἢ τούτοις παρ' ὧνπερ αὐτὸς λαμβάνειν ἠξίωσεν; ἐκ
ποίας δ' ἂν οἰκίας ἥδιον εἶδεν υἱὸν αὑτῷ κατὰ τοὺς
νόμους εἰσποιηθέντα μᾶλλον ἢ ταύτης, ἐξ ἧσπερ
καὶ φύσει παῖδας ἐζήτησεν αὑτῷ γενέσθαι;

47 Ὥστ' ἂν μὲν ἐμοὶ ψηφίσησθε τὸν κλῆρον, καὶ
πρὸς ἐκεῖνον ὑμῖν καλῶς ἕξει καὶ πρὸς τοὺς ἄλλους ἅπαντας οἷς προσήκει τι τούτων τῶν πραγ-
μάτων· ἂν δ' ὑπὸ ταύτης πεισθέντες ἐξαπατηθῆτε,
οὐ μόνον ἔμ' ἀδικήσετε ἀλλὰ καὶ Θρασύλοχον
[394] τὸν τὴν διαθήκην καταλιπόντα καὶ Σώπολιν καὶ
τὴν ἀδελφὴν τὴν ἐκείνων, ἣ νῦν ἐμοὶ συνοικεῖ, καὶ
τὴν μητέρ' αὐτῶν, ἣ πασῶν ἂν εἴη δυστυχεστάτη
γυναικῶν, εἰ μὴ μόνον ἐξαρκέσειεν αὐτῇ στέρε-
σθαι τῶν παίδων, ἀλλὰ καὶ τοῦτ' αὐτῇ προσγένοιτο,
ὥστ' ἐπιδεῖν ἄκυρον μὲν τὴν ἐκείνων γνώμην οὖσαν,

48 ἔρημον δὲ τὸν οἶκον γιγνόμενον, καὶ τὴν μὲν ἐπι-
χαίρουσαν τοῖς αὑτῆς κακοῖς ἐπιδικαζομένην τῶν
χρημάτων, ἐμὲ δὲ μηδενὸς δυνάμενον τῶν δικαίων
τυχεῖν, ὃς τοιαῦτ' ἔπραξα περὶ τοὺς ἐκείνης, ὥστ'
εἴ τίς με σκοποῖτο μὴ πρὸς ταύτην ἀλλὰ πρὸς τοὺς
πώποτε κατὰ δόσιν ἀμφισβητήσαντας, εὑρεθείην ἂν
οὐδενὸς χείρων αὐτῶν περὶ τοὺς φίλους γεγενημένος. καίτοι χρὴ τοὺς τοιούτους τιμᾶν καὶ περὶ
πολλοῦ ποιεῖσθαι πολὺ μᾶλλον ἢ τὰς ὑφ' ἑτέρων

49 δεδομένας δωρεὰς ἀφαιρεῖσθαι. ἄξιον δ' ἐστὶ καὶ
τῷ νόμῳ βοηθεῖν καθ' ὃν ἔξεστιν ἡμῖν καὶ παῖδας
εἰσποιήσασθαι καὶ βουλεύσασθαι περὶ τῶν ἡμετέρων αὐτῶν, ἐνθυμηθέντας ὅτι τοῖς ἐρήμοις τῶν
ἀνθρώπων ἀντὶ παίδων οὗτός ἐστιν· διὰ γὰρ τοῦτον
καὶ οἱ συγγενεῖς καὶ οἱ μηδὲν προσήκοντες μᾶλλον
ἀλλήλων ἐπιμελοῦνται.

50 Ἵνα δὲ παύσωμαι λέγων καὶ μηκέτι πλείω χρό-

to that family from which he himself chose his wife?
And from what family would he have more gladly
seen a son adopted according to law than that from
which he sought to beget children of his own body?

If, therefore, you award the inheritance to me,
you will stand well with Thrasyllus and with all
others who have any proper interest in this matter;
but if you permit yourselves to be deceived by the
persuasion of this woman, not only will you do injury
to me, but also to Thrasylochus, the testator, and to
Sopolis, and to their sister, who is now my wife,
and their mother, who would be the unhappiest of
women if it should not be enough for her to have
lost her children, but also must see this additional
sorrow, that their wishes are nullified, her family
left without an heir, and this woman, as she exults
over her misfortunes, making good at law her claim
to the property, while I am unable to obtain my just
rights, although my treatment of her sons has been
such that, if anyone should compare me—I will not
say with this woman, but with any who have ever
entered their claim to an inheritance on the strength of
a testamentary gift—I should be found to have been
inferior to none in my conduct toward my friends.
And yet men of my kind ought to be honoured and
esteemed rather than be robbed of the gifts which
others have bestowed upon them. It is expedient,
too, that you should uphold the law which permits
us to adopt children and to dispose wisely of our
property, reflecting that for men who are childless
this law takes the place of children; for it is owing
to this law that both kinsmen and those who are not
related take greater care of each other.

But that I may conclude and occupy no more time

νον διατρίβω, σκέψασθ' ὡς μεγάλα καὶ δίκαι' ἥκω
πρὸς ὑμᾶς ἔχων, πρῶτον μὲν φιλίαν πρὸς τοὺς
καταλιπόντας τὸν κλῆρον παλαιὰν καὶ πατρικὴν καὶ
πάντα τὸν χρόνον διατελέσασαν, ἔπειτ' εὐεργεσίας
πολλὰς καὶ μεγάλας καὶ περὶ δυστυχοῦντας ἐκείνους γεγενημένας, πρὸς δὲ τούτοις διαθήκας παρ'
αὐτῶν τῶν ἀντιδίκων ὁμολογουμένας, ἔτι δὲ νόμον
ταύταις βοηθοῦντα, ὃς δοκεῖ τοῖς Ἕλλησιν ἅπασι
51 καλῶς κεῖσθαι. τεκμήριον δὲ μέγιστον· περὶ γὰρ
ἄλλων πολλῶν διαφερόμενοι περὶ τούτου ταὐτὰ γιγνώσκουσιν. δέομαι οὖν ὑμῶν καὶ τούτων μεμνημένους καὶ τῶν ἄλλων τῶν εἰρημένων τὰ δίκαια
ψηφίσασθαι, καὶ τοιούτους μοι γενέσθαι δικαστάς,
οἵων περ ἂν αὐτοὶ τυχεῖν ἀξιώσαιτε.

in speaking, pray consider how strong and how just
are the claims with which I have come before you ;
there is, first, my friendship with those who have
left the inheritance, a friendship of ancient origin,
handed down from our fathers, and in all that time
never broken ; second, my many great acts of kindness done for them in their adversity ; third, there
is a will which my opponents themselves acknowledge ; and lastly, the law, which supports the will,
a law that in the opinion of all Greeks is regarded
as wisely made. Of my statement the best proof
is this—although the Greek states differ in opinion
about many other enactments, they are of one accord
concerning this one. I beg you, therefore, bearing
in mind both these considerations and the others I
have mentioned, to give a just verdict, and prove
yourselves to be for me such judges as you would
want to have for yourselves.

XX. AGAINST LOCHITES

INTRODUCTION

THE law-suit which evoked this speech is an Action for Assault. The plaintiff, who calls himself " a poor man and one of the people " (§ 19), brings suit for heavy damages (§ 16) against a rich young citizen named Lochites, who had struck him.

The beginning of the speech, in which presumably there would have been a presentation of the facts in the case and a citation of the testimony of witnesses, seems to be lacking. What we possess is a cleverly developed and amplified plea (αὔξησις). The speaker builds up, from a rather unimportant personal indignity (αἰκία), a case of wanton outrage (ὕβρις), or assault and battery, against the young aristocrat. Isocrates furnishes the speaker with a strong appeal to the judges emphasizing the necessity of restraining and punishing violence, especially under the rule of the democracy. The insolence of the aggressor is identified with the spirit and attitude of those oligarchs who twice overthrew the democracy.

The approximate date ^a of the speech is ascertainable from internal evidence. In § 11 the accused is said to have been " too young to have belonged to the oligarchy established at that time " (404–403 B.C.). There is also in the same section a reference to the destruction of the walls of Athens which were razed in 404 B.C. and not rebuilt until 393 B.C.

ᵃ Blass sets the date as soon after Eucleides (see *Die attische Beredsamkeit* ii. p. 217). For a discussion of the discourse see Jebb, *Attic Orators* ii. pp. 215-217.

20. ΚΑΤΑ ΛΟΧΙΤΟΥ

. . . . .

[395] Ὡς μὲν τοίνυν ἔτυπτέ με Λοχίτης, ἄρχων χειρῶν ἀδίκων, ἅπαντες ὑμῖν οἱ παρόντες μεμαρτυρήκασιν. τὸ δ' ἁμάρτημα τοῦθ' οὐχ ὅμοιον δεῖ νομίζειν τοῖς ἄλλοις οὐδὲ τὰς τιμωρίας ἴσας ποιεῖσθαι περί τε τοῦ σώματος καὶ τῶν χρημάτων, ἐπισταμένους ὅτι τοῦτο πᾶσιν ἀνθρώποις οἰκειότατόν ἐστι, καὶ τούς τε νόμους ἐθέμεθα καὶ περὶ τῆς ἐλευθερίας μαχόμεθα καὶ τῆς δημοκρατίας ἐπιθυμοῦμεν καὶ τἆλλα πάντα τὰ περὶ τὸν βίον ἕνεκα τούτου πράττομεν. ὥστ' εἰκὸς ὑμᾶς ἐστι τοὺς περὶ τοῦτ' ἐξαμαρτάνοντας, ὃ περὶ πλείστου ποιεῖσθε, τῇ μεγίστῃ ζημίᾳ κολάζειν.

2   Εὑρήσετε δὲ καὶ τοὺς θέντας ἡμῖν τοὺς νόμους ὑπὲρ τῶν σωμάτων μάλιστα σπουδάσαντας. πρῶτον μὲν γὰρ περὶ μόνου τούτου τῶν ἀδικημάτων καὶ δίκας καὶ γραφὰς ἄνευ παρακαταβολῆς ἐποίησαν, ἵν' ὅπως ἂν ἕκαστος ἡμῶν τυγχάνῃ καὶ δυνά-

---

ᵃ The court-deposit refers to money deposited in court by a claimant and forfeited by him in case of failure to establish his claim.

XX. AGAINST LOCHITES

(The first part of the speech is lacking ; see Introduction)

. . . . .

Well then, that Lochites struck me and was the aggressor all who were present when the event occurred have testified to you. But this offence should not be regarded as similar to other breaches of the law, nor should the penalty imposed for injury to the person be no greater than that which is inflicted for cheating a man of money ; for you know that one's person is of nearest concern to all men, and that it is for the protection of the person that we have established laws, that we fight for freedom, that we have our hearts set on the democratic form of government, and that all the activities of our lives are directed to this end. And so it is reasonable to expect you to punish with the greatest severity those who do wrong to you in respect to that which you prize most dearly.

You will find that our legislators also have had the greatest concern for our persons. For, in the first place, it is for this one kind of misdemeanour only that they have instituted public and private actions that require no preliminary court-deposit,[a] with the intent that each of us, according to what may

μενος καὶ βουλόμενος, οὕτως ἔχῃ τιμωρεῖσθαι τοὺς
ἀδικοῦντας. ἔπειτα τῶν μὲν ἄλλων ἐγκλημάτων
αὐτῷ τῷ παθόντι μόνον ὁ δράσας ὑπόδικός ἐστιν·
[396] περὶ δὲ τῆς ὕβρεως, ὡς κοινοῦ τοῦ πράγματος
ὄντος, ἔξεστι τῷ βουλομένῳ τῶν πολιτῶν γραψα-
μένῳ πρὸς τοὺς θεσμοθέτας εἰσελθεῖν εἰς ὑμᾶς.
3 οὕτω δ᾽ ἡγήσαντο δεινὸν εἶναι τὸ τύπτειν ἀλλήλους, ὥστε καὶ περὶ τῆς κακηγορίας νόμον ἔθεσαν
ὃς κελεύει τοὺς λέγοντάς τι τῶν ἀπορρήτων πεν-
τακοσίας δραχμὰς ὀφείλειν. καίτοι πηλίκας τινὰς
χρὴ ποιεῖσθαι τὰς τιμωρίας ὑπὲρ τῶν ἔργῳ παθόν-
των κακῶς, ὅταν ὑπὲρ τῶν λόγῳ μόνον ἀκηκοότων
οὕτως ὀργιζόμενοι φαίνησθε;

4 Θαυμαστὸν δ᾽ εἰ τοὺς μὲν ἐπὶ τῆς ὀλιγαρχίας
ὑβρίσαντας ἀξίους θανάτου νομίζετε, τοὺς δ᾽ ἐν
δημοκρατίᾳ ταῦτ᾽ ἐκείνοις ἐπιτηδεύοντας ἀζημίους
ἀφήσετε. καίτοι δικαίως ἂν μείζονος οὗτοι τιμωρίας τυγχάνοιεν· φανερώτερον γὰρ ἐπιδείκνυνται
τὴν αὐτῶν πονηρίαν. ὅστις γὰρ νῦν τολμᾷ παρα-
νομεῖν, ὅτ᾽ οὐκ ἔξεστι, τί ποτ᾽ ἂν ἐποίησεν, ὅθ᾽
οἱ κρατοῦντες τῆς πόλεως καὶ χάριν εἶχον τοῖς τὰ
τοιαῦτ᾽ ἐξαμαρτάνουσιν;

5 Ἴσως οὖν Λοχίτης ἐπιχειρήσει μικρὸν ποιεῖν τὸ
πρᾶγμα, διασύρων τὴν κατηγορίαν καὶ λέγων ὡς
οὐδὲν ἐκ τῶν πληγῶν κακὸν ἔπαθον, ἀλλὰ μείζους
ποιοῦμαι τοὺς λόγους ἢ κατὰ τὴν ἀξίαν τῶν γεγενημένων. ἐγὼ δ᾽ εἰ μὲν μηδεμία προσῆν ὕβρις τοῖς

ᵃ The Thesmothetes were the six junior archons. They
had jurisdiction over many offences against the state.
336

happen to be within his power and agreeable to his wish, may be able to exact punishment from those who wrong him. In the next place, in the case of other charges, the culprit may be prosecuted by the injured party only ; but where assault and battery is involved, as the public interest is affected, any citizen who so desires may give notice of a public suit to the Thesmothetes [a] and appear before your court. And our lawgivers regarded the giving of blows as an offence of such gravity that even for abusive language they made a law to the effect that those who used any of the forbidden opprobrious terms should pay a fine of five hundred drachmas. And yet how severe should the penalty be on behalf of those who have actually suffered bodily injury, when you show yourselves so angry for the protection of those who have merely suffered verbal injury ?

It would be astonishing if, while you judge to be worthy of death those who were guilty of battery under the oligarchy, you shall allow to go unpunished those who, under the democracy, are guilty of the same practices. And yet the latter would justly meet with a more severe punishment ; for they reveal more conspicuously their real baseness. This is what I mean : if anyone has the effrontery to transgress the law now, when it is not permissible, what would he have done, I ask you, when the government in power actually was grateful to such malefactors ?

It may be that Lochites will attempt to belittle the importance of the affair, and ridiculing my accusation will say that I suffered no injury from his blows and that I am unduly exaggerating the gravity of what occurred. My reply to this is, that if no assault and battery had been connected with the affair, I

πεπραγμένοις, οὐκ ἄν ποτ᾽ εἰσῆλθον εἰς ὑμᾶς· νῦν
δ᾽ οὐχ ὑπὲρ τῆς ἄλλης βλάβης τῆς ἐκ τῶν πληγῶν
γενομένης, ἀλλ᾽ ὑπὲρ τῆς αἰκίας καὶ τῆς ἀτιμίας
6 ἥκω παρ᾽ αὐτοῦ δίκην ληψόμενος, ὑπὲρ ὧν προσήκει τοῖς ἐλευθέροις μάλιστ᾽ ὀργίζεσθαι καὶ
μεγίστης τυγχάνειν τιμωρίας. ὁρῶ δ᾽ ὑμᾶς, ὅταν
του καταγνῶθ᾽ ἱεροσυλίαν ἢ κλοπήν, οὐ πρὸς τὸ μέγεθος ὧν ἂν λάβωσι τὴν τίμησιν ποιουμένους,
ἀλλ᾽ ὁμοίως ἁπάντων θάνατον καταγιγνώσκοντας,
καὶ νομίζοντας δίκαιον εἶναι τοὺς τοῖς αὐτοῖς ἔργοις ἐπιχειροῦντας ταῖς αὐταῖς ζημίαις κολάζεσθαι.
7 χρὴ τοίνυν καὶ περὶ τῶν ὑβριζόντων τὴν αὐτὴν
γνώμην ἔχειν, καὶ μὴ τοῦτο σκοπεῖν, εἰ μὴ σφόδρα
συνέκοψαν, ἀλλ᾽ εἰ τὸν νόμον παρέβησαν, μηδ᾽
ὑπὲρ τοῦ συντυχόντος μόνον ἀλλ᾽ ὑπὲρ ἅπαντος τοῦ
τρόπου δίκην παρ᾽ αὐτῶν λαμβάνειν, ἐνθυμουμέ-
8 νους ὅτι πολλάκις ἤδη μικραὶ προφάσεις μεγάλων
[397] κακῶν αἴτιαι γεγόνασι, καὶ διότι διὰ τοὺς τύπτειν
τολμῶντας εἰς τοῦτ᾽ ἤδη τινὲς ὀργῆς προήχθησαν
ὥστ᾽ εἰς τραύματα καὶ θανάτους καὶ φυγὰς καὶ
τὰς μεγίστας συμφορὰς ἐλθεῖν· ὧν οὐδὲν διὰ τὸν
φεύγοντα τὴν δίκην ἀγένητόν ἐστιν, ἀλλὰ κατὰ μὲν
τὸ τούτου μέρος ἅπαντα πέπρακται, διὰ δὲ τὴν
τύχην καὶ τὸν τρόπον τὸν ἐμὸν οὐδὲν τῶν ἀνηκέστων συμβέβηκεν.
9 Ἡγοῦμαι δ᾽ ὑμᾶς οὕτως ἂν ἀξίως ὀργισθῆναι
τοῦ πράγματος, εἰ διεξέλθοιτε πρὸς ὑμᾶς αὐτοὺς
ὅσῳ μεῖζόν ἐστι τοῦτο τῶν ἄλλων ἁμαρτημάτων.
εὑρήσετε γὰρ τὰς μὲν ἄλλας ἀδικίας μέρος τι τοῦ

ᵃ For the same argument cf. Lycurgus, *Against Leocrates*
65-66.

should never have come before you ; but as it is, it is not because of the mere injury inflicted by his blows that I am seeking satisfaction from him, but for the humiliation and the indignity ; and it is that sort of thing which free men should especially resent and for which they should obtain the greatest requital. I observe that you, when you find anyone guilty of the robbery of a temple or of theft, do not assess the fine according to the value of what is stolen, but that you condemn all alike to death, and that you consider it just that those who attempt to commit the same crimes should pay the same penalty.[a] You should, therefore, be of the same mind with respect to those who commit battery, and not consider whether they did not maul their victims thoroughly, but whether they transgressed the law, and you should punish them, not merely for the chance outcome of the attack, but for their character as a whole, reflecting that often ere now petty causes have been responsible for great evils, and that, because there are persons who have the effrontery to beat others, there have been cases where men have become so enraged that wounds, death, exile, and the greatest calamities have resulted. That no one of these consequences happened in my case is not due to the defendant ; on the contrary, so far as he is concerned they have all taken place, and it was only by the grace of fortune and my character that no irreparable harm has been done.

I think that you would be as indignant as the circumstances merit if you should reflect how much more reprehensible this misdemeanour is than any others. For you will find that while the other unjust acts impair life only partially, malicious

βίου βλαπτούσας, τὴν δ' ὕβριν ὅλοις τοῖς πράγμασι
λυμαινομένην, καὶ πολλοὺς μὲν οἴκους δι' αὐτὴν
διαφθαρέντας, πολλὰς δὲ πόλεις ἀναστάτους γεγε-
10 νημένας. καὶ τί δεῖ τὰς τῶν ἄλλων συμφορὰς
λέγοντα διατρίβειν; αὐτοὶ γὰρ ἡμεῖς δὶς ἤδη τὴν
δημοκρατίαν ἐπείδομεν καταλυθεῖσαν καὶ δὶς τῆς
ἐλευθερίας ἀπεστερήθημεν, οὐχ ὑπὸ τῶν ταῖς ἄλλαις
πονηρίαις ἐνόχων ὄντων, ἀλλὰ διὰ τοὺς κατα-
φρονοῦντας τῶν νόμων καὶ βουλομένους τοῖς μὲν
11 πολεμίοις δουλεύειν, τοὺς δὲ πολίτας ὑβρίζειν. ὧν
οὗτος εἷς ὢν τυγχάνει. καὶ γὰρ εἰ τῶν τότε κατα-
σταθέντων νεώτερός ἐστιν, ἀλλὰ τόν γε τρόπον ἔχει
τὸν ἐξ ἐκείνης τῆς πολιτείας. αὗται γὰρ αἱ φύσεις
εἰσὶν αἱ παραδοῦσαι μὲν τὴν δύναμιν τὴν ἡμετέραν
τοῖς πολεμίοις, κατασκάψασαι δὲ τὰ τείχη τῆς
πατρίδος, πεντακοσίους δὲ καὶ χιλίους ἀκρίτους
ἀποκτείνασαι τῶν πολιτῶν.

12 Ὧν εἰκὸς ὑμᾶς μεμνημένους τιμωρεῖσθαι μὴ
μόνον τοὺς τότε λυμηναμένους ἀλλὰ καὶ τοὺς νῦν
βουλομένους οὕτω διαθεῖναι τὴν πόλιν, καὶ τοσούτῳ
μᾶλλον τοὺς ἐπιδόξους γενήσεσθαι πονηροὺς τῶν
πρότερον ἡμαρτηκότων, ὅσῳ περ κρεῖττόν ἐστι τῶν
μελλόντων κακῶν ἀποτροπὴν εὑρεῖν ἢ τῶν ἤδη
13 γεγενημένων δίκην λαβεῖν. καὶ μὴ περιμείνηθ'
ἕως ἂν ἀθροισθέντες καὶ καιρὸν λαβόντες εἰς ὅλην
τὴν πόλιν ἐξαμάρτωσιν, ἀλλ' ἐφ' ἧς ἂν ὑμῖν προφάσεως παραδοθῶσιν, ἐπὶ ταύτης αὐτοὺς τιμω-
ρεῖσθε, νομίζοντες εὕρημ' ἔχειν, ὅταν τινὰ λάβητ'
ἐν μικροῖς πράγμασιν ἐπιδεδειγμένον ἅπασαν τὴν

---

^a In 411 B.C., by the régime of the Four Hundred, and in
340

assault vitiates all our concerns, since it has destroyed many households and rendered desolate many cities. And yet why need I waste time in speaking of the calamities of the other states ? For we ourselves have twice seen the democracy over-thrown[a] and twice we have been deprived of freedom, not by those who were guilty of other crimes, but by persons who contemned the laws and were willing to be slaves of the enemy while wantonly outraging their fellow-citizens. Lochites is one of these per-sons. For even though he was too young to have belonged to the oligarchy established at that time, yet his character at any rate is in harmony with their régime. For it was men of like disposition who betrayed our power to the enemy, razed the walls of the fatherland, and put to death without a trial fifteen hundred citizens.[b]

We may reasonably expect that you, remembering the past, will punish, not only those who then did us harm, but also those who wish now to bring our city into the same condition as then ; and you should punish potential criminals with greater severity than the malefactors of the past in so far as it is better to find how to avert future evils than to exact the penalty for past misdeeds. Do not wait for the time when these enemies shall unite, seize an opportune moment, and bring ruin upon the whole city, but whenever on any pretext they are delivered into your hands, punish them, thinking it a stroke of luck when you catch a man who in petty derelictions

---

[a] 404 B.C. when the Spartans, after the capture of Athens, established the Thirty Tyrants in power.

[b] Cf. *Areop.* 67, where the same number of victims is given ; cf. also *Panegyr.* 113.

14
[398] αὐτοῦ πονηρίαν. κράτιστον μὲν γὰρ ἦν, εἴ τι προσῆν ἄλλο σημεῖον τοῖς πονηροῖς τῶν ἀνθρώπων, πρὶν ἀδικηθῆναί τινα τῶν πολιτῶν, πρότερον κολάζειν αὐτούς· ἐπειδὴ δ' οὐχ οἷόν τ' ἐστὶν αἰσθέσθαι πρὶν κακῶς τινὰς παθεῖν ὑπ' αὐτῶν, ἀλλ' οὖν γ' ἐπειδὰν γνωρισθῶσι, προσήκει πᾶσι μισεῖν τοὺς τοιούτους καὶ κοινοὺς ἐχθροὺς νομίζειν.

15 Ἐνθυμεῖσθε δ' ὅτι τῶν μὲν περὶ τὰς οὐσίας κινδύνων οὐ μέτεστι τοῖς πένησι, τῆς δ' εἰς τὰ σώματ' αἰκίας ὁμοίως ἅπαντες κοινωνοῦμεν· ὥσθ' ὅταν μὲν τοὺς ἀποστεροῦντας τιμωρῆσθε, τοὺς πλουσίους μόνον ὠφελεῖτε, ὅταν δὲ τοὺς ὑβρίζοντας

16 κολάζητε, ὑμῖν αὐτοῖς βοηθεῖτε. ὧν ἕνεκα δεῖ περὶ πλείστου ποιεῖσθαι ταύτας τῶν δικῶν, καὶ περὶ μὲν τῶν ἄλλων συμβολαίων τοσούτου τιμᾶν, ὅσον προσήκει τῷ διώκοντι κομίσασθαι, περὶ δὲ τῆς ὕβρεως, ὅσον ἀποτείσας ὁ φεύγων παύσεσθαι

17 μέλλει τῆς παρούσης ἀσελγείας. ἂν οὖν περιαιρῆτε τὰς οὐσίας τῶν νεανιευομένων εἰς τοὺς πολίτας καὶ μηδεμίαν νομίζηθ' ἱκανὴν εἶναι ζημίαν, οἵτινες ἂν εἰς τὰ σώματ' ἐξαμαρτάνοντες τοῖς χρήμασι τὰς δίκας ὑπέχωσιν, ἅπανθ' ὅσα δεῖ τοὺς καλῶς

18 δικάζοντας διαπράξεσθε· καὶ γὰρ περὶ τοῦ παρόντος πράγματος ὀρθῶς γνώσεσθε καὶ τοὺς ἄλλους

---

* So also Euripides, *Medea* 516-519 :

  " O Zeus, ah wherefore hast thou given to men
  Plain signs for gold which is but counterfeit,

342

reveals his complete depravity. It would indeed have been best, if only some distinguishing mark were borne by men of base nature,[a] that we might punish them before any fellow-citizen has been injured by them. But since it is impossible to perceive who such men are before a victim has suffered at their hands, at any rate as soon as their character is recognized, it is the duty of all men to hate them and to regard them as enemies of all mankind.

Remember, too, that while the poor have no share in the danger of loss of property, yet fear of injury to our persons is common to all alike ; in consequence, whenever you punish thieves and cheats you benefit only the rich, but whenever you chastise those who commit mayhem, you give aid to yourselves. You should therefore treat trials such as this as of the highest importance ; and while in suits involving private contracts you should assess the plaintiff's damages at only what it is fitting that he should receive, when the case is assault and battery the defendant should be required to pay so large a sum that he will in future refrain from his present unbridled wantonness. If, then, you deprive of their property those who conduct themselves with wanton violence toward their fellow-citizens and regard no fine as severe enough to punish those who do injury to the persons of others and have to pay the penalty with their money, you will then have discharged in full measure the duty of conscientious judges. Indeed in the present case you will thus render the correct

But no assay-mark nature-graven shows
On man's form, to discern the base withal."
(Translation by Way in L.C.L.)

πολίτας κοσμιωτέρους ποιήσετε καὶ τὸν βίον τὸν
ὑμέτερον αὐτῶν ἀσφαλέστερον καταστήσετε. ἔστι
δὲ δικαστῶν νοῦν ἐχόντων περὶ τῶν ἀλλοτρίων τὰ
δίκαια ψηφιζομένους ἅμα καὶ τὰ σφέτερ' αὐτῶν
εὖ τίθεσθαι.

19 Καὶ μηδεὶς ὑμῶν εἰς τοῦτ' ἀποβλέψας, ὅτι πένης
εἰμὶ καὶ τοῦ πλήθους εἷς, ἀξιούτω τοῦ τιμήματος
ἀφαιρεῖν. οὐ γὰρ δίκαιον ἐλάττους ποιεῖσθαι τὰς
τιμωρίας ὑπὲρ τῶν ἀδόξων ἢ τῶν διωνομασμένων,
οὐδὲ χείρους ἡγεῖσθαι τοὺς πενομένους ἢ τοὺς
πολλὰ κεκτημένους. ὑμᾶς γὰρ ἂν αὐτοὺς ἀτιμά-
ζοιτ' εἰ τοιαῦτα γιγνώσκοιτε περὶ τῶν πολλῶν.

20 ἔτι δὲ καὶ πάντων ἂν εἴη δεινότατον, εἰ δημο-
κρατουμένης τῆς πόλεως μὴ τῶν αὐτῶν ἅπαντες
τυγχάνοιμεν, ἀλλὰ τῶν μὲν ἀρχῶν μετέχειν ἀξιοῖ-
μεν, τῶν δ' ἐν τοῖς νόμοις δικαίων ἀποστεροῖμεν
[399] ἡμᾶς αὐτούς, καὶ μαχόμενοι μὲν ἐθέλοιμεν ἀποθνήσκειν ὑπὲρ τῆς πολιτείας, ἐν δὲ τῇ ψήφῳ πλέον

21 νέμοιμεν τοῖς τὰς οὐσίας ἔχουσιν. οὐκ, ἄν γέ μοι
πεισθῆθ', οὕτω διακείσεσθε πρὸς ὑμᾶς αὐτούς,
οὐδὲ διδάξετε τοὺς νεωτέρους καταφρονεῖν τοῦ
πλήθους τῶν πολιτῶν, οὐδὲ ἀλλοτρίους ἡγήσεσθ'
εἶναι τοὺς τοιούτους τῶν ἀγώνων, ἀλλ' ὡς ὑπὲρ
αὑτοῦ δικάζων, οὕτως ἕκαστος ὑμῶν οἴσει τὴν
ψῆφον. ἅπαντας γὰρ ὁμοίως ἀδικοῦσιν οἱ τολμῶντες τοῦτον τὸν νόμον παραβαίνειν τὸν ὑπὲρ τῶν

22 σωμάτων τῶν ὑμετέρων κειμένον. ὥστ' ἂν σωφρονῆτε, παρακαλέσαντες ἀλλήλους ἐνσημανεῖσθε
Λοχίτῃ τὴν ὀργὴν τὴν ὑμετέραν αὐτῶν, εἰδότες ὅτι
πάντες οἱ τοιοῦτοι τῶν μὲν νόμων τῶν κειμένων

judgement, will cause our other citizens to be more decorous in conduct, and will make your own lives more secure. And it is the part of intelligent judges, while casting their votes for justice in causes not their own, at the same time to safeguard their own interests also.

Let no one of you think, just because he observes that I am a poor man and a man of the people, that the amount I claim should be reduced. For it is unjust that you should reckon the indemnification to be given to plaintiffs who are obscure as of less importance than that which men of distinction are to receive, and that the poor be thought inferior to the rich. For you would be lowering your own civic status if you should reach any such decisions where the many are concerned. Besides, it would be a most shocking state of affairs if in a democratic state we should not all enjoy equal rights; and if, while judging ourselves worthy of holding office, yet we should deprive ourselves of our legal rights; and if in battle we should all be willing to die for our democratic form of government and yet, in our votes as judges, especially favour men of property. No, if you will be advised by me, you will not assume that position toward your own selves. You will not teach the young men to have contempt for the mass of our citizens, nor consider that trials of this character are of no concern to you; on the contrary, each one of you will cast his ballot as if he were judging his own case. In truth, those who dare to transgress the law that protects your persons do injury to all alike. And so, if you are wise, exhort one another, and reveal to Lochites your own wrath, for you know that all individuals of his kind despise

καταφρονοῦσι, τὰ δ' ἐνθάδε γιγνωσκόμενα, ταῦτα νόμους εἶναι νομίζουσιν.

Ἐγὼ μὲν οὖν ὡς οἷός τ' ἦν εἴρηκα περὶ τοῦ πράγματος· εἰ δέ τις τῶν παρόντων ἔχει τί μοι συνειπεῖν, ἀναβὰς εἰς ὑμᾶς λεγέτω.

the established laws, but regard as law the decisions rendered here.

I have spoken as well as I could about the matter at issue ; if anyone present has anything to say on my behalf, let him mount the platform and address you.

XXI. AGAINST EUTHYNUS

INTRODUCTION

THE discourse *Against Euthynus*,[a] designated in the manuscripts as a plea " Without Witnesses," is an action brought to recover a deposit (παρακαταθήκης δίκη). The speaker is a friend of a certain Nicias who " was in need, the victim of injustice, and lacking in the ability to plead " (§ 1).

During the rule of the Thirty Tyrants Nicias, because of threats of his enemies, deposited the sum of three talents with the defendant Euthynus. Later, desiring to leave Attica, he asked for the return of his money. Euthynus restored only two talents. At the time Nicias was unable to take any action, except to complain bitterly to friends. After the restoration of the democracy Nicias brought suit.

The date is manifestly soon after the democrats were restored to power, 403 B.C.

The speaker's proof is made difficult because of the lack of witnesses which were customary in cases of deposit entrusted to private individuals.[b] In consequence, the speaker affirms that his case must rest solely on presumptive evidence.

[a] For a discussion of this speech, see Jebb, *Attic Orators* ii. pp. 221-223 and Blass, *Die attische Beredsamkeit* ii. pp. 219 ff. *Cf.* also Mathieu, *Isocrate* i. pp. 3-5.

[b] Witnesses were not used, however, in making deposits with bankers (*cf.* beginning of the *Trapeziticus*).

AGAINST EUTHYNUS

The authenticity of the speech has been suspected, but on insufficient grounds. It is cited by Aristotle (*Rhet.* ii. 19); by Isocrates himself (*Panegyr.* 188); and Diogenes Laertius (vi. 15) mentions an exercise, in reply to this speech of Isocrates, by Antisthenes. Philostratus (*Vit. Soph.* i. 17) gives the discourse high praise. As the speech is a very early example of his forensic oratory, it is not surprising that it does not conform in style and method to the later epideictic compositions of Isocrates.

We have evidence that Lysias wrote a speech for Euthynus in reply to Nicias. This discourse, not extant, was undoubtedly the reply of Euthynus in this case.

21. ΠΡΟΣ ΕΥΘΥΝΟΥΝ ΑΜΑΡΤΥΡΟΣ

[400] Οὐ προφάσεως ἀπορῶ, δι᾽ ἥντινα λέγω ὑπὲρ
Νικίου τουτουί· καὶ γὰρ φίλος ὤν μοι τυγχάνει καὶ
δεόμενος καὶ ἀδικούμενος καὶ ἀδύνατος εἰπεῖν, ὥστε
διὰ ταῦτα πάντα ὑπὲρ αὐτοῦ λέγειν ἀναγκάζομαι.
2 Ὅθεν οὖν τὸ συμβόλαιον αὐτῷ πρὸς Εὐθύνουν
γεγένηται, διηγήσομαι ὑμῖν ὡς ἂν δύνωμαι διὰ
βραχυτάτων. Νικίας γὰρ οὑτοσί, ἐπειδὴ οἱ τριάκοντα κατέστησαν καὶ αὐτὸν οἱ ἐχθροὶ ἐκ μὲν τῶν
μετεχόντων τῆς πολιτείας ἐξήλειφον, εἰς δὲ τὸν
μετὰ Λυσάνδρου κατάλογον ἐνέγραφον, δεδιὼς τὰ
παρόντα πράγματα τὴν μὲν οἰκίαν ὑπέθηκε, τοὺς δ᾽
οἰκέτας ἔξω τῆς γῆς ἐξέπεμψε, τὰ δ᾽ ἔπιπλα ὡς ἐμὲ
ἐκόμισε, τρία δὲ τάλαντα ἀργυρίου Εὐθύνῳ φυλάττειν ἔδωκεν, αὐτὸς δ᾽ εἰς ἀγρὸν ἐλθὼν διῃτᾶτο.
3 οὐ πολλῷ δὲ χρόνῳ ὕστερον βουλόμενος ἐκπλεῖν
ἀπῄτησε τἀργύριον· Εὐθύνους δὲ τὰ μὲν δύο τάλαντα ἀποδίδωσι, τοῦ δὲ τρίτου ἔξαρνος γίγνεται.
ἄλλο μὲν οὖν οὐδὲν εἶχε Νικίας ἐν τῷ τότε χρόνῳ
ποιῆσαι, προσιὼν δὲ πρὸς τοὺς ἐπιτηδείους ἐνεκάλει καὶ ἐμέμφετο καὶ ἔλεγεν ἃ πεπονθὼς εἴη.
καίτοι οὕτω τοῦτόν τε περὶ πολλοῦ ἐποιεῖτο καὶ
τὰ καθεστῶτα ἐφοβεῖτο, ὥστε πολὺ ἂν θᾶττον

---

[a] A list of citizens deprived of civic rights and enrolled
for military service under the Spartan general Lysander,
who after taking Athens had set up the government of the
Thirty. *Cf.* Xenophon, *Hell.* ii. 3.

XXI. AGAINST EUTHYNUS

(A Plea without Witnesses)

I have no lack of reasons for speaking in behalf of the plaintiff Nicias; for it so happens that he is my friend, that he is in need, that he is the victim of injustice, and that he has no ability as a speaker; for all these reasons, therefore, I am compelled to speak on his behalf.

The circumstances in which the transaction between Nicias and Euthynus came to be made I shall relate to you in as few words as I can. This Nicias, the plaintiff, after the Thirty Tyrants came into power and his enemies threatened to expunge his name from the number of those who were to have the rights of citizenship, and to include him in Lysander's *a* list, being in fear of the state of affairs, mortgaged his house, sent his slaves outside of Attica, conveyed his furniture to my house, gave in trust three talents of silver to Euthynus, and went to live in the country. Not long after this, desiring to take ship, he asked for the return of his money; Euthynus restored two talents, but denied that he had received the third. At that time Nicias was unable to take any further action, but he went to his friends and with complaints and recriminations told them how he had been treated. And yet he regarded Euthynus so highly and was in such fear of the government that he

ISOCRATES

ὀλίγων στερηθεὶς ἐσιώπησεν ἢ μηδὲν ἀπολέσας
ἐνεκάλεσεν.

4 Τὰ μὲν οὖν γεγενημένα ταῦτ' ἐστίν. ἀπόρως δ'
ἡμῖν ἔχει τὸ πρᾶγμα. Νικίᾳ γὰρ οὔτε παρακατα-
τιθεμένῳ τὰ χρήματα οὔτε κομιζομένῳ οὐδεὶς οὔτ'
ἐλεύθερος οὔτε δοῦλος παρεγένετο, ὥστε μήτ' ἐκ
βασάνων μήτ' ἐκ μαρτύρων οἷόν τ' εἶναι γνῶναι
περὶ αὐτῶν, ἀλλ' ἀνάγκη ἐκ τεκμηρίων καὶ ἡμᾶς
διδάσκειν καὶ ὑμᾶς δικάζειν, ὁπότεροι τἀληθῆ λέγουσιν.

5 Οἶμαι δὴ πάντας εἰδέναι ὅτι μάλιστα συκοφαντεῖν ἐπιχειροῦσιν οἱ λέγειν μὲν δεινοί, ἔχοντες δὲ
[401] μηδέν, τοὺς ἀδυνάτους μὲν εἰπεῖν, ἱκανοὺς δὲ χρήματα τελεῖν. Νικίας τοίνυν Εὐθύνου πλείω μὲν
ἔχει, ἧττον δὲ δύναται λέγειν· ὥστε οὐκ ἔστι δι' ὅτι
6 ἂν ἐπήρθη ἀδίκως ἐπ' Εὐθύνουν ἐλθεῖν. ἀλλὰ μὴν
καὶ ἐξ αὐτοῦ ἄν τις τοῦ πράγματος γνοίη, ὅτι πολὺ
μᾶλλον εἰκὸς ἦν Εὐθύνουν λαβόντα ἐξαρνεῖσθαι ἢ
Νικίαν μὴ δόντα αἰτιᾶσθαι. δῆλον γὰρ ὅτι πάντες
κέρδους ἕνεκ' ἀδικοῦσιν. οἱ μὲν οὖν ἀποστεροῦντες
ὧνπερ ἕνεκ' ἀδικοῦσιν ἔχουσιν, οἱ δ' ἐγκαλοῦντες
7 οὐδ' εἰ λήψεσθαι μέλλουσιν ἴσασιν. πρὸς δὲ τούτοις, ἀκαταστάτως ἐχόντων τῶν ἐν τῇ πόλει καὶ
δικῶν οὐκ οὐσῶν τῷ μὲν οὐδὲν ἦν πλέον ἐγκα-
λοῦντι, τῷ δὲ οὐδὲν ἦν δέος ἀποστεροῦντι. ὥστε
τὸν μὲν οὐδὲν ἦν θαυμαστόν, ὅτε καὶ οἱ μετὰ μαρ-

ᵃ Transactions with a banker were generally conducted
without witnesses; see Isocrates, *Trapez.* 2.

354

would sooner by far have been defrauded of a small sum and held his peace than have made complaints where no loss was suffered.

Such are the facts. But our cause presents difficulties. For Nicias, both when he was depositing the money and when he tried to get it back, had no one with him, either freeman or slave [a] ; thus it is impossible either by torture of slaves or by testimony to get at the facts, but it is by circumstantial evidence that we must plead and you must judge which side speaks the truth.

I think that you all know that malicious prosecution is most generally attempted by those who are clever speakers but possess nothing, whereas the defendants lack skill in speaking but are able to pay money. Well, Nicias is better off than Euthynus, but has less ability as a speaker ; so that there is no reason why he should have proceeded against Euthynus unjustly. No indeed, but from the very facts in the case anyone can see that it is far more probable that Euthynus received the money and then denied having done so than that Nicias did not entrust it to him and then entered his complaint. For it is self-evident that it is always for the sake of gain that men do wrong. Now those who defraud others are in possession of the fruit of their crimes, but their accusers do not even know if they shall get back anything. Besides, when conditions in the city were unsettled and the courts were suspended, it was useless for Nicias to sue Euthynus and the latter had no cause for fear though guilty of the fraud. It was not surprising, therefore, at a time when those who had borrowed money even in the presence of witnesses denied it, that Euthynus should have

τύρων δανεισάμενοι ἐξηρνοῦντο, τότε ἃ μόνος παρὰ
μόνου ἔλαβεν ἀποστερῆσαι· τὸν δ' οὐκ εἰκός, ὅτε
οὐδ' οἷς δικαίως ὠφείλετο οἷόν τ' ἦν πράττεσθαι,
τότε ἀδίκως ἐγκαλοῦντα οἴεσθαί τι λήψεσθαι.

8 Ἔτι δ' εἰ καὶ μηδὲν αὐτὸν ἐκώλυεν, ἀλλὰ καὶ
ἐξῆν καὶ ἐβούλετο συκοφαντεῖν, ὡς οὐκ ἂν ἐπ'
Εὐθύνουν ἦλθε ῥᾴδιον γνῶναι. οἱ γὰρ τοιαῦτα
πράττειν ἐπιθυμοῦντες οὐκ ἀπὸ τῶν φίλων ἄρχονται
ἀλλὰ μετὰ τούτων ἐπὶ τοὺς ἄλλους ἔρχονται, καὶ
τούτοις ἐγκαλοῦσιν, οὓς ἂν μήτ' αἰσχύνωνται μήτε
δεδίωσι, καὶ οὓς ἂν ὁρῶσι πλουσίους μέν, ἐρήμους
9 δὲ καὶ ἀδυνάτους πράττειν. Εὐθύνῳ τοίνυν τὰ-
ναντία τούτων ὑπάρχει· ἀνεψιὸς γὰρ ὢν Νικίου
τυγχάνει, λέγειν δὲ καὶ πράττειν μᾶλλον δύναται
τούτου, ἔτι δὲ χρήματα μὲν ὀλίγα, φίλους δὲ πολλοὺς κέκτηται. ὥστ' οὐκ ἔστιν ἐφ' ὅντινα ἂν
ἧττον ἢ ἐπὶ τοῦτον ἦλθεν· ἐπεὶ ἔμοιγε δοκεῖ, εἰδότι
τὴν τούτων οἰκειότητα, οὐδ' ἂν Εὐθύνους Νικίαν
ἀδικῆσαι, εἰ ἐξῆν ἄλλον τινὰ τοσαῦτα χρήματα
10 ἀποστερῆσαι. νῦν δ' ἀρχαιότερον[1] ἦν αὐτοῖς τὸ
πρᾶγμα. ἐγκαλεῖν μὲν γὰρ ἔξεστιν ἐξ ἁπάντων
ἐκλεξάμενον, ἀποστερεῖν δ' οὐχ οἷόν τ' ἄλλον ἢ τὸν
παρακαταθέμενον. ὥστε Νικίας μὲν συκοφαντεῖν
ἐπιθυμῶν οὐκ ἂν ἐπὶ τοῦτον ἦλθεν, Εὐθύνους δ'
11 ἀποστερεῖν ἐπιχειρῶν οὐκ ἄλλον εἶχεν.

Ὁ δὲ μέγιστον τεκμήριον καὶ πρὸς ἄπαντα
ἱκανόν· ὅτε γὰρ τὸ ἔγκλημα ἐγένετο, ὀλιγαρχία

---

[1] ἀρχαιότερον mss.: ἦν omitted in all but Λ and Lang's
cod. Generally considered corrupt: ἀπ' ἀρχῆς ἕτερον
Strange: ἄρ' ἦν ἕτερον Sauppe: ἆρα διάφορον ἦν or ἆρα
διέφερεν Blass: δ' ἆρα τυχαιότερον suggested by Capps:
ἀναγκαιότερον, i.e. "rather inevitable," proposed by Post.

356

robbed him of what he had received from him when
neither was accompanied by witnesses. And it is
not probable that at a time when not even those
to whom money was justly owed could recover it,
Nicias should have believed that he could obtain
anything by an unjust accusation.

And again, even if nothing had stood in his way
and he could have brought a false accusation against
him and wished to do so, it can easily be seen that
Nicias would not have proceeded against Euthynus.
For those who desire to act in this way do not begin
with their friends, but in alliance with them proceed
against others and accuse those for whom they have
neither respect nor fear, persons whom they see to
be rich, but friendless and helpless. Well then, in
the case of Euthynus the opposite is true ; he is the
cousin of Nicias and has greater ability in speech
and action, and although he has little money, he has
many friends. In consequence, he is the last person
whom Nicias would have proceeded against. And,
in my opinion, knowing as I do their intimacy, neither
would Euthynus ever have acted unjustly toward
Nicias if he could have defrauded someone else of so
large a sum. But as it was, their transaction was
simple.[a] It is possible to choose whomever you please
from the whole body of citizens for accusation, but
you can defraud only the man who has entrusted a
deposit with you. Thus Nicias, if he had desired to
get money by blackmail, would not have proceeded
against Euthynus, but the latter, when he resorted
to fraud, had no other victim available.

But here is the strongest evidence and sufficient
in every respect. When the charge was made, the

* See textual note.

καθειστήκει, ἐν ᾗ οὕτως ἑκάτερος αὐτῶν διέκειτο,
ὥστε Νικίας μέν, εἰ καὶ τὸν ἄλλον χρόνον εἴθιστο
συκοφαντεῖν, τότ' ἂν ἐπαύσατο, Εὐθύνους δέ, καὶ εἰ
12 μηδὲ πώποτε διενοήθη ἀδικεῖν, τότ' ἂν ἐπήρθη. ὁ
μὲν γὰρ διὰ τὰ ἁμαρτήματα ἐτιμᾶτο, ὁ δὲ διὰ τὰ
χρήματα ἐπεβουλεύετο. πάντες γὰρ ἐπίστασθε, ὅτι
ἐν ἐκείνῳ τῷ χρόνῳ δεινότερον ἦν πλουτεῖν ἢ
ἀδικεῖν· οἱ μὲν γὰρ τὰ ἀλλότρια ἐλάμβανον, οἱ δὲ
τὰ σφέτερ' αὐτῶν ἀπώλλυον. ἐφ' οἷς γὰρ ἦν ἡ
πόλις, οὐ τοὺς ἁμαρτάνοντας ἐτιμωροῦντο, ἀλλὰ
τοὺς ἔχοντας ἀφῃροῦντο, καὶ ἡγοῦντο τοὺς μὲν
ἀδικοῦντας πιστούς, τοὺς δὲ πλουτοῦντας ἐχθρούς.
13 ὥστε μὴ περὶ τοῦτ' εἶναι Νικίᾳ ὅπως συκοφαντῶν
τἀλλότρια λήψοιτο, ἀλλ' ὅπως μὴ οὐδὲν ἀδικῶν
κακόν τι πείσοιτο. τῷ μὲν γὰρ ὅσον Εὐθύνους
δυναμένῳ ἐξῆν ἅ τ' ἔλαβεν ἀποστερεῖν καὶ οἷς μὴ
συνέβαλεν ἐγκαλεῖν· οἱ δ' ὥσπερ Νικίας διακείμενοι ἠναγκάζοντο τοῖς τ' ὀφείλουσι τὰ χρέα
ἀφιέναι καὶ τοῖς συκοφαντοῦσι τὰ αὑτῶν διδόναι.
14 καὶ ταῦθ' ὅτι ἀληθῆ λέγω αὐτὸς ἂν ὑμῖν Εὐθύνους
μαρτυρήσειεν· ἐπίσταται γὰρ ὅτι Τιμόδημος τουτονὶ τριάκοντα μνᾶς ἐπράξατο, οὐ χρέος ἐγκαλῶν
ἀλλ' ἀπάξειν ἀπειλῶν. καίτοι πῶς εἰκὸς Νικίαν
εἰς τοῦτ' ἀνοίας ἐλθεῖν, ὥστ' αὐτὸν περὶ τοῦ σώ-

oligarchy was in power, in which the situation of the two men was as follows : Nicias, even if he had been accustomed in former times to bring malicious accusations, then would have given up the practice, whereas Euthynus, even if he had never before given a thought to wrongdoing, then would have been tempted to act thus. For his misdeeds were bringing him honours, but Nicias, because of his wealth, was the object of plotting. For you are all aware that, at that time, it was a greater danger to be wealthy than to engage in wrongdoing, for the evil-doers were seizing the property of others, whereas the rich were losing their own. For it was the custom of those in whose hands the control of the city was, not to punish those who were guilty of offences, but to despoil the possessors of property, and they regarded the criminals as loyal and the wealthy as inimical.[a] Consequently it was not the problem before Nicias how he might get possession of the property of others by bringing malicious accusations, but how he might not be made a victim of wrongdoing, although himself innocent. For while any man who possessed the influence of Euthynus could steal what he had received on deposit and also bring charges against those to whom he had lent nothing, yet those who were in Nicias' position were compelled to absolve their debtors of just debts and to surrender their own property to blackmailers. Euthynus himself could testify to the truth of what I say ; for he knows that Timodemus extorted thirty minas from Nicias, not by demanding the payment of a debt, but by threatening him with summary arrest. And yet is it probable that Nicias went so far in folly that he was bringing malicious charges against others when

15 ματος κινδυνεύοντα ἑτέρους συκοφαντεῖν, καὶ μὴ
δυνάμενον τὰ αὑτοῦ σῴζειν τοῖς ἀλλοτρίοις ἐπιβουλεύειν, καὶ πρὸς τοῖς ὑπάρχουσιν ἐχθροῖς ἑτέρους διαφόρους ποιεῖσθαι, καὶ τούτοις ἀδίκως
ἐγκαλεῖν παρ' ὧν οὐδ' ὁμολογούντων ἀποστερεῖν
οἷός τ' ἂν ἦν δίκην λαβεῖν, καὶ τότε πλέον ἔχειν
ζητεῖν, ὅτε οὐδὲ ἴσον ἐξῆν αὐτῷ, καὶ ὅτε ἃ οὐκ
ἔλαβεν ἀποτίνειν ἠναγκάζετο, τότε καὶ ἃ μὴ
συνέβαλεν ἐλπίζειν πράξασθαι;

16   Περὶ μὲν οὖν τούτων ἱκανὰ τὰ εἰρημένα. ἴσως
δ' Εὐθύνους ἐρεῖ, ἃ καὶ πρότερον ἤδη, ὅτι οὐκ
ἄν ποτ' ἀδικεῖν ἐπιχειρῶν τὰ μὲν δύο μέρη τῆς
[403] παρακαταθήκης ἀπέδωκε, τὸ δὲ τρίτον μέρος ἀπ-
εστέρησεν, ἀλλ' εἴτε ἀδικεῖν ἐπεθύμει εἴτε δίκαιος
ἐβούλετο εἶναι, περὶ ἁπάντων ἂν τὴν αὐτὴν γνώ-
17 μην ἔσχεν. ἐγὼ δ' ἡγοῦμαι πάντας ὑμᾶς εἰδέναι
ὅτι πάντες ἄνθρωποι, ὅταν περ ἀδικεῖν ἐπιχει-
ρῶσιν, ἅμα καὶ τὴν ἀπολογίαν σκοποῦνται· ὥστ'
οὐκ ἄξιον θαυμάζειν, εἰ τούτων ἕνεκα τῶν λόγων
οὕτως Εὐθύνους ἠδίκησεν. ἔτι δ' ἔχοιμ' ἂν ἐπιδεῖξαι καὶ ἑτέρους, οἳ χρήματα λαβόντες τὰ μὲν
πλεῖστ' ἀπέδοσαν, ὀλίγα δ' ἀπεστέρησαν, καὶ ἐν
μικροῖς μὲν συμβολαίοις ἀδικήσαντας, ἐν μεγάλοις
18 δὲ δικαίους γενομένους· ὥστ' οὐ μόνος οὐδὲ πρῶτος Εὐθύνους τοιαῦτα πεποίηκεν. ἐνθυμεῖσθαι δὲ
χρή, εἰ ἀποδέξεσθε τῶν τὰ τοιαῦτα λεγόντων, ὅτι
νόμον θήσετε, πῶς χρὴ ἀδικεῖν· ὥστε τοῦ λοιποῦ

his own life was in jeopardy ; that he was plotting
to get the goods of others when he was unable to
protect his own ; that he was making other enemies
in addition to those he already had ; that he was
unjustly accusing persons from whom, even if they
confessed the theft, he could not have exacted
punishment ; and that he was trying to get the
better of others at the time when even to have
equality with them was beyond his power ; and,
finally, at the time when he was being forced to pay
back what he had not received, he hoped to collect
what he had not lent ?

Enough has been said concerning these matters.
Perhaps Euthynus will repeat what indeed he has
already said, that, if he had been trying to defraud
Nicias, he never would have returned two-thirds
of the deposit, while withholding merely the third
part, but that whether he was intent upon acting
unjustly or wished to act justly, he would have had
the same intention in regard to the whole amount.
But you all know, I think, that all men, when they
set about committing a crime, at the same time are
looking about for a plea in defence ; consequently,
it should occasion no surprise that Euthynus, in
view of this very argument, committed the crime.
Besides, I could point out other men also who, after
having received money, have restored the major
portion of it, but retained a small part, and men who,
though guilty of dishonesty in petty contracts, yet
in important ones have shown themselves honest ;
therefore, Euthynus is not the only person, nor yet
the first, who has acted so. You must remember
that, if you ever countenance such a plea by defendants, you will be establishing a legal provision as to

χρόνου τὰ μὲν ἀποδώσουσι, τὰ δ' ὑπολείψονται.
λυσιτελήσει γὰρ αὐτοῖς, εἰ μέλλουσιν, οἷς ἂν ἀπο-
δῶσι τεκμηρίοις χρώμενοι, ὧν ἂν ἀποστερῶσι μὴ
δώσειν δίκην.

19 Σκέψασθε δὲ καί, ὡς ὑπὲρ Νικίου ῥᾴδιον εἰπεῖν
ὅμοια τῇ Εὐθύνου ἀπολογίᾳ. ὅτε γὰρ ἀπελάμβανε
τὰ δύο τάλαντα, οὐδεὶς αὐτῷ παρεγένετο· ὥστ'
εἴπερ καὶ ἐβούλετο καὶ ἐδόκει αὐτῷ συκοφαντεῖν,
δῆλον ὅτι οὐδ' ἂν ταῦτα ὡμολόγει κεκομίσθαι,
ἀλλὰ περὶ ἁπάντων ἂν τοὺς αὐτοὺς λόγους ἐποιεῖτο,
καὶ περὶ πλειόνων τε χρημάτων Εὐθύνους ἂν ἐκιν-
δύνευεν, καὶ ἅμα οὐκ ἂν εἶχεν οἷσπερ νυνὶ τεκμηρίοις χρῆσθαι.

20 Καὶ μὲν δὴ καὶ Νικίαν μὲν οὐδ' ἂν εἷς δύναιτο
ἀποδεῖξαι, δι' ἥντινά ποτε αἰτίαν ἐνεκάλεσεν,
Εὐθύνουν δὲ ῥᾴδιον γνῶναι, ὧν ἕνεκα τοῦτον τὸν
τρόπον ἠδίκησεν. ὅτε γὰρ Νικίας ἦν ἐν ταῖς
συμφοραῖς, πάντες οἱ συγγενεῖς καὶ οἱ ἐπιτήδειοι
ἀκηκοότες ἦσαν ὅτι τὸ ἀργύριον, ὃ ἦν αὐτῷ, τούτῳ
21 παρακατέθετο. ἐγίγνωσκεν οὖν Εὐθύνους, ὅτι μὲν
ἔκειτο τὰ χρήματα παρ' αὐτῷ, πολλοὺς ᾐσθημέ-
νους, ὁπόσα δὲ οὐδένα πεπυσμένον. ὥσθ' ἡγεῖτο
ἀπὸ μὲν τοῦ ἀριθμοῦ ἀφαιρῶν οὐ γνωσθήσεσθαι,
πάντα δ' ἀποστερῶν καταφανὴς γενήσεσθαι. ἐβούλετο οὖν ἱκανὰ λαβὼν ἀπολογίαν ὑπολείπεσθαι
μᾶλλον ἢ μηδὲν ἀποδοὺς μηδ' ἀρνηθῆναι δύνασθαι.

---

[a] The loss of a formal conclusion, or Epilogue, to the
speech is suggested by the abrupt ending.

the way a fraud should be committed ; consequently, in the future, holders of deposits will indeed return a part, but will retain a part for themselves. For it will be to their advantage, if they can use their repayment of some as presumptive proof so that they will not be punished for their stealing the rest.

Consider, also, that it is easy to use on behalf of Nicias arguments similar to those employed in the defence of Euthynus. For instance, when Nicias recovered the two talents, no one was present as his witness ; so that, if he wanted to make a malicious accusation and that seemed best to him, it is obvious that he would not have acknowledged the receipt of even the two talents, but would have made the same plea for the entire amount ; in that case, Euthynus would now be liable to lose even a larger sum, and at the same time he would not be able to use the presumptive proof on which he now depends.

And, furthermore, no one can point to any culpable motive whatever that led Nicias to enter an accusation against Euthynus, but as to Euthynus, it is easy to see the reasons which induced him to commit a crime in that manner. For when Nicias was in adversity, all his relations and friends had heard him say that he had deposited his money with Euthynus. Euthynus knew, therefore, that many persons were aware that the money was in his keeping, but that no one knew the amount ; in consequence he thought that if he diminished the amount he would not be found out, but if he withheld the whole sum, his guilt would be manifest. Therefore, he chose to take enough and have left a plea in his defence rather than to pay nothing back and be left without a possibility of denial.[a]

THE LETTERS OF ISOCRATES

GENERAL INTRODUCTION

Nine *Letters* of Isocrates have been preserved. It is true that in his many extant discourses Isocrates himself furnishes more information of a personal nature than is generally the case with writers of antiquity, but his *Letters* serve to amplify what is elsewhere found and give some new facts. In general, however, the *Letters* are " less personal than general in tone and subject-matter, and might be classed with his political writings." [a]

The *Letters* are all addressed by Isocrates to rulers and princes. Four were written to kings and warlords in furtherance of his long cherished plan, advocated for thirty-four years, that a strong leader should unite the discordant states of Greece in a common cause, and with a powerful army assembled from all Greece invade Asia and conquer Persia. This idea impelled the educator and publicist to send *Epistle* 1 to Dionysius the Elder, tyrant of Syracuse ; *Epistles* 2 and 3 to King Philip of Macedon ; and *Epistle* 9 to Archidamas of Sparta.

Epistle 4, to Antipater, regent of Macedon, is the most informal and personal of the *Letters* and is a letter of recommendation on behalf of a pupil.

Epistle 5 has particular interest in that it is addressed to Alexander, who was, at the time the letter

---

[a] See General Introd., Isocrates (Vol. I, p. xxxi, L.C.L.).

was written, a boy of about fourteen years of age, and in all probability had just been placed in the charge of Aristotle as tutor. In this short letter Isocrates refers to the favourable reports which he had heard concerning the young prince and prophesies that " if, as you grow older, you hold fast to your present course, you will surpass the rest in wisdom as far as your father has surpassed all men."

In *Epistles* 6 (*To the Children of Jason*, in Thessaly) and 7 (*To Timotheus*, ruler of Heracleia on the Euxine), Isocrates assumes his favourite rôle of mentor, and gives counsel to those even of exalted station. *Epistle* 8 (*To the Rulers of the Mytilenaeans*) was written on behalf of the musician Agenor and his family and is a plea to those in authority to permit them to return home from exile.

In their probable chronological order the *Letters* may be placed in the following sequence : *Epistle* 1 (368 B.C.) ; 6 (359 B.C.) ; 9 (356 B.C.) ; 8 (350 B.C.) ; 7 (345 B.C.) ; 2 (342 B.C.) ; 5 (342 B.C.) ; 4 (340 B.C.) ; 3 (338 B.C.). Isocrates was 68 years of age at the time of writing the earliest extant letter ; the last letter was written just before his death at the great age of 98 years.

In conclusion, a few words should be said about the formerly much-discussed question of the authenticity of these *Letters* which have come down to us with Isocrates designated as their author. Since some letters and documents from antiquity have been proved by modern scholarship to be indubitably spurious,[a] there has been a tendency to be sceptical

---

[a] *Cf.* the *Letters of Phalaris*, and the forged letters and documents in the oration of Demosthenes, *On the Crown* ; *cf.* also the controversy which has raged over the letters of Plato.

367

concerning all literary compositions of this nature. In the case of the nine *Letters* of Isocrates, however, I am convinced that they are all genuine and that the scepticism of some scholars and the objections raised by them on historical and stylistic grounds are without justification.[a]

L. V. H.

[a] For readers who may be especially interested in the question of the genuineness of the *Letters* of Isocrates these references are provided. The following scholars judge all the letters to be genuine: Blass (*Die attische Beredsamkeit*); Drerup (*Isocratis Opera Omnia*); and Beloch (*Griechische Geschichte*). Ed. Meyer (*Geschichte des Altertums*) accepted all the letters he refers to—1, 9, and 6. Bury (*History of Greece*) accepts 1 and 3, all he mentions. Mathieu (*Isocrate, Philippe et Lettres à Philippe*) accepts 3, 4, 6, and 9. Scholars who have rejected some or all of the *Letters* are: Wilamowitz (*Letters* 3, 4, and 9); Münscher (3, 4, 6, and 9 in Pauly-Wissowa, *Real-Encyc., s.v. Isokrates*). For complete and detailed discussion of the question, with specific references, see the Columbia University Dissertation of L. F. Smith, *The Genuineness of the Ninth and Third Letters of Isocrates* (1940); Smith believes all the letters genuine.

LETTER 1. TO DIONYSIUS

INTRODUCTION

THE first of the extant *Letters* of Isocrates is addressed to Dionysius the Elder, who was tyrant of Syracuse in Sicily from 405 B.C. to 367 B.C. The letter, as we have it, is incomplete; it is merely the introduction to a communication which was evidently of considerable length. From the general tenor of the beginning of the letter it is obvious that Isocrates went on to a discussion of his favourite theme, namely, the urgent need of a united Greece which would make feasible a common military expedition against Persia.

In his *Panegyricus* Isocrates had urged Athens to no avail to assume the leadership in this cause and in the *To Philip* (129) he asserts that he had petitioned Athens first of all Greek powers. This letter to Dionysius is evidently an appeal to the Sicilian tyrant to take the lead.[a]

Isocrates wrote this letter in his old age, as he tells us in § 1, and it is later than the *Panegyricus* (380 B.C.). § 8 of the letter helps to give the probable date. Isocrates says that the Lacedaemonians are no longer in power (Sparta was defeated at Leuctra in 371 B.C.). In 368 B.C. Dionysius was again waging war with the Carthaginians and at first met with success. This would seem to be the time when the letter was written.

[a] Isocrates refers to this letter in his discourse *To Philip* 81.

1. ΙΣΟΚΡΑΤΗΣ ΔΙΟΝΥΣΙΩΙ ΧΑΙΡΕΙΝ

[404] Εἰ μὲν νεώτερος ἦν, οὐκ ἂν ἐπιστολὴν ἔπεμπον,
ἀλλ' αὐτὸς ἄν σοι πλεύσας ἐνταῦθα διελέχθην·
ἐπειδὴ δ' οὐ κατὰ τοὺς αὐτοὺς χρόνους ὅ τε τῆς
ἡλικίας τῆς ἐμῆς καιρὸς καὶ τῶν σῶν πραγμάτων
συμβέβηκεν, ἀλλ' ἐγὼ μὲν προαπείρηκα, τὰ δὲ
πράττεσθαι νῦν ἀκμὴν εἴληφεν, ὡς οἷόν τ' ἐστὶν ἐκ
τῶν παρόντων, οὕτω σοι πειράσομαι δηλῶσαι περὶ
αὐτῶν.

2 Οἶδα μὲν οὖν ὅτι τοῖς συμβουλεύειν ἐπιχειροῦσι
πολὺ διαφέρει μὴ διὰ γραμμάτων ποιεῖσθαι τὴν
συνουσίαν ἀλλ' αὐτοὺς πλησιάσαντας, οὐ μόνον ὅτι
περὶ τῶν αὐτῶν πραγμάτων ῥᾷον ἄν τις παρὼν
πρὸς παρόντα φράσειεν ἢ δι' ἐπιστολῆς δηλώσειεν,
οὐδ' ὅτι πάντες τοῖς λεγομένοις μᾶλλον ἢ τοῖς
γεγραμμένοις πιστεύουσι, καὶ τῶν μὲν ὡς εἰσηγη-
μάτων, τῶν δ' ὡς ποιημάτων ποιοῦνται τὴν ἀκρό-
3 ασιν· ἔτι δὲ πρὸς τούτοις ἐν μὲν ταῖς συνουσίαις
[405] ἤν ἀγνοηθῇ τι τῶν λεγομένων ἢ μὴ πιστευθῇ,
παρὼν ὁ τὸν λόγον διεξιὼν ἀμφοτέροις τούτοις
ἐπήμυνεν, ἐν δὲ τοῖς ἐπιστελλομένοις καὶ γεγραμμένοις ἤν τι συμβῇ τοιοῦτον, οὐκ ἔστιν ὁ διορθώ-
σων· ἀπόντος γὰρ τοῦ γράψαντος ἔρημα τοῦ
372

LETTER 1. ISOCRATES SENDS GREETING TO DIONYSIUS

If I were younger, I should not be sending you a letter, but should myself take ship and converse with you there ; but inasmuch as it so happens that the fruitful period of my life and that of your own affairs have not coincided—since I am already spent with years, and with you it is the high time for action—I shall try to disclose to you my views about the situation as well as I can in the circumstances.

I know, to be sure, that when men essay to give advice, it is far preferable that they should come in person rather than send a letter, not only because it is easier to discuss the same matters face to face than to give their views by letter, nor yet because all men give greater credence to the spoken rather than to the written word, since they listen to the former as to practical advice and to the latter as to an artistic composition [a] ; but also, in addition to these reasons, in personal converse, if anything that is said is either not understood or not believed, the one who is presenting the arguments, being present, can come to the rescue in either case ; but when written missives are used and any such misconception arises, there is no one to correct it,[b] for since the

[a] In connexion with this, *To Philip* 25-26 should be read.
[b] *Cf.* Plato, *Phaedrus* 275 E.

βοηθήσοντός ἐστιν. οὐ μὴν ἀλλ' ἐπειδὴ σὺ μέλ-
λεις αὐτῶν ἔσεσθαι κριτής, πολλὰς ἐλπίδας ἔχω
φανήσεσθαι λέγοντας ἡμᾶς τι τῶν δεόντων· ἡγοῦμαι γὰρ ἁπάσας ἀφέντα σε τὰς δυσχερείας τὰς
προειρημένας αὐταῖς ταῖς πράξεσι προσέξειν τὸν
νοῦν.

4 Καίτοι τινὲς ἤδη με τῶν σοὶ πλησιασάντων
ἐκφοβεῖν ἐπεχείρησαν, λέγοντες ὡς σὺ τοὺς μὲν
κολακεύοντας τιμᾷς, τῶν δὲ συμβουλευόντων κατα-
φρονεῖς. ἐγὼ δ' εἰ μὲν ἀπεδεχόμην τοὺς λόγους
τούτους ἐκείνων, πολλὴν ἂν ἡσυχίαν εἶχον· νῦν δ'
οὐδεὶς ἄν με πείσειεν, ὡς οἷόν τ' ἐστὶ τοσοῦτον καὶ
τῇ γνώμῃ καὶ ταῖς πράξεσι διενεγκεῖν, ἂν μή τις
τῶν μὲν μαθητής, τῶν δ' ἀκροατής, τῶν δ' εὑρετὴς
γένηται, καὶ πανταχόθεν προσαγάγηται καὶ συλ-
λέξηται, δι' ὧν οἷόν τ' ἐστὶν ἀσκῆσαι τὴν αὑτοῦ
διάνοιαν.

5 Ἐπήρθην μὲν οὖν ἐπιστέλλειν σοι διὰ ταῦτα.
λέγειν δὲ μέλλω περὶ μεγάλων πραγμάτων καὶ
περὶ ὧν οὐδενὶ τῶν ζώντων ἀκοῦσαι μᾶλλον ἢ σοὶ
προσήκει. καὶ μὴ νόμιζέ με προθύμως οὕτω σε
παρακαλεῖν, ἵνα γένῃ συγγράμματος ἀκροατής· οὐ
γὰρ οὔτ' ἐγὼ τυγχάνω φιλοτίμως διακείμενος
πρὸς τὰς ἐπιδείξεις οὔτε σὺ λανθάνεις ἡμᾶς ἤδη
6 πλήρης ὢν τῶν τοιούτων. πρὸς δὲ τούτοις κἀκεῖνο
πᾶσι φανερόν, ὅτι τοῖς μὲν ἐπιδείξεως δεομένοις αἱ
πανηγύρεις ἁρμόττουσιν, ἐκεῖ γὰρ ἄν τις ἐν πλείστοις τὴν αὑτοῦ δύναμιν διασπείρειεν, τοῖς δὲ δια-
πράξασθαί τι βουλομένοις πρὸς τοῦτον διαλεκτέον,
ὅστις τάχιστα μέλλει τὰς πράξεις ἐπιτελεῖν τὰς

writer is not at hand, the defender is lacking. Nevertheless, since you are to be the judge in this matter, I have great hope that I shall prove to be saying something of value, as I think you will disregard all the difficulties just mentioned and will direct your attention to the matters themselves.

And yet, certain persons who have been admitted to your presence have attempted to frighten me, saying that while you honour flatterers, you despise those who offer you advice. If I had believed their words, I should have remained quiet; but as it is, no one could persuade me that it is possible that a man should so surpass others in both judgement and action, unless he has become a learner, a listener, and a discoverer, and has drawn to himself and collected from every possible source those means which will enable him to exercise his own intellectual ability.

It was for these reasons, then, that I have been moved to write you. I intend to speak to you about important matters, matters about which no living person may more fittingly hear than you. And do not think that I am earnestly urging you in this way that you may become a listener to a rhetorical composition; for I am not, as it happens, in a mood to seek glory through rhetorical show-pieces, nor am I unaware that you on your part are sated with such offerings. Furthermore, one thing is evident to all, that while our public festivals offer fitting occasions to those who want to make an oratorical display (for there, in the presence of the greatest numbers, they may spread the fame of their eloquence abroad), yet those who wish to bring some serious thing to pass should address the man who is likely most promptly to accomplish in deed that which the word has pro-

7 ὑπὸ τοῦ λόγου δηλωθείσας. εἰ μὲν οὖν μιᾷ τινι
τῶν πόλεων εἰσηγούμην, πρὸς τοὺς ἐκείνης προ-
εστῶτας τοὺς λόγους ἂν ἐποιούμην· ἐπειδὴ δ' ὑπὲρ
τῆς τῶν Ἑλλήνων σωτηρίας παρεσκεύασμαι συμβουλεύειν, πρὸς τίν' ἂν δικαιότερον διαλεχθείην
[406] ἢ πρὸς τὸν πρωτεύοντα τοῦ γένους καὶ μεγίστην
ἔχοντα δύναμιν;

8 Καὶ μὴν οὐδ' ἀκαίρως φανησόμεθα μεμνημένοι
περὶ τούτων. ὅτε μὲν γὰρ Λακεδαιμόνιοι τὴν
ἀρχὴν εἶχον, οὐ ῥᾴδιον ἦν ἐπιμεληθῆναί σοι τῶν
περὶ τὸν τόπον τὸν ἡμέτερον, οὐδὲ τούτοις ἐναντία
πράττειν ἅμα καὶ Καρχηδονίοις πολεμεῖν· ἐπειδὴ
δὲ Λακεδαιμόνιοι μὲν οὕτω πράττουσιν ὥστ'
ἀγαπᾶν, ἢν τὴν χώραν τὴν αὐτῶν ἔχωσιν, ἡ δ'
ἡμετέρα πόλις ἡδέως ἂν αὐτήν σοι παράσχοι
συναγωνιζομένην, εἴ τι πράττοις ὑπὲρ τῆς Ἑλλάδος ἀγαθόν, πῶς ἂν παραπέσοι καλλίων καιρὸς τοῦ
νῦν σοι παρόντος;

9 Καὶ μὴ θαυμάσῃς, εἰ μήτε δημηγορῶν μήτε
στρατηγῶν μήτ' ἄλλως δυνάστης ὢν οὕτως ἐμ-
βριθὲς αἴρομαι πρᾶγμα καὶ δυοῖν ἐπιχειρῶ τοῖν
μεγίστοιν, ὑπέρ τε τῆς Ἑλλάδος λέγειν καὶ σοὶ
συμβουλεύειν. ἐγὼ γὰρ τοῦ μὲν πράττειν τι τῶν
κοινῶν εὐθὺς ἐξέστην, δι' ἃς δὲ προφάσεις πολὺ ἂν
ἔργον εἴη μοι λέγειν, τῆς δὲ παιδεύσεως τῆς τῶν

---

[a] Cf. To Philip 12-13, for the same sentiment.
[b] This statement seems to indicate that the spirit of universal Hellenism was growing.
[c] But in To Philip 65 Isocrates, in scathing language,
disparages Dionysius.
[d] For these sentiments see To Philip 81, where Isocrates
specifically refers to this letter.

posed.[a] No, if I were offering advice to some particular state, I should address its leading men, but since I have determined to give counsel looking to the salvation of all Hellenes, to whom could I more appropriately address myself than to him who is the foremost of our race[b] and the possessor of the greatest power?[c]

In truth, it will be seen that not inopportunely I make mention of these matters. For when the Lacedaemonians were in power, it was not easy for you to take upon yourself the responsibility for the affairs in our region, nor to oppose the Lacedaemonians and at the same time fight the Carthaginians. But now, when the Lacedaemonians are in such a plight that they are content if they can remain in possession of their own land, and when our city would gladly join with you as ally in any struggle that you should care to make in behalf of the welfare of Greece, how could there befall a more favourable opportunity than that which now presents itself to you?

Do not think it strange[d] that I, who am not an orator who moves public assemblies, nor a leader of armies, nor otherwise a man of power, am undertaking so difficult an affair and am attempting two of the most serious things—to speak on behalf of Greece and at the same time to give counsel to you. For at the beginning of my career I stood aloof from participation in public affairs (the reasons for this would be tedious to relate),[e] but of that culture

---

[e] Isocrates states that a weak voice and a lack of assurance prevented him from entering upon a public career. These disabilities are frequently mentioned by the writer, e.g., Panath. 9-10; Epist. 8. 7 (οὔτε γὰρ φωνὴν ἔσχον ἱκανὴν οὔτε τόλμαν); To Philip 81; cf. General Introd., Vol. I, p. xix.

μὲν μικρῶν καταφρονούσης, τῶν δὲ μεγάλωι
ἐφικνεῖσθαι πειρωμένης οὐκ ἂν φανείην ἄμοιρος
10 γεγενημένος. ὥστ' οὐδὲν ἄτοπον, εἴ τι τῶν συμφερόντων ἰδεῖν ἂν μᾶλλον δυνηθείην τῶν εἰκῇ μὲν
πολιτευομένων, μεγάλην δὲ δόξαν εἰληφότων
δηλώσομεν δ' οὐκ εἰς ἀναβολάς, εἴ τινος ἄξιοι
τυγχάνομεν ὄντες, ἀλλ' ἐκ τῶν ῥηθήσεσθαι μελλόντων . . .

which contemns the petty things and attempts to achieve the great things I should not be found to be entirely destitute. Consequently, it would not be surprising if I should be better able to see something to our advantage than those whose public life has been but guesswork, though they have acquired great renown. And so, without further delay, but from what will presently be said, I shall make it clear whether I really am worth listening to. . . .

LETTER 2. TO PHILIP, I

INTRODUCTION

In the collection of *Letters* of Isocrates two (*Epistles* 2 and 3) are addressed to Philip.

In *Letter* 2, Isocrates rebukes King Philip of Macedon, recently wounded in fighting barbarians, for his recklessness in unnecessarily assuming personal risks in war. Now Philip was occupied with a Thracian war from 342 to 339 B.C. and it is obvious from the tone of the letter, and the references to the friendly relations between Athens and Philip, that the war between Athens and Macedon, declared in 340 B.C., had not broken out. Furthermore, in § 20 of the letter, the orator refers to recent relations between Philip and the Thessalians which were effected in 342 B.C. In consequence, this letter may be assigned to the year 342 B.C. [a]

After counselling Philip to greater prudence in warfare, Isocrates appeals for more amicable relations between Macedon and Athens, and suggests that Philip should lead a common Greek expedition against Persia.

[a] Blass gives the end of the year 342 B.C., as does Jebb. Mathieu, *Isocrate, Philippe et Lettres à Philippe* 39 prefers the latter part of 344 B.C.

2. ΦΙΛΙΠΠΩΙ

[406] Οἶδα μὲν ὅτι πάντες εἰώθασι πλείω χάριν ἔχειν
τοῖς ἐπαινοῦσιν ἢ τοῖς συμβουλεύουσιν, ἄλλως τε
[407] κἂν μὴ κελευσθεὶς ἐπιχειρῇ τις τοῦτο ποιεῖν. ἐγὼ
δ᾽ εἰ μὲν μὴ καὶ πρότερον ἐτύγχανόν σοι παρη-
νεκὼς μετὰ πολλῆς εὐνοίας, ἐξ ὧν ἐδόκεις μοι τὰ
πρέποντα μάλιστ᾽ ἂν σαυτῷ πράττειν, ἴσως οὐδ᾽
ἂν νῦν ἐπεχείρουν ἀποφαίνεσθαι περὶ τῶν σοὶ
2 συμβεβηκότων· ἐπειδὴ δὲ προειλόμην φροντίζειν
τῶν σῶν πραγμάτων καὶ τῆς πόλεως ἕνεκα τῆς
ἐμαυτοῦ καὶ τῶν ἄλλων Ἑλλήνων, αἰσχυνθείην
ἄν, εἰ περὶ μὲν τῶν ἧττον ἀναγκαίων φαινοίμην σοι
συμβεβουλευκώς, ὑπὲρ δὲ τῶν μᾶλλον κατεπειγόν-
των μηδένα λόγον ποιοίμην, καὶ ταῦτ᾽ εἰδὼς ἐκεῖνα
μὲν ὑπὲρ δόξης ὄντα, ταῦτα δ᾽ ὑπὲρ τῆς σῆς σωτηρίας, ἧς ὀλιγωρεῖν ἅπασιν ἔδοξας τοῖς ἀκούσασι
3 τὰς περὶ σοῦ ῥηθείσας βλασφημίας. οὐδεὶς γὰρ
ἔστιν, ὅστις οὐ κατέγνω προπετέστερόν σε κινδυνεύειν ἢ βασιλικώτερον, καὶ μᾶλλόν σοι μέλειν τῶν
περὶ τὴν ἀνδρίαν ἐπαίνων ἢ τῶν ὅλων πραγμάτων.
ἔστι δ᾽ ὁμοίως αἰσχρὸν περιστάντων τε τῶν
πολεμίων μὴ διαφέροντα γενέσθαι τῶν ἄλλων,

ᵃ Cf. Epist. 9. 6.
ᵇ A reference to the orator's discourse To Philip (cf.
Vol. I, pp. 244 ff., L.C.L.).

LETTER 2. TO PHILIP, I

I KNOW that all men are accustomed to be more grateful to those who praise them than to those who give them counsel,[a] especially if one offers his advice unbidden. And if I had not on a former occasion [b] given you with most kindly intent such counsel as I believed would lead to a course of action worthy of one in your position, perhaps even now I should not be undertaking to declare my view concerning what has happened to you. But since I then did decide to concern myself with your affairs, in the interests of my own state and of the other Greeks as well, I should be ashamed if, when comparatively unimportant things were the issue, I am known to have offered you advice, yet now I should have nothing to say concerning more urgent matters, particularly since I realize that in the former case your reputation alone was at stake, whereas at present it is your personal safety, which you have been thought to esteem too lightly by all who heard the abusive reproaches directed against you. In truth there is no one who has not condemned you as being more reckless in assuming risks than is becoming to a king, and as caring more for men's praise of your courage than for the general welfare. For it is equally disgraceful, when your enemies threaten on every side, not to prove

385

ISOCRATES

μηδεμιᾶς τε συμπεσούσης ἀνάγκης αὐτὸν ἐμβαλεῖν
εἰς τοιούτους ἀγῶνας, ἐν οἷς κατορθώσας μὲν οὐδὲν
ἂν ἦσθα μέγα διαπεπραγμένος, τελευτήσας δὲ τὸν
βίον ἅπασαν ἂν τὴν ὑπάρχουσαν εὐδαιμονίαν συν-
4 ανεῖλες. χρὴ δὲ μὴ καλὰς ἁπάσας ὑπολαμβάνειν
τὰς ἐν τοῖς πολέμοις τελευτάς, ἀλλὰ τὰς μὲν ὑπὲρ
τῆς πατρίδος καὶ τῶν γονέων καὶ τῶν παίδων
ἐπαίνων ἀξίας, τὰς δὲ ταῦτά τε πάντα βλαπτούσας
καὶ τὰς πράξεις τὰς πρότερον κατωρθωμένας
καταρρυπαινούσας αἰσχρὰς νομίζειν καὶ φεύγειν
ὡς αἰτίας πολλῆς ἀδοξίας γιγνομένας.
5 Ἡγοῦμαι δέ σοι συμφέρειν μιμεῖσθαι τὰς πόλεις,
ὃν τρόπον διοικοῦσι τὰ περὶ τοὺς πολέμους. ἅπασαι γάρ, ὅταν στρατόπεδον ἐκπέμπωσιν, εἰώθασι
τὸ κοινὸν καὶ τὸ βουλευσόμενον ὑπὲρ τῶν ἐνεστώτων εἰς ἀσφάλειαν καθιστάναι· διὸ δὴ συμβαίνει μὴ
μιᾶς ἀτυχίας συμπεσούσης ἀνῃρῆσθαι καὶ τὴν
δύναμιν αὐτῶν, ἀλλὰ πολλὰς ὑποφέρειν δύνασθαι
συμφορὰς καὶ πάλιν αὐτὰς ἐκ τούτων ἀναλαμβάνειν.
6 ὃ καὶ σὲ δεῖ σκοπεῖν, καὶ μηδὲν μεῖζον ἀγαθὸν τῆς
σωτηρίας ὑπολαμβάνειν, ἵνα καὶ τὰς νίκας τὰς
συμβαινούσας κατὰ τρόπον διοικῇς καὶ τὰς ἀτυχίας
[408] τὰς συμπιπτούσας ἐπανορθοῦν δύνῃ.[1] ἴδοις δ᾽ ἂν
καὶ Λακεδαιμονίους περὶ τῆς τῶν βασιλέων σωτηρίας πολλὴν ἐπιμέλειαν ποιουμένους καὶ τοὺς
ἐνδοξοτάτους τῶν πολιτῶν φύλακας αὐτῶν καθ-

[1] καὶ τὰς . . . δύνῃ is added by Γ: Blass omits, as does Mathieu.

* The many wounds suffered in battle by Philip are vividly related by Demosthenes, De Corona 67.
[b] The sentiment is a commonplace in early Greek elegiac
386

yourself superior to all the rest, and, when no urgent
need has arisen, to hurl yourself into combats of such
a kind that, if you succeeded, you would have accomplished nothing of importance, but if you lost your
life, you would have destroyed all your present good
fortune.[a] Not every death in war must be regarded
as honourable; on the contrary, although when death
is incurred for fatherland, for parents, and for children
it is worthy of praise,[b] yet when it brings harm to
all of these and tarnishes the brilliance of past successes, it should be thought disgraceful and should
be avoided as being the cause of great discredit.

I think that you would profitably imitate the
fashion in which our city-states conduct the business
of warfare. They all are accustomed, when they send
forth an army, to take measures to secure the safety
of the government and of the authority which is to
decide what is to be done in the emergency. In
consequence, if a single mischance befalls, their
power is not also wholly destroyed; on the contrary,
they can sustain many misfortunes and again recover
their strength. This principle you too should take
into consideration, and consider no blessing more
important than your safety, in order that you may
not only duly make use of the victories which may
be yours but also may rectify the mischances that
may befall you. You might observe that the Lacedaemonians also are extremely solicitous for the
safety of their kings,[c] and appoint the most distinguished of the citizens as their bodyguards, and that

poetry; cf. the fragments of the verse of Callinus and
Tyrtaeus.

[c] For this example see Isocrates, *On the Peace* 143 and
To Philip 80.

ἱστάντας, οἷς αἴσχιόν ἐστιν ἐκείνους τελευτήσαντας
7 περιιδεῖν ἢ τὰς ἀσπίδας ἀποβαλεῖν. ἀλλὰ μὴν οὐδ᾽
ἐκεῖνά σε λέληθεν ἃ Ξέρξῃ τε τῷ καταδουλώσα-
σθαι τοὺς Ἕλληνας βουληθέντι καὶ Κύρῳ τῷ τῆς
βασιλείας ἀμφισβητήσαντι συνέπεσεν. ὁ μὲν γὰρ
τηλικαύταις ἥτταις καὶ συμφοραῖς περιπεσών,
ἡλίκας οὐδεὶς οἶδεν ἄλλοις γενομένας, διὰ τὸ περι-
ποιῆσαι τὴν αὑτοῦ ψυχὴν τήν τε βασιλείαν κατέσχε καὶ τοῖς παισὶ τοῖς αὑτοῦ παρέδωκε καὶ τὴν
Ἀσίαν οὕτω διῴκησεν ὥστε μηδὲν ἧττον αὐτὴν
8 εἶναι φοβερὰν τοῖς Ἕλλησιν ἢ πρότερον· Κῦρος
δὲ νικήσας ἅπασαν τὴν βασιλέως δύναμιν καὶ
κρατήσας ἂν τῶν πραγμάτων, εἰ μὴ διὰ τὴν αὑτοῦ προπέτειαν, οὐ μόνον αὐτὸν ἀπεστέρησε
τηλικαύτης δυναστείας, ἀλλὰ καὶ τοὺς συνακολου-
θήσαντας εἰς τὰς ἐσχάτας συμφορὰς κατέστησεν.
ἔχοιμι δ᾽ ἂν παμπληθεῖς εἰπεῖν οἳ μεγάλων στρατοπέδων ἡγεμόνες γενόμενοι διὰ τὸ προδιαφθαρῆναι
πολλὰς μυριάδας αὑτοῖς συναπώλεσαν.

9 Ὧν ἐνθυμούμενον χρὴ μὴ τιμᾶν τὴν ἀνδρίαν τὴν
μετ᾽ ἀνοίας ἀλογίστου καὶ φιλοτιμίας ἀκαίρου
γιγνομένην, μηδὲ πολλῶν κινδύνων ἰδίων ὑπαρχόντων ταῖς μοναρχίαις ἑτέρους ἀδόξους καὶ στρα-
τιωτικοὺς αὑτῷ προσεξευρίσκειν, μηδ᾽ ἁμιλλᾶσθαι
τοῖς ἢ βίου δυστυχοῦς ἀπαλλαγῆναι βουλομένοις ἢ
μισθοφορᾶς ἕνεκα μείζονος εἰκῆ τοὺς κινδύνους
10 προαιρουμένοις, μηδ᾽ ἐπιθυμεῖν τοιαύτης δόξης, ἧς
πολλοὶ καὶ τῶν Ἑλλήνων καὶ τῶν βαρβάρων τυγχάνουσιν, ἀλλὰ τῆς τηλικαύτης τὸ μέγεθος, ἣν
μόνος ἂν τῶν νῦν ὄντων κτήσασθαι δυνηθείης· μηδ᾽
ἀγαπᾶν λίαν τὰς τοιαύτας ἀρετὰς ὧν καὶ τοῖς

* Cf. To Philip 90.

for them it is a greater disgrace to suffer the kings to meet death than to throw away their shields. And surely you are not unaware of what happened to Xerxes when he wished to enslave the Greeks and to Cyrus when he laid claim to the kingdom. Thus Xerxes, although he had suffered defeats and calamities of such magnitude the like of which have never been known to befall other kings, because he preserved his life, not only retained his throne and handed it over to his children, but also so administered Asia that it was no less formidable to the Greeks than before. Cyrus, however, after he had conquered all the military might of the king, would have gained mastery of the throne had it not been for his rashness,[a] which caused him not only to forfeit that mighty empire, but brought his followers into extreme danger. And I could mention very many men who, becoming commanders of great armies, because they were slain before they need have died, brought destruction at the same time upon countless numbers of their followers.

Bearing these examples in mind, you should not honour that courage which accompanies heedless folly and unseasonable ambition, nor, when so many hazards which are inherent in monarchy are at hand, should you devise for yourself still others that bring no glory and belong to the common soldier ; nor should you vie with those who wish to escape from an unhappy existence or who rashly incur danger in the hope of a higher wage ; nor should you desire such glory as many, both Greeks and barbarians, obtain, but rather that exalted renown which you alone of living men could win. Nor should you be enamoured of such virtues as even ignoble men share,

φαύλοις μέτεστιν, ἀλλ' ἐκείνας ὧν οὐδεὶς ἂν πονη-
11 ρὸς κοινωνήσειεν· μηδὲ ποιεῖσθαι πολέμους ἀδόξους
καὶ χαλεπούς, ἐξὸν ἐντίμους καὶ ῥᾳδίους, μηδ' ἐξ
ὧν τοὺς μὲν οἰκειοτάτους εἰς λύπας καὶ φροντίδας
καταστήσεις, τοὺς δ' ἐχθροὺς ἐν ἐλπίσι μεγάλαις
[409] ποιήσεις, οἵας καὶ νῦν αὐτοῖς παρέσχες· ἀλλὰ τῶν
μὲν βαρβάρων, πρὸς οὓς νῦν πολεμεῖς, ἐπὶ τοσοῦτον
ἐξαρκέσει σοι κρατεῖν, ὅσον ἐν ἀσφαλείᾳ καταστῆσαι τὴν σαυτοῦ χώραν, τὸν δὲ βασιλέα τὸν¹ νῦν
μέγαν προσαγορευόμενον καταλύειν ἐπιχειρήσεις,
ἵνα τήν τε σαυτοῦ δόξαν μείζω ποιήσῃς καὶ τοῖς
Ἕλλησιν ὑποδείξῃς πρὸς ὃν χρὴ πολεμεῖν.

12 Πρὸ πολλοῦ δ' ἂν ἐποιησάμην ἐπιστεῖλαί σοι
ταῦτα πρὸ τῆς στρατείας, ἵν' εἰ μὲν ἐπείσθης, μὴ
τηλικούτῳ κινδύνῳ περιέπεσες, εἰ δ' ἠπίστησας,
μὴ συμβουλεύειν ἐδόκουν ταὐτὰ τοῖς ἤδη διὰ τὸ
πάθος ὑπὸ πάντων ἐγνωσμένοις, ἀλλὰ τὸ συμβεβη-
κὸς ἐμαρτύρει τοὺς λόγους ὀρθῶς ἔχειν τοὺς ὑπ'
ἐμοῦ περὶ αὐτῶν εἰρημένους.

13 Πολλὰ δ' ἔχων εἰπεῖν διὰ τὴν τοῦ πράγματος
φύσιν παύσομαι λέγων· οἶμαι γὰρ καὶ σὲ καὶ
τῶν ἑταίρων τοὺς σπουδαιοτάτους ῥᾳδίως ὁπόσ'
ἂν βούλησθε προσθήσειν τοῖς εἰρημένοις. πρὸς δὲ
τούτοις φοβοῦμαι τὴν ἀκαιρίαν· καὶ γὰρ νῦν κατὰ
μικρὸν προϊὼν ἔλαθον ἐμαυτὸν οὐκ εἰς ἐπιστολῆς
συμμετρίαν ἀλλ' εἰς λόγου μῆκος ἐξοκείλας.

14 Οὐ μὴν ἀλλὰ καίπερ τούτων οὕτως ἐχόντων οὐ

---

¹ βασιλέα τὸν is added by Blass : cf. Epist. 3. 5.

* The Persians, of course, are meant.

but only of those of which no base person may partake; nor wage inglorious and difficult wars when honourable and easy ones are possible, nor those which will cause grief and anxiety to your closest friends and arouse great hope in your enemies, as even now you have done. Nay, as to the barbarians with whom you are now waging war, it will suffice you to gain the mastery over them only so far as to secure the safety of your own territory, but the king who is now called Great you will attempt to overthrow, that you may both enhance your own renown and may point out to the Greek world who the enemy is against whom they should wage war.[a]

I should have greatly preferred to send you this letter before your campaign in order that, had you heeded my advice, you might not have incurred so great danger, or if you had rejected it, I should not now seem to be advising that same caution which has already, because of the wound you received, been approved by all; but, instead, your misfortune would be bearing witness to the truth of what I had said about the matter.

Although I have much more to say, because of the nature of the subject, I will cease; for I think that you and the ablest[b] of your companions will readily add as much as you wish to what I have said. Besides, I fear my advice may be inopportune; for even now I have unawares gradually drifted beyond[c] the due proportions of a letter and run into a lengthy discourse.

Nevertheless, although this is the case, I must not

---

[b] *Cf. To Philip* 19 for the same expression.

[c] The same nautical figure is found in *Areop.* 18 and *Antid.* 268.

παραλειπτέον ἐστὶ τὰ περὶ τῆς πόλεως, ἀλλὰ
πειρατέον παρακαλέσαι σε πρὸς τὴν οἰκειότητα
καὶ τὴν χρῆσιν αὐτῆς. οἶμαι γὰρ πολλοὺς εἶναι
τοὺς ἀπαγγέλλοντας καὶ λέγοντας οὐ μόνον τὰ δυσχερέστατα τῶν περὶ σοῦ παρ᾽ ἡμῖν εἰρημένων, ἀλλὰ
καὶ παρ᾽ αὑτῶν προστιθέντας· οἷς οὐκ εἰκὸς προσ-
15 έχειν τὸν νοῦν. καὶ γὰρ ἂν ἄτοπον ποιοίης, εἰ τὸν
μὲν δῆμον τὸν ἡμέτερον ψέγοις ὅτι ῥαδίως πείθεται
τοῖς διαβάλλουσιν, αὐτὸς δὲ φαίνοιο πιστεύων τοῖς
τὴν τέχνην ταύτην ἔχουσι, καὶ μὴ γιγνώσκοις ὡς
ὅσῳπερ ἂν τὴν πόλιν εὐαγωγοτέραν ὑπὸ τῶν
τυχόντων οὖσαν ἀποφαίνωσι, τοσούτῳ μᾶλλόν σοι
συμφερόντως ἔχουσαν αὐτὴν ἐπιδεικνύουσιν. εἰ
γὰρ οἱ μηδὲν ἀγαθὸν οἷοί τ᾽ ὄντες ποιῆσαι διαπράτ-
τονται τοῖς λόγοις ὅ τι ἂν βουληθῶσιν, ἦ που σέ
γε προσήκει τὸν πλεῖστ᾽ ἂν ἔργῳ δυνάμενον εὐ-
εργετῆσαι μηδενὸς ἀποτυχεῖν παρ᾽ ἡμῶν.
16 Ἡγοῦμαι δὲ δεῖν πρὸς μὲν τοὺς πικρῶς τῆς
πόλεως ἡμῶν κατηγοροῦντας ἐκείνους ἀντιτάτ-
[410] τεσθαι τοὺς πάντα τἀναντί᾽ εἶναι[1] λέγοντας καὶ
τοὺς μήτε μεῖζον μήτ᾽ ἔλαττον αὐτὴν ἠδικηκέναι
φάσκοντας· ἐγὼ δ᾽ οὐδὲν ἂν εἴποιμι τοιοῦτον·
αἰσχυνθείην γὰρ ἄν, εἰ τῶν ἄλλων μηδὲ τοὺς θεοὺς
ἀναμαρτήτους εἶναι νομιζόντων αὐτὸς τολμῴην
λέγειν, ὡς οὐδὲν πώποθ᾽ ἡ πόλις ἡμῶν πεπλημμέ-
17 ληκεν. οὐ μὴν ἀλλ᾽ ἐκεῖν᾽ ἔχω περὶ αὐτῆς εἰπεῖν,
ὅτι χρησιμωτέραν οὐκ ἂν εὕροις ταύτης οὔτε τοῖς
Ἕλλησιν οὔτε τοῖς σοῖς πράγμασιν· ᾧ μάλιστα
προσεκτέον τὸν νοῦν ἐστιν. οὐ γὰρ μόνον συν-

---

[1] πάντα τἀναντί᾽ εἶναι Capps, following Corais: πάντα τε
ταῦτ᾽ εἶναι (ΓΕ) is read by Blass, although he thinks it corrupt: Post suggests τοὺς σπάνιά τε ταῦτ᾽ εἶναι.

omit discussion of the affairs of the city of Athens ; on the contrary, I must try to urge you to cultivate friendly relations and intimacy with her. For I think there are many who report to you and tell you not only the most disparaging of the things said of you among us, but also add their own inventions ; but it is not reasonable for you to pay any attention to these persons. For you would in fact be acting inconsistently if you should find fault with our people for lending a ready ear to your calumniators, but yourself should be found giving credence to those who practise this art and should not perceive that the more easily influenced by nobodies such persons declare our city to be, the better suited to your ends they prove it. For if those who are powerless to be of any service to Athens can accomplish by words alone what they wish, surely it is right to expect that you, who are able in very deed to confer upon her the greatest benefits, would not fail to gain from us anything whatever.

To the bitter accusers of our city I think I should place in contrast those who say that the very opposite is true, that is, those who assert that she has done no wrong at all, whether great or small. For my part, I would not make any such claim ; for I should be ashamed if, while men in general do not regard even the gods as blameless, I should dare to affirm that our city had never transgressed at all.[a] Nevertheless, this I can say of Athens—that you could not find a city more useful to all the Greeks and to your enterprises ; and to this fact you should give your special attention. For not only as your ally would

---

[a] This statement is repeated in *Panath.* 64, where Isocrates says of it, " as I have already said in another place."

ἀγωνιζομένη γίγνοιτ' ἂν αἰτία σοι πολλῶν ἀγαθῶν,
18 ἀλλὰ καὶ φιλικῶς ἔχειν δοκοῦσα μόνον· τούς τε
γὰρ ὑπὸ σοὶ νῦν ὄντας ῥᾷον ἂν κατέχοις, εἰ μηδεμίαν ἔχοιεν ἀποστροφήν, τῶν τε βαρβάρων οὓς
βουληθείης θᾶττον ἂν καταστρέψαιο. καίτοι πῶς
οὐ χρὴ προθύμως ὀρέγεσθαι τῆς τοιαύτης εὐνοίας,
δι' ἣν οὐ μόνον τὴν ὑπάρχουσαν ἀρχὴν ἀσφαλῶς καθέξεις, ἀλλὰ καὶ πολλὴν ἑτέραν ἀκινδύνως
19 προσκτήσει; θαυμάζω δ' ὅσοι τῶν τὰς δυνάμεις
ἐχόντων τὰ μὲν τῶν ξενιτευομένων στρατόπεδα
μισθοῦνται καὶ χρήματα πολλὰ δαπανῶσι, συν-
ειδότες ὅτι πλείους ἠδίκηκε τῶν πιστευσάντων
αὐτοῖς ἢ σέσωκε, τὴν δὲ πόλιν τὴν τηλικαύτην
δύναμιν κεκτημένην μὴ πειρῶνται θεραπεύειν, ἢ
καὶ μίαν ἑκάστην τῶν πόλεων καὶ σύμπασαν τὴν
20 Ἑλλάδα πολλάκις ἤδη σέσωκεν. ἐνθυμοῦ δ' ὅτι
πολλοῖς καλῶς βεβουλεῦσθαι δοκεῖς ὅτι δικαίως
κέχρησαι Θετταλοῖς καὶ συμφερόντως ἐκείνοις,
ἀνδράσιν οὐκ εὐμεταχειρίστοις, ἀλλὰ μεγαλοψύχοις
καὶ στάσεως μεστοῖς. χρὴ τοίνυν καὶ περὶ ἡμᾶς
πειρᾶσθαι γίγνεσθαί σε τοιοῦτον, ἐπιστάμενον ὅτι
τὴν μὲν χώραν Θετταλοί, τὴν δὲ δύναμιν ἡμεῖς
ὅμορόν σοι τυγχάνομεν ἔχοντες, ἣν ἐκ παντὸς τρό-
21 που ζήτει προσαγαγέσθαι. πολὺ γὰρ κάλλιόν ἐστι
τὰς εὐνοίας τὰς τῶν πόλεων αἱρεῖν ἢ τὰ τείχη. τὰ
μὲν γὰρ τοιαῦτα τῶν ἔργων οὐ μόνον ἔχει φθόνον,
ἀλλὰ καὶ τῶν τοιούτων τὴν αἰτίαν τοῖς στρατο-
πέδοις ἀνατιθέασιν· ἣν δὲ τὰς οἰκειότητας καὶ

---

[a] Cf. *To Philip* 129, where three examples are given—
Marathon, Salamis, and Cnidus.

she bring about many advantages to you, but even
if she merely was believed to be on friendly terms
with you. For you might then more easily keep in
subjection those who are now under your sway, if
they should have no refuge, and of the barbarians
you could more quickly conquer any you should wish.
Yet is there any reason why you should not eagerly
grasp at a relationship of goodwill such that you
will hold securely not only your present dominion,
but also without risk acquire another great one? I
marvel that so many who maintain great forces hire
mercenary armies and expend so much money on
them, although they know that such help has been
the cause of greater injury than of salvation to those
who relied upon them, and have made no effort to
gain the friendship of a city which possesses such
power that it has ere now often saved every Hellenic
state and indeed all Greece.[a] Consider, too, that to
many you appear to have been well advised because
your treatment of the Thessalians[b] has been just and
advantageous to them, although they are a people
not easy to handle, but high-spirited and seditious.
You should, therefore, endeavour to show yourself
equally prudent towards us also, knowing as you do
that, while the Thessalians have the territory next
to you, it is we who are next to you in strength and
influence, and that is what you should seek in every
way to win for yourself. For it is a much greater
glory to capture the goodwill of cities than their
walls[c]; for achievements like the latter not only en-
gender ill-will, but men attribute the credit for them
to your armies; yet if you are able to win friend-

---

[b] *Cf. To Philip* 20.
[c] For this sentiment *cf. To Philip* 68.

τὰς εὐνοίας κτήσασθαι δυνηθῇς, ἅπαντες τὴν σὴν διάνοιαν ἐπαινέσονται.

22 Δικαίως δ' ἄν μοι πιστεύοις οἷς εἴρηκα περὶ τῆς [411] πόλεως· φανήσομαι γὰρ οὔτε κολακεύειν αὐτὴν ἐν τοῖς λόγοις εἰθισμένος, ἀλλὰ πλεῖστα πάντων ἐπιτετιμηκώς, οὔτ' εὖ παρὰ τοῖς πολλοῖς καὶ τοῖς εἰκῇ δοκιμάζουσι φερόμενος, ἀλλ' ἀγνοούμενος ὑπ' αὐτῶν καὶ φθονούμενος ὥσπερ σύ. πλὴν τοσοῦτον διαφέρομεν, ὅτι πρὸς σὲ μὲν διὰ τὴν δύναμιν καὶ τὴν εὐδαιμονίαν οὕτως ἔχουσι, πρὸς δ' ἐμέ, διότι προσποιοῦμαι τὸ βέλτιον αὐτῶν φρονεῖν καὶ πλείους ὁρῶσιν ἐμοὶ διαλέγεσθαι βουλομένους ἢ σφίσιν

23 αὐτοῖς. ἠβουλόμην δ' ἂν ἡμῖν ὁμοίως ῥάδιον εἶναι τὴν δόξαν ἣν ἔχομεν παρ' αὐτοῖς διαφεύγειν. νῦν δὲ σὺ μὲν οὐ χαλεπῶς, ἢν βουληθῇς, αὐτὴν διαλύσεις, ἐμοὶ δ' ἀνάγκη καὶ διὰ τὸ γῆρας καὶ δι' ἄλλα πολλὰ στέργειν τοῖς παροῦσιν.

24 Οὐκ οἶδ' ὅ τι δεῖ πλείω λέγειν πλὴν τοσοῦτον, ὅτι καλόν ἐστι τὴν βασιλείαν καὶ τὴν εὐδαιμονίαν τὴν ὑπάρχουσαν ὑμῖν παρακαταθέσθαι τῇ τῶν Ἑλλήνων εὐνοίᾳ.

ships and goodwill, all will praise the wisdom shown by you.

You may well believe me in what I have said concerning Athens ; for you will find that I have not been accustomed to flatter her in my discourses ; on the contrary, more than anyone else I have censured her [a] ; nor am I highly esteemed by the masses or by those who form their opinions offhand, but, like yourself, I am misunderstood and disliked by them. But we are dissimilar in this, that they are thus disposed toward you because of your power and prosperity, but toward me because I lay claim to a wisdom greater than their own, and they see that more people wish to converse with me than with themselves. I could wish that it were equally easy for us both to dispel the prejudice in which we are held by these ; but as it is, you will put an end to it without difficulty if you wish, but I must be content with the standing I now have because of my old age and for many other reasons.

I know not what more I need to say, except this only—that it will be a fine thing for you to entrust your royal power and your existing prosperity into the keeping of the goodwill of the Hellenic race.

---

[a] For example, in his *On the Peace* 13-14, and in other sections of that discourse.

LETTER 3. TO PHILIP, II

INTRODUCTION

This short letter to Philip was written in the autumn of 338 B.C., not long after the Athenian defeat at Chaeronea. Isocrates was ninety-eight years of age, in feeble health, and died shortly thereafter. It is the latest of all his extant writings.

Again the orator urges Philip, with a united Hellas, to undertake a military expedition against Asia and the Persians, a theme dear to his heart and already expounded at length in the *Panegyricus* (380 B.C.) and in his discourse *To Philip* (346 B.C.).

The authenticity of this letter has been questioned, on insufficient grounds, by some scholars.[a] It is accepted by Blass, Jebb, and Mathieu.

[a] *e.g.*, Wilamowitz, A. Schaefer, and K. Münscher. For a recent and complete discussion see L. F. Smith, *The Genuineness of the Ninth and Third Letters of Isocrates* (1940). See also the General Introd. to the *Letters*.

3. ΦΙΛΙΠΠΩΙ

[411] Ἐγὼ διελέχθην μὲν καὶ πρὸς Ἀντίπατρον περί τε τῶν τῇ πόλει καὶ τῶν σοὶ συμφερόντων ἐξαρκούντως, ὡς ἐμαυτὸν ἔπειθον, ἠβουλήθην δὲ καὶ πρὸς σὲ γράψαι περὶ ὧν μοι δοκεῖ πρακτέον εἶναι μετὰ τὴν εἰρήνην, παραπλήσια μὲν τοῖς ἐν τῷ λόγῳ γεγραμμένοις, πολὺ δ' ἐκείνων συντομώτερα.

2 Κατ' ἐκεῖνον μὲν γὰρ τὸν χρόνον συνεβούλευον ὡς χρὴ διαλλάξαντά σε τὴν πόλιν τὴν ἡμετέραν καὶ τὴν Λακεδαιμονίων καὶ τὴν Θηβαίων καὶ τὴν Ἀργείων εἰς ὁμόνοιαν καταστῆσαι τοὺς Ἕλληνας, ἡγούμενος, ἂν τὰς προεστώσας πόλεις πείσῃς οὕτω φρονεῖν, ταχέως καὶ τὰς ἄλλας ἐπακολουθήσειν.

[412] τότε μὲν οὖν ἄλλος ἦν καιρός, νῦν δὲ συμβέβηκε μηκέτι δεῖν πείθειν· διὰ γὰρ τὸν ἀγῶνα τὸν γεγενημένον ἠναγκασμένοι πάντες εἰσὶν εὖ φρονεῖν καὶ τούτων ἐπιθυμεῖν ὧν ὑπονοοῦσί σε βούλεσθαι πράττειν καὶ λέγειν, ὡς δεῖ παυσαμένους τῆς μανίας καὶ τῆς πλεονεξίας, ἣν ἐποιοῦντο πρὸς ἀλλήλους, εἰς τὴν Ἀσίαν τὸν πόλεμον ἐξενεγκεῖν.

3 καὶ πολλοὶ πυνθάνονται παρ' ἐμοῦ πότερον ἐγώ σοι

---

[a] Antipater, to whom *Letter* 4 is addressed, trusted minister of Philip, had been the Macedonian envoy to Athens for the Peace of Philocrates (346 B.C.) and was again in Athens in connexion with peace preliminaries after Chaeronea.

402

LETTER 3. TO PHILIP, II

I HAVE discussed with Antipater [a] the course which is expedient for our city and for you, at sufficient length, I am convinced ; but I wished to write to you also regarding the action which I think should be taken after the conclusion of peace, and while this advice is similar to that in my discourse,[b] it is, however, expressed much more concisely.

At that time, you recall, I counselled you that, after you had reconciled our city with Sparta, Thebes, and Argos, you should bring all the Greeks into concord, as I was of opinion that if you should persuade the principal cities to be favourably inclined to such a course, the others also would quickly follow. At that time, however, the state of affairs was different, and now it has come to pass that the need of persuasion no longer exists ; for on account of the battle [c] which has taken place, all are compelled to be prudent and to desire that which they surmise you wish to do and to say, namely, that they must desist from the madness and the spirit of aggrandizement, which they were wont to display in their relations with each other, and must carry the war into Asia. Many inquire of me whether I advised

[b] *To Philip*, written in 346 B.C.
[c] The battle of Chaeronea, autumn of 338 B.C., where the Athenian army was crushed by the phalanxes of Macedon.

παρήνεσα ποιεῖσθαι τὴν στρατείαν τὴν ἐπὶ τοὺς
βαρβάρους ἢ σοῦ διανοηθέντος συνεῖπον· ἐγὼ δ'
οὐκ εἰδέναι μέν φημι τὸ σαφές, οὐ γὰρ συγγεγενῆ-
σθαί σοι πρότερον, οὐ μὴν ἀλλ' οἴεσθαι σὲ μὲν
ἐγνωκέναι περὶ τούτων, ἐμὲ δὲ συνειρηκέναι ταῖς
σαῖς ἐπιθυμίαις. ταῦτα δ' ἀκούοντες ἐδέοντό μου
πάντες παρακελεύεσθαί σοι καὶ προτρέπειν ἐπὶ τῶν
αὐτῶν τούτων μένειν, ὡς οὐδέποτ' ἂν γενομένων
οὔτε καλλιόνων ἔργων οὔτ' ὠφελιμωτέρων τοῖς
Ἕλλησιν οὔτ' ἐν καιρῷ μᾶλλον πραχθησομένων.

4 Εἰ μὲν οὖν εἶχον τὴν αὐτὴν δύναμιν ἥνπερ πρότερον, καὶ μὴ παντάπασιν ἦν ἀπειρηκώς, οὐκ ἂν
δι' ἐπιστολῆς διελεγόμην, ἀλλὰ παρὼν αὐτὸς παρ-
ώξυνον ἄν σε καὶ παρεκάλουν ἐπὶ τὰς πράξεις
ταύτας. νῦν δ' ὡς δύναμαι παρακελεύομαί σοι μὴ
καταμελῆσαι τούτων, πρὶν ἂν τέλος ἐπιθῇς αὐτοῖς.
ἔστι δὲ πρὸς μὲν ἄλλο τι τῶν ὄντων ἀπλήστως ἔχειν
οὐ καλόν, αἱ γὰρ μετριότητες παρὰ τοῖς πολλοῖς
εὐδοκιμοῦσι, δόξης δὲ μεγάλης καὶ καλῆς ἐπιθυμεῖν
καὶ μηδέποτ' ἐμπίπλασθαι προσήκει τοῖς πολὺ τῶν
5 ἄλλων διενεγκοῦσιν· ὅπερ σοὶ συμβέβηκεν. ἡγοῦ
δὲ τόθ' ἕξειν ἀνυπέρβλητον αὐτὴν καὶ τῶν σοὶ
πεπραγμένων ἀξίαν, ὅταν τοὺς μὲν βαρβάρους
ἀναγκάσῃς εἱλωτεύειν τοῖς Ἕλλησι πλὴν τῶν σοὶ
συναγωνισαμένων, τὸν δὲ βασιλέα τὸν νῦν μέγαν
προσαγορευόμενον ποιήσῃς τοῦτο πράττειν ὅ τι ἂν
σὺ προστάττῃς. οὐδὲν γὰρ ἔσται λοιπὸν ἔτι πλὴν
θεὸν γενέσθαι. ταῦτα δὲ κατεργάσασθαι πολὺ

---

* Isocrates was 98 years of age at this time and died soon
after writing this letter.

you to make the expedition against the barbarians or whether it was your idea and I concurred. I reply that I do not know for certain, since before then I had not been acquainted with you, but that I supposed that you had reached a decision in this matter and that I in my speech had fallen in with your desires. On hearing this, all entreated me to encourage you and to exhort you to hold fast to this same resolution, since they believe that no achievement could be more glorious, more useful to the Greeks, or more timely than this will be.

If I possessed the same vigour which I formerly had and were not utterly spent with years,[a] I should not be speaking with you by letter, but in your presence should myself be spurring and summoning you to undertake these tasks. But even as it is, I do exhort you, as best I can, not to put these matters aside until you bring them to a successful conclusion. To have an insatiate desire for anything else in the world is ignoble—for moderation is generally esteemed—but to set the heart upon a glory that is great and honourable, and never to be satiated with it, befits those men who have far excelled all others.[b] And that is true of you. Be assured that a glory unsurpassable and worthy of the deeds you have done in the past will be yours when you shall compel the barbarians—all but those who have fought on your side—to be serfs of the Greeks, and when you shall force the king who is now called Great to do whatever you command. For then will naught be left for you except to become a god.[c] And to accom-

---

[b] *Cf. To Philip* 135.

[c] For this extravagant statement *cf. To Philip* 113–114 and 151.

ῥᾷόν ἐστιν ἐκ τῶν παρόντων ἢ προελθεῖν ἐπὶ τὴν
δύναμιν καὶ τὴν δόξαν ἣν νῦν ἔχεις, ἐκ τῆς βασιλείας τῆς ἐξ ἀρχῆς ὑμῖν ὑπαρξάσης.

6
[413]   Χάριν δ' ἔχω τῷ γήρᾳ ταύτην μόνην, ὅτι προήγαγεν εἰς τοῦτό μου τὸν βίον, ὥσθ' ἃ νέος ὢν
διενοούμην καὶ γράφειν ἐπεχείρουν ἔν τε τῷ πανη-
γυρικῷ λόγῳ καὶ τῷ πρὸς σὲ πεμφθέντι, ταῦτα νῦν
τὰ μὲν ἤδη γιγνόμενα διὰ τῶν σῶν ἐφορῶ πράξεων,
τὰ δ' ἐλπίζω γενήσεσθαι.

  ᵃ The same statement is found in *To Philip* 115.
  ᵇ The *Panegyricus* was published in 380 B.C. Isocrates
was then 56 years of age, but had begun its composition
many years before.

plish all this from your present status is much easier for you than it was for you to advance to the power and renown you now possess from the kingship which you had in the beginning.[a]

I am grateful to my old age for this reason alone, because it has prolonged my life to this moment, so that the dreams of my youth, which I attempted to commit to writing both in my *Panegyricus* [b] and in the discourse which was sent to you, I am now seeing in part already coming to fulfilment through your achievements and in part I have hopes of their future realization.[c]

---

[a] See General Introd., Vol. I, p. x.

LETTER 4. TO ANTIPATER

INTRODUCTION

THIS is the most informal and personal of the *Letters* of Isocrates. It is a letter of recommendation to Antipater,[a] regent of Macedonia in Philip's absence, whose acquaintance Isocrates had made in Athens on the several occasions when Antipater had been sent as Macedonian envoy.

The letter is written on behalf of a certain Diodotus, a pupil of Isocrates, and for the son of Diodotus, who are not known otherwise. The protection and favour of Antipater are solicited and the good character, frankness, and usefulness of Diodotus are emphasized.

The authenticity of the letter has been challenged, without good reason, on stylistic grounds, because of its informality and the occurrence of a few rare and colloquial words and expressions.[b] That the letter is genuine is maintained by Blass, Jebb, Drerup, and Mathieu.[c]

The date is indicated in the first sentence—" now when we are at war with you "—as being soon after the renewal of war between Philip and Athens in 340, or 339 B.C.

[a] See *Epist.* 3. 1, note.
[b] *e.g.*, λιγυρώτατον (§ 4, see note); σωμάτιον (" poor body " § 11), and ἄττα οἴνη (§ 11).
[c] *Cf.* General Introd. to the *Letters*, Vol. III, L.C.L.

4. ΑΝΤΙΠΑΤΡΩΙ

Ἐγώ, καίπερ ἐπικινδύνου παρ' ἡμῖν ὄντος εἰς
Μακεδονίαν πέμπειν ἐπιστολήν, οὐ μόνον νῦν ὅτε
πολεμοῦμεν πρὸς ὑμᾶς, ἀλλὰ καὶ τῆς εἰρήνης οὔσης,
ὅμως γράψαι πρὸς σὲ προειλόμην περὶ Διοδότου,
δίκαιον εἶναι νομίζων ἅπαντας μὲν περὶ πολλοῦ
ποιεῖσθαι τοὺς ἐμαυτῷ πεπλησιακότας καὶ γεγενημένους ἀξίους ἡμῶν, οὐχ ἥκιστα δὲ τοῦτον καὶ διὰ
τὴν εὔνοιαν τὴν εἰς ἡμᾶς καὶ διὰ τὴν ἄλλην ἐπι-
2 εἴκειαν. μάλιστα μὲν οὖν ἠβουλόμην ἂν αὐτὸν
συσταθῆναί σοι δι' ἡμῶν· ἐπειδὴ δὲ δι' ἑτέρων
ἐντετύχηκέ σοι, λοιπόν ἐστί μοι μαρτυρῆσαι περὶ
αὐτοῦ καὶ βεβαιῶσαι τὴν γεγενημένην αὐτῷ πρὸς
σὲ γνῶσιν. ἐμοὶ γὰρ πολλῶν καὶ παντοδαπῶν
συγγεγενημένων ἀνδρῶν καὶ δόξας ἐνίων μεγάλας
ἐχόντων, τῶν μὲν ἄλλων ἁπάντων οἱ μέν τινες περὶ
αὐτὸν τὸν λόγον, οἱ δὲ περὶ τὸ διανοηθῆναι καὶ
πρᾶξαι δεινοὶ γεγόνασιν, οἱ δ' ἐπὶ μὲν τοῦ βίου
σώφρονες καὶ χαρίεντες, πρὸς δὲ τὰς ἄλλας χρήσεις
3 καὶ διαγωγὰς ἀφυεῖς παντάπασιν· οὗτος δ' οὕτως

---

[a] War between Athens and Macedon had recommenced
in 340 B.C.

[b] This Diodotus is otherwise unknown.

[c] For Isocrates' pupils, who became famous, see General
Introd., Vol. I, p. xxix, L.C.L. Some of these were the
orators Isaeus, Lycurgus, and Hypereides; the historians

LETTER 4. TO ANTIPATER

ALTHOUGH it is dangerous for us here in Athens to send a letter to Macedonia, not only now when we are at war with you,[a] but even in time of peace, nevertheless I have decided to write to you concerning Diodotus,[b] as I think it only right to esteem highly all those who have been my pupils and who have shown themselves worthy disciples, and not the least among them this man both because of his devotion to me and of the general probity of his character. I wish that if possible I might have been the means of his introduction to you ; since, however, he has already met you through the kindness of others, it remains for me to give my testimony concerning him and to strengthen the acquaintance which he already has with you. For although many men of various countries have been my pupils [c] and some of these are of great repute, and while of all the others some have proved to be distinguished for eloquence alone, and others in intellect and in practical affairs, and still others have indeed been men of sobriety of life and cultivated tastes, but for general usefulness in the practical affairs of life utterly devoid of natural ability, yet Diodotus has been endowed with

Ephorus and Theopompus; the philosopher Speusippus; and the statesman and general Timotheus ; in *Antid.* 93-94 Isocrates himself gives a list of his first students.

εὐάρμοστον τὴν φύσιν ἔσχηκεν ὥστ᾽ ἐν ἅπασι τοῖς εἰρημένοις τελειότατος εἶναι.

Καὶ ταῦτ᾽ οὐκ ἂν ἐτόλμων λέγειν, εἰ μὴ τὴν ἀκριβεστάτην πεῖραν αὐτός τ᾽ εἶχον αὐτοῦ καὶ [414] σὲ λήψεσθαι προσεδόκων, τὰ μὲν αὐτὸν χρώμενον 4 αὐτῷ, τὰ δὲ καὶ παρὰ τῶν ἄλλων τῶν ἐμπείρων αὐτοῦ πυνθανόμενον, ὧν οὐδεὶς ὅστις οὐκ ἂν ὁμολογήσειεν, εἰ μὴ λίαν εἴη φθονερός, καὶ εἰπεῖν καὶ βουλεύσασθαι μηδενὸς ἧττον αὐτὸν δύνασθαι καὶ δικαιότατον καὶ σωφρονέστατον εἶναι καὶ χρημάτων ἐγκρατέστατον, ἔτι δὲ συνημερεῦσαι καὶ συμβιῶναι πάντων ἥδιστον καὶ λιγυρώτατον,ᵃ πρὸς δὲ τούτοις πλείστην ἔχειν παρρησίαν, οὐχ ἣν οὐ προσῆκεν, ἀλλὰ τὴν εἰκότως ἂν μέγιστον γιγνομένην σημεῖον τῆς εὐνοίας τῆς πρὸς τοὺς 5 φίλους· ἣν τῶν δυναστῶν οἱ μὲν ἀξιόχρεων τὸν ὄγκον τὸν τῆς ψυχῆς ἔχοντες τιμῶσιν ὡς χρησίμην οὖσαν, οἱ δ᾽ ἀσθενέστεροι τὰς φύσεις ὄντες ἢ κατὰ τὰς ὑπαρχούσας ἐξουσίας δυσχεραίνουσιν, ὡς ὧν οὐ προαιροῦνταί τι ποιεῖν βιαζομένην αὐτούς, οὐκ εἰδότες ὡς οἱ μάλιστα περὶ τοῦ συμφέροντος ἀντιλέγειν τολμῶντες, οὗτοι πλείστην ἐξουσίαν αὐτοῖς τοῦ πράττειν ἃ βούλονται παρα- 6 σκευάζουσιν. εἰκὸς γὰρ διὰ μὲν τοὺς ἀεὶ πρὸς ἡδονὴν λέγειν προαιρουμένους οὐχ ὅπως τὰς μοναρχίας δύνασθαι διαμένειν, αἳ πολλοὺς τοὺς ἀναγκαίους ἐφέλκονται κινδύνους, ἀλλ᾽ οὐδὲ τὰς πολιτείας, αἳ μετὰ πλείονος ἀσφαλείας εἰσί, διὰ δὲ τοὺς ἐπὶ

ᵃ λιγυρός in this sense is unusual; it usually refers to the voice.

a nature so well balanced that in all the attributes I have named he is quite perfect.

All this I should not dare to say of him if I did not possess the most precise knowledge of him gained by experience, and if I were not anticipating that you would gain the same, partly through your own association with him and partly from the testimony of his acquaintances, of whom there is no one who would not agree, unless he be exceedingly envious, that Diodotus is inferior to none in eloquence and counsel, and that he is very honest, temperate, and self-controlled in respect to money ; nay more, to spend the day with and to live with he is a most charming and agreeable *a* companion. In addition to these good qualities he possesses frankness in the highest degree, not that outspokenness which is objectionable, but that which would rightly be regarded as the surest indication of devotion to his friends. This is the sort of frankness which princes, if they have worthy and fitting greatness of soul, honour as being useful, while those whose natural gifts are weaker than the powers they possess take such frankness ill, as if it forced them to act in some degree contrary to their desires—ignorant as they are that those who dare to speak out most fearlessly in opposition to measures in which expediency is the issue are the very persons who can provide them with more power than others to accomplish what they wish. For it stands to reason that it is because of those who always and by choice speak to please that not only monarchies cannot endure—since monarchies are liable to numerous inevitable dangers—but even constitutional governments as well, though they enjoy greater security : whereas it is owing to those

τῷ βελτίστῳ παρρησιαζομένους πολλὰ σῴζεσθαι
καὶ τῶν ἐπιδόξων διαφθαρήσεσθαι πραγμάτων.
ὧν ἕνεκα προσῆκε μὲν παρὰ πᾶσι τοῖς μονάρχοις
πλέον φέρεσθαι τοὺς τὴν ἀλήθειαν ἀποφαινομέ-
νους τῶν ἅπαντα μὲν πρὸς χάριν, μηδὲν δὲ χάριτος
ἄξιον λεγόντων· συμβαίνει δ᾽ ἔλαττον ἔχειν αὐτοὺς
παρ᾽ ἐνίοις αὐτῶν.

7 Ὃ καὶ Διοδότῳ παθεῖν συνέπεσε παρά τισι τῶν
περὶ τὴν Ἀσίαν δυναστῶν, οἷς περὶ πολλὰ χρήσιμος
γενόμενος οὐ μόνον τῷ συμβουλεύειν ἀλλὰ καὶ τῷ
πράττειν καὶ κινδυνεύειν, διὰ τὸ παρρησιάζεσθαι
πρὸς αὐτοὺς περὶ ὧν ἐκείνοις συνέφερε, καὶ τῶν
οἴκοι τιμῶν ἀπεστέρηται καὶ πολλῶν ἄλλων ἐλπίδων, καὶ μεῖζον ἴσχυσαν αἱ τῶν τυχόντων ἀνθρώ-
8 πων κολακεῖαι τῶν εὐεργεσιῶν τῶν τούτου. διὸ
[415] δὴ καὶ πρὸς ὑμᾶς ἀεὶ προσιέναι διανοούμενος
ὀκνηρῶς εἶχεν, οὐχ ὡς ἅπαντας ὁμοίους εἶναι
νομίζων τοὺς ὑπὲρ αὐτὸν ὄντας, ἀλλὰ διὰ τὰς πρὸς
ἐκείνους γεγενημένας δυσχερείας καὶ πρὸς τὰς παρ᾽
ὑμῶν ἐλπίδας ἀθυμότερος ἦν, παραπλήσιον, ὡς
ἐμοὶ δοκεῖ, πεπονθὼς τῶν πεπλευκότων τισίν, οἳ
τὸ πρῶτον, ὅταν χρήσωνται χειμῶσιν, οὐκέτι θαρ-
ροῦντες εἰσβαίνουσιν εἰς θάλατταν, καίπερ εἰδότες
ὅτι καὶ καλοῦ πλοῦ πολλάκις ἐπιτυχεῖν ἔστιν.
οὐ μὴν ἀλλ᾽ ἐπειδὴ συνέστηκέ σοι, καλῶς ποιεῖ.

9 λογίζομαι γὰρ αὐτῷ συνοίσειν, μάλιστα μὲν τῇ
φιλανθρωπίᾳ τῇ σῇ στοχαζόμενος, ἣν ἔχειν ὑπ-

who speak with absolute frankness in favour of what
is best that many things are preserved even of those
which seemed doomed to destruction. For these
reasons it is indeed fitting that in the courts of all
monarchs those who declare the truth should be
held in greater esteem than those who, though they
aim to gratify in all they say, yet say naught that
merits gratitude ; in fact, however, the former find
less favour with some princes.

This experience Diodotus has met with in his
relations with some of the potentates of Asia, to
whom he had often been of service, not only in offering counsel, but also in venturing upon dangerous
deeds ; because of his frankness of speech in matters
involving their best interests he has been both
deprived of honours he had at home and cheated
of many hopes elsewhere, and the flattery of men
of no consequence had greater weight than his
own good services. That, then, is the reason why
Diodotus, although from time to time he entertained
the thought of presenting himself to you, hesitated
to do so, not because he believed that all his superiors
were alike, but because the difficulties which he had
experienced with these rulers caused him to be
rather faint-hearted with reference also to the hopes
he placed in you. That feeling was, I fancy, like that
of some persons who have been at sea, who when
they have once experienced a tempest, no longer
with confidence embark upon a voyage, even though
they know that one may often meet with a fair
sailing. Nevertheless, now that he has met you, he
is taking the right course. For I reason that this
will be to his advantage, chiefly conjecturing so on
the strength of that kindliness which you have been

εἴληψαι παρὰ τοῖς ἔξωθεν ἀνθρώποις, ἔπειτα νομίζων οὐκ ἀγνοεῖν ὑμᾶς ὅτι πάντων ἥδιστόν ἐστι
καὶ λυσιτελέστατον πιστοὺς ἅμα καὶ χρησίμους
φίλους κτᾶσθαι ταῖς εὐεργεσίαις καὶ τοὺς τοιούτους
εὖ ποιεῖν, ὑπὲρ ὧν πολλοὶ καὶ τῶν ἄλλων ὑμῖν
χάριν ἕξουσιν. ἅπαντες γὰρ οἱ χαρίεντες τοὺς τοῖς
σπουδαίοις τῶν ἀνδρῶν καλῶς ὁμιλοῦντας ὁμοίως
ἐπαινοῦσι καὶ τιμῶσιν ὥσπερ αὐτοὶ τῶν ὠφελειῶν
ἀπολαύοντες.

10 Ἀλλὰ γὰρ Διόδοτον αὐτὸν οἶμαι μάλιστά σε προ-
τρέψεσθαι πρὸς τὸ φροντίζειν αὐτοῦ. συνέπειθον
δὲ καὶ τὸν υἱὸν αὐτοῦ τῶν ὑμετέρων ἀντέχεσθαι
πραγμάτων καὶ παραδόνθ' ὑμῖν αὐτὸν ὥσπερ
μαθητὴν εἰς τοὔμπροσθε πειραθῆναι προελθεῖν. ὁ
δὲ ταῦτά μου λέγοντος ἐπιθυμεῖν μὲν ἔφασκε τῆς
ὑμετέρας φιλίας, οὐ μὴν ἀλλὰ παραπλήσιόν τι
πεπονθέναι πρὸς αὐτὴν καὶ πρὸς τοὺς στεφανίτας
11 ἀγῶνας. ἐκείνους τε γὰρ νικᾶν μὲν ἂν βούλεσθαι,
καταβῆναι δ' εἰς αὐτοὺς οὐκ ἂν τολμῆσαι διὰ τὸ
μὴ μετεσχηκέναι ῥώμης ἀξίας τῶν στεφάνων, τῶν
τε παρ' ὑμῶν τιμῶν εὔξασθαι μὲν ἂν τυχεῖν,
ἐφίξεσθαι δ' αὐτῶν οὐ προσδοκᾶν· τήν τε γὰρ
ἀπειρίαν τὴν αὑτοῦ καταπεπλῆχθαι καὶ τὴν λαμ-
πρότητα τὴν ὑμετέραν, ἔτι δὲ καὶ τὸ σωμάτιον οὐκ
εὐκρινὲς ὂν ἀλλ' ἔχον ἄττα σίνη νομίζειν ἐμποδιεῖν
αὐτὸν πρὸς πολλὰ τῶν πραγμάτων.

12 Οὗτος μὲν οὖν, ὅ τι ἂν αὐτῷ δοκῇ συμφέρειν,
τοῦτο πράξει· σὺ δ' ἄν τε περὶ ὑμᾶς ἄν θ' ἡσυχίαν
[416] ἔχων διατρίβῃ περὶ τούτους τοὺς τόπους, ἐπιμελοῦ
καὶ τῶν ἄλλων μὲν ἁπάντων ὧν ἂν τυγχάνῃ δεόμενος, μάλιστα δὲ τῆς ἀσφαλείας καὶ τῆς τούτου
καὶ τῆς τοῦ πατρὸς αὐτοῦ, νομίσας ὥσπερ παρα-

supposed among foreigners to possess ; and partly believing you are not unaware that the most agreeable and profitable of all things is to win by one's kind deeds friends who are at the same time both loyal and useful, and to befriend men of such character that on their account many others also will be grateful to you. For all men of discrimination praise and honour those who are on intimate terms with superior men just as much as if they themselves were deriving profit from the services rendered.

But I think that Diodotus himself will best induce you to take an interest in him. His son also I have advised to espouse your cause and by putting himself in your hands as a pupil, to try to advance himself. When I gave him this advice he declared that while he craved your friendship, yet he felt toward that very much as he does toward the athletic contests in which crowns are awarded to the victors ; victory in them he would gladly win, but to enter the lists to gain them he would not dare, because he had not acquired the strength that would deserve the crowns. Similarly, while he longed to obtain the honours it is yours to bestow, yet he did not expect to attain them ; for he is appalled not only by his own inexperience but also by the splendour of your position ; furthermore, he believes that his poor body, not being sound but somewhat defective, will impede him in many activities.

He will do, however, whatever he thinks expedient ; and do you, I beg, whether he resides with you or remains inactive in that region, have a care for everything else which he may chance to need and especially for the personal safety of himself and of his father, considering them to be, as it were, a

καταθήκην ἔχειν τούτους[1] παρά τε τοῦ γήρως ἡμῶν, ὃ προσηκόντως ἂν πολλῆς τυγχάνοι προνοίας, καὶ τῆς δόξης τῆς ὑπαρχούσης, εἴ τινος ἄρα σπουδῆς ἐστιν ἀξία, καὶ τῆς εὐνοίας τῆς πρὸς ὑμᾶς 13 ἣν ἔχων ἅπαντα τὸν χρόνον διατετέλεκα. καὶ μὴ θαυμάσῃς, μήτ᾽ εἰ μακροτέραν γέγραφα τὴν ἐπιστολὴν μήτ᾽ εἴ τι περιεργότερον καὶ πρεσβυτικώτερον εἰρήκαμεν ἐν αὐτῇ· πάντων γὰρ τῶν ἄλλων ἀμελήσας ἑνὸς μόνον ἐφρόντισα, τοῦ φανῆναι σπουδάζων ὑπὲρ ἀνδρῶν φίλων καὶ προσφιλεστάτων μοι γεγενημένων.

[1] τούτους Auger : τοῦτον MSS.

sacred trust committed to you by my old age, which might fittingly receive much consideration, and by the reputation I possess (if this, to be sure, is worthy of any interest) and by the goodwill which I have never ceased to have for you. And do not be surprised either if the letter I have written is too long, or if in it I have expressed myself in a somewhat too officious way and after the fashion of an old man; for everything else I have neglected and have had thought for this one thing alone—to show my zeal on behalf of men who are my friends and who have become very dear to me.

LETTER 5.   TO ALEXANDER

INTRODUCTION

THIS brief letter to Alexander accompanied one [a] sent to his father Philip, who was in Thrace or the Chersonese, in 342 B.C. Alexander at this time was a boy of fourteen and, in all probability, had just been placed under Aristotle as instructor. This affords Isocrates opportunity again to express his disapproval of *eristic*,[b] and to affirm the great value of rhetorical training as he himself taught it.

[a] *i.e.*, probably *Letter 2.*
[b] For *eristic* in the bad sense, *captious argumentation* or *disputation for its own sake*, see *Against the Sophists* 1 (and note), Isocrates, Vol. II, p. 162, L.C.L. It is probable that Alexander was studying eristics under Aristotle !

5. ΑΛΕΞΑΝΔΡΩΙ

[416] Πρὸς τὸν πατέρα σου γράφων ἐπιστολὴν ἄτοπον
ᾠμην ποιήσειν, εἰ περὶ τὸν αὐτὸν ὄντα σὲ τόπον
ἐκείνῳ μήτε προσερῶ μήτ' ἀσπάσομαι μήτε γράψω
τι τοιοῦτον, ὃ ποιήσει τοὺς ἀναγνόντας μὴ νομίζειν
ἤδη με παραφρονεῖν διὰ τὸ γῆρας μηδὲ παντάπασι
ληρεῖν, ἀλλ' ἔτι τὸ καταλελειμμένον μου μέρος καὶ
λοιπὸν ὂν οὐκ ἀνάξιον εἶναι τῆς δυνάμεως ἣν ἔσχον
νεώτερος ὤν.[a]

2   Ἀκούω δέ σε πάντων λεγόντων ὡς φιλάνθρωπος
εἶ καὶ φιλαθήναιος καὶ φιλόσοφος, οὐκ ἀφρόνως
ἀλλὰ νοῦν ἔχοντως. τῶν τε γὰρ πολιτῶν ἀπο-
δέχεσθαί σε τῶν ἡμετέρων οὐ τοὺς ἠμεληκότας αὐτῶν καὶ πονηρῶν πραγμάτων ἐπιθυμοῦντας, ἀλλ'
[417] οἷς συνδιατρίβων τ' οὐκ ἂν λυπηθείης, συμβάλλων
τε καὶ κοινωνῶν πραγμάτων οὐδὲν ἂν βλαβείης
οὐδ' ἀδικηθείης, οἵοις περ χρὴ πλησιάζειν τοὺς εὖ
3   φρονοῦντας· τῶν τε φιλοσοφιῶν[b] οὐκ ἀποδοκιμάζειν
μὲν οὐδὲ τὴν περὶ τὰς ἔριδας, ἀλλὰ νομίζειν εἶναι
πλεονεκτικὴν ἐν ταῖς ἰδίαις διατριβαῖς, οὐ μὴν

---

[a] In his later years Isocrates frequently refers to his
advanced age. At this time (342 B.C.) he was perhaps
94 years of age.

[b] i.e., philosophical studies, in the broad sense.

426

LETTER 5. TO ALEXANDER

Since I am writing to your father I thought I should be acting in a strange manner if, when you are in the same region as he, I should fail either to address you or to send you a greeting, or to write you something calculated to convince any reader that I am now not out of my mind through old age [a] and that I do not babble like a fool, but that, on the contrary, the share of intelligence that still is left to me is not unworthy of the ability which as a younger man I possessed.

I hear everyone say of you that you are a friend of mankind, a friend of Athens, and a friend of learning, not foolishly, but in sensible fashion. For they say that the Athenians whom you admit to your presence are not those men who have neglected their higher interests [b] and have a lust for base things, but those rather whose constant companionship would not cause you regret and with whom association and partnership would not result in harm or injury to you—just such men, indeed, as should be chosen as associates by the wise. As regards systems of philosophy, they say that while you do not indeed reject *eristic*,[c] but hold that it is valuable in private discussions, you regard it nevertheless as unsuitable

[c] For *eristic*, " disputation for its own sake," see *Helen* 6, with note.

ἁρμόττειν οὔτε τοῖς τοῦ πλήθους προεστῶσιν οὔτε
τοῖς τὰς μοναρχίας ἔχουσιν· οὐδὲ γὰρ συμφέρον
οὐδὲ πρέπον ἐστὶ τοῖς μεῖζον τῶν ἄλλων φρονοῦσιν
οὔτ᾽ αὐτοῖς ἐρίζειν πρὸς τοὺς συμπολιτευομένους
οὔτε τοῖς ἄλλοις ἐπιτρέπειν πρὸς αὐτοὺς ἀντιλέγειν.

4 Ταύτην μὲν οὖν οὐκ ἀγαπᾶν σε τὴν διατριβήν,
προαιρεῖσθαι δὲ τὴν παιδείαν τὴν περὶ τοὺς λόγους,
οἷς χρώμεθα περὶ τὰς πράξεις τὰς προσπιπτούσας
καθ᾽ ἑκάστην τὴν ἡμέραν καὶ μεθ᾽ ὧν βουλευόμεθα
περὶ τῶν κοινῶν· δι᾽ ἣν νῦν τε δοξάζειν περὶ τῶν
μελλόντων ἐπιεικῶς, τοῖς τ᾽ ἀρχομένοις προστάττειν οὐκ ἀνοήτως ἃ δεῖ πράττειν ἑκάστους, ἐπι-
στήσει, περὶ δὲ τῶν καλῶν καὶ δικαίων καὶ τῶν
τούτοις ἐναντίων ὀρθῶς κρίνειν, πρὸς δὲ τούτοις
τιμᾶν τε καὶ κολάζειν ὡς προσῆκόν ἐστιν ἑκάτε-
5 ρους. σωφρονεῖς οὖν νῦν ταῦτα μελετῶν· ἐλπίδας
γὰρ τῷ τε πατρὶ καὶ τοῖς ἄλλοις παρέχεις, ὡς, ἂν
πρεσβύτερος γενόμενος ἐμμείνῃς τούτοις, τοσοῦτον
προέξεις τῇ φρονήσει τῶν ἄλλων, ὅσον περ ὁ πατήρ
σου διενήνοχεν ἁπάντων.

for either those who are leaders of the people or for monarchs; for it is not expedient or becoming that those who regard themselves as superior to all others should themselves dispute with their fellow-citizens or suffer anyone else to contradict them.

But this branch of learning, I am told, you are not content with, but you choose rather the training which rhetoric gives, which is of use in the practical affairs of everyday life and aids us when we deliberate concerning public affairs. By means of this study you will come to know how at the present time to form reasonably sound opinions about the future, how not ineptly to instruct your subject peoples what each should do, how to form correct judgements about the right and the just and their opposites and, besides, to reward and chastise each class as it deserves. You act wisely, therefore, in devoting yourself to these studies; for you give hope to your father and to all the world that if, as you grow older, you hold fast to this course, you will as far surpass your fellow-men in wisdom as your father has surpassed all mankind.[a]

[a] For Isocrates' views on Education, with numerous references to his writings, see Norlin's General Introd. (Isocrates, Vol. I, pp. xxiii ff., L.C.L.).

LETTER 6. TO THE CHILDREN OF JASON

INTRODUCTION

JASON, tyrant of Pherae in Thessaly, was assassinated in 370 B.C. [a] and was succeeded by his brothers Polydorus and Polyphron. But deeds of violence continued. Polyphron, having murdered his brother, was himself slain by Alexander, son of Polydorus. Alexander, however, was murdered (359 B.C.) at the instigation of his wife Thebê (daughter of Jason) by her half-brothers.

It is to Thebê and her half-brother Tisiphonus (the children of Jason), who had assumed the power, that this letter was written, in 359 B.C.,[b] urging them to a moderate course in governing their state.

[a] See Diodorus xv. 60, and Xenophon, *Hell.* vi. 4. 33 for facts concerning Jason and his successors.
[b] Jebb, *Attic Orators* ii. p. 242, rather than Blass, is here followed.

6. ΤΟΙΣ ΙΑΣΟΝΟΣ ΠΑΙΣΙΝ

[417] Ἀπήγγειλέ τίς μοι τῶν πρεσβευσάντων ὡς ὑμᾶς
ὅτι καλέσαντες αὐτὸν ἄνευ τῶν ἄλλων ἐρωτήσαιτ'
[418] εἰ πεισθείην ἂν ἀποδημῆσαι καὶ διατρῖψαι παρ'
ὑμῖν. ἐγὼ δ' ἕνεκα μὲν τῆς Ἰάσονος καὶ Πολυ-
αλκοῦς ξενίας ἡδέως ἂν ἀφικοίμην ὡς ὑμᾶς· οἶμαι
γὰρ ἂν τὴν ὁμιλίαν τὴν γενομένην ἅπασιν ἡμῖν συν-
2 ενεγκεῖν· ἀλλὰ γὰρ ἐμποδίζει με πολλά, μάλιστα
μὲν τὸ μὴ δύνασθαι πλανᾶσθαι καὶ τὸ μὴ πρέπειν
ἐπιξενοῦσθαι τοῖς τηλικούτοις, ἔπειθ' ὅτι πάντες
οἱ πυθόμενοι τὴν ἀποδημίαν δικαίως ἄν μου κατα-
φρονήσειαν, εἰ προῃρημένος τὸν ἄλλον χρόνον ἡσυχίαν ἄγειν ἐπὶ γήρως ἀποδημεῖν ἐπιχειροίην, ὅτ'
εἰκὸς ἦν, εἰ καὶ πρότερον ἄλλοθί που διέτριβον,
νῦν οἴκαδε σπεύδειν, οὕτως ὑπογυίου μοι τῆς τε-
3 λευτῆς οὔσης. πρὸς δὲ τούτοις φοβοῦμαι καὶ τὴν
πόλιν· χρὴ γὰρ τἀληθῆ λέγειν. ὁρῶ γὰρ τὰς
συμμαχίας τὰς πρὸς αὐτὴν γιγνομένας ταχέως
διαλυομένας. εἰ δή τι συμβαίη καὶ πρὸς ὑμᾶς
τοιοῦτον, εἰ καὶ τὰς αἰτίας καὶ τοὺς κινδύνους
διαφυγεῖν δυνηθείην, ὃ χαλεπόν ἐστιν, ἀλλ' οὖν
αἰσχυνθείην ἄν, εἴτε διὰ τὴν πόλιν δόξαιμί τισιν
ὑμῶν ἀμελεῖν, εἴτε δι' ὑμᾶς τῆς πόλεως ὀλιγωρεῖν.
μὴ κοινοῦ δὲ τοῦ συμφέροντος ὄντος οὐκ οἶδ' ὅπως

434

LETTER 6. TO THE CHILDREN OF JASON

ONE of our envoys who were sent to you has brought me word that you, summoning him apart from the others, asked whether I could be persuaded to go abroad and reside with you. And I for the sake of my friendship with Jason and Polyalces would gladly come to you ; for I think such an association would benefit us all. Many things hinder me, however, especially my inability to travel and that it is unseemly that men of my age should dwell in a foreign land ; next, because all who heard of my residence abroad would justly despise me if, having chosen to pass my former life in tranquillity, I should undertake in old age to spend my life abroad, when it would be reasonable for me, even if I had been accustomed to live somewhere else, now to hasten home, since the end of my life is now so near at hand. Moreover, I have fears for Athens, since the truth must be told ; for I see that alliances made with her are soon dissolved. So, if anything of that kind should happen between Athens and you, even if I could escape the ensuing accusations and dangers, which would be difficult, yet I should be ashamed if I should be thought by any either to be neglectful of you on account of my city, or on your account to be indifferent to the interests of Athens. For in the absence of a common ground of interest I do not see

ἂν ἀμφοτέροις ἀρέσκειν δυνηθείην. αἱ μὲν οὖν
αἰτίαι, δι' ἃς οὐκ ἔξεστί μοι ποιεῖν ἃ βούλομαι,
τοιαῦται συμβεβήκασιν.

4 Οὐ μὴν περὶ τῶν ἐμαυτοῦ μόνον ἐπιστείλας οἶμαι
δεῖν ἀμελῆσαι τῶν ὑμετέρων, ἀλλ' ἅπερ ἂν παρα-
γενόμενος πρὸς ὑμᾶς διελέχθην, πειράσομαι καὶ
νῦν περὶ τῶν αὐτῶν τούτων ὅπως ἂν δύνωμαι
διεξελθεῖν. μηδὲν δ' ὑπολάβητε τοιοῦτον, ὡς ἄρ'
ἐγὼ ταύτην ἔγραψα τὴν ἐπιστολὴν οὐχ ἕνεκα τῆς
ὑμετέρας ξενίας, ἀλλ' ἐπίδειξιν ποιήσασθαι βουλόμενος. οὐ γὰρ εἰς τοῦθ' ἥκω μανίας ὥστ' ἀγνοεῖν
ὅτι κρείττω μὲν γράψαι τῶν πρότερον διαδεδο-
μένων οὐκ ἂν δυναίμην, τοσοῦτον τῆς ἀκμῆς
ὑστερῶν, χείρω δ' ἐξενεγκὼν πολὺ φαυλοτέραν ἂν
5 λάβοιμι δόξαν τῆς νῦν ἡμῖν ὑπαρχούσης. ἔπειτ'
εἴπερ ἐπιδείξει προσεῖχον τὸν νοῦν ἀλλὰ μὴ πρὸς
ὑμᾶς ἐσπούδαζον, οὐκ ἂν ταύτην ἐξ ἁπασῶν προειλόμην τὴν ὑπόθεσιν, περὶ ἧς χαλεπόν ἐστιν ἐπιεικῶς εἰπεῖν, ἀλλὰ πολὺ καλλίους ἑτέρας ἂν εὗρον
[419] καὶ μᾶλλον λόγον ἐχούσας. ἀλλὰ γὰρ οὔτε πρότερον οὐδὲ πώποτ' ἐφιλοτιμήθην ἐπὶ τούτοις, ἀλλ' ἐφ'
ἑτέροις μᾶλλον, ἃ τοὺς πολλοὺς διαλέληθεν, οὔτε
νῦν ἔχων ταύτην τὴν διάνοιαν ἐπραγματευσάμην,
6 ἀλλ' ὑμᾶς μὲν ὁρῶν ἐν πολλοῖς καὶ μεγάλοις πράγμασιν ὄντας, αὐτὸς δ' ἀποφήνασθαι βουλόμενος
ἣν ἔχω γνώμην περὶ αὐτῶν. ἡγοῦμαι δὲ συμβουλεύειν μὲν ἀκμὴν ἔχειν, αἱ γὰρ ἐμπειρίαι παιδεύ-
ουσι τοὺς τηλικούτους καὶ ποιοῦσι μᾶλλον τῶν
ἄλλων δύνασθαι καθορᾶν τὸ βέλτιστον, εἰπεῖν δὲ
περὶ τῶν προτεθέντων ἐπιχαρίτως καὶ μουσικῶς
καὶ διαπεπονημένως οὐκέτι τῆς ἡμετέρας ἡλικίας

436

how I could please both sides. Such, then, are the reasons why I cannot do as I wish.

But I do not think that I should write to you about my own affairs only and be indifferent to yours; on the contrary, just as I would have done had I come to you, I will now try to discuss these same matters to the best of my ability. And pray do not entertain any such notion as that I have written this letter, not on account of your friendship, but for the purpose of making a rhetorical display. For I have not become so demented as not to know that I could not write anything better than my previously published discourses, being now so far past my prime, and that if I produce anything much inferior in merit, I should find my present reputation grievously impaired. Besides, if I were intent upon producing a composition for display instead of having your interest at heart, I should not have chosen of all available subjects that one which is difficult to treat passably well, but I should have found other themes, much nobler and more logical. But the truth is that never at any time have I prided myself on the compositions of the former kind, but rather upon the latter, which most people have disregarded, nor have I undertaken my present theme with that intention, but because I see that your troubles are many and serious and wish to give you my own opinion concerning them. And I think that for the giving of counsel I am in my prime—for men of my age are trained by experience, which enables them to perceive more clearly than the younger men the best course of action —but to speak upon any proposed subject with grace, elegance, and finish is no longer to be ex-

ἐστίν, ἀλλ' ἀγαπῷην ἄν, εἰ μὴ παντάπασιν ἐκλε-
λυμένως διαλεχθείην περὶ αὐτῶν.

7 Μὴ θαυμάζετε δ' ἄν τι φαίνωμαι λέγων ὧν πρότερον ἀκηκόατε· τῷ μὲν γὰρ ἴσως ἄκων ἂν ἐντύ-
χοιμι, τὸ δὲ καὶ προειδώς, εἰ πρέπον εἰς τὸν λόγον
εἴη, προσλάβοιμι· καὶ γὰρ ἂν ἄτοπος εἴην, εἰ τοὺς
ἄλλους ὁρῶν τοῖς ἐμοῖς χρωμένους αὐτὸς μόνος
ἀπεχοίμην τῶν ὑπ' ἐμοῦ πρότερον εἰρημένων.
τούτου δ' ἕνεκα ταῦτα προεῖπον, ὅτι τὸ πρῶτον
8 ἐπιφερόμενον ἓν τῶν τεθρυλημένων ἐστίν. εἴθισμαι
γὰρ λέγειν πρὸς τοὺς περὶ τὴν φιλοσοφίαν τὴν
ἡμετέραν διατρίβοντας ὅτι τοῦτο πρῶτον δεῖ
σκέψασθαι, τί τῷ λόγῳ καὶ τοῖς τοῦ λόγου μέρεσι
διαπρακτέον ἐστίν· ἐπειδὰν δὲ τοῦθ' εὕρωμεν καὶ
διακριβωσώμεθα, ζητητέον εἶναί φημι τὰς ἰδέας
δι' ὧν ταῦτ' ἐξεργασθήσεται καὶ λήψεται τέλος
ὅπερ ὑπεθέμεθα. καὶ ταῦτα φράζω μὲν ἐπὶ τῶν
λόγων, ἔστι δὲ τοῦτο στοιχεῖον καὶ κατὰ τῶν ἄλλων ἁπάντων καὶ κατὰ τῶν ὑμετέρων πραγμάτων.
9 οὐδὲν γὰρ οἷόν τ' ἐστὶ πραχθῆναι νοῦν ἐχόντως, ἂν
μὴ τοῦτο πρῶτον μετὰ πολλῆς προνοίας λογίσησθε
καὶ βουλεύσησθε, πῶς χρὴ τὸν ἐπίλοιπον χρόνον
ὑμῶν αὐτῶν προστῆναι καὶ τίνα βίον προελέσθαι καὶ
ποίας δόξης ὀριγνηθῆναι καὶ ποτέρας τῶν τιμῶν
ἀγαπῆσαι, τὰς παρ' ἑκόντων γιγνομένας ἢ τὰς παρ'
ἀκόντων τῶν πολιτῶν· ταῦτα δὲ διορισαμένους τότ'

---

[a] Cf. To Philip 10.
[b] For this apology see Antid. 74 and To Philip 93-94
(with Norlin's note), Vol. I, p. 302, L.C.L.
[c] Literally " philosophy "; but for the meaning of " philo-

pected at my age[a]; indeed, I shall be content if I discuss these matters in a not altogether negligent fashion.

Do not be surprised if I am found saying something which you have heard before ; for one statement I may perhaps chance upon unwittingly, another I may consciously employ, if it is pertinent to the discussion. Certainly I should be foolish if, although I see others using my thoughts, I alone should refrain from employing what I have previously said.[b] This is the reason, then, for these introductory words, that the very first precept I shall present is one of those most often repeated. I am accustomed, that is, to tell the students in my school of rhetoric[c] that the first question to be considered is—what is the object to be accomplished by the discourse as a whole and by its parts ? And when we have discovered this and the matter has been accurately determined, I say that we must seek the rhetorical elements whereby that which we have set out to do may be elaborated and fulfilled. And this procedure I prescribe with reference to discourse, yet it is a principle applicable not only to all other matters, but also to your own affairs. For nothing can be intelligently accomplished unless first, with full forethought, you reason and deliberate how you ought to direct your own future, what mode of life you should choose, what kind of repute you should set your heart upon, and which kind of honours you should be contented with—those freely granted by your fellow-citizens or those wrung from them against their will ; and when these principles have been determined,

sophy " in Isocrates see the General Introd. to Vol. I, pp. xxvi ff., of Isocrates (L.C.L.).

ἤδη τὰς πράξεις τὰς καθ' ἑκάστην τὴν ἡμέραν
[420] σκεπτέον, ὅπως συντενοῦσι πρὸς τὰς ὑποθέσεις τὰς
10 ἐξ ἀρχῆς γενομένας. καὶ τοῦτον μὲν τὸν τρόπον
ζητοῦντες καὶ φιλοσοφοῦντες ὥσπερ σκοποῦ κει-
μένου στοχάσεσθε τῇ ψυχῇ καὶ μᾶλλον ἐπιτεύξεσθε
τοῦ συμφέροντος· ἂν δὲ μηδεμίαν ποιήσησθε τοιαύτην ὑπόθεσιν, ἀλλὰ τὸ προσπῖπτον ἐπιχειρῆτε
πράττειν, ἀναγκαῖόν ἐστιν ὑμᾶς ταῖς διανοίαις
πλανᾶσθαι καὶ πολλῶν διαμαρτάνειν πραγμάτων.
11 Ἴσως ἂν οὖν τις τῶν εἰκῇ ζῆν προῃρημένων τοὺς
μὲν τοιούτους λογισμοὺς διασύρειν ἐπιχειρήσειεν,
ξιώσειε δ' ἂν ἤδη με συμβουλεύειν περὶ τῶν προειρημένων. ἔστιν οὖν οὐκ ὀκνητέον ἀποφήνασθαι
περὶ αὐτῶν ἃ τυγχάνω γιγνώσκων. ἐμοὶ γὰρ
αἱρετώτερος ὁ βίος εἶναι δοκεῖ καὶ βελτίων ὁ τῶν
ἰδιωτευόντων ἢ τῶν τυραννούντων, καὶ τὰς τιμὰς
ἡδίους ἡγοῦμαι τὰς ἐν ταῖς πολιτείαις ἢ τὰς ἐν ταῖς
μοναρχίαις· καὶ περὶ τούτων λέγειν ἐπιχειρήσω.
12 καίτοι μ' οὐ λέληθεν ὅτι πολλοὺς ἔξω τοὺς ἐν-
αντιουμένους, καὶ μάλιστα τοὺς περὶ ὑμᾶς ὄντας.
οἶμαι γὰρ οὐχ ἥκιστα τούτους ἐπὶ τὴν τυραννίδα
παροξύνειν ὑμᾶς· σκοποῦσι γὰρ οὐ πανταχῇ τὴν
φύσιν τοῦ πράγματος, ἀλλὰ πολλὰ παραλογίζονται
σφᾶς αὐτούς. τὰς μὲν γὰρ ἐξουσίας καὶ τὰ κέρδη
καὶ τὰς ἡδονὰς ὁρῶσι καὶ τούτων ἀπολαύσεσθαι
προσδοκῶσι, τὰς δὲ ταραχὰς καὶ τοὺς φόβους καὶ
τὰς συμφορὰς τὰς τοῖς ἄρχουσι συμπιπτούσας καὶ
τοῖς φίλοις αὐτῶν οὐ θεωροῦσιν, ἀλλὰ πεπόνθασιν
ὅπερ οἱ τοῖς αἰσχίστοις καὶ παρανομωτάτοις τῶν
13 ἔργων ἐπιχειροῦντες. καὶ γὰρ ἐκεῖνοι τὰς μὲν

then and only then should your daily actions be considered, in order that they may be in conformity with the original plan. If in this way you seriously search and study, you will take mental aim, as at a mark, at what is expedient for you, and will be the more likely to hit it. And if you have no such plan, but attempt to act in casual fashion, inevitably you will go astray in your purposes and fail in many undertakings.

Perhaps some one of those who choose to live planlessly may attempt to disparage such reasoning and ask that I give my advice forthwith with regard to what has just been said. Hence I must not shrink from declaring my honest opinion about it. To me the life of a private citizen seems preferable and better than that of a king, and I regard the honours received under constitutional governments as more gratifying than those under monarchies.[a] It is of these honours I shall endeavour to speak. And yet I am not unaware that I shall have many adversaries, especially among those who are in your circle, because these persons especially, I think, urge you to despotic power ; for they do not examine from all sides the real nature of the question, but in many ways deceive themselves. For it is the powers, the profits, and the pleasures that they see in royalty and expect to enjoy them, whereas they fail to observe the disturbances, the fears, and the misfortunes which befall rulers and their friends. Instead they suffer from the same delusion as do men who set their hands to the most disgraceful and lawless deeds. These in fact are

[a] Isocrates was a firm believer in democracy, but often complains that the Athens of his later life has grievous faults ; see General Introd., Vol. I, p. xxxviii.

πονηρίας τὰς τῶν πραγμάτων οὐκ ἀγνοοῦσιν, ἐλπί-
ζουσι δ' ὅσον μὲν ἀγαθόν ἐστιν ἐν αὐτοῖς, τοῦτο μὲν
ἐκλήψεσθαι, τὰ δὲ δεινὰ πάντα τὰ προσόντα τῷ
πράγματι καὶ τὰ κακὰ διαφεύξεσθαι, καὶ διοική-
σειν τὰ περὶ σφᾶς αὐτοὺς οὕτως, ὥστε τῶν μὲν
κινδύνων εἶναι πόρρω, τῶν δ' ὠφελειῶν ἐγγύς.
14 τοὺς μὲν οὖν ταύτην ἔχοντας τὴν διάνοιαν ζηλῶ
τῆς ῥᾳθυμίας, αὐτὸς δ' αἰσχυνθείην ἄν, εἰ συμβουλεύων ἑτέροις ἐκείνων ἀμελήσας τὸ ἐμαυτῷ
συμφέρον ποιοίην καὶ μὴ παντάπασιν ἔξω θεὶς
[121] ἐμαυτὸν καὶ τῶν ὠφελειῶν καὶ τῶν ἄλλων ἁπάντων
τὰ βέλτιστα παραινοίην.

Ὡς οὖν ἐμοῦ ταύτην ἔχοντος τὴν γνώμην, οὕτω
μοι προσέχετε τὸν νοῦν. . . .

not ignorant of the wickedness of their acts, but hope to extract all the profit therein and yet to be exempt from all the dangers and ills which inhere in such acts, and to manage their affairs in such fashion as to keep the perils at a distance and the benefits within easy reach. As for those who have this conception of the matter, I envy them their easy-going philosophy, but I myself should be ashamed if, while offering counsel to others, I should be negligent of their interests and look to my own advantage instead of putting myself altogether beyond the reach of both the personal benefits and all other considerations and advising the best course of action.

Being aware, therefore, that I hold this conviction, I beg you to give me your attention. . . . [*Then followed in the letter the practical advice of Isocrates to the future rulers of Thessaly, presumably setting forth the advantages of a government under a constitution,* i.e., *a limited monarchy.*]

LETTER 7. TO TIMOTHEUS

INTRODUCTION

THIS letter is written to Timotheüs, who was ruler of Heracleia on the Euxine Sea. Clearchus, the father of Timotheüs, had been a pupil of Isocrates and was generally esteemed for his kindliness and humanity.[a] But when he returned to Heracleia, and became tyrant, in 364 B.C., he ruled for twelve years with great cruelty. At his death, in 353 B.C., he was succeeded by his brother Satyrus, as regent, who, after holding power for some seven years, gave up the throne to Timotheüs, son of Clearchus, who reigned from about 346 to 338 B.C. The government under Timotheüs was milder and more democratic, and Isocrates writes to congratulate him on this wise policy, to renew old ties of friendship, and to give him, in typical fashion, good advice for his future conduct. The bearer of the letter, Autocrator, a friend of Isocrates, is recommended to the good graces of the king.

The date of the letter is evidently about 345 B.C. and its authenticity is not open to question.[b]

[a] See § 12 of this letter.
[b] For the evidence on which these statements are based see Blass, *Die attische Beredsamkeit* ii. p. 330 and Jebb, *Attic Orators* ii. p. 247.

7. ΤΙΜΟΘΕΩΙ

[421] Περὶ μὲν τῆς οἰκειότητος τῆς ὑπαρχούσης ἡμῖν πρὸς ἀλλήλους οἶμαί σε πολλῶν ἀκηκοέναι, συγχαίρω δέ σοι πυνθανόμενος, πρῶτον μὲν ὅτι τῇ δυναστείᾳ τῇ παρούσῃ κάλλιον χρῇ τοῦ πατρὸς καὶ φρονιμώτερον, ἔπειθ᾽ ὅτι προαιρεῖ δόξαν καλὴν κτήσασθαι μᾶλλον ἢ πλοῦτον μέγαν συναγαγεῖν. σημεῖον γὰρ οὐ μικρὸν ἐκφέρεις ἀρετῆς, ἀλλ᾽ ὡς δυνατὸν μέγιστον, ταύτην ἔχων τὴν γνώμην· ὥστ᾽ ἢν ἐμμείνῃς τοῖς περὶ σοῦ νῦν λεγομένοις, οὐκ ἀπορήσεις τῶν ἐγκωμιασομένων τήν τε φρόνησιν 2 τὴν σὴν καὶ τὴν προαίρεσιν ταύτην. ἡγοῦμαι δὲ καὶ τὰ διηγγελμένα περὶ τοῦ πατρός σου συμβαλεῖσθαι μεγάλην πίστιν πρὸς τὸ δοκεῖν εὖ φρονεῖν σε καὶ διαφέρειν τῶν ἄλλων· εἰώθασι γὰρ οἱ πλεῖστοι τῶν ἀνθρώπων οὐχ οὕτως ἐπαινεῖν καὶ τιμᾶν τοὺς ἐκ τῶν πατέρων τῶν εὐδοκιμούντων γεγονότας, ὡς τοὺς ἐκ τῶν δυσκόλων καὶ χαλεπῶν, ἤν περ φαίνωνται μηδὲν ὅμοιοι τοῖς γονεῦσιν ὄντες. μᾶλλον γὰρ ἐπὶ πάντων κεχαρισμένον αὐτοῖς ἐστι τὸ παρὰ λόγον συμβαῖνον ἀγαθὸν τῶν εἰκότως καὶ προσηκόντως γιγνομένων.

3 Ὧν ἐνθυμούμενον χρὴ ζητεῖν καὶ φιλοσοφεῖν ἐξ

448

LETTER 7.   TO TIMOTHEUS

OF the friendly relations which exist between your family and me I think you have heard from many sources, and I congratulate you as I receive word, first that you are making use of the princely power you now possess in better and wiser fashion than your father,[a] and also, that you choose rather to win good repute than to amass great wealth.   In making this your purpose you give no slight indication of virtue, but the very greatest ; so that, if you are faithful to your present reputation, you will not lack those who will praise both your wisdom and this choice.   I think that the reports which have been noised abroad about your father will also contribute a great deal of credibility to the general opinion of your good judgement and superiority to all others ; for most men are wont to praise and honour, not so much the sons of fathers who are of good repute, as those born of harsh and cruel fathers, provided that they show themselves to be similar in no respect to their parents.   For any boon which comes to men contrary to reason always gives them greater pleasure than those which duly come to pass in accordance with their expectation.

Bearing this in mind, you should search and study

[a] The rule of Clearchus (tyrant of Heracleia on the Euxine), father of Timotheüs, had been extremely cruel.

449

ὅτου τρόπου καὶ μετὰ τίνων καὶ τίσι συμβούλοις
χρώμενος τάς τε τῆς πόλεως ἀτυχίας ἐπανορθώσεις
καὶ τοὺς πολίτας ἐπί τε τὰς ἐργασίας καὶ τὴν
[422] σωφροσύνην προτρέψεις καὶ ποιήσεις αὐτοὺς ἥδιον
ζῆν καὶ θαρραλεώτερον ἢ τὸν παρελθόντα χρόνον·
ταῦτα γάρ ἐστιν ἔργα τῶν ὀρθῶς καὶ φρονίμως
4 τυραννευόντων. ὧν ἔνιοι καταφρονήσαντες οὐδὲν
ἄλλο σκοποῦσι, πλὴν ὅπως αὐτοί θ' ὡς μετὰ
πλείστης ἀσελγείας τὸν βίον διάξουσι, τῶν τε
πολιτῶν τοὺς βελτίστους καὶ πλουσιωτάτους καὶ
φρονιμωτάτους λυμανοῦνται καὶ δασμολογήσουσι,
κακῶς εἰδότες ὅτι προσήκει τοὺς εὖ φρονοῦντας καὶ
τὴν τιμὴν ταύτην ἔχοντας μὴ τοῖς τῶν ἄλλων
κακοῖς αὑτοῖς ἡδονὰς παρασκευάζειν, ἀλλὰ ταῖς
αὑτῶν ἐπιμελείαις τοὺς πολίτας εὐδαιμονεστέρους
5 ποιεῖν, μηδὲ πικρῶς μὲν καὶ χαλεπῶς διακεῖσθαι
πρὸς ἅπαντας, ἀμελεῖν δὲ τῆς αὑτῶν σωτηρίας,
ἀλλ' οὕτω μὲν πράως καὶ νομίμως ἐπιστατεῖν τῶν
πραγμάτων ὥστε μηδένα τολμᾶν αὐτοῖς ἐπιβουλεύειν, μετὰ τοσαύτης δ' ἀκριβείας τὴν τοῦ σώματος
ποιεῖσθαι φυλακὴν ὡς ἁπάντων αὐτοὺς ἀνελεῖν
βουλομένων. ταύτην γὰρ τὴν διάνοιαν ἔχοντες
αὐτοί τ' ἂν ἔξω τῶν κινδύνων εἶεν καὶ παρὰ τοῖς
ἄλλοις εὐδοκιμοῖεν· ὧν ἀγαθὰ μείζω χαλεπὸν
6 εὑρεῖν ἐστίν. ἐνεθυμήθην δὲ μεταξὺ γράφων, ὡς
εὐτυχῶς ἅπαντά σοι συμβέβηκεν. τὴν μὲν γὰρ
εὐπορίαν ἣν ἀναγκαῖον ἦν κτήσασθαι μετὰ βίας
καὶ τυραννικῶς καὶ μετὰ πολλῆς ἀπεχθείας ὁ
πατήρ σοι καταλέλοιπε, τὸ δὲ χρῆσθαι τούτοις
καλῶς καὶ φιλανθρώπως ἐπὶ σοὶ γέγονεν· ὧν χρή
σε πολλὴν ποιεῖσθαι τὴν ἐπιμέλειαν.

ᵃ Cf. *On the Peace* 91 for the same sentiment.

in what fashion, with the aid of whom, and by employing what counsellors you are to repair your city's misfortunes, to spur your citizens on to their labours and to temperate conduct, and to cause them to live more happily and more confidently than in the past; for this is the duty of good and wise kings. Some, disdaining these obligations, look to nothing else save how they may themselves lead lives of the greatest licentiousness and may mistreat and pillage by taxation the best and wealthiest and most sagacious of their subjects, being ill aware that wise men who hold that high office should not, at the cost of injury to all the rest, provide pleasures for themselves, but rather should by their own watchful care make their subjects happier [a]; nor should they, while being harshly and cruelly disposed toward all, yet be careless of their own safety; on the contrary, their conduct of affairs should be so gentle and so in accordance with the law that no one will venture to plot against them; yet they should rigorously guard their persons as if everybody wished to kill them. For if they should adopt this policy, they would themselves be free from danger and at the same time be highly esteemed by all; blessings greater than these it would be difficult to discover. I have been thinking, as I write, how happily everything has fallen out for you. The wealth which could only have been acquired forcibly and despotically and at the cost of much hatred, has been left to you by your father, but to use it honourably and for the good of mankind has devolved upon you [b]; and to this task you should devote yourself with great diligence.

[a] *Cf. Evag.* 25 for a somewhat similar passage.

7 Ἃ μὲν οὖν ἐγὼ γιγνώσκω, ταῦτ' ἐστίν· ἔχει δ'
οὕτως. εἰ μὲν ἐρᾷς χρημάτων καὶ μείζονος δυναστείας καὶ κινδύνων δι' ὧν αἱ κτήσεις τούτων εἰσίν,
ἑτέρους σοι συμβούλους παρακλητέον· εἰ δὲ ταῦτα
μὲν ἱκανῶς ἔχεις, ἀρετῆς δὲ καὶ δόξης καλῆς καὶ
τῆς παρὰ τῶν πολλῶν εὐνοίας ἐπιθυμεῖς, τοῖς τε
λόγοις τοῖς ἐμοῖς προσεκτέον τὸν νοῦν ἐστι καὶ
τοῖς καλῶς τὰς πόλεις τὰς αὑτῶν διοικοῦσιν ἁμιλ-
λητέον καὶ πειρατέον αὐτῶν διενεγκεῖν.

8 Ἀκούω δὲ Κλέομμιν τὸν ἐν Μηθύμνῃ ταύτην
ἔχοντα τὴν δυναστείαν περί τε τὰς ἄλλας πράξεις
καλὸν κἀγαθὸν εἶναι καὶ φρόνιμον, καὶ τοσοῦτον
ἀπέχειν τοῦ τῶν πολιτῶν τινας ἀποκτείνειν ἢ
φυγαδεύειν ἢ δημεύειν τὰς οὐσίας ἢ ποιεῖν ἄλλο τι
[423] κακόν, ὥστε πολλὴν μὲν ἀσφάλειαν παρέχειν τοῖς
συμπολιτευομένοις, κατάγειν δὲ τοὺς φεύγοντας,
ἀποδιδόναι δὲ τοῖς μὲν κατιοῦσι τὰς κτήσεις ἐξ ὧν
9 ἐξέπεσον, τοῖς δὲ πριαμένοις τὰς τιμὰς τὰς ἑκάστοις γιγνομένας, πρὸς δὲ τούτοις καθοπλίζειν
ἅπαντας τοὺς πολίτας, ὡς οὐδενὸς μὲν ἐπιχειρή-
σοντος περὶ αὐτὸν νεωτερίζειν, ἢν δ' ἄρα τινὲς
τολμήσωσιν, ἡγούμενον λυσιτελεῖν αὐτῷ τεθνάναι
τοιαύτην ἀρετὴν ἐνδειξαμένῳ τοῖς πολίταις μᾶλλον
ἢ ζῆν πλείω χρόνον τῇ πόλει τῶν μεγίστων κακῶν
αἴτιον γενόμενον.

10 Ἔτι δ' ἂν πλείω σοι περὶ τούτων διελέχθην, ἴσως
δ' ἂν καὶ χαριέστερον, εἰ μὴ παντάπασιν ἔδει με διὰ
ταχέων γράψαι τὴν ἐπιστολήν. νῦν δὲ σοὶ μὲν
αὖθις συμβουλεύσομεν, ἂν μὴ κωλύσῃ με τὸ γῆρας,
ἐν δὲ τῷ παρόντι περὶ τῶν ἰδίων δηλώσομεν.
Αὐτοκράτωρ γὰρ ὁ τὰ γράμματα φέρων οἰκείως
11 ἡμῖν ἔχει· περί τε γὰρ τὰς διατριβὰς τὰς αὐτὰς

These, then, are my views ; but this is the application : If your heart is set upon money and greater power and dangers too, through which these possessions are acquired, you must summon other advisers ; but if you already have enough of these and wish virtue, fair reputation, and the goodwill of your subjects in general, you should heed my words and emulate those rulers who govern their states well and should endeavour to surpass them.

I hear that Cleommis, who in Methymna holds this royal power, is noble and wise in all his actions, and that so far from putting any of his subjects to death, or exiling them, or confiscating their property, or injuring them in any other respect, he provides great security for his fellow-citizens, and restores the exiles, returning to those who come back their lost possessions, and in each case recompenses the purchasers the price they had paid. In addition, he gives arms to all the citizens, thinking that none will try to revolt from him ; but even if any should dare it, he believes that his death after having shown such generosity to the citizens would be preferable to continued existence after becoming the author of the greatest evils to his city.

I should have discussed these matters with you at greater length, and perhaps also in a more attractive style, were I not under the stern necessity of writing the letter in haste. As it is, I will counsel you at a later time if my old age does not prevent ; for the present I will speak concerning our personal relations. Autocrator, the bearer of this letter, is my friend ; we have been interested in the same

ISOCRATES

γεγόναμεν καὶ τῇ τέχνῃ πολλάκις αὐτοῦ κέχρημαι
καὶ τὸ τελευταῖον περὶ τῆς ἀποδημίας τῆς ὡς σὲ
σύμβουλος ἐγενόμην αὐτῷ. διὰ δὴ ταῦτα πάντα
βουλοίμην ἄν σε καλῶς αὐτῷ χρήσασθαι καὶ συμφερόντως ἀμφοτέροις ἡμῖν,[1] καὶ γενέσθαι φανερόν,
ὅτι μέρος τι καὶ δι᾽ ἐμὲ γίγνεταί τι τῶν δεόντων
12 αὐτῷ. καὶ μὴ θαυμάσῃς, εἰ σοὶ μὲν οὕτως ἐπιστέλλω
προθύμως, Κλεάρχου δὲ μηδὲν πώποτ᾽ ἐδεήθην.
σχεδὸν γὰρ ἅπαντες οἱ παρ᾽ ὑμῶν καταπλέοντες σὲ
μὲν ὅμοιόν φασιν εἶναι τοῖς βελτίστοις τῶν ἐμοὶ
πεπλησιακότων, Κλέαρχον δὲ κατὰ μὲν ἐκεῖνον τὸν
χρόνον, ὅτ᾽ ἦν παρ᾽ ἡμῖν, ὡμολόγουν, ὅσοι περ
ἐνέτυχον, ἐλευθεριώτατον εἶναι καὶ πραότατον καὶ
φιλανθρωπότατον τῶν μετεχόντων τῆς διατριβῆς·
ἐπειδὴ δὲ τὴν δύναμιν ἔλαβε, τοσοῦτον ἔδοξε μετα-
πεσεῖν ὥστε πάντας θαυμάζειν τοὺς πρότερον αὐτὸν
13 γιγνώσκοντας. πρὸς μὲν οὖν ἐκεῖνον διὰ ταύτας
τὰς αἰτίας ἀπηλλοτριώθην· σὲ δ᾽ ἀποδέχομαι καὶ
πρὸ πολλοῦ ποιησαίμην ἂν οἰκείως διατεθῆναι πρὸς
ἡμᾶς. δηλώσεις δὲ καὶ σὺ διὰ ταχέων, εἰ τὴν
[424] αὐτὴν γνώμην ἔχεις ἡμῖν· Αὐτοκράτορός τε γὰρ
ἐπιμελήσει καὶ πέμψεις ἐπιστολὴν ὡς ἡμᾶς,
ἀνανεούμενος τὴν φιλίαν καὶ ξενίαν τὴν πρότερον
ὑπάρχουσαν. ἔρρωσο, κἄν του δέῃ τῶν παρ᾽ ἡμῖν,
ἐπίστελλε.

[1] ἡμῖν: ὑμῖν ΕΓ[1] is read by Blass.

454

pursuits and I have often profited by his skill, and, finally, I have advised him about his visit to you. For all those reasons I would have you use him well and in a manner profitable to us both, and that it may become evident that his needs are being realized in some measure through my efforts. And do not marvel that I am so ready to write to you, though I never made any request of your father Clearchus. For almost all who have sailed hither from your court say that you resemble my best pupils. But as for Clearchus when he visited us, all who met him agreed that he was at that time the most liberal, kindly, and humane of the members of my school; but when he gained his power he seemed to change in disposition so greatly that all who had previously known him marvelled. For these reasons I was estranged from him; but you I esteem and I should highly value your friendly disposition toward myself. And you yourself will soon make it clear if you reciprocate my regard; for you will be considerate of Autocrator, and send me a letter renewing our former friendship and hospitality. Farewell; if you wish anything from here, write.

LETTER 8. TO THE RULERS OF
THE MYTILENAEANS

INTRODUCTION

In this letter Isocrates addresses the oligarchic government of Mytilenê in Lesbos, which had overthrown the democracy not long before. Since the oligarchs had shown unexpected clemency and moderation [a] the orator, on the insistent request of his grandsons, begs for the restoration from exile of the distinguished musician Agenor, their teacher, and his family.

The authenticity of *Letter* 8 is unquestioned. The date appears to be 350 B.C., as may be determined from § 8, where Isocrates says that " if Conon and Timotheüs were still living and Diophantus had returned from Asia " they would support his plea. Timotheüs, son of Conon, had died in 354 B.C., and Diophantus the Athenian was serving the king of Egypt against Artaxerxes Ochus in 351–350 B.C.[b]

[a] See § 3. [b] *Cf.* Diodorus xvi. 48.

459

8. ΤΟΙΣ ΜΥΤΙΛΗΝΑΙΩΝ ΑΡΧΟΥΣΙΝ

Οἱ παῖδες οἱ Ἀφαρέως, υἱδεῖς δ' ἐμοί, παιδευθέντες ὑπ' Ἀγήνορος τὰ περὶ τὴν μουσικήν, ἐδεήθησάν μου γράμματα πέμψαι πρὸς ὑμᾶς, ὅπως ἄν, ἐπειδὴ καὶ τῶν ἄλλων τινὰς κατηγάγετε φυγάδων, καὶ τοῦτον καταδέξησθε καὶ τὸν πατέρα καὶ τοὺς ἀδελφούς. λέγοντος δέ μου πρὸς αὐτοὺς ὅτι δέδοικα μὴ λίαν ἄτοπος εἶναι δόξω καὶ περίεργος, ζητῶν εὑρίσκεσθαι τηλικαῦτα τὸ μέγεθος παρ' ἀνδρῶν οἷς οὐδὲ πώποτε πρότερον οὔτε διελέχθην οὔτε συνήθης ἐγενόμην, ἀκούσαντες ταῦτα πολὺ
2 μᾶλλον ἐλιπάρουν. ὡς δ' οὐδὲν αὐτοῖς ἀπέβαινεν ὧν ἤλπιζον, ἅπασιν ἦσαν καταφανεῖς ἀηδῶς διακείμενοι καὶ χαλεπῶς φέροντες. ὁρῶν δ' αὐτοὺς λυπουμένους μᾶλλον τοῦ προσήκοντος, τελευτῶν ὑπεσχόμην γράψειν τὴν ἐπιστολὴν καὶ πέμψειν ὑμῖν. ὑπὲρ μὲν οὖν τοῦ μὴ δικαίως ἂν δοκεῖν μωρὸς εἶναι μηδ' ὀχληρὸς ταῦτ' ἔχω λέγειν.
3 Ἡγοῦμαι δὲ καλῶς ὑμᾶς βεβουλεῦσθαι καὶ διαλλαττομένους τοῖς πολίταις τοῖς ὑμετέροις, καὶ πειρωμένους τοὺς μὲν φεύγοντας ὀλίγους ποιεῖν, τοὺς δὲ συμπολιτευομένους πολλούς, καὶ μιμου-

LETTER 8. TO THE RULERS OF
THE MYTILENAEANS

THE sons of Aphareus,[a] my grandsons, who were
instructed in music by Agenor,[b] have asked me to
write to you and beg that, since you have restored
some of the other exiles, you will also allow Agenor,
his father, and his brothers to return home. When
I told them that I feared I should appear ridiculous
and meddlesome in seeking so great a favour from
men with whom I have never before spoken or been
acquainted, they, upon hearing my reply, were all the
more insistent. And when they could obtain nothing
of what they hoped, they clearly showed to all that
they were displeased and sorely disappointed. So
when I saw that they were unduly distressed I finally
promised to write the letter and send it to you.
That I may not justly seem foolish and irksome I
make this explanation.

I think you have been well advised both in becoming reconciled to your fellow-citizens and, while trying to reduce the number of exiles, in increasing that
of the participants in public life and also in imitating

[a] Aphareus, son of the sophist Hippias and the son-in-law
and adoptive son of Isocrates, was a tragic poet of some
distinction.
[b] Agenor and his school were well known as musicians
before Aristoxenus.

461

μένους τὰ περὶ τὴν στάσιν τὴν πόλιν τὴν ἡμετέραν.
μάλιστα δ' ἄν τις ὑμᾶς ἐπαινέσειεν ὅτι τοῖς κατιοῦ-
σιν ἀποδίδοτε τὴν οὐσίαν· ἐπιδείκνυσθε γὰρ καὶ
ποιεῖτε πᾶσι φανερὸν ὡς οὐ τῶν κτημάτων ἐπι-
[425] θυμήσαντες τῶν ἀλλοτρίων, ἀλλ' ὑπὲρ τῆς πόλεως
4 δείσαντες ἐποιήσασθε τὴν ἐκβολὴν αὐτῶν. οὐ μὴν
ἀλλ' εἰ καὶ μηδὲν ὑμῖν ἔδοξε τούτων μηδὲ προσ-
εδέχεσθε μηδένα τῶν φυγάδων, τούτους γε νομίζω
συμφέρειν ὑμῖν κατάγειν. αἰσχρὸν γὰρ τὴν μὲν
πόλιν ὑμῶν ὑπὸ πάντων ὁμολογεῖσθαι μουσικω-
τάτην εἶναι καὶ τοὺς ὀνομαστοτάτους ἐν αὐτῇ παρ'
ὑμῖν τυγχάνειν γεγονότας, τὸν δὲ προέχοντα τῶν
νῦν ὄντων περὶ τὴν ἱστορίαν τῆς παιδείας ταύτης
φεύγειν ἐκ τῆς τοιαύτης πόλεως, καὶ τοὺς μὲν
ἄλλους Ἕλληνας τοὺς διαφέροντας περί τι τῶν
καλῶν ἐπιτηδευμάτων, κἂν μηδὲν προσήκωσι,
ποιεῖσθαι πολίτας, ὑμᾶς δὲ τοὺς εὐδοκιμοῦντάς τε
παρὰ τοῖς ἄλλοις καὶ μετασχόντας τῆς αὐτῆς
5 φύσεως περιορᾶν παρ' ἑτέροις μετοικοῦντας. θαυμάζω δ' ὅσαι τῶν πόλεων μειζόνων δωρεῶν ἀξιοῦσι
τοὺς ἐν τοῖς γυμνικοῖς ἀγῶσι κατορθοῦντας μᾶλλον
ἢ τοὺς τῇ φρονήσει καὶ τῇ φιλοπονίᾳ τι τῶν χρησίμων εὑρίσκοντας, καὶ μὴ συνορῶσιν ὅτι πεφύκασιν αἱ μὲν περὶ τὴν ῥώμην καὶ τὸ τάχος δυνάμεις
συναποθνήσκειν τοῖς σώμασιν, αἱ δ' ἐπιστῆμαι
παραμένειν ἅπαντα τὸν χρόνον ὠφελοῦσαι τοὺς
6 χρωμένους αὐταῖς. ὧν ἐνθυμουμένους χρὴ τοὺς
νοῦν ἔχοντας περὶ πλείστου μὲν ποιεῖσθαι τοὺς
καλῶς καὶ δικαίως τῆς αὐτῶν πόλεως ἐπιστατοῦν-

Athens [a] in handling the sedition. You are especially deserving of praise because you are restoring their property to the exiles who return ; for thus you show and make clear to all that you had expelled them, not because you coveted the property of others, but because you feared for the welfare of the city. Nevertheless, even if you had adopted none of the measures, and had received back no one of the exiles, the restoration of these individuals is to your advantage, I think; for it is disgraceful that while your city is universally acknowledged to be most devoted to music and the most notable artists in that field have been born among you,[b] yet he who is the foremost authority of living men in that branch of culture is an exile from such a city ; and that while all other Greeks confer citizenship upon men who are distinguished in any of the noble pursuits, even though they are foreigners, yet you suffer those who are both famous among the other Greeks and share in your own racial origin to live abroad in exile. I marvel that so many cities judge those who excel in the athletic contests to be worthy of greater rewards than those who, by painstaking thought and endeavour, discover some useful thing,[c] and that they do not see at a glance that while the faculties of strength and speed naturally perish with the body, yet the arts and sciences abide for eternity, giving benefit to those who cultivate them. Intelligent men, therefore, bearing in mind these considerations, should esteem most highly, first those who administer

[a] A reference to the moderation of the Athenian democracy in 403 B.C.

[b] *e.g.*, Terpander, Alcaeus, and Sappho.

[c] For this same complaint see *Panegyr.* 1-2, Vol. I, p. 121, L.C.L. with note, and *Antid.* 250.

τας, δευτέρους δὲ τοὺς τιμὴν καὶ δόξαν αὐτῇ καλὴν συμβαλέσθαι δυναμένους· ἅπαντες γὰρ ὥσπερ
δείγματι τοῖς τοιούτοις χρώμενοι καὶ τοὺς ἄλλους
τοὺς συμπολιτευομένους ὁμοίους εἶναι τούτοις
νομίζουσιν.

7 Ἴσως οὖν εἴποι τις ἂν ὅτι προσήκει τοὺς εὑρέσθαι
τι βουλομένους μὴ τὸ πρᾶγμα μόνον ἐπαινεῖν ἀλλὰ
καὶ σφᾶς αὐτοὺς ἐπιδεικνύναι δικαίως ἂν τυγχάνοντας, περὶ ὧν ποιοῦνται τοὺς λόγους. ἔχει δ'
οὕτως. ἐγὼ τοῦ μὲν πολιτεύεσθαι καὶ ῥητορεύειν
ἀπέστην· οὔτε γὰρ φωνὴν ἔσχον ἱκανὴν οὔτε τόλμαν·
οὐ μὴν παντάπασιν ἄχρηστος ἔφυν οὐδ' ἀδόκιμος,
ἀλλὰ τοῖς τε λέγειν προῃρημένοις ἀγαθόν τι περὶ
ὑμῶν καὶ τῶν ἄλλων συμμάχων φανείην ἂν καὶ
σύμβουλος καὶ συναγωνιστὴς γεγενημένος, αὐτός
[426] τε πλείους λόγους πεποιημένος ὑπὲρ τῆς ἐλευθερίας
καὶ τῆς αὐτονομίας τῆς τῶν Ἑλλήνων ἢ σύμπαντες
8 οἱ τὰ βήματα κατατετριφότες. ὑπὲρ ὧν ὑμεῖς ἂν
μοι δικαίως πλείστην ἔχοιτε χάριν· μάλιστα γὰρ
ἐπιθυμοῦντες διατελεῖτε τῆς τοιαύτης καταστάσεως.
οἶμαι δ' ἄν, εἰ Κόνων μὲν καὶ Τιμόθεος ἐτύγχανον
ζῶντες, Διόφαντος δ' ἧκεν ἐκ τῆς Ἀσίας, πολλὴν
ἂν αὐτοὺς ποιήσασθαι σπουδήν, εὑρέσθαι με βουλομένους ὧν τυγχάνω δεόμενος. περὶ ὧν οὐκ οἶδ'
ὅ τι δεῖ πλείω λέγειν· οὐδεὶς γὰρ ὑμῶν οὕτως ἐστὶ
νέος οὐδ' ἐπιλήσμων, ὅστις οὐκ οἶδε τὰς ἐκείνων
εὐεργεσίας.

9 Οὕτω δ' ἄν μοι δοκεῖτε κάλλιστα βουλεύσασθαι
περὶ τούτων, εἰ σκέψαισθε, τίς ἐστιν ὁ δεόμενος

---

[a] See *Epist.* 1. 9 (with note *e*).
[b] See General Introd., Vol. I, p. xxxii, L.C.L., for the
sympathies of Isocrates, which embraced all Hellas.

well and justly the affairs of their own city, and, second, those who are able to contribute to its honour and glory; for all the world uses such men as examples and all their fellow-citizens are judged to be of like excellence.

But perhaps someone may object, saying that those who wish to obtain a favour should not merely praise the thing, but should also show that they themselves would be justly entitled to that for which they petition. But here is the situation. It is true that I have abstained from political activity and from practising oratory: for my voice was inadequate and I lacked assurance.[a] I have not been altogether useless, however, and without repute; on the contrary, you will find that I have been the counsellor and coadjutor of those who have been chosen to speak well of you and of our other allies, and that I have myself composed more discourses on behalf of the freedom and independence of the Greeks[b] than all those together who have worn smooth the floor of our platforms. For this you would justly be grateful to me in the highest degree; for you constantly and earnestly desire such a settled policy. And I think that, if Conon and Timotheüs were still alive, and Diophantus[c] had returned from Asia, they would have supported me most enthusiastically, since they would wish that I might obtain all I request. On this topic I do not know what more I need say; for there is no one among you so young or so forgetful as not to know the benefactions of those great men.

But I think that you would arrive at the best decision as to this matter if you should consider

* See Introduction to this letter.

καὶ ὑπὲρ ποίων τινῶν ἀνθρώπων. εὑρήσετε γὰρ
ἐμὲ μὲν οἰκειότατα κεχρημένον τοῖς μεγίστων
ἀγαθῶν αἰτίοις γεγενημένοις ὑμῖν τε καὶ τοῖς ἄλλοις, ὑπὲρ ὧν δὲ δέομαι τοιούτους ὄντας, οἵους
τοὺς μὲν πρεσβυτέρους καὶ τοὺς περὶ τὴν πολιτείαν
ὄντας μὴ λυπεῖν, τοῖς δὲ νεωτέροις διατριβὴν
παρέχειν ἡδεῖαν καὶ χρησίμην καὶ πρέπουσαν τοῖς
τηλικούτοις.

10 Μὴ θαυμάζετε δ' εἰ προθυμότερον καὶ διὰ μακροτέρων γέγραφα τὴν ἐπιστολήν· βούλομαι γὰρ
ἀμφότερα, τοῖς τε παισὶν ἡμῶν χαρίσασθαι καὶ
ποιῆσαι φανερὸν αὐτοῖς ὅτι, κἂν μὴ δημηγορῶσι
μηδὲ στρατηγῶσιν ἀλλὰ μόνον μιμῶνται τὸν τρόπον τὸν ἐμόν, οὐκ ἠμελημένως διάξουσιν ἐν τοῖς
Ἕλλησιν. ἓν ἔτι λοιπόν· ἂν ἄρα δόξῃ τι τούτων
ὑμῖν πράττειν, Ἀγήνορί τε δηλώσατε καὶ τοῖς
ἀδελφοῖς ὅτι μέρος τι καὶ δι' ἐμὲ τυγχάνουσιν ὧν
ἐπεθύμουν.

who your petitioner is and for what men the favour is asked. For you will find that I have had the most intimate relations with those who have been the authors of the greatest benefits to both you and the other allies, and that while those for whom I intercede are men of such character as to give no offence to their elders and to those in governmental authority, to the younger men they furnish agreeable and useful occupation that befits those of their age.

Do not wonder that I have written this letter with considerable warmth and at some length; for I desire to accomplish two things : not only to do our children a favour, but also to make it clear to them that even if they do not become orators in the Assembly or generals, but merely imitate my manner of life, they will not lead neglected lives among the Greeks. One thing more—if it should seem best to you to grant any of these requests, let Agenor and his brothers understand that it is owing in some measure to me that they are obtaining what they desire.

LETTER 9. TO ARCHIDAMUS

INTRODUCTION

ARCHIDAMUS III succeeded his father Agesilaus as one of the kings of Sparta. Isocrates had previously written for him, probably in 366 B.C., his Sixth Oration, *Archidamus*, a deliberative speech. He now addresses him in this letter, which, like *Letters* 1 and 6, lacks a conclusion and was, therefore, probably only a preface to a longer discourse on his favourite topic [a]—that Archidamus should lead a united Hellas against Persia.

The date of this letter (356 B.C.) is furnished by Isocrates himself. In § 16 he says that he is eighty years of age. Despite the writer's statement that he is "altogether worn out," the communication, although it seems to show signs of hasty composition, is full of life and vigour.[b] The evil plight at this time of Hellas as a whole, and of the Greeks dwelling along the seaboard of Asia, is vividly depicted.

The arguments adduced by some scholars to cast doubt upon the authenticity of this letter are without validity.[c]

[a] *Cf.* General Introd., Vol. I, pp. xxxiv ff., and *To Philip* 130.

[b] Especially is this true of the carefully elaborated Introduction (§§ 1-7).

[c] See L. F. Smith, *The Genuineness of the Ninth and Third Letters of Isocrates* (1940).

9. ΑΡΧΙΔΑΜΩΙ

[434] Εἰδώς, ὦ Ἀρχίδαμε, πολλοὺς ὡρμημένους ἐγκωμιάζειν σὲ καὶ τὸν πατέρα καὶ τὸ γένος ὑμῶν, εἱλόμην τοῦτον μὲν τὸν λόγον, ἐπειδὴ λίαν ῥᾴδιος ἦν, ἐκείνοις παραλιπεῖν, αὐτὸς δέ σε διανοοῦμαι παρακαλεῖν ἐπὶ στρατηγίας καὶ στρατείας οὐδὲν ὁμοίας ταῖς νῦν ἐνεστηκυίαις, ἀλλ᾽ ἐξ ὧν μεγάλων ἀγαθῶν αἴτιος γενήσει καὶ τῇ πόλει τῇ σαυτοῦ καὶ 2 τοῖς Ἕλλησιν ἅπασιν. ταύτην δ᾽ ἐποιησάμην τὴν αἵρεσιν, οὐκ ἀγνοῶν τῶν λόγων τὸν εὐμεταχειριστότερον, ἀλλ᾽ ἀκριβῶς εἰδὼς ὅτι πράξεις μὲν εὑρεῖν καλὰς καὶ μεγάλας καὶ συμφερούσας χαλεπὸν καὶ σπάνιόν ἐστιν, ἐπαινέσαι δὲ τὰς ἀρετὰς τὰς ὑμετέρας ῥᾳδίως οἷός τ᾽ ἂν ἐγενόμην. οὐ γὰρ ἔδει με παρ᾽ ἐμαυτοῦ πορίζεσθαι τὰ λεχθησόμενα περὶ αὐτῶν, ἀλλ᾽ ἐκ τῶν ὑμῖν πεπραγμένων τοσαύτας ἂν καὶ τοιαύτας ἀφορμὰς ἔλαβον ὥστε τὰς περὶ τῶν ἄλλων εὐλογίας μηδὲ κατὰ μικρὸν ἐναμίλλους 3 γενέσθαι τῇ περὶ ὑμᾶς ῥηθείσῃ. πῶς γὰρ ἄν τις ἢ τὴν εὐγένειαν ὑπερεβάλετο τῶν γεγονότων ἀφ᾽ Ἡρακλέους καὶ Διὸς ἣν πάντες ἴσασι μόνοις ὑμῖν

---

[a] For Archidamus see Introduction to this letter and Isocrates' discourse *Archidamus* in Vol. I, p. 343, L.C.L.

[b] The Spartan kings claimed descent from Heracles, the son of Zeus and Alcmena ; *cf. Panegyr.* 62 and *Archidamus* 8.

472

LETTER 9. TO ARCHIDAMUS

SINCE I know, Archidamus,[a] that many persons are eager to sing the praises of you, your father, and your family, I have chosen to leave to them that topic, since it would be a very easy one to treat. I myself, however, intend to exhort you to feats of generalship and military campaigns which are in no respect similar to those which are impending now, but, on the contrary, are such as will make you the author of great benefits, not only to your own state, but also to all the Greek world. This is the choice of subject I have made, although I am not unaware which of the two discourses is the easier to deal with ; nay, I know perfectly well that to discover actions which are noble, great, and advantageous is difficult and given to few men, whereas to praise your virtues I should have found an easy task. For there would have been no need of deriving from my own resources all that was to be said about them, but in your own past achievements I should have found topics for treatment so many and of such a kind that the eulogies pronounced upon other men would not have rivalled in the slightest degree the praise that I should have lavished upon you. For how could anyone have surpassed in nobility of birth the descendants of Heracles[b] and Zeus—and all men know that to your family alone confessedly

473

ὁμολογουμένως ὑπάρχουσαν, ἢ τὴν ἀρετὴν τῶν ἐν
Πελοποννήσῳ τὰς Δωρικὰς πόλεις κτισάντων καὶ
τὴν χώραν ταύτην κατασχόντων, ἢ τὸ πλῆθος τῶν
κινδύνων καὶ τῶν τροπαίων τῶν διὰ τὴν ὑμετέραν
4 ἡγεμονίαν καὶ βασιλείαν σταθέντων; τίς δ' ἂν
ἠπόρησε, διεξιέναι βουληθεὶς τὴν ἀνδρίαν ὅλης τῆς
πόλεως καὶ σωφροσύνην καὶ πολιτείαν τὴν ὑπὸ τῶν
προγόνων τῶν ὑμετέρων συνταχθεῖσαν; πόσοις δ'
[435] ἂν λόγοις ἐξεγένετο χρήσασθαι περὶ τὴν φρόνησιν
τοῦ σοῦ πατρὸς καὶ τὴν ἐν ταῖς συμφοραῖς διοίκησιν
καὶ τὴν μάχην τὴν ἐν τῇ πόλει γενομένην ἧς ἡγεμὼν
σὺ καταστὰς καὶ μετ' ὀλίγων πρὸς πολλοὺς
κινδυνεύσας καὶ πάντων διενεγκὼν αἴτιος ἐγένου
τῇ πόλει τῆς σωτηρίας, οὗ κάλλιον ἔργον οὐδεὶς ἂν
5 ἐπιδείξειεν· οὔτε γὰρ πόλεις ἑλεῖν οὔτε πολλοὺς
ἀποκτεῖναι τῶν πολεμίων οὕτω μέγα καὶ σεμνόν
ἐστιν ὡς ἐκ τῶν τοιούτων κινδύνων σῶσαι τὴν
πατρίδα, μὴ τὴν τυχοῦσαν ἀλλὰ τὴν τοσοῦτον ἐπ'
ἀρετῇ διενεγκοῦσαν. περὶ ὧν μὴ κομψῶς, ἀλλ'
ἁπλῶς διελθών, μηδὲ τῇ λέξει κοσμήσας, ἀλλ'
ἐξαριθμήσας μόνον καὶ χύδην εἰπὼν οὐδεὶς ὅστις
οὐκ ἂν εὐδοκιμήσειεν.

6 Ἐγὼ τοίνυν δυνηθεὶς ἂν καὶ περὶ τούτων ἐξαρκούντως διαλεχθῆναι, κἀκεῖνο γιγνώσκων, πρῶτον
μὲν ὅτι ῥᾷόν ἐστι περὶ τῶν γεγενημένων εὐπόρως
ἐπιδραμεῖν ἢ περὶ τῶν μελλόντων νουνεχόντως
εἰπεῖν, ἔπειθ' ὅτι πάντες ἄνθρωποι πλείω χάριν
ἔχουσι τοῖς ἐπαινοῦσιν ἢ τοῖς συμβουλεύουσι, τοὺς

belongs this honour—or in valour the founders of the
Dorian cities in the Peloponnese who occupied that
land, or in the multitude of the perilous deeds and
the trophies erected as a result of your leadership
and rule ? Who would lack material if he wished
to recount in full the tale of the courage of your
entire state, and of its moderation, and its constitution established by your ancestors ? How long a
story would be needed to tell of your father's wisdom,
of his handling of affairs in adversity, and of that
battle in Sparta*a* in which you, leading a few against
many, exposed yourself to danger, and, surpassing
all, proved to be the author of your city's salvation—a deed than which no man could point to
one more glorious ! For neither capture of cities
nor slaughter of a multitude of the enemy is
so great and so sublime as the saving of one's
fatherland from perils so dire—and no ordinary
fatherland, but one so greatly distinguished for its
valour. Any man who should relate these achievements, not in polished style, but simply, and without
stylistic embellishment, merely telling the tale of
them and speaking in random fashion, could not fail
to win renown.

Now I might have spoken passably about even
these matters, since I knew, in the first place, that
it is easier to treat copiously in cursory fashion
occurrences of the past than intelligently to discuss
the future and, in the second place, that all men
are more grateful to those who praise them than to
those who advise them*b*—for the former they approve

a In 362 B.C. the troops of Epaminondas, the Theban
general, were routed by Archidamus with 100 hoplites ;
cf. Xenophon, *Hell.* vii. 5. 9.
b Cf. *Epist.* 2. 1.

μὲν γὰρ ὡς εὔνους ὄντας ἀποδέχονται, τοὺς δ' ἂν
7 μὴ κελευσθέντες παραινῶσιν, ἐνοχλεῖν νομίζουσιν,
ἀλλ' ὅμως ἅπαντα ταῦτα προειδὼς τῶν μὲν πρὸς
χάριν ἂν ῥηθέντων ἀπεσχόμην, περὶ δὲ τοιούτων
μέλλω λέγειν, περὶ ὧν οὐδεὶς ἂν ἄλλος τολμήσειεν,
ἡγούμενος δεῖν τοὺς ἐπιεικείας καὶ φρονήσεως
ἀμφισβητοῦντας μὴ τοὺς ῥᾴστους προαιρεῖσθαι τῶν
λόγων, ἀλλὰ τοὺς ἐργωδεστάτους, μηδὲ τοὺς
ἡδίστους τοῖς ἀκούουσιν, ἀλλ' ἐξ ὧν ὠφελήσουσι
καὶ τὰς πόλεις τὰς αὐτῶν καὶ τοὺς ἄλλους Ἕλληνας·
ἐφ' οἷσπερ ἐγὼ τυγχάνω νῦν ἐφεστηκώς.

8 Θαυμάζω δὲ καὶ τῶν ἄλλων τῶν πράττειν ἢ
λέγειν δυναμένων, εἰ μηδὲ πώποτ' αὐτοῖς ἐπῆλθεν
ἐνθυμηθῆναι περὶ τῶν κοινῶν πραγμάτων, μηδ'
ἐλεῆσαι τὰς τῆς Ἑλλάδος δυσπραξίας οὕτως
αἰσχρῶς καὶ δεινῶς διατιθεμένης, ἧς οὐδεὶς παρα-
λέλειπται τόπος, ὃς οὐ γέμει καὶ μεστός ἐστι
πολέμου καὶ στάσεων καὶ σφαγῶν καὶ κακῶν
ἀναριθμήτων· ὧν πλεῖστον μέρος μετειλήφασιν οἱ
[43] τῆς Ἀσίας τὴν παραλίαν οἰκοῦντες, οὓς ἐν ταῖς
συνθήκαις ἅπαντας ἐκδεδώκαμεν οὐ μόνον τοῖς
βαρβάροις ἀλλὰ καὶ τῶν Ἑλλήνων τοῖς τῆς μὲν
φωνῆς τῆς ἡμετέρας κοινωνοῦσι, τῷ δὲ τρόπῳ τῷ
9 τῶν βαρβάρων χρωμένοις· οὕς, εἰ νοῦν εἴχομεν,
οὐκ ἂν περιεωρῶμεν ἀθροιζομένους οὐδ' ὑπὸ τῶν
τυχόντων στρατηγουμένους, οὐδὲ μείζους καὶ κρείττους συντάξεις στρατοπέδων γιγνομένας ἐκ τῶν
476

as being well-disposed, but the latter, if the advice comes unbidden, they look upon as officious—nevertheless, although I was already fully aware of all these considerations, I have refrained from topics which would surely be flattering and now I propose to speak of such matters as no one else would dare to discuss, because I believe that those who make pretensions to fairness and practical wisdom should choose, not the easiest subjects, but the most arduous, nor yet those which are the sweetest to the ears of the listeners, but such as will avail to benefit, not only their own states, but also all the other Greeks. And such is the subject, in fact, to which I have fixed my attention at the present time.

I marvel also at those men who have ability in action or in speech that it has never occurred to them seriously to take to heart the conditions which affect all Greeks alike, or even to feel pity for the evil plight of Hellas, so shameful and dreadful, no part of which now remains that is not teeming full of war, uprisings, slaughter, and evils innumerable.[a] The greatest share of these ills is the lot of the dwellers along the seaboard of Asia, whom by the treaty [b] we have delivered one and all into the hands, not only of the barbarians, but also of those Greeks who, though they share our speech, yet adhere to the ways of the barbarians. These renegades, if we had any sense, we should not be permitting to come together into bands or, led by any chance leaders, to form armed contingents, composed of roving forces more numerous and powerful than are the troops of

---

[a] For this same complaint see *Panegyr.* 170-171.
[b] The Peace of Antalcidas, 387 B.C.

πλανωμένων ἢ τῶν πολιτευομένων· οἱ τῆς μὲν
βασιλέως χώρας μικρὸν μέρος λυμαίνονται, τὰς δὲ
πόλεις τὰς Ἑλληνίδας, εἰς ἣν ἂν εἰσέλθωσιν, ἀναστάτους ποιοῦσι, τοὺς μὲν ἀποκτείνοντες, τοὺς δὲ
10 φυγαδεύοντες, τῶν δὲ τὰς οὐσίας διαρπάζοντες, ἔτι
δὲ παῖδας καὶ γυναῖκας ὑβρίζοντες, καὶ τὰς μὲν
εὐπρεπεστάτας καταισχύνοντες, τῶν δ' ἄλλων ἃ
περὶ τοῖς σώμασιν ἔχουσι περισπῶντες, ὥσθ' ἃς
πρότερον οὐδὲ κεκοσμημένας ἦν ἰδεῖν τοῖς ἀλλοτρίοις, ταύτας ὑπὸ πολλῶν ὁρᾶσθαι γυμνάς, ἐνίας
δ' αὐτῶν ἐν ῥάκεσι περιφθειρομένας δι' ἔνδειαν
τῶν ἀναγκαίων.

11 Ὑπὲρ ὧν πολὺν ἤδη χρόνον γιγνομένων οὔτε
πόλις οὐδεμία τῶν προεστάναι τῶν Ἑλλήνων
ἀξιουσῶν ἠγανάκτησεν, οὔτ' ἀνὴρ τῶν πρωτευόν-
των οὐδεὶς βαρέως ἤνεγκε, πλὴν ὁ σὸς πατήρ· μόνος
γὰρ Ἀγησίλαος ὢν ἡμεῖς ἴσμεν ἐπιθυμῶν ἅπαντα
τὸν χρόνον διετέλεσε τοὺς μὲν Ἕλληνας ἐλευθερῶ-
σαι, πρὸς δὲ τοὺς βαρβάρους πόλεμον ἐξενεγκεῖν.
οὐ μὴν ἀλλὰ κἀκεῖνος ἑνὸς πράγματος διήμαρτεν.

12 καὶ μὴ θαυμάσῃς, εἰ πρὸς σὲ διαλεγόμενος μνησθήσομαι τῶν οὐκ ὀρθῶς ὑπ' αὐτοῦ γνωσθέντων·
εἴθισμαί τε γὰρ μετὰ παρρησίας ἀεὶ ποιεῖσθαι τοὺς
λόγους, καὶ δεξαίμην ἂν δικαίως ἐπιτιμήσας ἀπ-
εχθέσθαι μᾶλλον ἢ παρὰ τὸ προσῆκον ἐπαινέσας

13 χαρίσασθαι. τὸ μὲν οὖν ἐμὸν οὕτως ἔχον ἐστίν,
ἐκεῖνος δ' ἐν ἅπασι τοῖς ἄλλοις διενεγκὼν καὶ
γενόμενος ἐγκρατέστατος καὶ δικαιότατος καὶ
πολιτικώτατος διττὰς ἔσχεν ἐπιθυμίας, χωρὶς μὲν
ἑκατέραν καλὴν εἶναι δοκοῦσαν, οὐ συμφωνούσας

ᵃ Cf. To Philip 120-121.

our own citizen forces. These armies do damage to only a small part of the domain of the king of Persia, but every Hellenic city they enter they utterly destroy, killing some, driving others into exile, and robbing still others of their possessions[a]; furthermore, they treat with indignity children and women, and not only dishonour the most beautiful women, but from the others they strip off the clothing which they wear on their persons, so that those who even when fully clothed were not to be seen by strangers, are beheld naked by many men; and some women, clad in rags, are seen wandering in destitution from lack of the bare necessities of life.[b]

With regard to this unhappy situation, which has now obtained for a long time, not one of the cities which lays claim to the leadership of the Hellenes has shown indignation, nor has any of its leading men been wroth, except your father. For Agesilaüs alone of all whom we know unceasingly to the end longed to liberate the Greeks and to wage war against the barbarians. Nevertheless, even he erred in one respect. And do not be surprised if I, in my communication to you, mention matters in which his judgement was at fault; for I am accustomed always to speak with the utmost frankness and I should prefer to be disliked for having justly censured than to win favour through having given unmerited praise. My view, then, is as follows: Agesilaus, who had won distinction in all other fields, and had shown himself to be in the highest degree self-controlled, just, and statesmanlike, conceived two strong desires, each of them taken by itself seeming admirable, but being

[b] See Introd. to *Panegyr.*, Vol. I, p. 117; *cf. Panegyr.* 167-168.

δ' ἀλλήλαις οὐδ' ἅμα πράττεσθαι δυναμένας· ἠβού-
[437] λετο γὰρ βασιλεῖ τε πολεμεῖν καὶ τῶν φίλων τοὺς
φεύγοντας εἰς τὰς πόλεις καταγαγεῖν καὶ κυρίους
14 καταστῆσαι τῶν πραγμάτων. συνέβαινεν οὖν ἐκ
μὲν τῆς πραγματείας τῆς ὑπὲρ τῶν ἑταίρων ἐν
κακοῖς καὶ κινδύνοις εἶναι τοὺς Ἕλληνας, διὰ δὲ
τὴν ταραχὴν τὴν ἐνθάδε γιγνομένην μὴ σχολὴν
ἄγειν μηδὲ δύνασθαι πολεμεῖν τοῖς βαρβάροις.
ὥστ' ἐκ τῶν ἀγνοηθέντων κατ' ἐκεῖνον τὸν χρόνον
ῥᾴδιον καταμαθεῖν ὅτι δεῖ τοὺς ὀρθῶς βουλευο-
μένους μὴ πρότερον ἐκφέρειν πρὸς βασιλέα πόλεμον,
πρὶν ἂν διαλλάξῃ τις τοὺς Ἕλληνας καὶ παύσῃ τῆς
μανίας καὶ τῆς φιλονικίας ἡμᾶς. περὶ ὧν ἐγὼ καὶ
πρότερον εἴρηκα καὶ νῦν ποιήσομαι τοὺς λόγους.

15 Καίτοι τινὲς τῶν οὐδεμιᾶς μὲν παιδείας μετ-
εσχηκότων, δύνασθαι δὲ παιδεύειν τοὺς ἄλλους
ὑπισχνουμένων, καὶ ψέγειν μὲν τἀμὰ τολμώντων,
μιμεῖσθαι δὲ γλιχομένων, τάχ' ἂν μανίαν εἶναι
φήσειαν τὸ μέλειν ἐμοὶ τῶν τῆς Ἑλλάδος συμφορῶν, ὥσπερ παρὰ τοὺς ἐμοὺς λόγους ἢ βέλτιον ἢ
χεῖρον αὐτὴν πράξουσαν. ὧν δικαίως ἂν ἅπαντες
πολλὴν ἀνανδρίαν καὶ μικροψυχίαν καταγνοῖεν, ὅτι
προσποιούμενοι φιλοσοφεῖν αὐτοὶ μὲν ἐπὶ μικροῖς
φιλοτιμοῦνται, τοῖς δὲ δυναμένοις περὶ τῶν μεγί-
16 στων συμβουλεύειν φθονοῦντες διατελοῦσιν. οὗτοι
μὲν οὖν βοηθοῦντες ταῖς αὑτῶν ἀσθενείαις καὶ

incompatible and incapable of achievement at the same time. For he wished not only to wage war on the Persian king but also to restore to their respective cities his friends who were in exile and to establish them as masters of affairs.[a] The result, therefore, of his exertions on behalf of his friends was that the Greeks were involved in misfortunes and in fighting, and on account of the confusion which prevailed here had not the leisure nor yet the strength to wage war against the barbarians. So, in consequence of the conditions which were at that time not recognized, it is easy to perceive that men of good counsel should not wage war against the king of Persia until some-one shall have first reconciled the Greeks with each other and have made us cease from our madness and contentiousness. On these topics I have spoken before and now I intend to discuss them.

And yet certain persons who, although they have no share at all in learning, yet profess to be able to teach everybody else, and although they dare to find fault with my efforts, yet are eager to imitate them, will perhaps call it madness for me to concern myself with the misfortunes of Greece, as if Greece would be either better or worse off as a result of words of mine! Justly, however, would all men condemn these persons as guilty of great cowardice and meanness of spirit, for while they make pretence to serious intellectual interests, they pride themselves on petty things and consistently show malice and envy against those who have the ability to give counsel concerning matters of the greatest importance. These men, then, in their endeavour to give aid and comfort to their own weaknesses and indol-

---

[a] This same explanation is given in *To Philip* 87.

ῥᾳθυμίαις ἴσως τοιαῦτ' ἐροῦσιν· ἐγὼ δ' οὕτως ἐπ'
ἐμαυτῷ μέγα φρονῶ, καίπερ ἔτη γεγονὼς ὀγδοή-
κοντα καὶ παντάπασιν ἀπειρηκώς, ὥστ' οἶμαι καὶ
λέγειν ἐμοὶ προσήκειν μάλιστα περὶ τούτων καὶ
καλῶς βεβουλεῦσθαι πρὸς σὲ ποιούμενον τοὺς
λόγους, καὶ τυχὸν ἀπ' αὐτῶν γενήσεσθαί τι τῶν
δεόντων.

17 Ἡγοῦμαι δὲ καὶ τοὺς ἄλλους Ἕλληνας, εἰ δεήσειεν αὐτοὺς ἐξ ἁπάντων ἐκλέξασθαι τόν τε τῷ
λόγῳ κάλλιστ' ἂν δυνηθέντα παρακαλέσαι τοὺς
Ἕλληνας ἐπὶ τὴν τῶν βαρβάρων στρατείαν καὶ τὸν
τάχιστα μέλλοντα τὰς πράξεις ἐπιτελεῖν τὰς συμφέρειν δοξάσας, οὐκ ἂν ἄλλους ἀνθ' ἡμῶν προ-
κριθῆναι. καίτοι πῶς οὐκ ἂν αἰσχρὸν ποιήσαιμεν,
εἰ τούτων ἀμελήσαιμεν οὕτως ἐντίμων ὄντων ὧν
[438] ἅπαντες ἂν ἡμᾶς ἀξιώσαιεν; τὸ μὲν οὖν ἐμὸν
18 ἔλαττόν ἐστιν· ἀποφήνασθαι γὰρ ἃ γιγνώσκει τις
οὐ πάνυ τῶν χαλεπῶν πέφυκεν· σοὶ δὲ προσήκει
προσέχοντι τὸν νοῦν τοῖς ὑπ' ἐμοῦ λεγομένοις
βουλεύσασθαι, πότερον ὀλιγωρητέον ἐστὶ τῶν
Ἑλληνικῶν πραγμάτων γεγονότι μέν, ὥσπερ ὀλίγῳ
πρότερον ἐγὼ διῆλθον, ἡγεμόνι δὲ Λακεδαιμονίων
ὄντι, βασιλεῖ δὲ προσαγορευομένῳ, μεγίστην δὲ
τῶν Ἑλλήνων ἔχοντι δόξαν, ἢ τῶν μὲν ἐνεστώτων
πραγμάτων ὑπεροπτέον, μείζοσι δ' ἐπιχειρητέον.

19 Ἐγὼ μὲν γάρ φημι χρῆναί σε πάντων ἀφέμενον
τῶν ἄλλων δυοῖν τούτοιν προσέχειν τὸν νοῦν, ὅπως
τοὺς μὲν Ἕλληνας ἀπαλλάξεις τῶν πολέμων καὶ
τῶν ἄλλων κακῶν τῶν νῦν αὐτοῖς παρόντων, τοὺς

ence, will perhaps speak in such fashion. I for my
part, however, pride myself so greatly on my ability
that, even though I am now eighty years of age and
altogether worn out, I think it is especially fitting
to speak my mind on these matters, and also that I
have been well advised in directing my appeal to
you, and that it may well be that from my counsel
some of the necessary measures will be taken.

And I believe that if the rest of the Greek world
also should be called upon to choose from all mankind
both the man who by his eloquence would best be
able to summon the Greeks to the expedition against
the barbarians, and also the leader who would be
likely most quickly to bring to fulfilment the measures
recognized as expedient, they would choose no others
but you and me. Yet surely we should be acting
disgracefully, should we not, if we should neglect
these duties in which our honour is involved, should
all men regard us as worthy of them ? My part, it
is true, is the smaller; for to declare what one thinks
is usually not so very difficult. But for you it is
fitting, giving attention to all that I have said, to
deliberate upon the question whether you should
shrink from the conduct of the affairs of Hellas—
you, whose noble lineage I have a little while ago
described, leader of the Lacedaemonians, addressed
by the name King, and a man who enjoys the
greatest renown of all the Hellenes—or, disdaining
the matters you now have in hand, you should put
your hand to greater undertakings.

I for my part say that, disregarding everything
else, you should give your attention to these two
tasks—to rid the Hellenes from their wars and from
all the other miseries with which they are now

δὲ βαρβάρους παύσεις ὑβρίζοντας καὶ πλείω κεκτημένους ἀγαθὰ τοῦ προσήκοντος. ὡς δ᾽ ἐστὶ ταῦτα
δυνατὰ καὶ συμφέροντα καὶ σοὶ καὶ τῇ πόλει καὶ
τοῖς ἄλλοις ἅπασιν, ἐμὸν ἔργον ἤδη διδάξαι περὶ
αὐτῶν ἐστιν. . . .

afflicted, and to put a stop to the insolence of the barbarians and to their possession of wealth beyond their due. That these things are practicable and expedient for you, for your city, and for all the Hellenes at large, it is now my task to explain. . . .

[The conclusion is missing]

GENERAL INDEX

TO

ISOCRATES, VOLUMES I, II, AND III

The numbers refer to volume and page of this edition

GENERAL INDEX